Macmillan Mathema[...]s

Paul [...] [...]ddle

MACMILLAN

Contents

Introduction

Macmillan Mathematics is a complete mathematics scheme for pupils from Grades 1 to 6. It is wide ranging and written not only to develop a thorough understanding of mathematics, but also to try to foster interest, enthusiasm and confidence in mathematics. It has a thorough mathematical structure, and careful progression and development to ensure continuity and curriculum coverage.

Components

- The **Teacher's Book** gives clear guidance on planning, practical activities and the use of the pupil material for each unit of work.
- The **Pupil's Books** provide a clear explanation of the key steps needed to learn specific skills and concepts, as well as practice, reinforcement and enrichment activities to consolidate these skills and concepts.
- The **Pupil's CD-ROM** provides further reinforcement and assessment of the skills and concepts developed within each unit, with the provision of interactive exercises.

Planning and organisation

For each year group, the curriculum has been organised into six blocks of work that are progressed over the year. Each block is organised into four teaching units that each covers a week of lessons. Within each unit is contained the set of objectives that guide planning, teaching and pupils' learning. These blocks support an extended period of learning when pupils' progress can be assessed and those pupils who are not keeping up with their peers can receive the additional attention and support they need. The fourth unit in each block is an 'assess and review' unit, allowing teachers to assess and monitor pupils' progress, and their ability to use and apply the skills and concepts learnt in the previous three units.

Teaching sequence

Term 1

September	October	November	December
Block A	Block B		Block C

Term 2

January	February	March	April	May
Block D	Block E		Block F	

Successful teaching and learning with Macmillan Mathematics

Macmillan Mathematics is intended to be used in the context of quality first teaching, with activities to support teachers in their efforts to develop pupils' learning, confidence and love of mathematics. The authors give these principles to outline their thoughts on teaching and learning mathematics:

1 Plan and provide a balanced, practical experience that incorporates the acquisition, consolidation and application of knowledge and skills, with opportunities to use and extend thinking and reasoning.
2 Model ways to explore mathematics and look for patterns, rules and properties; direct their learning by providing examples that enable them to identify appropriate methods and understand rules and ideas.
3 Give pupils the opportunity to consolidate their learning, with frequent and regular periods of practice that are short, sharp and focused.
4 Ensure that pupils recognise how their learning builds on previous learning and help them to see connections; ensure that they feel appropriately supported and challenged by the work they are given.
5 Engage with pupils' thinking; give them sufficient time for discussion and time to think about their ideas and methods by prompting and by asking probing questions.
6 Demonstrate the correct use of mathematical vocabulary and the interpretation and use of symbols, images, diagrams and models as tools to support their mathematical thinking and communication.
7 Share the excitement of mathematics, capturing pupils' imagination by teaching creatively and with enthusiasm.

Structure of Teacher's Book

Objectives: The objectives from the syllabus covered by this unit.

Vocabulary: The key words to use and develop with pupils. List these on the wall or board for the pupils to read.

Lessons: The focus for each lesson. Share these with your pupils at the start of each lesson.

Oral and mental starters: Suggested starter activities for the first 5 minutes of each lesson (see below).

Resources: Practical resource suggestions to help support the teaching and learning of this unit.

Prior learning: The step before this unit of work. Use this as a basis for some questions at the start of the unit to assess the pupils' prior knowledge and understanding.

Background notes: Linking theory with practice, this briefly outlines some common difficulties and misconceptions for this unit of work and gives key teaching points.

Supporting the topic: Lists possible suggestions for using and applying the mathematics in real life.

End of unit evaluation: Learning outcomes for this unit of work, with key area of assessment linked to the objectives. This is followed by lesson notes, containing practical activities and references to the Pupil's Book.

Oral and mental starters

These are suggestions for whole-class mental maths activities for the first 5 or 10 minutes of each lesson. They are interactive and lively oral activities, with questions, games and practical activities that actively involve the pupils. They enable pupils to become confident and agile with mental calculation and number, as well as consolidating work done on shape, measures and handling data. The starters have a number of purposes.

- They can prepare the pupils for the unit of work ahead, rehearsing and sharpening skills.
- They can be used as a method of 'keeping sharp' the skills and concepts introduced in previous units.
- They reinforce the importance of the language of mathematics, with regular use of the vocabulary.
- They allow you to assess pupils' knowledge of an area you intend to teach in the main part of the lesson.

Basic resources such as number cards, counters and number lines are important. These are only suggestions for each lesson. Once you have used some of the activities, refine and develop them and plan your own starters to support your teaching.

Hands up (reading and writing numbers to 999): Write a set of numbers on the board, e.g. 91, 450, 18, 678, 803, 555, 900. Ask a pupil to point to a given number. Ask the class to raise their hands if they agree. Repeat with other numbers.

Hold up (reading and writing numbers to 999): Ask each pupil to write a given number then hold it up for you to see. Repeat with other numbers.

One more (conservation of number): Ask a pupil to stand at the front. Ask the class 'How many children?' Ask another pupil to the front. 'How many children now?' Encourage them to answer without counting. Repeat, asking 1 more pupil out each time, emphasising that there is no need to count the new group because the previous group number was known, they just need to add 1 more. Ask one pupil at a time to leave the group, the pupils working out 1 less each time.

Zero!: Ask the class to count from 0 to an appropriate number and then count back, clapping with each number.

What's the order? (ordering numbers to 999): Write a set of numbers in random order on the board. Explain that the numbers are to be put in order, starting with the smallest. Ask the class to suggest which should come first, second etc. Write the numbers out in the order suggested. Ask 'Is this correct?' Alter if necessary.

Start here: Ask the class to count on from different starting numbers, e.g. start at 487 and count to 509. Develop to include counting back to the starting number.

Steps: Ask the class to count on from a given starting number in twos and then back. Use different steps as appropriate, e.g. fives, tens, hundreds.

Arrows away (place value to 999): Show a 2- or 3-digit number using arrow cards, e.g. 435. Ask 'What is this number? What does the 4 mean?' (4 hundred). Move the bottom card to reveal 400. 'What does the 3 mean?' (thirty or 3 tens). Move the top arrow card to reveal 30. Replace the top card. 'What is the value of the 5?' (5 ones or units). Repeat with other numbers.

Hidden fingers (addition/subtraction facts within 10): Hold up 2 hands, palms facing you. Ask 'How many fingers (including thumbs) can you see?' Hide a number of fingers by bending them down towards you. 'How many can you see now? How many can't you see?' Repeat with different numbers.

Flash facts (addition, subtraction and multiplication facts): Ask number fact questions (e.g. $5 + 4$, $12 + 3$, $5 + 8$, $17 - 6$, $15 - 7$, 2×7, 5×8, 3×5) for pupils to answer together or by holding up a number card when you give a signal. Allow a little time before your signal, then reduce the time as confidence increases.

Pairs for sums (addition): Give an appropriate number. Pupils choose 2 numbers which add to that total. They could hold up number cards, write 2 numbers and hold them up, or give individual answers orally.

Product pairs (multiplication): As 'Pairs for sums' but pupils show two numbers which make the given number when multiplied together.

My way (adding and subtracting 2-digit numbers mentally): Write a 2-digit addition or subtraction calculation on the board for pupils to work out mentally. Ask for the answer then ask volunteers to explain how they worked it out. Record the method on the board as each explanation is given, e.g. for $46 + 23$ 'I added 46 and 20 which is 66' (record $46 + 20 = 66$) 'then I added 3 to give 69' (record $66 + 3 = 69$).

Name it (identifying shapes from descriptions): Describe a shape using mathematical properties (but don't show the shape), e.g. 'This shape has 3 faces. Two of its faces are circles. It can roll. What shape is it?'

Double it: Give a few numbers for the class to double and respond together, then give a number for an individual pupil to double. Repeat with different numbers.

Halve it: Give even numbers for pupils to halve, as a whole class, individually, or a mixture of both.

Quarter it: Give multiples of four for pupils to quarter, as a whole class, individually or a mixture of both.

Tell me a story: Write a calculation on the board, e.g. $24 - 8 = 16$; $14 + 28 = 42$; $5 \times 6 = 30$. Ask pupils to make up a 'number story' for the calculation, e.g. 'We made 24 biscuits. 8 of them have been eaten, so there are 16 left.' Invite a few pupils to tell their stories.

What's the question?: Provide an appropriate number, e.g. 10. Say 'The answer is 10. What's the question?' Pupils give number statements which have 10 as the answer, e.g. $6 + 4$, 5×2, $12 - 2$, half of 20 etc. Record each on the board. Collect as many suggestions as possible within a time limit.

Language (understanding mathematical vocabulary): Give instructions or ask questions using mathematical terms such as: multiply, multiple, plus, total, sum, subtract, difference, fraction, metre, centimetre, litre, kilogram, polygon, line, ray, segment, e.g. 'Multiply 3 by 5. What is the difference between 16 and 36? What is the name of a polygon with 5 sides? Which of these is a ray? Which is a segment?' etc.

In time: Set the teaching clock to o'clock, half past, quarter past and quarter to times. Ask pupils to give the time in both analogue and digital form (e.g. quarter past 10; 10:15). Ask questions such as 'What time is half/quarter of an hour later? What time will it be in 2 hours?'

Pupil's Book 2A

Block A Numbers and addition

Maths Topic	National Standards from Government Guidelines	
Unit	*Curriculum area*	*End of year objectives / success criteria*
1 Numbers to 100	Understanding numbers, methods of displaying them and the relations between them	Develop a primary understanding of counting in tens to 100 and place value up to 99. Read and write numbers composed of units and tens in both numbers (figure) and letter form.
2 Numbers to 999	Understanding numbers, methods of displaying them and the relations between them	Read and write 100 and its multiples up to 900. Develop a primary understanding of counting in tens to 100 and place value up to 999. Read and write numbers composed of units, tens and hundreds in both numbers (figure) and letter form.
3 Addition to 99	Understanding numerical operations and the relations between them Calculate skilfully and make reasonable assessments Use of symbols and shapes to display simple mathematical situations	Understand the meaning of adding 2 or 3 numbers whose sum does not exceed 99, with or without renaming. Choose the basic operation needed to solve a mathematical or everyday problem (word problems). Check the result of any addition problem. Use different and suitable methods for addition like Mental Maths or use of paper and pencil (written). Use approximation in solving addition of numbers. Identify numerical examples showing the properties of addition up to 99, without explicitly naming them.
4 Assess and review	Revision and assessment of previous 3 units – problems, formative and summative assessment. Activities to monitor, assess, evaluate and consolidate pupils' knowledge and understanding.	

During this block of work, pupils will experience:

1 Counting, reading, writing and ordering numbers to 100.
2 Reading and displaying numbers on an abacus.
3 Reading and writing numbers to 999.
4 Understanding place value in numbers to 999.
5 Adding numbers with a sum < 100 without renaming, then with renaming.

Unit 1 **Numbers to 100**

Term 1 Block A **Numbers and addition** **Unit 1 Numbers to 100** Unit 2 Numbers to 999 Unit 3 Addition to 99 Unit 4 Assess and review	**Objectives** *At the end of the unit, students should be able to…* Develop a primary understanding of counting in tens to 100 and place value. Read and write numbers composed of units and tens in both number (figure) and letter form.
Vocabulary Names for numbers to 100, tens, units, digits, place value, abacus	**Lessons** 1 Counting to 20 2 Counting in tens 3 Counting to 100 4 Reading numbers to 99 5 Using an abacus
Oral and mental starters One more Zero! Start here Hands up Hold up	**Resources** Abacus A large 10 × 10 grid numbered 1–100 on display Tens and units apparatus (e.g. ten rods and unit cubes, or bundles of ten sticks and unit sticks) Arrow cards *Pupil's Book pages 4–13*
Prior learning Counting, reading, writing and ordering numbers to 99 Counting in tens to 100 Understanding place value in 2-digit numbers (Grade 1)	**Background notes** This unit revises and consolidates learning undertaken in Grade 1. The concept of place value, which is included in this unit, needs much reinforcement to ensure that all pupils are confident in their understanding and to help to avoid errors in calculation. The use of materials such as an abacus, arrow cards and materials grouped in tens and hundreds are very helpful in the development of this concept.
End of unit evaluation Check that pupils are able to: 1 Read, write and order numbers to 100. 2 Count in tens to 100. 3 Know the value of each digit in a 2-digit number.	**Supporting the topic** Explain that the work in this unit is designed to remind pupils about the numbers they learnt about in Grade 1. Discuss situations in everyday life when things need to be counted, e.g. the number of pupils in the class, the number of hens in a farmer's field, the numbering of houses or flats for identification. Use the classroom 1–100 grid whenever appropriate across the curriculum to consolidate understanding.

Lesson 1 **Counting to 20**

Pupil's Book pages 4 and 5 **Oral and mental starter: One more**

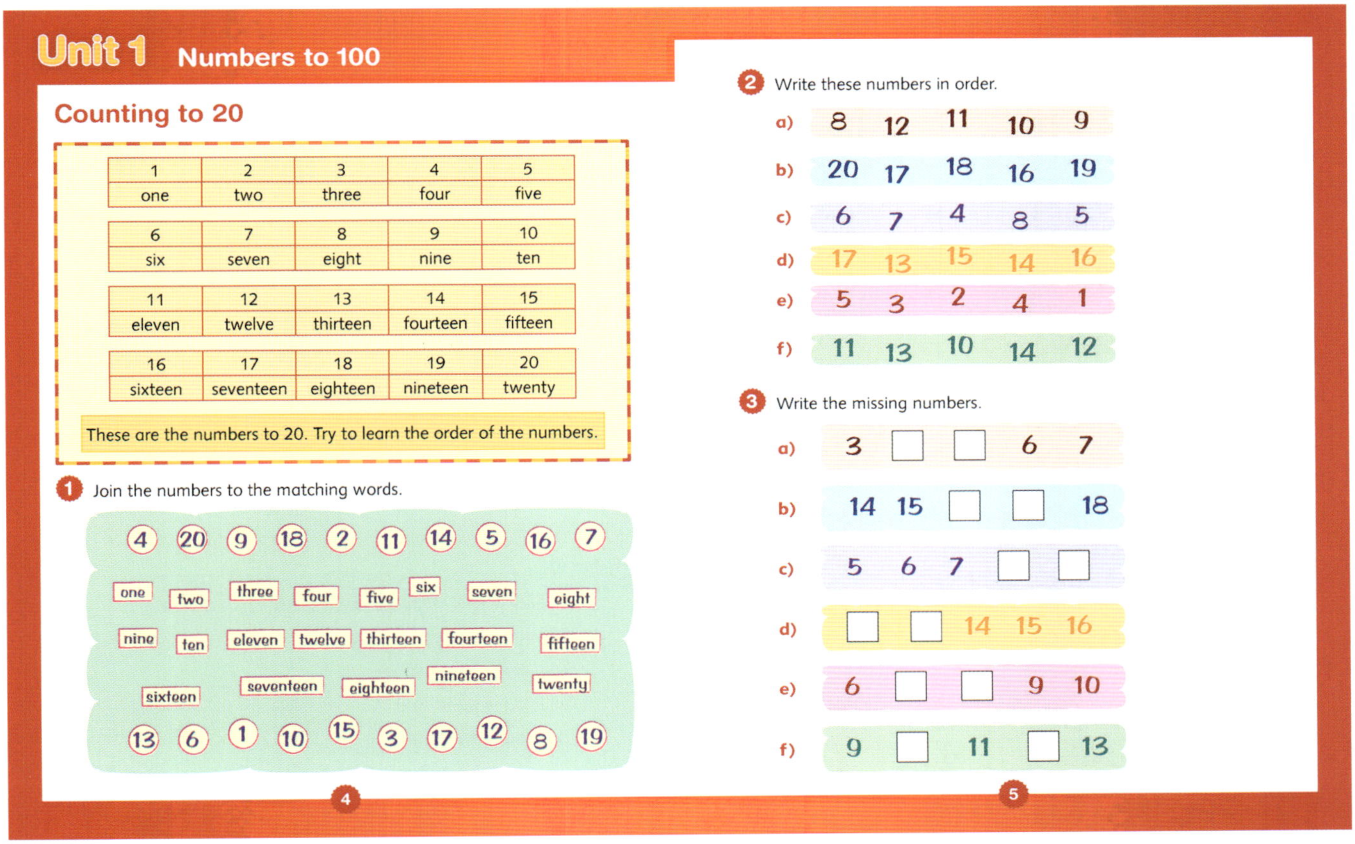

Unit 1 Numbers to 100

Counting to 20

1 one	2 two	3 three	4 four	5 five
6 six	7 seven	8 eight	9 nine	10 ten
11 eleven	12 twelve	13 thirteen	14 fourteen	15 fifteen
16 sixteen	17 seventeen	18 eighteen	19 nineteen	20 twenty

These are the numbers to 20. Try to learn the order of the numbers.

1 Join the numbers to the matching words.

4 20 9 18 2 11 14 5 16 7

one two three four five six seven eight

nine ten eleven twelve thirteen fourteen fifteen

sixteen seventeen eighteen nineteen twenty

13 6 1 10 15 3 17 12 8 19

2 Write these numbers in order.

a) 8 12 11 10 9

b) 20 17 18 16 19

c) 6 7 4 8 5

d) 17 13 15 14 16

e) 5 3 2 4 1

f) 11 13 10 14 12

3 Write the missing numbers.

a) 3 ☐ ☐ 6 7

b) 14 15 ☐ ☐ 18

c) 5 6 7 ☐ ☐

d) ☐ ☐ 14 15 16

e) 6 ☐ ☐ 9 10

f) 9 ☐ 11 ☐ 13

4 5

Activities

- Ask the class to count together to 40 as you point to the numbers in turn on the class 1–100 grid. Ask them to close their eyes and count to 20.
- Ask questions such as 'Which number comes after 7? What is 1 more than 12? What is 1 less than 9? Which number comes between 12 and 14?' etc.
- Ask the pupils to count round the class, the first pupil saying 1, the second saying 2 etc until all pupils have had a turn. Ask 'How many pupils are here today?'
- Repeat, starting with the last pupil and finishing with the first. Repeat with pupils in a different order. Prompt any pupils who need help and note them for support during the lesson.
- Look at page 4. Ask the class to say the numbers 1–20 as they point to each in the introduction. Write the names (in words) of some of the numbers on the board and ask the class to read them together, then find them on the grid.
- At the end of the lesson ask individual pupils to read a completed sequence from question 2 or 3.

Answers

1 1 → one, 2 → two, 3 → three, 4 → four, 5 → five, 6 → six, 7 → seven, 8 → eight, 9 → nine, 10 → ten, 11 → eleven, 12 → twelve, 13 → thirteen, 14 → fourteen, 15 → fifteen, 16 → sixteen, 17 → seventeen, 18 → eighteen, 19 → nineteen, 20 → twenty

2 a) 8, 9, 10, 11, 12 b) 16, 17, 18, 19, 20
c) 4, 5, 6, 7, 8 d) 13, 14, 15, 16, 17
e) 1, 2, 3, 4, 5 f) 10, 11, 12, 13, 14

3 a) 4, 5 b) 16, 17 c) 8, 9 d) 12, 13
e) 7, 8 f) 10, 12

Lesson 2 **Counting in tens**

Pupil's Book pages 6 and 7 **Oral and mental starter: Zero!**

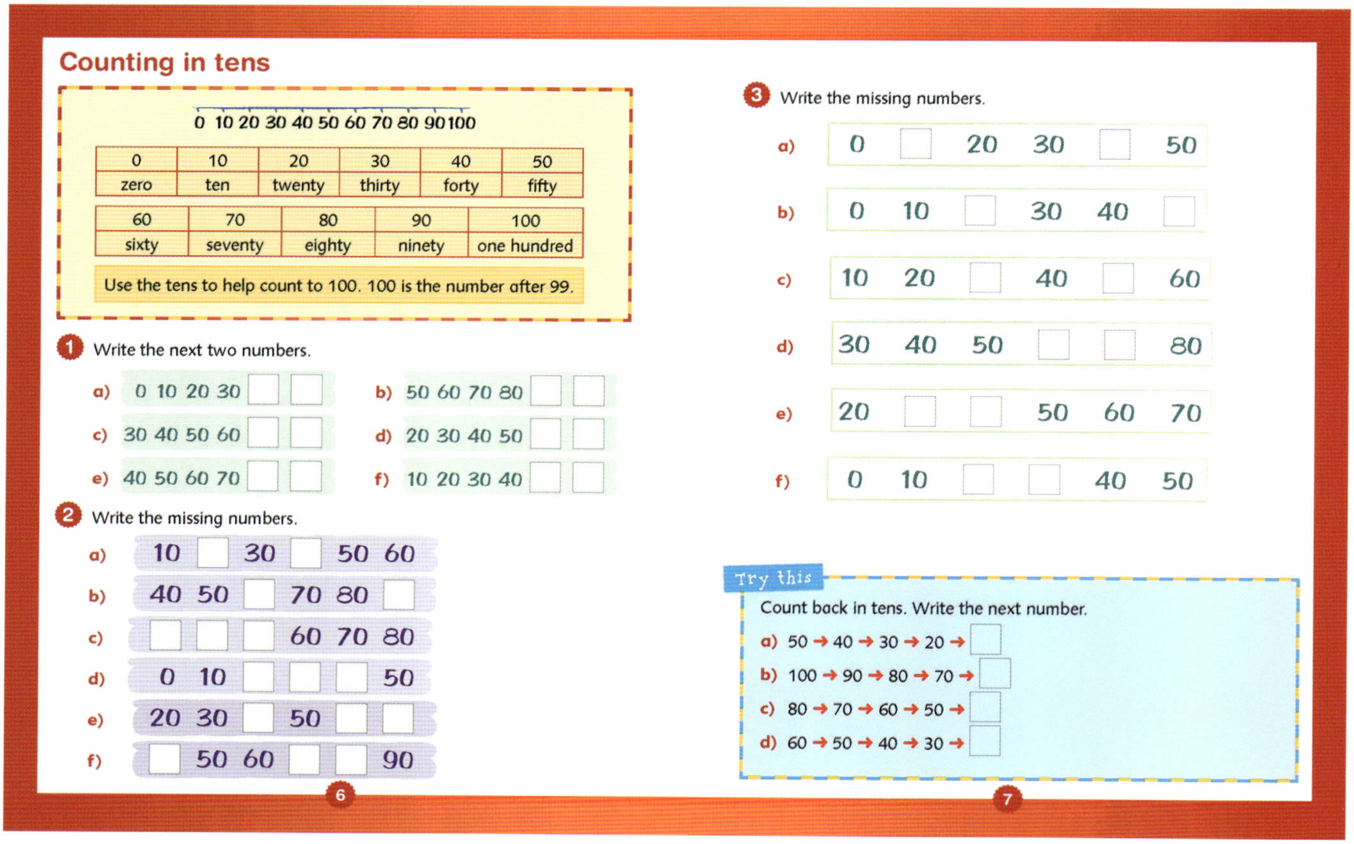

Counting in tens

0 10 20 30 40 50 60 70 80 90 100

0	10	20	30	40	50
zero	ten	twenty	thirty	forty	fifty

60	70	80	90	100
sixty	seventy	eighty	ninety	one hundred

Use the tens to help count to 100. 100 is the number after 99.

1 Write the next two numbers.

a) 0 10 20 30 ___ ___ b) 50 60 70 80 ___ ___
c) 30 40 50 60 ___ ___ d) 20 30 40 50 ___ ___
e) 40 50 60 70 ___ ___ f) 10 20 30 40 ___ ___

2 Write the missing numbers.

a) 10 ___ 30 ___ 50 60
b) 40 50 ___ 70 80 ___
c) ___ ___ ___ 60 70 80
d) 0 10 ___ ___ ___ 50
e) 20 30 ___ 50 ___ ___
f) ___ 50 60 ___ ___ 90

6

3 Write the missing numbers.

a) 0 ___ 20 30 ___ 50
b) 0 10 ___ 30 40 ___
c) 10 20 ___ 40 ___ 60
d) 30 40 50 ___ ___ 80
e) 20 ___ ___ 50 60 70
f) 0 10 ___ ___ 40 50

Try this

Count back in tens. Write the next number.

a) 50 → 40 → 30 → 20 → ___
b) 100 → 90 → 80 → 70 → ___
c) 80 → 70 → 60 → 50 → ___
d) 60 → 50 → 40 → 30 → ___

7

Activities

- Give ten rods (or a bundle of 10 sticks or straws) to groups of 4 or 5 pupils so that all pupils can clearly see and count them. 'How many cubes are there in your rod (or sticks in your bundle)?' Establish that there are 10.
- Ask one pupil from each group to bring their rod to the front. Ask the first to hold up the rod. 'How many cubes are in this rod?' Indicate the number 10 on the class 1–100 grid. Ask the next pupil to hold up his/her rod alongside the first. 'How many cubes now?' Count on ten from 10 on the class grid, i.e. counting 11 as 1, 12 as 2 etc to illustrate that 10 + 10 = 20. Repeat with the rest of the rods to establish the pattern of counting in tens.
- Ask the class to count in 10s to 100 as you indicate each number on the class grid. 'What is 10 more than 90?' Discuss that 100 has 3 digits. 'What is 10 more than: 10 … 30 … 60?' etc.
- Look at the number track on page 6. Explain that each space from one multiple of 10 to the next represents 10 unit spaces.
- At the end of the lesson ask the class to close their eyes then count in 10s from 0 to 100 and then back.

Answers

1 a) 40, 50 b) 90, 100 c) 70, 80
 d 60, 70 e) 80, 90 f) 50, 60

2 a) 20, 40 b) 60, 90 c) 30, 40, 50
 d) 20, 30, 40 e) 40, 60, 70 f) 40, 70, 80

3 a) 10, 40 b) 20, 50 c) 30, 50
 d) 60, 70 e) 30, 40 f) 20, 30

Try this

a) 10 b) 60 c) 40 d) 20

Lesson 3 **Counting to 100**

Pupil's Book pages 8 and 9 **Oral and mental starter: Start here**

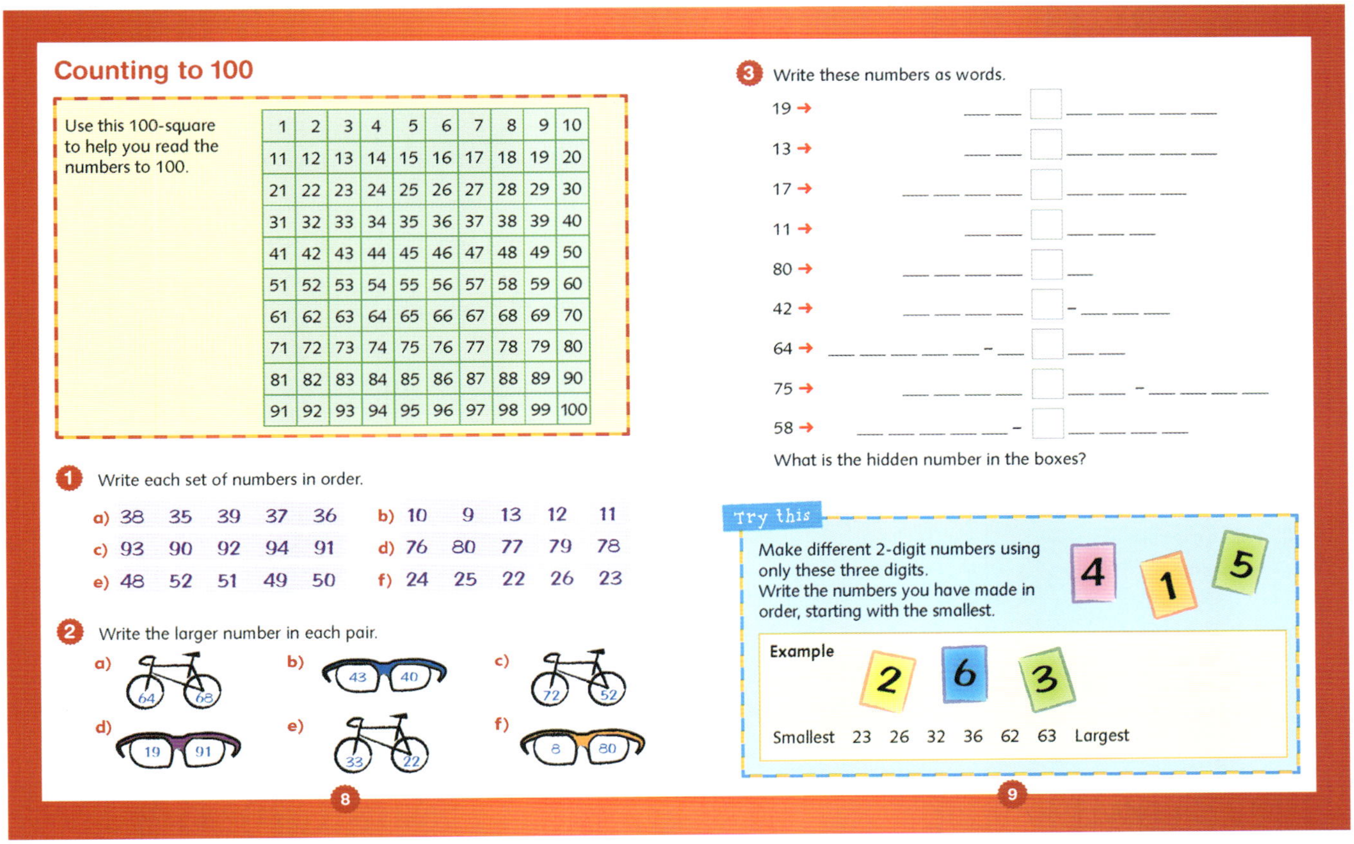

Counting to 100

Use this 100-square to help you read the numbers to 100.

1	2	3	4	5	6	7	8	9	10
11	12	13	14	15	16	17	18	19	20
21	22	23	24	25	26	27	28	29	30
31	32	33	34	35	36	37	38	39	40
41	42	43	44	45	46	47	48	49	50
51	52	53	54	55	56	57	58	59	60
61	62	63	64	65	66	67	68	69	70
71	72	73	74	75	76	77	78	79	80
81	82	83	84	85	86	87	88	89	90
91	92	93	94	95	96	97	98	99	100

1 Write each set of numbers in order.

a) 38 35 39 37 36 b) 10 9 13 12 11
c) 93 90 92 94 91 d) 76 80 77 79 78
e) 48 52 51 49 50 f) 24 25 22 26 23

2 Write the larger number in each pair.

8

3 Write these numbers as words.

19 →
13 →
17 →
11 →
80 →
42 →
64 →
75 →
58 →

What is the hidden number in the boxes?

Try this

Make different 2-digit numbers using only these three digits.
Write the numbers you have made in order, starting with the smallest.

9

Activities

- Look at page 8. Talk about the arrangement of numbers on the 1–100 grid, emphasising that they increase by 1 along each row and from the end of one row to the beginning of the next. 'Can you see any patterns? How do they work?' Discuss and clarify pupils' suggestions. Ask pupils to point to a particular number on the grid and count on 5 more numbers. Repeat with other starting numbers.
- Ask pupils to use the grid on page 8 to answer questions such as 'Which number comes after 30? … before 40? … after 62? … between 73 and 75? … before 100?' 'What is 1 more than 52? … 2 more than 29? … 1 less than 81?' etc.
- At the end of the lesson ask for the numbers made in 'Try this' in order, starting with the smallest.

Answers

1 a) 35, 36, 37, 38, 39 b) 9, 10, 11, 12, 13
c) 90, 91, 92, 93, 94 d) 76, 77, 78, 79, 80
e) 48, 49, 50, 51, 52 f) 22, 23, 24, 25, 26

2 a) 68 b) 43 c) 72 d) 91 e) 33 f) 80

3 nineteen, thirteen, seventeen, eleven, eighty, forty-two, sixty-four, seventy-five, fifty-eight; 91

Try this

14, 15, 41, 45, 51, 54

Lesson 4 **Place value**

Pupil's Book pages 10 and 11 **Oral and mental starter: Hands up**

Place value

Example 1
58 = 50 + 8

tens	units
5	8

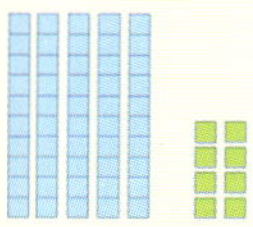

The 5 stands for 50
The 8 stands for 8
58
58 is fifty-eight

Example 2
67 = 60 + 7

tens	units
6	7

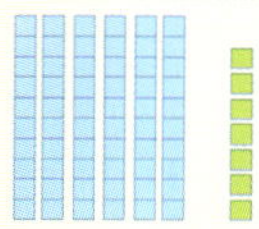

The 6 stands for 60
The 7 stands for 7
67
67 is sixty-seven

1 Write these words as numbers.

a) forty-three b) ninety-six c) fifty-two
d) eighty-seven e) twenty-four f) sixty-nine

2 Write these numbers as words.

a) 71 b) 38 c) 59
d) 95 e) 22 f) 87

3 Write each number as tens and ones.

Example 89 → 80 + 9

a) 47 → □ + □ b) 91 → □ + □
c) 75 → □ + □ d) 82 → □ + □
e) 66 → □ + □ f) 58 → □ + □

4 Write the missing numbers.

a) 2 0 + 1 = □□
b) 3 0 + □ = 3 6
c) □□ + 9 = 4 9
d) 8 0 + 2 = □□
e) 7 0 + □ = 7 4
f) □□ + 7 = 5 7

g) 30 + □ = 31 h) 80 + 5 = □□
i) 60 + □ = 67 j) □□ + 8 = 18
k) 90 + 2 = □□ l) □□ + 4 = 74

Activities

- Look at page 10. Ask 'Which number is the same as 5 tens?' Illustrate 58 with the set of arrow cards then go through the explanation in the example with the class. Repeat for 67.
- Ask a pupil to say any 2-digit number. 'How many tens are there in that number? How many units?' Record on the board in tens and units boxes as shown in the examples on page 10. Ask another pupil to show the number on the arrow cards. Record the number as a multiple of ten with the units below and a total below that (as in the examples), then write the number in words. Repeat with a few more numbers and pupils.
- Write 37 on the board. Ask 'What is the value of the 3 in 37? What is the value of the 7?' Ask pupils to suggest other numbers which have 7 units and record them on the board, then other numbers with 3 tens.
- Explain that in question 4 the boxes stand for missing digits. Write an example on the board such as

  5 0
  \+ ❑
  5 4

  and work through it with the class.

Answers

1 a) 43 b) 96 c) 52 d) 87 e) 24 f) 69
2 a) seventy-one b) thirty-eight c) fifty-nine
d) ninety-five e) twenty-two f) eighty-seven
3 a) 40 + 7 b) 90 + 1 c) 70 + 5
d) 80 + 2 e) 60 +6 f) 50 + 8
4 a) 21 b) 6 c) 40 d) 82 e) 4 f) 50
g) 1 h) 85 i) 7 j) 10 k) 92 l) 70

Lesson 5 **Using an abacus**

Pupil's Book pages 12 and 13 **Oral and mental starter: Hold up**

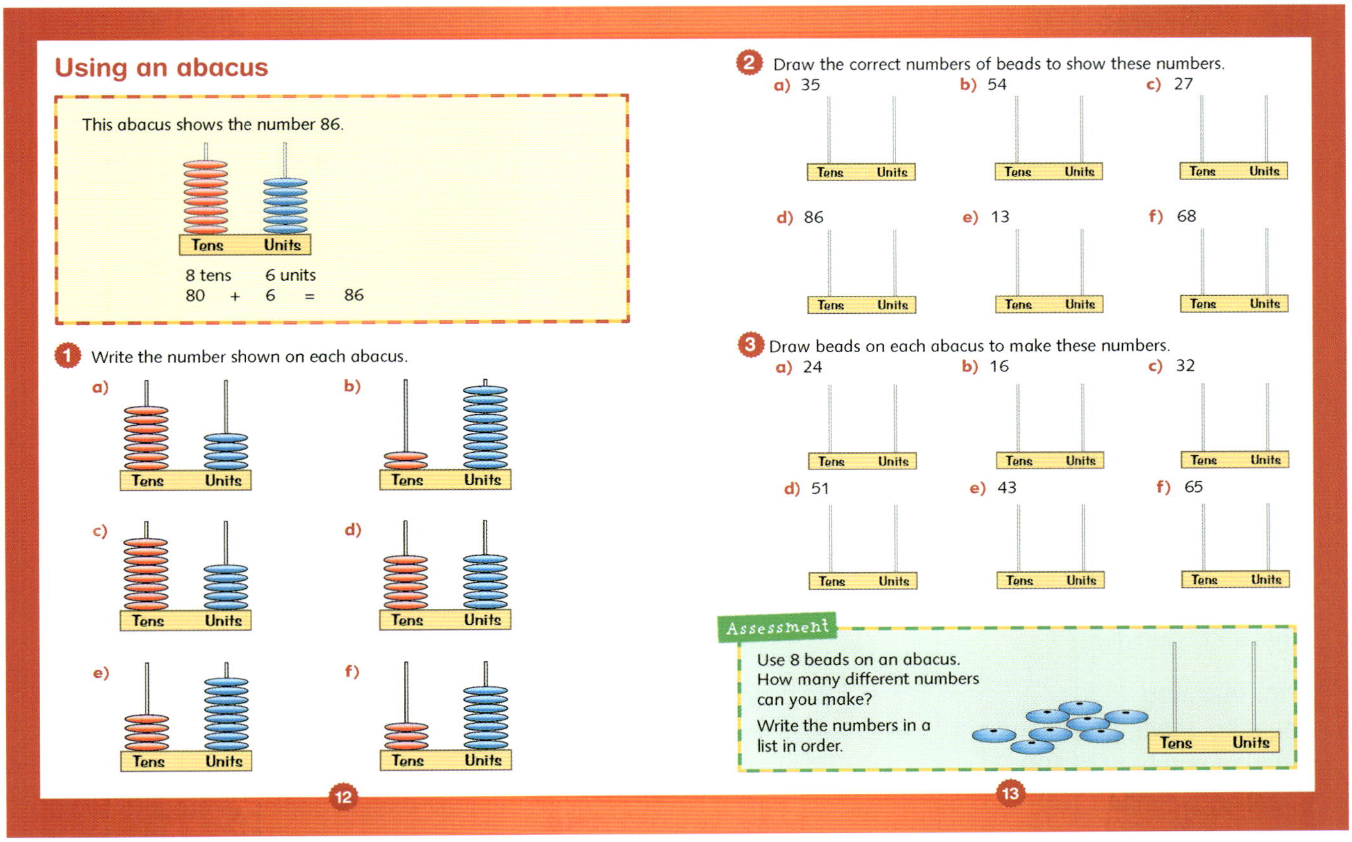

Using an abacus

This abacus shows the number 86.

Tens Units

8 tens 6 units
80 + 6 = 86

1 Write the number shown on each abacus.

a) Tens Units b) Tens Units
c) Tens Units d) Tens Units
e) Tens Units f) Tens Units

2 Draw the correct numbers of beads to show these numbers.

a) 35 b) 54 c) 27
d) 86 e) 13 f) 68

3 Draw beads on each abacus to make these numbers.

a) 24 b) 16 c) 32
d) 51 e) 43 f) 65

Assessment

Use 8 beads on an abacus.
How many different numbers can you make?
Write the numbers in a list in order.

Tens Units

12 13

Activities

- Ask the class to count to 30 as you place one bead at a time on the abacus. After 9 is reached on the units spike, revise that 10 is shown by removing the 9 units beads and placing 1 bead on the tens spike. Reinforce this in a similar way after 19 and 29.
- Place the beads to show any 2-digit number, e.g. 42, and ask pupils to say the number. Repeat with a few more 2-digit numbers.
- Ask pairs of pupils to come to the front, one to say a number, the other to show it on the abacus. Ask the class to raise their hands if they agree.
- Look at page 12. Go through the example in the introduction then draw a similar abacus picture on the board for another number. 'How many tens are there?' Record below the tens spike. 'How many units?' Record below the units spike with a plus sign between the two numbers. 'What is the number?' Record the number.

Answers

1 a) 74 b) 29 c) 85 d) 66 e) 48 f) 37

2 a) 3 + 5 b) 5 + 4 c) 2 + 7
d) 8 + 6 e) 1 + 3 f) 6 + 8

3 a) 2 + 4 b) 1 + 6 c) 3 + 2
d) 5 + 1 e) 4 + 3 f) 6 + 5

Assessment

8, 17, 26, 35, 44, 53, 62, 71, 80

Unit 2 **Numbers to 999**

Term 1 Block A **Numbers and addition** Unit 1 Numbers to 100 **Unit 2 Numbers to 999** Unit 3 Addition to 99 Unit 4 Assess and review	**Objectives** *At the end of the unit, students should be able to…* Read and write 100 and its multiples up to 900. Develop a primary understanding of counting in tens and place value up to 999. Read and write numbers composed of units, tens and hundreds in both number (figure) and letter form.
Vocabulary Names for numbers to 999, hundreds, tens, units, digits, place value, abacus	**Lessons** 1 Numbers to 200 2 Reading numbers to 200 3 Numbers to 999 4 Reading numbers to 999 5 Using an abacus
Oral and mental starters Arrows away (to 99) What's the order (2-digit numbers) Steps Pairs for sums What's the question?	**Resources** Abacus A large 10 × 10 grid numbered 1–100 on display Arrow cards to 999 *Pupil's book pages 14–23*
Prior learning Counting, reading, writing and ordering numbers to 100 Counting in tens to 100 Understanding place value in 2-digit numbers	**Background notes** The concept of place value can be very difficult for some pupils to grasp. It needs careful teaching with much reinforcement to ensure that all pupils are confident in their understanding in order to avoid errors in calculation. The use of materials such as a 1–100 number grid, an abacus and arrow cards is very helpful in the development of this concept. Further work on 3-digit numbers, including ordering, is provided in Block D Unit 13.
End of unit evaluation: Check that pupils are able to: 1 Read, write and order numbers to 999. 2 Count in hundreds to 900. 3 Know the value of each digit in a 3-digit number.	**Supporting the topic** Discuss real-life examples of numbers to 999, e.g. prices of expensive items, house/flat numbers, number of pupils in the school, distances between major towns etc.

Lesson 1 **Numbers to 200**

Pupil's Book pages 14 and 15 **Oral and mental starter: Arrows away (to 99)**

Unit 2 Numbers to 999

Numbers to 200

These show hundreds, tens and units.

1 hundred 2 tens 4 units
100 + 20 + 4

Remember 10 tens make 1 hundred.

1 Write the numbers shown on each mat.

Example

Hundreds	Tens	Units
1	3	6

100 + 30 + 6 = 136

a) 1 + 7 + 1 = ____
b) 1 + 5 + 8 = ____
c) ____ + ____ + ____ = ____
d) ____ + ____ + ____ = ____
e) ____ + ____ + ____ = ____
f) ____ + ____ + ____ = ____

14

2 Write the numbers shown on each mat.

Hundreds	Tens	Units

a) ____ + ____ + ____ = ____
b) ____ + ____ + ____ = ____
c) ____ + ____ + ____ = ____
d) ____ + ____ + ____ = ____

Try this

Write the numbers for each abacus.

Example

100 + 50 + 4
154

a) b) c) d)

15

Activities

- Put 8 beads on the tens spike on the abacus. Ask the class to count on from 80 to 100 as you show each number on the abacus. 'Does anyone know the next number?' Establish that 1 more than 100 is 101 and write it on the board. Explain to the class that when we count from 100 in ones we follow the same pattern as counting from 0 to 100, but each number begins with 1 hundred.
- Say the numbers from 100 to 125 as you continue the abacus count, asking pupils to join in when they feel confident. Record the numbers on the board in order and ask the class to say them together. Point out how each number is written with a 1 for 100, then two digits after that.
- 'Which number is 1 more than 125? Which number will come after that?' Ask the class to count from 125 to 140 together.
- Explain the introduction on page 14. Ask pupils to look carefully at the block representing 100. 'Can you see why it is 100?' Establish that it is made up of ten rods, each rod being divided into 10 units. Ask the class to count in tens to 100 as they touch each row of 10 on the block in turn. Look at the classroom 1–100 grid. It has the same number of squares as the 100 block.

Answers

1 a) 171 b) 158
c) 1 + 6 + 4 = 164 d) 1 + 3 + 9 = 139
e) 1 + 4 + 5 = 145 f) 1 + 1 + 3 = 113

2 a) 1 + 4 + 5 = 145 b) 1 + 3 + 2 = 132
c) 1 + 9 + 4 = 194 d) 1 + 2 + 5 = 125

Try this

a) 196 b) 147 c) 183 d) 125

Lesson 2 **Place value to 200**

Pupil's Book pages 16 and 17 **Oral and mental starter: What's the order? (to 100)**

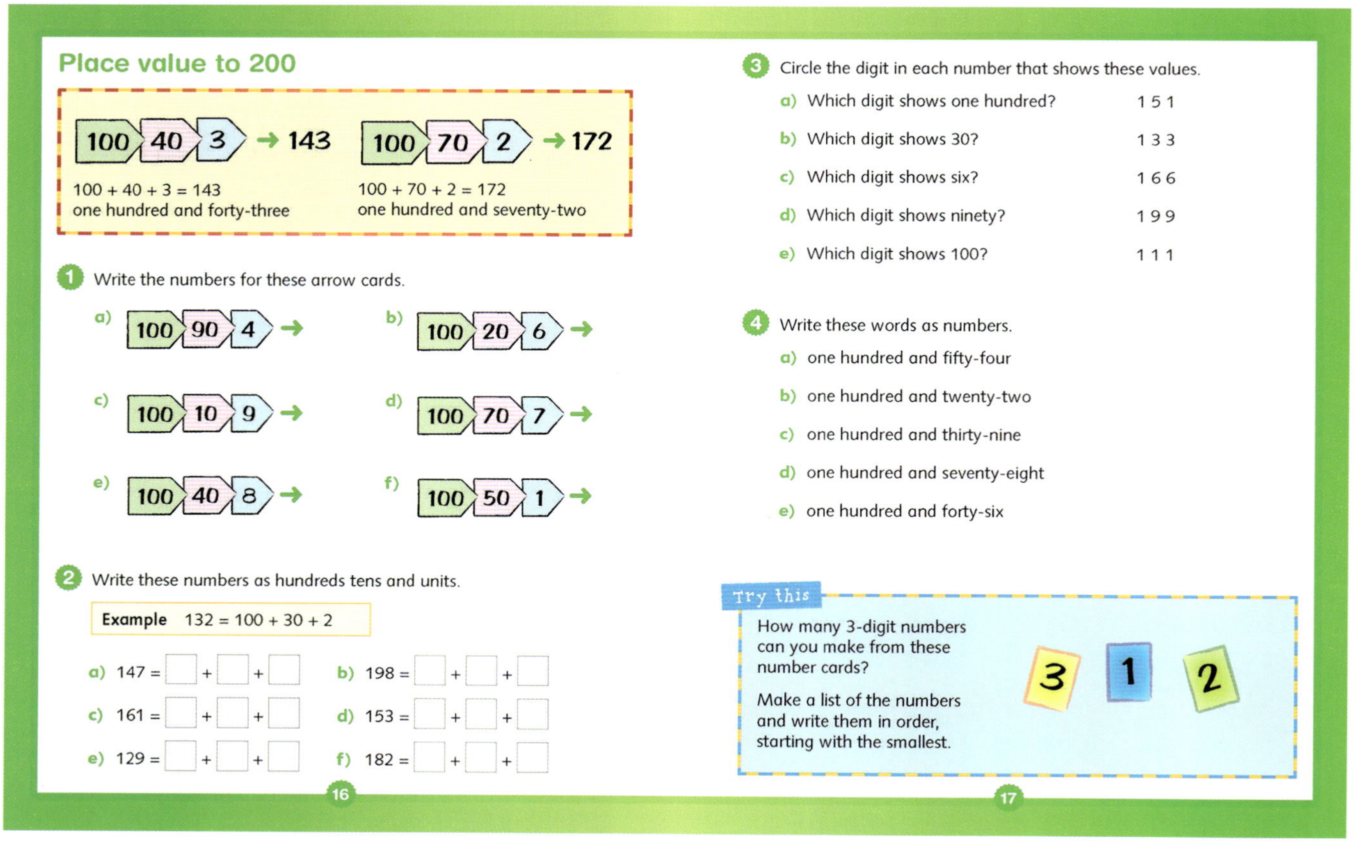

Place value to 200

100 40 3 → 143
100 + 40 + 3 = 143
one hundred and forty-three

100 70 2 → 172
100 + 70 + 2 = 172
one hundred and seventy-two

1. Write the numbers for these arrow cards.
   a) 100 90 4 →
   b) 100 20 6 →
   c) 100 10 9 →
   d) 100 70 7 →
   e) 100 40 8 →
   f) 100 50 1 →

2. Write these numbers as hundreds tens and units.

   Example 132 = 100 + 30 + 2

   a) 147 = ☐ + ☐ + ☐
   b) 198 = ☐ + ☐ + ☐
   c) 161 = ☐ + ☐ + ☐
   d) 153 = ☐ + ☐ + ☐
   e) 129 = ☐ + ☐ + ☐
   f) 182 = ☐ + ☐ + ☐

3. Circle the digit in each number that shows these values.
   a) Which digit shows one hundred? 1 5 1
   b) Which digit shows 30? 1 3 3
   c) Which digit shows six? 1 6 6
   d) Which digit shows ninety? 1 9 9
   e) Which digit shows 100? 1 1 1

4. Write these words as numbers.
   a) one hundred and fifty-four
   b) one hundred and twenty-two
   c) one hundred and thirty-nine
   d) one hundred and seventy-eight
   e) one hundred and forty-six

Try this

How many 3-digit numbers can you make from these number cards?

Make a list of the numbers and write them in order, starting with the smallest.

16 17

Activities

- Look at page 16. Talk about the arrow cards and demonstrate with your cards how they show the correct notation for each number when the arrows are placed over each other. Write 124 on the board and ask a pupil to read the number. Ask another pupil to select three arrow cards and place them correctly to show 124. Repeat with other numbers such as 156, 135, 191, 116.
- Show a variety of numbers to 200 on the arrow cards placed over each other appropriately and ask the class to read the number then say the value of each digit. Remove the appropriate card each time to show its value.
- Check that pupils are writing the 3-digit numbers correctly as they work (a common error at this stage of learning is to write 143 as 10043).
- At the end of the lesson ask pupils to look at the 3-digit numbers in question 2. 'Which is the smallest number? How do you know?' Record 129 on the board. Repeat for the next smallest up to the largest number.

Answers

1 a) 194 b) 126 c) 119 d) 177 e) 148 f) 151

2 a) 100 + 40 + 7 b) 100 + 90 + 8 c) 100 + 60 + 1
d) 100 + 50 + 3 e) 100 + 20 + 9 f) 100 + 80 + 2

3 a) **1** 5 1 b) 1 **3** 3 c) 1 6 **6** d) 1 **9** 9 e) **1** 1 1

4 a) 154 b) 122 c) 139 d) 178 e) 146

Try this

123, 132, 213, 231, 312, 321

Lesson 3 **Numbers to 999**

Pupil's Book pages 18 and 19 **Oral and mental starter: Steps**

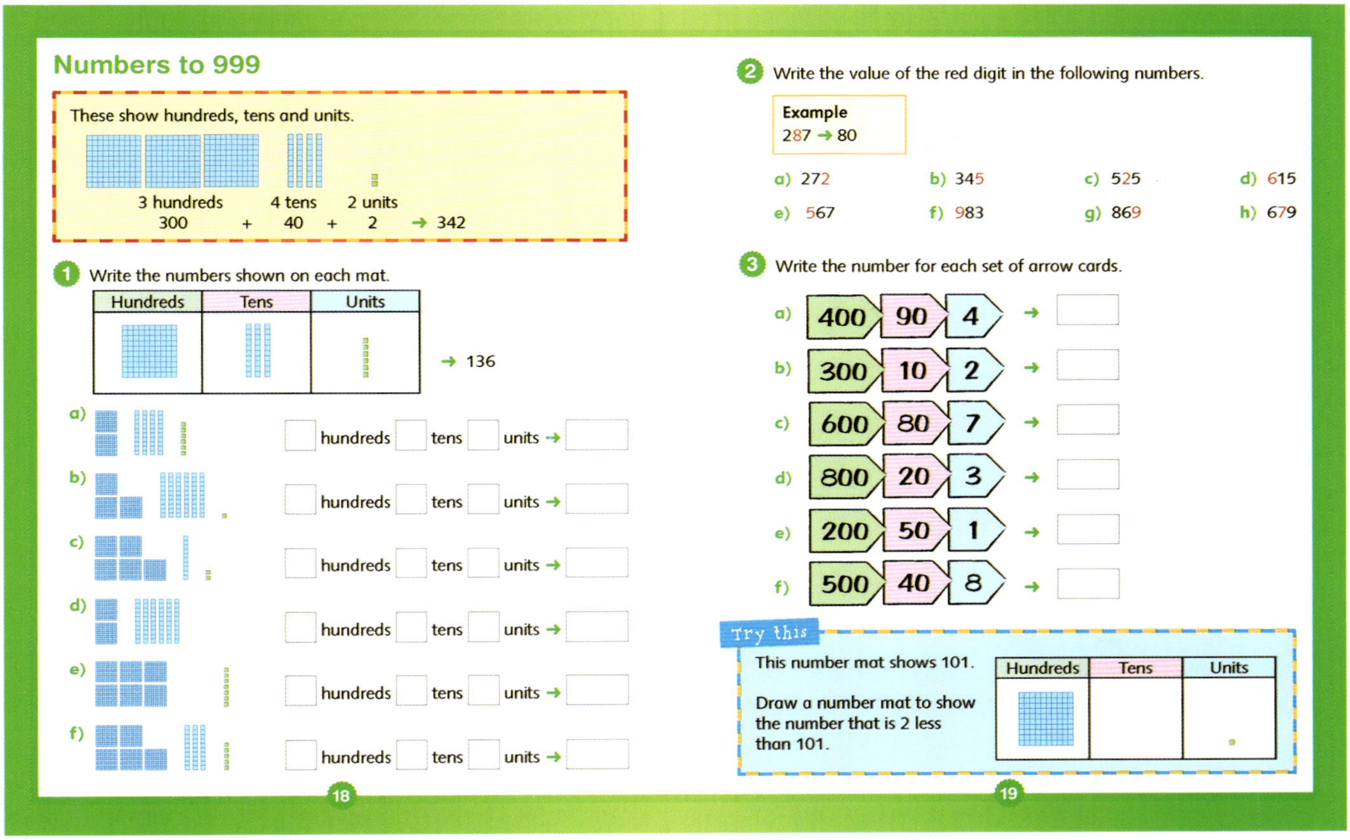

Numbers to 999

These show hundreds, tens and units.

3 hundreds 4 tens 2 units
300 + 40 + 2 → 342

1 Write the numbers shown on each mat.

Hundreds	Tens	Units

→ 136

a) ☐ hundreds ☐ tens ☐ units → ☐
b) ☐ hundreds ☐ tens ☐ units → ☐
c) ☐ hundreds ☐ tens ☐ units → ☐
d) ☐ hundreds ☐ tens ☐ units → ☐
e) ☐ hundreds ☐ tens ☐ units → ☐
f) ☐ hundreds ☐ tens ☐ units → ☐

2 Write the value of the red digit in the following numbers.

Example
287 → 80

a) 272 b) 345 c) 525 d) 615
e) 567 f) 983 g) 869 h) 679

3 Write the number for each set of arrow cards.

a) 400 90 4 → ☐
b) 300 10 2 → ☐
c) 600 80 7 → ☐
d) 800 20 3 → ☐
e) 200 50 1 → ☐
f) 500 40 8 → ☐

Try this

This number mat shows 101.

Draw a number mat to show the number that is 2 less than 101.

Hundreds	Tens	Units

18 19

Activities

- Ask the class to count from 185 to 200. 'What is 1 more than 200?' Record 201 on the board and display it on the abacus. 'How many tens are there in 201? What will the next number be … and the next?' Stress that the pattern is the same as counting from 100 to 200, but this time all the numbers begin with 2 hundreds. Record 202 and 203 on the board and continue the count.
- 'Which number comes after 250? … 259? What happens after 300?' Establish that the counting pattern continues as before. 'What is the next hundred after 300?' Continue until 900. Record 100 and all its multiples to 900 in order on the board. Ask the class to count in hundreds together.
- Go through the introduction on page 18 with the class. Check that pupils record the 3-digit numbers correctly as they answer question 1.
- At the end of the lesson write numbers such as 368, 741, 403, 299, 610 on the board and ask the class to say them together. Ask them to say the number which is 1 more than each, then 1 less than each. 'Which is the smallest number? How do you know?' Record 299 on the board and stress that this is the smallest because it has the lowest hundreds digit. Repeat for the next smallest up to the largest number.

Answers

1 a) 246 b) 361 c) 512 d) 260 e) 607 f) 535
2 a) 2 b) 5 c) 20 d) 600 e) 500 f) 900
g) 9 h) 70
3 a) 494 b) 312 c) 687 d) 823 e) 251 f) 548

Try this

Check that children have drawn 9 rods and 9 units.

Lesson 4 **Place value to 999**

Pupil's Book pages 20 and 21 **Oral and mental starter: Pairs for sums**

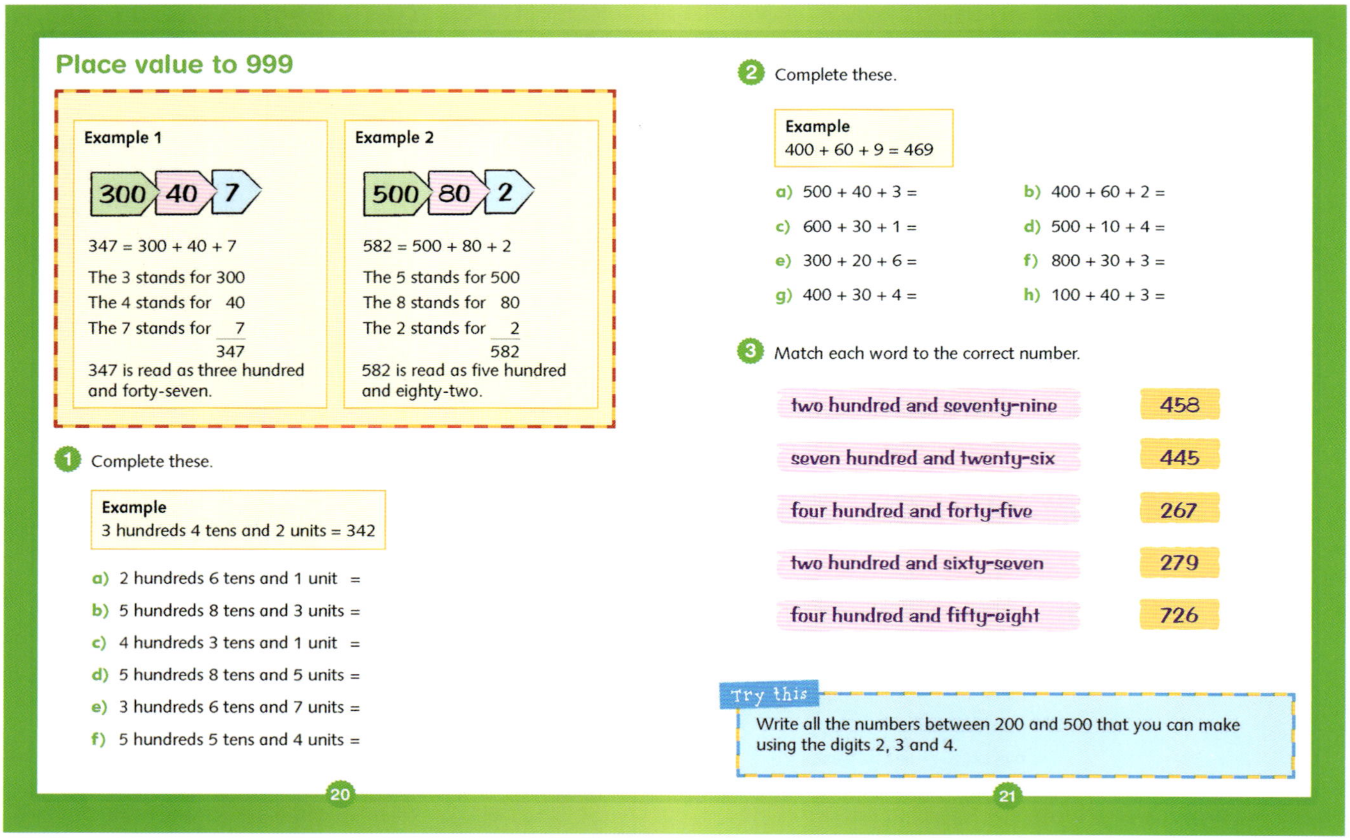

Place value to 999

Example 1

347 = 300 + 40 + 7

The 3 stands for 300
The 4 stands for 40
The 7 stands for 7
347

347 is read as three hundred and forty-seven.

Example 2

582 = 500 + 80 + 2

The 5 stands for 500
The 8 stands for 80
The 2 stands for 2
582

582 is read as five hundred and eighty-two.

1 Complete these.

Example
3 hundreds 4 tens and 2 units = 342

a) 2 hundreds 6 tens and 1 unit =
b) 5 hundreds 8 tens and 3 units =
c) 4 hundreds 3 tens and 1 unit =
d) 5 hundreds 8 tens and 5 units =
e) 3 hundreds 6 tens and 7 units =
f) 5 hundreds 5 tens and 4 units =

20

2 Complete these.

Example
400 + 60 + 9 = 469

a) 500 + 40 + 3 =
b) 400 + 60 + 2 =
c) 600 + 30 + 1 =
d) 500 + 10 + 4 =
e) 300 + 20 + 6 =
f) 800 + 30 + 3 =
g) 400 + 30 + 4 =
h) 100 + 40 + 3 =

3 Match each word to the correct number.

two hundred and seventy-nine	458
seven hundred and twenty-six	445
four hundred and forty-five	267
two hundred and sixty-seven	279
four hundred and fifty-eight	726

Try this
Write all the numbers between 200 and 500 that you can make using the digits 2, 3 and 4.

21

Activities

- Show a variety of 3-digit numbers on arrow cards placed over each other appropriately. Ask the class to say each number then give the value of each digit. Remove the appropriate card each time to show its value.
- Ask volunteers to show given 3-digit numbers on the arrow cards, e.g. 623, 174, 937, 508, 290 etc.
- Look at page 20 and go through the introduction with the class.
- Check that pupils are writing the 3-digit numbers correctly as they work.
- At the end of the lesson ask pupils to look at the 3-digit numbers in question 2. 'Which is the smallest number? How do you know?' Record 143 on the board. Repeat for the next smallest up to the largest number. Establish that when the hundreds digit is the same we compare the value of the tens digits to determine the order (as in 514 and 543).

Answers

1 a) 261 b) 583 c) 431 d) 585 e) 367 f) 554

2 a) 543 b) 462 c) 631 d) 514 e) 326 f) 833 g) 434 h) 143

3 two hundred and seventy-nine → 279,
seven hundred and twenty-six → 726,
four hundred and forty-five → 445,
two hundred and sixty-seven → 267,
four hundred and fifty-eight → 458

Try this

234, 243, 324, 342, 423, 432

Lesson 5 **Using an abacus**

Pupil's Book pages 22 and 23 **Oral and mental starter: What's the question?**

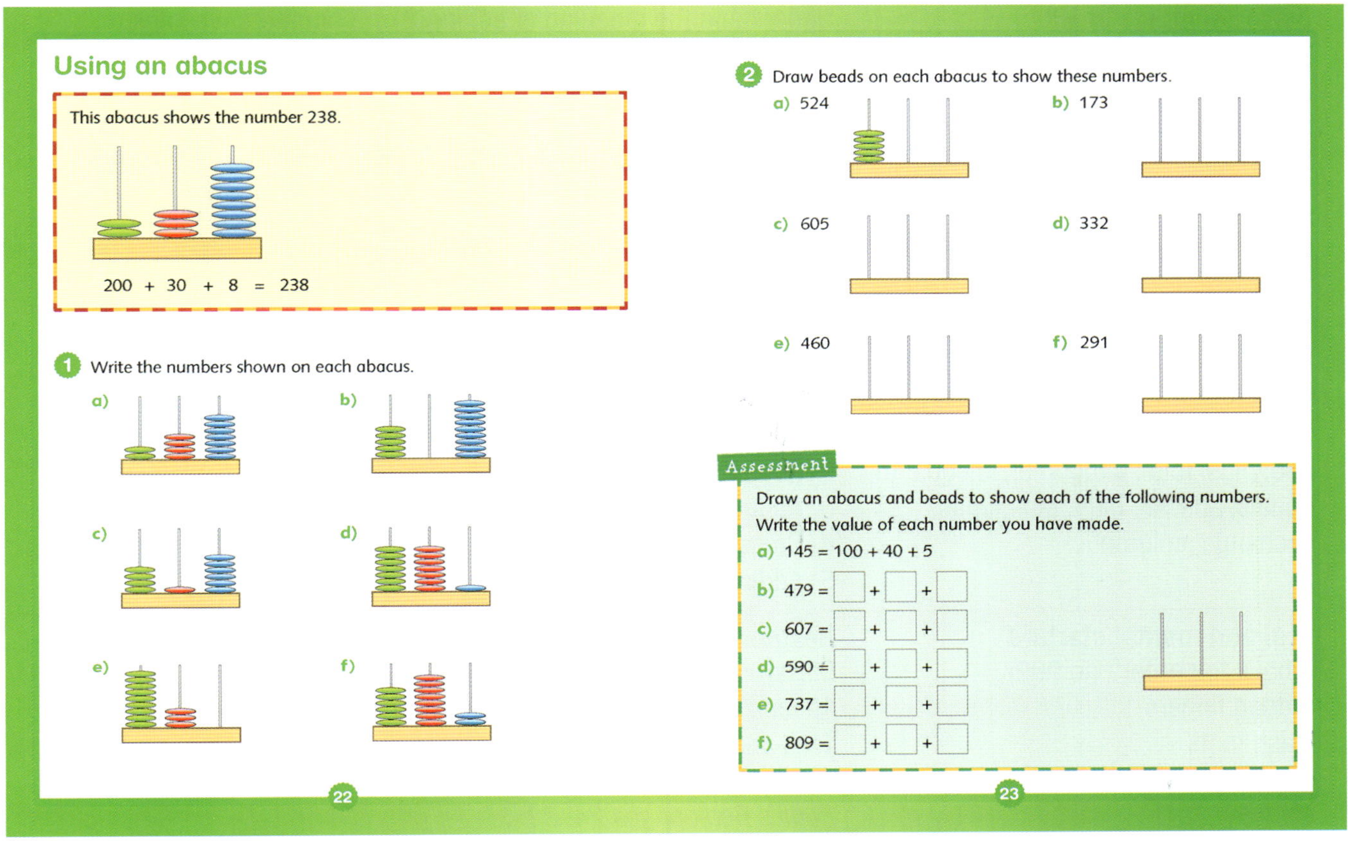
Using an abacus

This abacus shows the number 238.

200 + 30 + 8 = 238

1 Write the numbers shown on each abacus.

a) b) c) d) e) f)

2 Draw beads on each abacus to show these numbers.

a) 524 b) 173 c) 605 d) 332 e) 460 f) 291

Assessment

Draw an abacus and beads to show each of the following numbers. Write the value of each number you have made.

a) 145 = 100 + 40 + 5

b) 479 = ☐ + ☐ + ☐

c) 607 = ☐ + ☐ + ☐

d) 590 = ☐ + ☐ + ☐

e) 737 = ☐ + ☐ + ☐

f) 809 = ☐ + ☐ + ☐

22 23

Activities

- Ask the class to count in ones to 10, then in tens to 100, then in hundreds to 900, as you place appropriate beads on the abacus. 'Which is the units spike? Which is the hundreds? Which is the tens?'
- Show a variety of 3-digit numbers on the abacus. Ask the class to say each number then give the value of each digit.
- Ask volunteers to show given 3-digit numbers on the abacus, e.g. 376, 589, 138, 490, 812, 603 etc.
- Look at page 22 and go through the introduction with the class.

Answers

1 a) 247 b) 509 c) 416 d) 771 e) 930 f) 682

2 a) 2 + 4 b) 1 + 7 + 3 c) 6 + 0 + 5 d) 3 + 3 + 2 e) 4 + 6 + 0 f) 2 + 9 + 1

Assessment

b) 400 + 70 + 9 c) 600 + 0 + 7 d) 500 + 90 + 0 e) 700 + 30 + 7 f) 800 + 0 + 9

Unit 3 **Addition to 99**

Term 1 Block A
Numbers and addition
Unit 1 Numbers to 100
Unit 2 Numbers to 999
Unit 3 Addition to 99
Unit 4 Assess and review

Objectives
At the end of the unit, students should be able to...
Understand the meaning of adding 2 or 3 numbers whose sum doesn't exceed 99, with or without renaming.
Choose the basic operation needed to solve a mathematical or everyday problem (word problems).
Check the result of any addition problem.
Use different and suitable methods for addition like Mental Maths or use of paper and pencil (written).
Use approximation in solving addition of numbers.
Identify numerical examples showing the properties of addition up to 99, without explicitly naming them.

Vocabulary
Names for numbers to 99, addition, add, plus, total, altogether, is equal to, equals, answer, digit, tens, units, exchange, column

Lessons
1 Adding tens
2 Adding numbers to 99: no exchange
3 Adding to the next ten
4 Crossing the ten: TU + U
5 Adding 2-digit numbers

Oral and mental starters
What's the order? (to 999)
Hidden fingers
Flash facts
Arrows away
My way

Resources
Classroom 1–100 grid
Abacus
Tens and units apparatus (e.g. ten rods and unit cubes, or bundles of ten sticks and unit sticks)
Pupil's Book pages 24–33

Prior learning
Adding 2-digit numbers without renaming (Grade 1)
Understanding place value in 2-digit numbers

Background notes
Errors in addition calculations involving exchange are often due to a lack of understanding of place value. The content of this scheme covers place value thoroughly and by now pupils should be confident with the concept.
Encourage pupils to:
- use known addition facts when doing written calculations,
- learn addition facts to 20,
- use the fact that addition can be done in any order,
- count on when adding numbers whose sums are not known,
- align the digits in 2-digit numbers correctly when doing calculations which are set out vertically.

End of unit evaluation
Check that pupils are able to:
1 Add multiples of ten to 2-digit numbers (totals < 100).
2 Add pairs of 2-digit numbers without renaming (totals < 100).
3 Add pairs of 2-digit numbers with renaming (totals < 100).

Supporting the topic
Use opportunities in everyday classroom activities to add 2-digit numbers, e.g. 28 pupils in our class, 31 in the next, how many altogether? Talk about situations in real life where 2-digit numbers need to be added, e.g. the total cost of 2 or 3 items.

Lesson 1 Adding tens

Pupil's Book pages 24 and 25 **Oral and mental starter: What's the order? (to 999)**

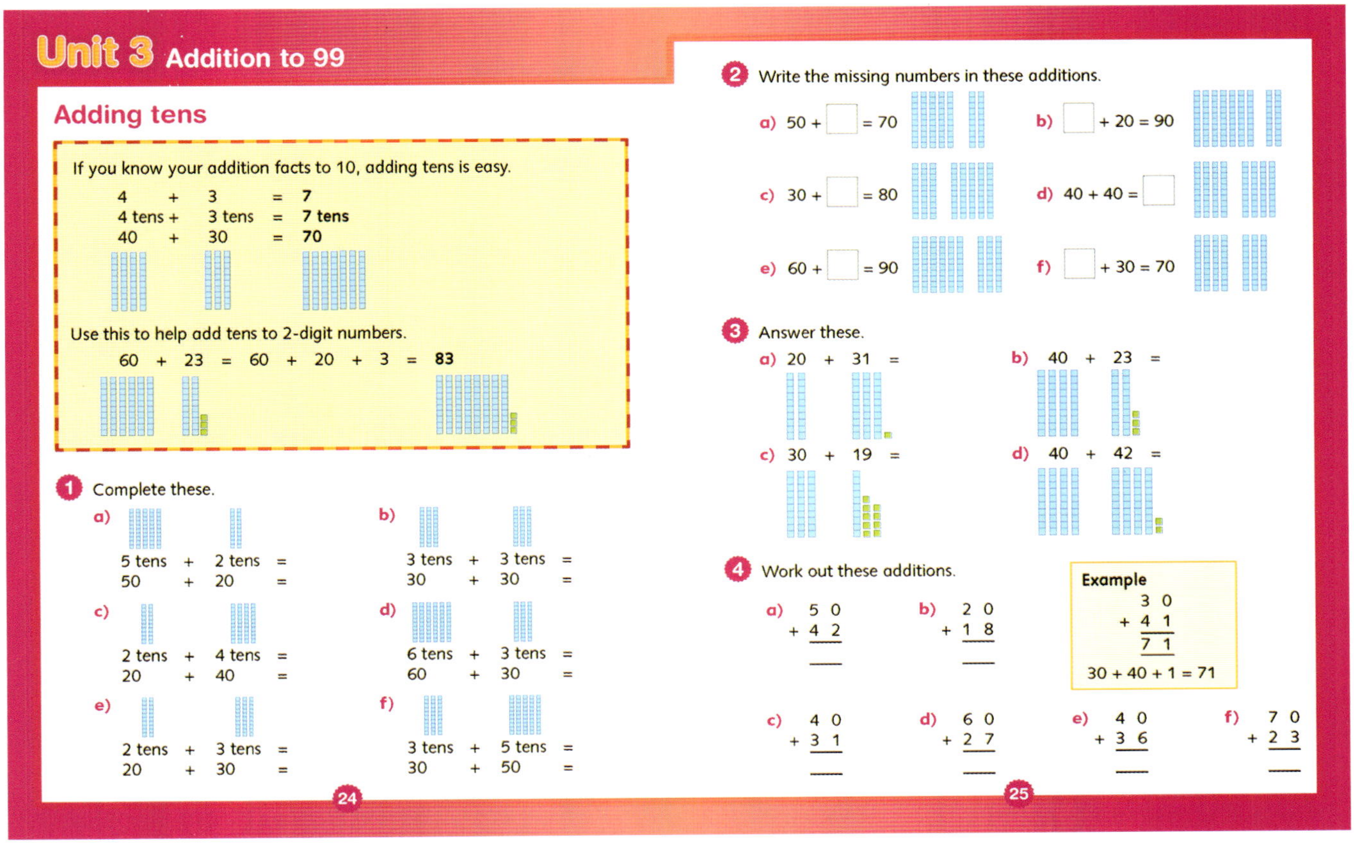

Unit 3 Addition to 99

Adding tens

If you know your addition facts to 10, adding tens is easy.

4 + 3 = **7**
4 tens + 3 tens = **7 tens**
40 + 30 = **70**

Use this to help add tens to 2-digit numbers.

60 + 23 = 60 + 20 + 3 = **83**

1 Complete these.

a) 5 tens + 2 tens =
50 + 20 =

b) 3 tens + 3 tens =
30 + 30 =

c) 2 tens + 4 tens =
20 + 40 =

d) 6 tens + 3 tens =
60 + 30 =

e) 2 tens + 3 tens =
20 + 30 =

f) 3 tens + 5 tens =
30 + 50 =

24

2 Write the missing numbers in these additions.

a) 50 + ☐ = 70
b) ☐ + 20 = 90
c) 30 + ☐ = 80
d) 40 + 40 = ☐
e) 60 + ☐ = 90
f) ☐ + 30 = 70

3 Answer these.

a) 20 + 31 =
b) 40 + 23 =
c) 30 + 19 =
d) 40 + 42 =

4 Work out these additions.

a) 50 + 42
b) 20 + 18
c) 40 + 31
d) 60 + 27
e) 40 + 36
f) 70 + 23

Example
30 + 41 = 71
30 + 40 + 1 = 71

25

Activities

- Look at the classroom 1–100 grid. Ask the class to count in 10s to 100 together as you indicate each number. Ask them to count in 10s from different multiples of 10, e.g. from 20, from 40 etc. Ask questions such as: 'What is the next 10 after 40? … ten more than 60? … the 10 before 20? … two tens more than 70?'
- Indicate 3 on the 1–100 grid. 'What is 10 more than 3?' Reinforce the answer by counting on 10 from 3 on the grid. Record 3 + 10 = 13 on the board. Ask 'What is 13 + 10 … 23 + 10 … 33 + 10?' Record each addition on the board below 3 + 10 = 13. 'What do you notice about the pattern? What happens when we add 10 to any number?' Establish that the tens digit increases by 1, the units digit is unchanged. Indicate 46 on the 1–100 grid. 'What is 46 + 10?' Repeat using other starting numbers from the grid.
- Go through the introduction on page 24, emphasising the teaching points and how to use the illustrations to help with the additions. Ask questions such as: 'What is 7 + 2? So what is 70 + 20? … 70 + 23? … 70 + 25?' 'What is 3 + 3? So what is 30 + 30? … 30 + 31? … 30 + 38?'
- Ask pupils to look page 25. Remind them that there are two ways of setting out additions as shown and that when columns are used the tens and units must line up correctly.

Answers

1 a) 70, 70 b) 60, 60 c) 60, 60 d) 90, 90
e) 50, 50 f) 80, 80

2 a) 20 b) 70 c) 50 d) 80 e) 30 f) 40

3 a) 51 b) 63 c) 49 d) 82

4 a) 92 b) 38 c) 71 d) 87 e) 76 f) 93

Lesson 2 **Adding numbers to 99: no exchange**

Pupil's Book pages 26 and 27 **Oral and mental starter: Hidden fingers**

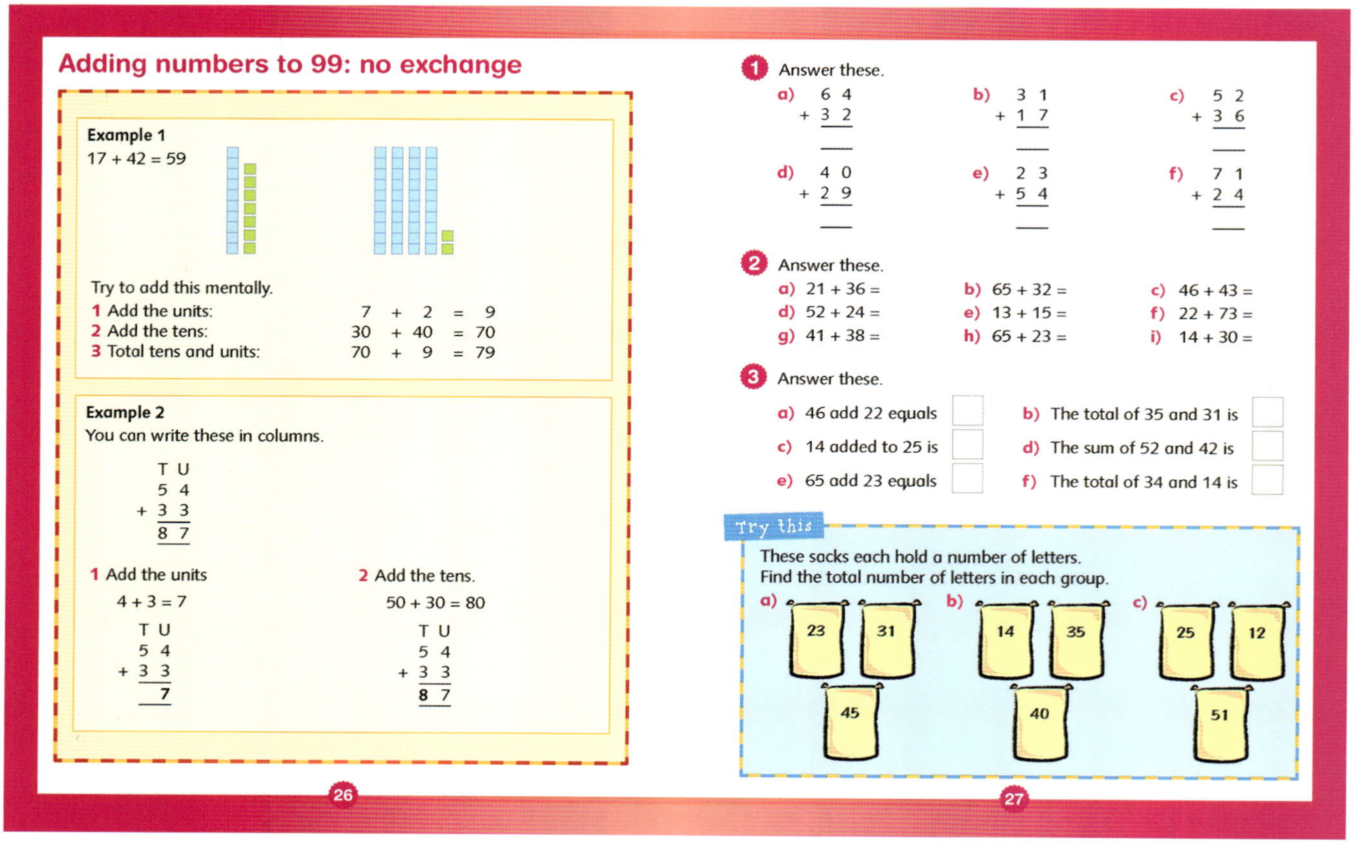

Adding numbers to 99: no exchange

Example 1

17 + 42 = 59

Try to add this mentally.

1 Add the units: 7 + 2 = 9

2 Add the tens: 30 + 40 = 70

3 Total tens and units: 70 + 9 = 79

Example 2

You can write these in columns.

```
  T U
  5 4
+ 3 3
  8 7
```

1 Add the units

4 + 3 = 7

```
  T U
  5 4
+ 3 3
    7
```

2 Add the tens.

50 + 30 = 80

```
  T U
  5 4
+ 3 3
  8 7
```


1 Answer these.

a) 64 + 32 b) 31 + 17 c) 52 + 36

d) 40 + 29 e) 23 + 54 f) 71 + 24

2 Answer these.

a) 21 + 36 = b) 65 + 32 = c) 46 + 43 =

d) 52 + 24 = e) 13 + 15 = f) 22 + 73 =

g) 41 + 38 = h) 65 + 23 = i) 14 + 30 =

3 Answer these.

a) 46 add 22 equals ☐ b) The total of 35 and 31 is ☐

c) 14 added to 25 is ☐ d) The sum of 52 and 42 is ☐

e) 65 add 23 equals ☐ f) The total of 34 and 14 is ☐

Try this

These sacks each hold a number of letters.
Find the total number of letters in each group.

Activities

- Write 43 + 31 on the board. Ask two pupils to come to the front and take rods (or bundles of sticks) and cubes (or loose sticks), one to show 43, the other 31. Ask them to hold them up with the rods in one hand, the cubes in the other. 'How many cubes are there altogether? How many rods?' Ask the two at the front to put their rods together then their cubes to demonstrate the total. Record 74 as the answer to the sum. Repeat with other pairs of pupils and other 2-digit additions in which the units total is less than 10.
- Look at page 26 and discuss the first example, relating it to the previous activity. Ask the class to try a few simple sums mentally, giving the answers orally, e.g. 21 + 14, 42 + 20, 25 + 12, 51 + 11. Each time ask how they worked out the answer. Clarify that in example 2 the answer would be worked out on the same sum, not two separate sums. The sums have been written separately to illustrate each stage of the calculation.
- At the end of the lesson discuss the 'Try this' results and ask pupils to explain how they worked out the answers.

Answers

1 a) 96 b) 48 c) 88 d) 69 e) 77 f) 95

2 a) 57 b) 97 c) 89 d) 76 e) 28 f) 95
g) 79 h) 88 i) 44

3 a) 68 b) 66 c) 39 d) 94 e) 88 f) 48

Try this

a) 99 b) 89 c) 88

Lesson 3 **Adding to the next ten**

Pupil's Book pages 28 and 29 **Oral and mental starter: Flash facts**

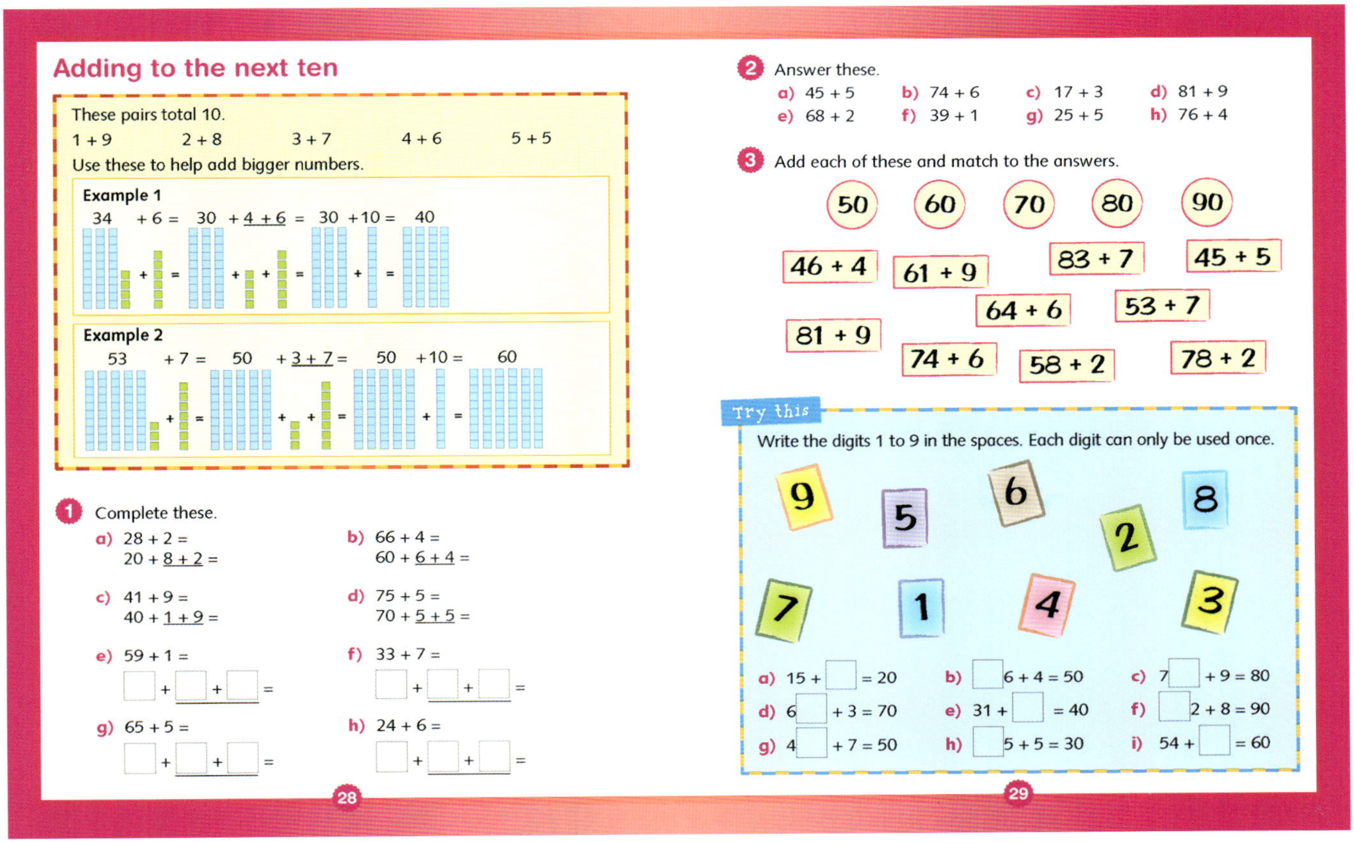

Adding to the next ten

These pairs total 10.

1 + 9   2 + 8   3 + 7   4 + 6   5 + 5

Use these to help add bigger numbers.

Example 1

34 + 6 = 30 + <u>4 + 6</u> = 30 + 10 = 40

Example 2

53 + 7 = 50 + <u>3 + 7</u> = 50 + 10 = 60

1 Complete these.

a) 28 + 2 =
20 + <u>8 + 2</u> =

b) 66 + 4 =
60 + <u>6 + 4</u> =

c) 41 + 9 =
40 + <u>1 + 9</u> =

d) 75 + 5 =
70 + <u>5 + 5</u> =

e) 59 + 1 =
☐ + ☐ + ☐ =

f) 33 + 7 =
☐ + ☐ + ☐ =

g) 65 + 5 =
☐ + ☐ + ☐ =

h) 24 + 6 =
☐ + ☐ + ☐ =

28

2 Answer these.

a) 45 + 5	b) 74 + 6	c) 17 + 3	d) 81 + 9
e) 68 + 2	f) 39 + 1	g) 25 + 5	h) 76 + 4

3 Add each of these and match to the answers.

50 60 70 80 90

46 + 4 61 + 9 83 + 7 45 + 5 64 + 6 53 + 7 81 + 9 74 + 6 58 + 2 78 + 2

Try this

Write the digits 1 to 9 in the spaces. Each digit can only be used once.

9 5 6 2 8 7 1 4 3

a) 15 + ☐ = 20	b) ☐6 + 4 = 50	c) 7☐ + 9 = 80
d) 6☐ + 3 = 70	e) 31 + ☐ = 40	f) ☐2 + 8 = 90
g) 4☐ + 7 = 50	h) ☐5 + 5 = 30	i) 54 + ☐ = 60

29

Activities

- Look at page 28. Talk about the pairs of numbers which total 10 and how they are used in the examples.
- Write 1 + 9 = on the board, ask for the answer and record. '1 plus 9 is 10, so what is 11 + 9?' 'How did you work it out?' Record 11 + 9 = 10 + 1 + 9 = 10 + 10 = 20 on the board. Repeat with 21 + 9, 31 + 9, …, 91 + 9. Emphasise the pattern in the calculations, each using 1 + 9 then adding 10 to the tens digit of the first number. Repeat with calculations such as 7 + 3 = 10, 37 + 3 = ?, 67 + 3 = ?, 47 + 3 = ?
- At the end of the lesson ask questions such as 34 + 6, 77 + 3, 18 + 2, 65 + 5, 92 + 8, 56 + 4 etc for the class to answer orally together on your signal. Aim for a quick response.

Answers

1 a) 30 b) 70 c) 50 d) 80
e) 50 + 9 + 1 = 60 f) 30 + 3 + 7 = 40
g) 60 + 5 + 5 = 70 h) 20 + 4 + 6 = 30

2 a) 50 b) 80 c) 20 d) 90 e) 70
f) 40 g) 30 h) 80

3 46 + 4 → 50, 61 + 9 → 70, 83 + 7 → 90, 45 + 5 → 50, 64 + 6 → 70, 53 + 7 → 60, 81 + 9 → 90, 74 + 6 → 80, 58 + 2 → 60, 78 + 2 → 80

Try this

a) 5 b) 4 c) 1 d) 7 e) 9 f) 8
g) 3 h) 2 i) 6

Lesson 4 **Crossing the ten: TU + U**

Pupil's Book pages 30 and 31 **Oral and mental starter: Arrows away**

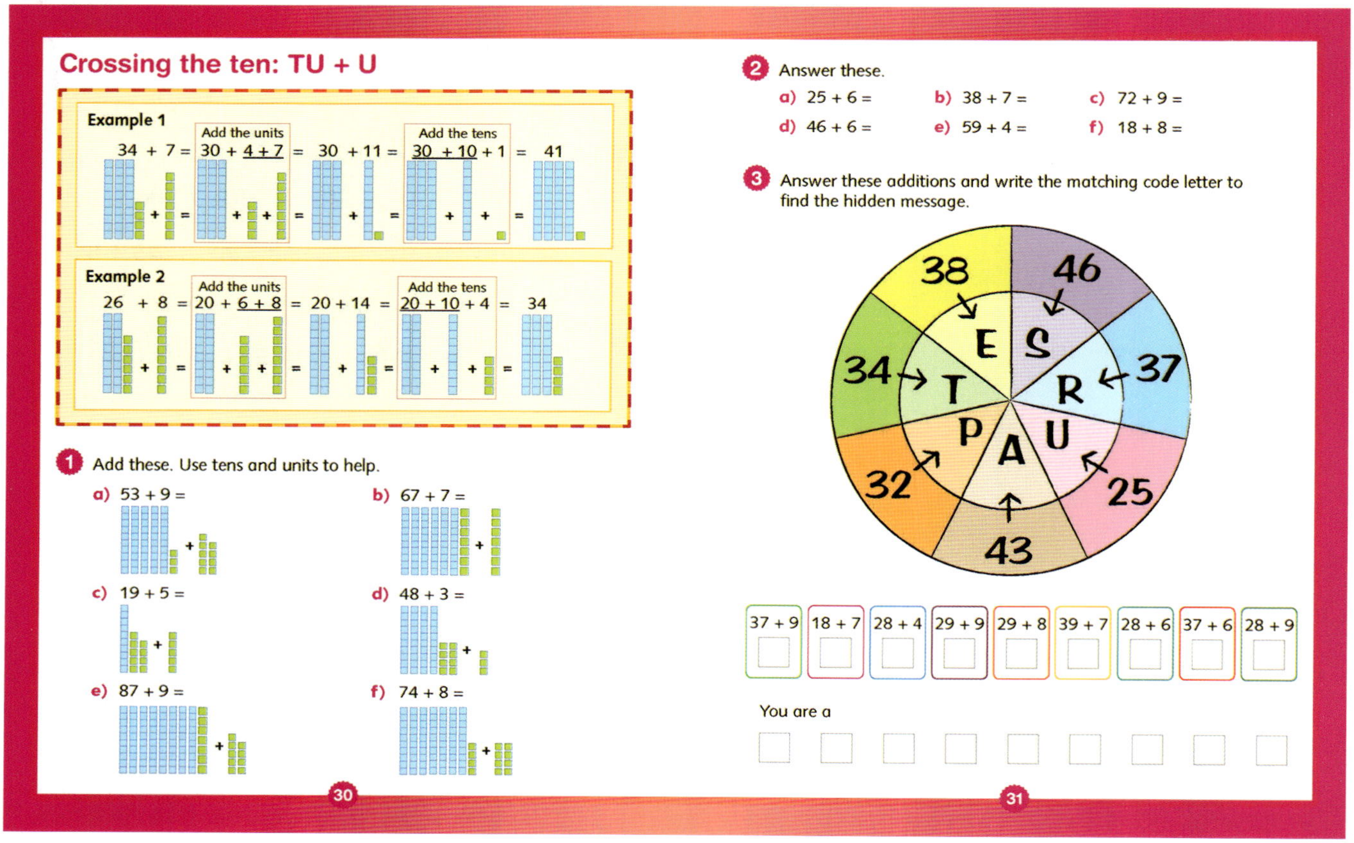
Crossing the ten: TU + U

Example 1

34 + 7 = 30 + 4 + 7 = 30 + 11 = 30 + 10 + 1 = 41

Add the units / Add the tens

Example 2

26 + 8 = 20 + 6 + 8 = 20 + 14 = 20 + 10 + 4 = 34

Add the units / Add the tens

1 Add these. Use tens and units to help.

a) 53 + 9 =
b) 67 + 7 =
c) 19 + 5 =
d) 48 + 3 =
e) 87 + 9 =
f) 74 + 8 =

2 Answer these.

a) 25 + 6 =
b) 38 + 7 =
c) 72 + 9 =
d) 46 + 6 =
e) 59 + 4 =
f) 18 + 8 =

3 Answer these additions and write the matching code letter to find the hidden message.

37 + 9 | 18 + 7 | 28 + 4 | 29 + 9 | 29 + 8 | 39 + 7 | 28 + 6 | 37 + 6 | 28 + 9

You are a

30
31

Activities

- Ask pupils in pairs to use tens and units materials to show 27 and 5. 'How many single cubes do you have altogether?' Ask them to exchange 10 of the cubes for a ten rod. 'How many rods do you have now? How many single cubes? How many cubes altogether?' Record 27 + 5 = 20 + 7 + 5 = 20 + 10 + 2 = 32 on the board, explaining how this recording relates to the activity. Repeat for another sum, e.g. 16 + 5.
- Look at page 30. Go through each example with the class.
- Towards the end of the lesson ask for answers to 28 + 9, 57 + 9, 45 + 9 for pupils to work out mentally. 'Has anyone found a quick way to add 9 to a number?' Establish that it is easier to add 10 then subtract 1 from the result because 9 is 1 less than 10. Ask pupils to use that strategy to answer further questions, e.g. 63 + 9, 46 + 9, 89 + 9.

Answers

1	a) 62	b) 74	c) 24	d) 51	e) 96	f) 82			
2	a) 31	b) 45	c) 81	d) 52	e) 63	f) 26			
3	46	25	32	38	37	46	34	43	37
	S	U	P	E	R	S	T	A	R

Lesson 5 **Adding 2-digit numbers**

Pupil's Book pages 32 and 33 **Oral and mental starter: My way**

Adding 2-digit numbers

Example 1

28 + 35 → 20 + 8
+ 30 + 5
50 + 13

8 + 5 = 13
20 + 30 = 50
50 + 13 = 63

Example 2

34 + 37 → 30 + 4
+ 30 + 7
60 + 11

4 + 7 = 11
30 + 30 = 60
60 + 11 = 71

1 Complete these.

a) 46 + 29 → 40 + 6
+ 20 + 9
☐ + ☐ → ☐

b) 18 + 73 → 10 + 8
+ 70 + 3
☐ + ☐ → ☐

c) 45 + 47 → 40 + 5
+ 40 + 7
☐ + ☐ → ☐

d) 38 + 38 → 30 + 8
+ 30 + 8
☐ + ☐ → ☐

e) 26 + 35 → 20 + 6
+ 30 + 5
☐ + ☐ → ☐

f) 54 + 19 → 50 + 4
+ 10 + 9
☐ + ☐ → ☐

g) 37 + 47 → 30 + 7
+ 40 + 7
☐ + ☐ → ☐

h) 54 + 28 → 50 + 4
+ 20 + 8
☐ + ☐ → ☐

32

2 Complete these addition walls. Each number is the sum of the two numbers below it.

a)

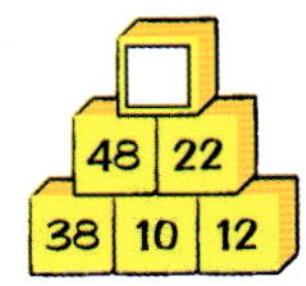

b)

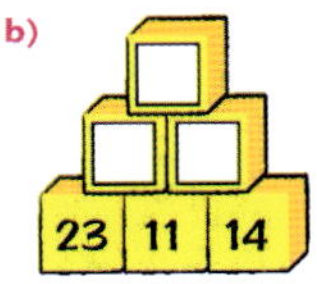

c)

Assessment

Use the grid to answer these.

21	24	13
34	75	50
43	62	51

a) Which two numbers total 86? ☐ and ☐

b) Write pairs of numbers that total the centre number. ☐ and ☐, ☐ and ☐

c) What is the total of the three numbers on the top row? ☐

d) What is the total of each pair of opposite corner numbers? ☐ and ☐

33

Activities

- Ask 'What is 30 + 15? How did you work it out?' Record on the board and revise that when whole tens are added to a number, the tens digits are added and the units digit is unchanged. Ask similar questions such as 20 + 18, 30 + 11, 60 + 16 etc.
- Look at page 32. Go through the examples in the introduction. Provide two or three more examples using the expanded method on the board, e.g. 26 + 18, 54 + 27, 38 + 45, 47 + 44.
- Provide an example of an addition wall on the board and clarify how it is completed in preparation for question 2 on page 33.
- At the end of the lesson ask questions such as 27 + 14, 58 + 25, 45 + 36, 63 + 27 etc. for the class to answer orally together on your signal.

Answers

1 a) 60 + 15 = 75 b) 80 + 11 = 91 c) 80 + 12 = 92
d) 60 + 16 = 76 e) 50 + 11 = 61 f) 60 + 13 = 73
g) 70 + 14 = 84 h) 70 + 12 = 82

2 a) 70 b) 59, 34, 25 c) 79, 29, 50

Assessment

a) 24 and 62 b) 24 and 51, 62 and 13
c) 58 d) 72 and 56

Unit 4 **Assess and review**

Term 1 Block A
Numbers and addition
Unit 1 Numbers to 100
Unit 2 Numbers to 999
Unit 3 Addition to 99
Unit 4 Assess and review

Final evaluation
Check that pupils are able to:
1 Count in tens to 100
2 Count, read, write and order numbers to 100
3 Count in hundreds to 900
4 Count, read, write and order numbers to 999
5 Add multiples of ten to 2-digit numbers (totals < 100)
6 Add pairs of 2-digit numbers without renaming (totals < 100)
7 Add pairs of 2-digit numbers with renaming (totals < 100)

Vocabulary
Names for numbers to 999, hundreds, tens, units, digits, addition, add, plus, sum, total

Resources
Abacus
Classroom 1–100 grid
Tens and units apparatus (e.g. ten rods and unit cubes, or bundles of ten sticks and unit sticks)
Pupil's Book pages 34–39

Pupil's Book pages 34–39
1 Write a few 2-digit numbers in words and ask the class to read them aloud together. (page 34)
2 Write the following sequences on the board: 5 6 _ 8 _ _ 11 _; _ 10 _ 30 40 50 _
Ask for the missing numbers and the rule for each sequence. (page 35)
3 Write 'three hundred and forty-one' on the board and ask the class to read it together. (page 36)
4 Write 673 on the board and ask for the value of each digit in random order. (page 37)
Write 47 + 26 on the board, then

```
  40 + 7
+ 20 + 6
  __ + _ = __
```

Work through the method with the class. (page 38)
5 Remind pupils to align the digits carefully when setting out calculations in columns. (page 38)
6 Clarify that the number on the roof of each tower is to be added to each number in the windows. (page 39)

Assessment activities
Use these to assess pupils' knowledge and understanding:
Count in tens to 100.
Read these six 2-digit numbers (in figures).
Write these numbers in figures (2-digit numbers written in words).
Put them in order starting with the smallest.
What is the value of: the 6 in 86; the 8?
Count in hundreds to 900.
Read these six 3-digit numbers (written in figures).
Write these numbers in figures (3-digit numbers written in words). Put them in order starting with the smallest.
What is the value of: the 5 in 458; the 4; the 8? Show me this number on the abacus.
Show me how you would do these additions:
40 + 35 = ; 36 + 23 =
56 + 4 = ; 67 + 5 =
28 + 34 =

Assess and review activities

Use these activities taken from the previous three weeks to monitor, evaluate and consolidate pupils' knowledge and understanding.

- Ask the class to count in 10s from 0 to 100 as you indicate each number on the class grid. 'What is 10 more than 90?' Discuss that 100 has 3 digits. 'What is 10 more than 10? … 30? … 60?' etc.
- Write 37 on the board. 'What is the value of the 3 in 37? What is the value of the 7?' Ask pupils to suggest other numbers which have 7 units and record them on the board, then other numbers with 3 tens.
- Ask the class to count to 30 as you place one bead at a time on the abacus. After 9 is reached on the units spike, revise that 10 is shown by removing the units beads and placing 1 bead on the tens spike. Reinforce this in a similar way after 19 and 29.
- Put 8 beads on the tens spike on the abacus. Ask the class to count on from 80 to 100 as you show each number on the abacus. 'Does anyone know the next number?' Establish that 1 more than 100 is 101 and write it on the board. Explain to the class that when we count from 100 in ones we follow the same pattern as counting from 0 to 100, but each number begins with 100.
- Show a variety of numbers to 200 on the arrow cards placed over each other appropriately and ask the class to read the number then say the value of each digit. Remove the appropriate card each time to show its value.
- 'Which number comes after 250? … 259? … 284? … 289? … 295? … 299? What happens after 300?' Establish that the counting pattern continues as before. What is the next hundred after 300? … and the next?' Continue to 900. Record 100 and all its multiples to 900 in order on the board. Ask the class to count in hundreds together. Ask them to close their eyes and repeat.
- Write numbers such as 368, 741, 403, 299, 610 on the board and ask the class to say them together. Ask them to say the number which is 1 more than each, then 1 less than each. 'Which is the smallest number? How do you know?' Record 299 on the board and stress that this is the smallest because it has the lowest hundreds digit. Repeat for the next smallest up to the largest number.
- Ask the class to count in ones to 10, then in tens to 100, then in hundreds to 900 as you place appropriate beads on the abacus. 'Which is the units spike? Which is the hundreds? Which is the tens?'
- Show a variety of 3-digit numbers on the abacus. Ask the class to say each number then give the value of each digit.
- Ask volunteers to show given 3-digit numbers on the abacus, e.g. 376, 589, 138, 490, 812, 603 etc.
- Indicate 3 on the 1–100 grid. 'What is 10 more than 3?' Reinforce the answer by counting on 10 from 3 on the grid. Record 3 + 10 = 13 on the board. Ask 'What is 13 + 10? … 23 + 10? … 33 + 10?' Record each addition on the board below 3 + 10 = 13. 'What do you notice about the pattern? What happens when we add 10 to any number?' Establish that the tens digit increases by 1, the units digit is unchanged. Indicate 46 on the grid. 'What is 46 + 10?' Repeat using other starting numbers.
- Write 1 + 9 = on the board, ask for the answer and record. '1 plus 9 is 10, so what is 11 + 9? How did you work it out?' Record 11 + 9 = 10 + 1 + 9 = 10 + 10 = 20 on the board. Repeat with 21 + 9, 31 + 9, …, 91 + 9. Emphasise the pattern in the calculations, each using 1 + 9 then adding 10 to the tens digit of the first number. Repeat with calculations such as 7 + 3 = 10, 37 + 3 = ?, 67 + 3 = ?, 47 + 3 = ?
- Ask pupils in pairs to use tens and units materials to show 27 and 5. 'How many single cubes do you have altogether?' Ask them to exchange 10 of the cubes for a ten rod. 'How many rods do you have now? How many single cubes? How many cubes altogether?' Record 27 + 5 = 20 + 7 + 5 = 20 + 10 + 2 = 32 on the board, explaining how this recording relates to the activity. Repeat for another sum, e.g. 16 + 5.

Unit 4 Assess and review

Numbers to 100

1 Join each word to the matching number.

19 31 13 90 91 33 93 39

nineteen, thirty-three, thirty-nine, ninety, ninety-one, thirty-one, thirteen, ninety-three

2 Write these words as numbers.
Write them in order, starting with the smallest.

twenty-three, forty-two, twenty, thirty-eight, eleven, seventeen, forty-one, twenty-seven, thirty-six, nineteen, sixteen, forty-nine

3 Write the missing numbers in each sequence.

a) 30 ☐ 50 60 ☐ ☐ 90

b) 19 20 ☐ 22 23 ☐ ☐

c) 40 50 ☐ ☐ 80 ☐ 100

d) 47 ☐ 49 ☐ ☐ 52 53

e) 10 ☐ ☐ 40 50 ☐ ☐

f) 78 79 ☐ ☐ 82 ☐ ☐

4 Write the value of the red digit in each of these numbers.

Example 37 → 30

a) 42 b) 19 c) 54 d) 82
e) 66 f) 13 g) 74 h) 89
i) 60 j) 97 k) 49 l) 91

Try this

Use 6 beads on an abacus.

List the different numbers you can make with 6 beads. Write the numbers in order.

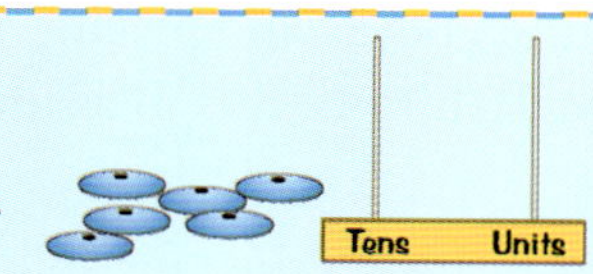

34

35

Numbers to 999

1 Complete these.

Example 348 = 3 hundreds + 4 tens + 8 units

a) 275 = ☐ hundreds + ☐ tens + ☐ units
b) 326 = ☐ hundreds + ☐ tens + ☐ units
c) 239 = ☐ hundreds + ☐ tens + ☐ units
d) 487 = ☐ hundreds + ☐ tens + ☐ units
e) 265 = ☐ hundreds + ☐ tens + ☐ units
f) 536 = ☐ hundreds + ☐ tens + ☐ units
g) 978 = ☐ hundreds + ☐ tens + ☐ units
h) 353 = ☐ hundreds + ☐ tens + ☐ units
i) 844 = ☐ hundreds + ☐ tens + ☐ units
j) 692 = ☐ hundreds + ☐ tens + ☐ units

2 Write these as numbers.

Example Six hundred and thirty-five = 635

a) Eight hundred and twenty-five
b) Six hundred and thirty-two
c) Seven hundred and twenty-two
d) Four hundred and eighty-five
e) Six hundred and sixty-three
f) Two hundred and seventy-five
g) Nine hundred and fourteen
h) Five hundred and forty

3 Draw an abacus and beads to show each of the following numbers.
Write the value of each digit in the numbers you have made.

Example 132

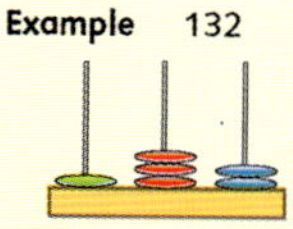

100 + 30 + 2

a) 145 b) 479

c) 167 d) 290

e) 337 f) 509 g) 690 h) 718

4 Circle the digit in each number that shows these values.

a) Which digit shows seven hundred? 7 5 7
b) Which digit shows 80? 8 8 9
c) Which digit shows four? 2 4 4
d) Which digit shows fifty? 5 5 5
e) Which digit shows 300? 3 3 3

Try this

Write all the numbers between 500 and 900 that you can make with the digits 5, 7 and 8.

5 7 8

36

37

Addition to 99

1 Answer these.

a) 52 + 31 =
b) 21 + 17 =
c) 42 + 36 =
d) 52 + 37 =
e) 36 + 32 =
f) 75 + 23 =

2 Complete these.

a) 36 + 19 → 30 + 6
+ 10 + 9
☐ + ☐ → ☐

b) 18 + 43 → 10 + 8
+ 40 + 3
☐ + ☐ → ☐

c) 25 + 17 → 20 + 5
+ 10 + 7
☐ + ☐ → ☐

d) 23 + 28 → 20 + 3
+ 20 + 8
☐ + ☐ → ☐

e) 26 + 35 → 20 + 6
+ 30 + 5
☐ + ☐ → ☐

f) 34 + 19 → 30 + 4
+ 10 + 9
☐ + ☐ → ☐

3 32 21 26 23 34

Use these numbers to answer the questions.

a) What is the largest total you can make when adding two of these numbers?
b) What is the smallest answer you can make when adding two of these numbers?
c) Which two numbers make 60 when added together?
d) Find two pairs of numbers that each total 55.

4 Complete these total towers.

a) +4	b) +8	c) +20	d) +40
63 → 67	91 → 99	19 → 39	27 → 67
44 → ☐	25 → ☐	35 → ☐	14 → ☐
38 → ☐	16 → ☐	72 → ☐	53 → ☐
76 → ☐	53 → ☐	48 → ☐	36 → ☐
59 → ☐	64 → ☐	61 → ☐	49 → ☐

Try this

25 + 43 = 68

Find other ways to make 68 by adding together numbers.

38 39

Answers pages 34 and 35

1 19 → nineteen, 31 → thirty-one, 13 → thirteen, 90 → ninety, 91 → ninety-one, 33 → thirty-three, 93 → ninety-three, 39 → thirty-nine

2 11, 16, 17, 19, 20, 23, 27, 36, 38, 41, 42, 49

3 a) 40, 70, 80 b) 21, 24, 25 c) 60, 70, 90
d) 48, 50, 51 e) 20, 30, 60, 70 f) 80, 81, 83, 84

4 a) 2 b) 9 c) 50 d) 2 e) 60 f) 10
g) 70 h) 80 i) 60 j) 7 k) 9 l) 90

Try this

6, 15, 24, 33, 42, 51, 60

Answers pages 36 and 37

1 a) 2 hundreds + 7 tens + 5 units
b) 3 hundreds + 2 tens + 6 units
c) 2 hundreds + 3 tens + 9 units
d) 4 hundreds + 8 tens + 7 units
e) 2 hundreds + 6 tens + 5 units
f) 5 hundreds + 3 tens + 6 units
g) 9 hundreds + 7 tens + 8 units
h) 3 hundreds + 5 tens + 3 units
i) 8 hundreds + 4 tens + 4 units
j) 6 hundreds + 9 tens + 2 units

2 a) 825 b) 632 c) 722 d) 485
e) 663 f) 275 g) 914 h) 540

3 a) 100 + 40 + 5 = 145 b) 400 + 70 + 9 = 479
c) 100 + 60 + 7 = 167 d) 200 + 90 + 0 = 290
e) 300 + 30 + 7 = 337 f) 500 + 0 + 9 = 509
g) 600 + 90 + 0 = 690 h) 700 + 10 + 8 = 718

4 a) 7 5 7 b) 8 8 9 c) 2 4 4 d) 5 5 5 e) 3 3 3

Try this

578, 587, 758, 785, 857, 875

Answers pages 38 and 39

1 a) 83 b) 38 c) 78 d) 89 e) 68 f) 98

2 a) 40 + 15 = 55 b) 50 + 11 = 61 c) 30 + 12 = 42
d) 40 + 11 = 51 e) 50 + 11 = 61 f) 40 + 13 = 53

3 a) 66 b) 44 c) 26 and 34 d) 32 and 23, 21 and 34

4 a) 48, 42, 80, 63 b) 33, 24, 61, 72
c) 55, 92, 68, 81 d) 54, 93, 76, 89

Block B Number operations

Maths Topic	National Standards from Government Guidelines	
Unit	*Curriculum area*	*End of year objectives / success criteria*
5 Subtraction within 99	Understanding numerical operations and the relations between them Calculate skilfully and make reasonable assessments Use of symbols and shapes to display simple mathematical situations	Subtract tens on a number line. Subtract a 2-digit number without renaming. Choose the basic operation needed to solve a mathematical or everyday problem. Check the results of any subtraction problem. Use different and suitable methods for subtraction, like Mental Maths or use of pencil and paper (written). Use approximation in solving subtraction of numbers. Comprehend that the relation between addition and subtraction is an inverse relation.
6 Multiplication	Understanding numbers, methods of displaying them and the relations between them Use of symbols and shapes to display simple mathematical situations	Comprehend that multiplication is repeated addition. State the products of multiplication up to table 9. Understand the concepts of multiplying by 1 and 0. Give numerical examples showing the properties of multiplication up to table 9 without naming the property.
7 Number facts	Understanding numbers, methods of displaying them and the relations between them Understanding numerical operations and the relations between them Calculate skilfully and make reasonable assessments Use of symbols and shapes to display simple mathematical situations	Use different and suitable methods for addition, subtraction and/or multiplication of numbers, like Mental Maths or use of pencil and paper (written). Comprehend that the relation between addition and subtraction is an inverse relation and apply this using shapes and symbols. Understand and state the products of multiplication up to table 9. Understand the concepts of multiplying by 1 and 0. Give numerical examples showing the properties of multiplication up to table 9 without naming the property.
8 Assess and review	Revision and assessment of previous 3 units – problems, formative and summative assessment. Monitor, assess, evaluate and consolidate pupils' knowledge and understanding.	

During this block of work, pupils will experience:

1 Finding the difference between numbers within 20.
2 Subtracting tens from multiples of 10.
3 Subtracting units, then tens, then tens and units without exchange, from 2-digit numbers.
4 Understanding the nature of multiplication through grouping, repeated addition and arrays.
5 Using the multiplication sign for equal addition.
6 The effect of multiplying by 0 and by 1.
7 Developing strategies to find unknown addition facts within 20 quickly.
8 Using the inverse relationship between addition and subtraction for quick recall of subtraction facts.
9 Developing knowledge of multiplication facts within the 2×, 3×, 4×, 5× and 10× tables.

Unit 5 **Subtraction within 99**

Term 1 Block B **Number operations** **Unit 5 Subtraction within 99** Unit 6 Multiplication Unit 7 Number facts Unit 8 Assess and review	**Objectives** *At the end of the unit, students should be able to…* Subtract tens and display the operation on the number line. Subtract a 2-digit number from a larger one without renaming Choose a basic operation to solve a mathematical problem. Check the results of any subtraction problem. Use different and suitable methods for subtraction of numbers, like Mental Maths or use of pencil and paper (written). Use approximation in solving subtraction of numbers. Comprehend that the relation between addition and subtraction is an inverse relation and apply this up to 99 using shapes and symbols.
Vocabulary take away, subtract, difference, count on, digit, tens, units, (place) value, subtraction facts, opposite, inverse	**Lessons** 1 Subtraction within 20 2 Subtracting tens 3 Subtracting: TU – U 4 Subtracting TU and tens 5 Subtracting 2-digit numbers: no exchange
Oral and mental starters Start here Flash facts What's the question? Tell me a story Name it	**Resources** Tens and units apparatus (e.g. ten rods and unit cubes, or bundles of ten sticks and unit sticks) Abacus Arrow cards *Pupil's Book pages 40–49*
Prior learning Understanding subtraction as taking away and as finding the difference Understanding that subtraction is the inverse of addition Subtracting 2-digit numbers (Grade 1)	**Background notes** This unit revises and consolidates work on subtraction covered in Grade 1. Knowledge of subtraction facts is very important as children develop to subtraction calculations with 2-digit numbers. Pupils were made aware in Grade 1 that subtraction is the inverse of addition, understanding this concept makes it easy to use known addition facts to work out subtraction facts. Many pupils will now know many of the addition/subtraction facts within 20.
End of unit evaluation Check that pupils are able to: 1 Subtract with 2-digit numbers without renaming. 2 Use mental methods and written methods for subtraction appropriately.	**Supporting the topic** Encourage pupils to: ● count back (take away) or count on (find the difference) when subtracting numbers involving unknown facts, ● recognise when subtractions can be done mentally, ● use known addition/subtraction facts whenever possible, ● learn addition/subtraction facts in odd moments at school and at home. Use opportunities in everyday activities to subtract, e.g. 'There are 38 people on a bus, 14 get off at the market, how many are still on the bus?'

Lesson 1 **Subtraction within 20**

Pupil's Book pages 40 and 41 **Oral and mental starter: Start here**

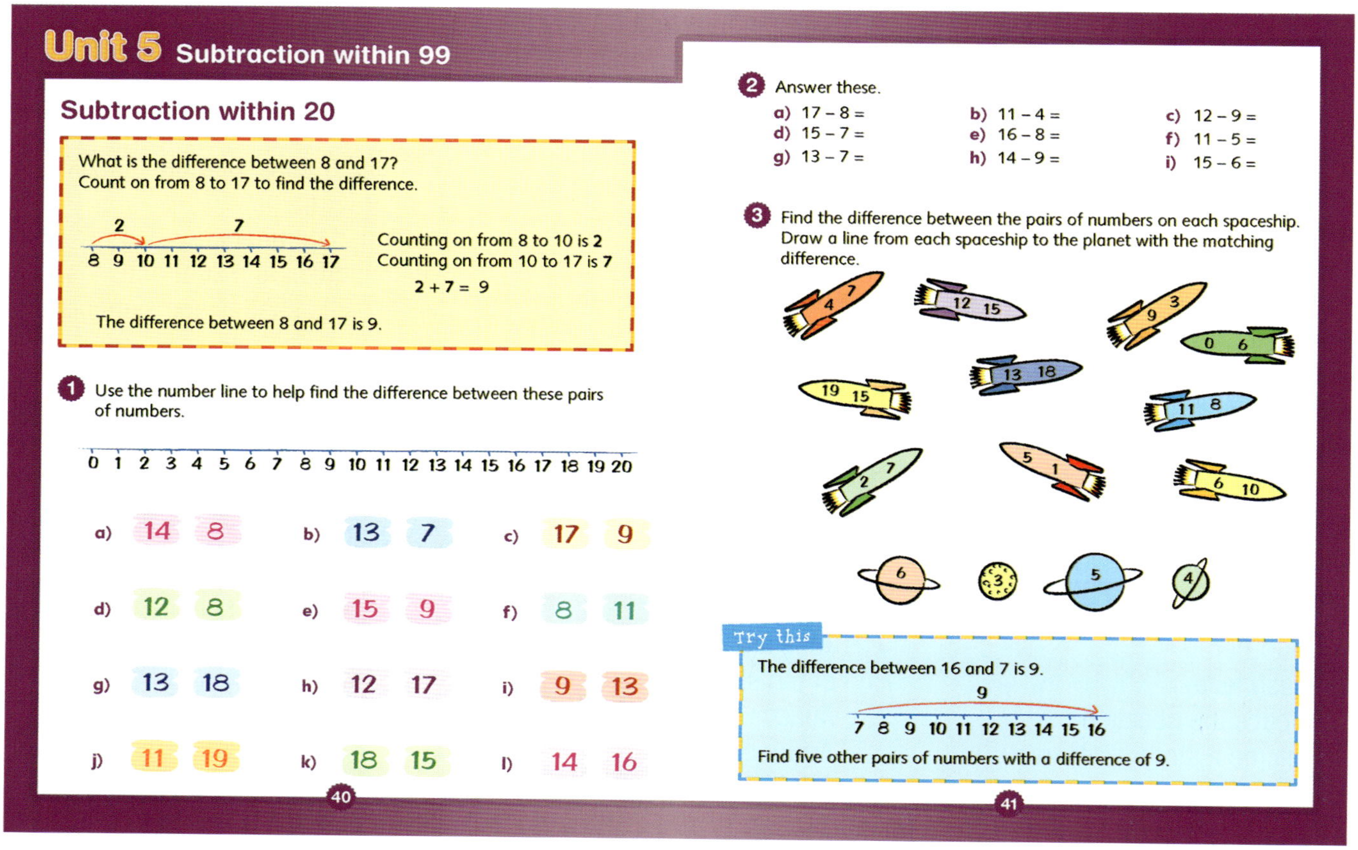
Unit 5 Subtraction within 99

Subtraction within 20

What is the difference between 8 and 17?
Count on from 8 to 17 to find the difference.

2 7
8 9 10 11 12 13 14 15 16 17

Counting on from 8 to 10 is **2**
Counting on from 10 to 17 is **7**
2 + 7 = 9

The difference between 8 and 17 is 9.

1 Use the number line to help find the difference between these pairs of numbers.

0 1 2 3 4 5 6 7 8 9 10 11 12 13 14 15 16 17 18 19 20

a) 14 8 b) 13 7 c) 17 9
d) 12 8 e) 15 9 f) 8 11
g) 13 18 h) 12 17 i) 9 13
j) 11 19 k) 18 15 l) 14 16

2 Answer these.

a) 17 − 8 = b) 11 − 4 = c) 12 − 9 =
d) 15 − 7 = e) 16 − 8 = f) 11 − 5 =
g) 13 − 7 = h) 14 − 9 = i) 15 − 6 =

3 Find the difference between the pairs of numbers on each spaceship. Draw a line from each spaceship to the planet with the matching difference.

4 7 12 15 9 3 0 6 19 15 13 18 11 8 2 7 5 1 6 10

6 3 5 4

Try this

The difference between 16 and 7 is 9.

9
7 8 9 10 11 12 13 14 15 16

Find five other pairs of numbers with a difference of 9.

40 41

Activities

- 'What happens when we take away 0 from a number? How do we subtract 1 from a number? What is 8 – 2? How did you work it out?' Establish that subtracting 0 leaves a number unchanged, subtracting 1 is simply 1 less and subtracting 2 is counting back 2, so 0, 1 or 2 can be subtracted from any number very quickly.
- Ask an addition fact, write it on the board, then ask for the two related subtraction facts, e.g. 'What is 5 + 2?' (Record the answer.) 'So what is 7 – 2? … 7 – 5?' Record these alongside the addition fact on the board. Stress that knowing an addition fact means that you also know two subtraction facts using the same three numbers. Repeat with other facts, e.g. 3 + 6, 5 + 4, 10 + 6 etc. Each time reinforce the addition by counting on from the largest number for the benefit of pupils who do not yet know the facts.
- Look at page 40. Go through the introduction with the class. Explain that because these subtractions are a bit harder than those in the previous two activities they might find the number line helpful.

Answers

1 a) 6 b) 6 c) 8 d) 4 e) 6 f) 3
g) 5 h) 5 i) 4 j) 8 k) 3 l) 2

2 a) 9 b) 7 c) 3 d) 8 e) 8
f) 6 g) 6 h) 5 i) 9

3 Planet 6: spaceships 0 and 6, 9 and 3
Planet 3: spaceships 4 and 7, 12 and 15, 11 and 8
Planet 5: spaceships 13 and 18, 2 and 7
Planet 4: spaceships 19 and 15, 6 and 10, 5 and 1

Lesson 2 **Subtracting tens**

Pupil's Book pages 42 and 43 **Oral and mental starter: Flash facts**

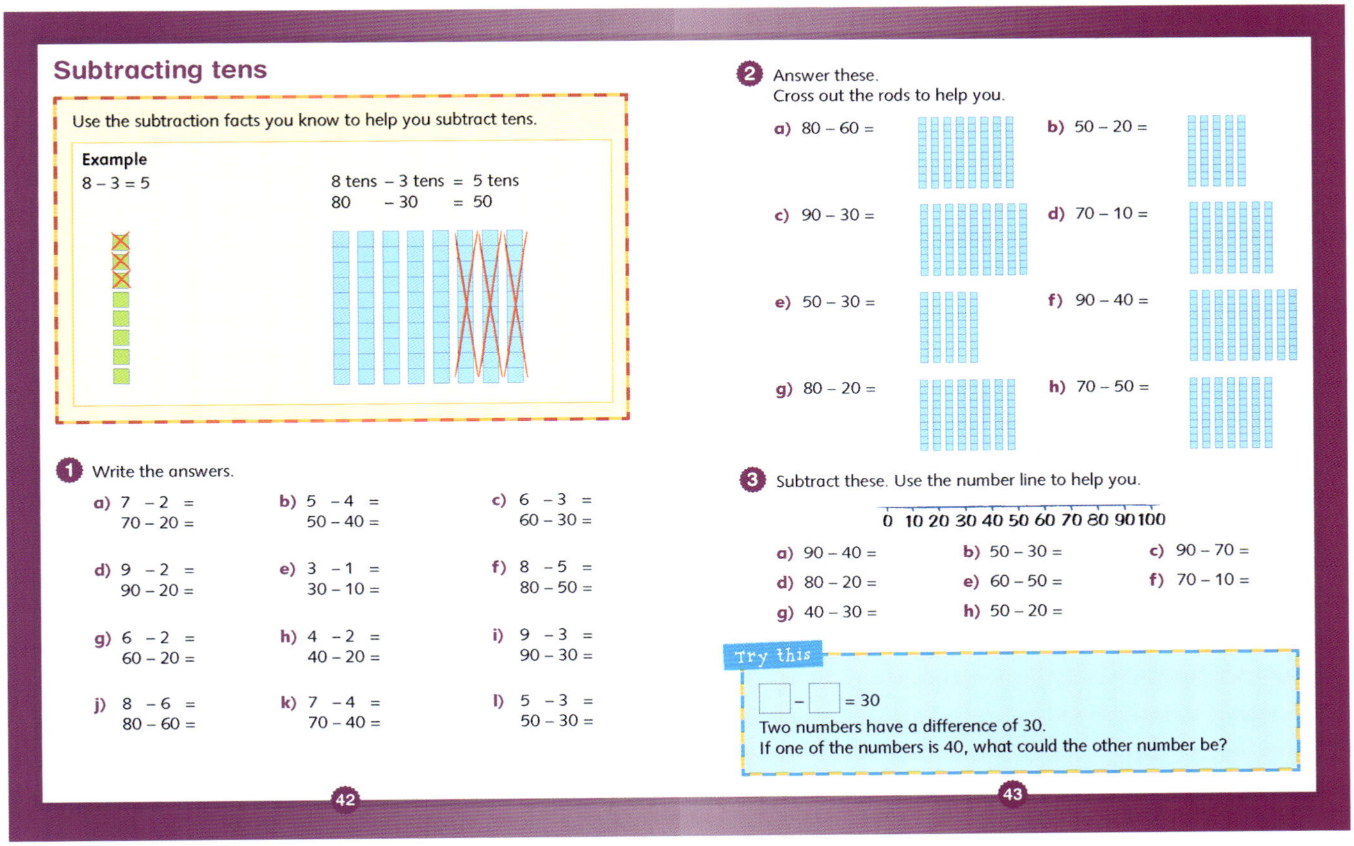

Subtracting tens

Use the subtraction facts you know to help you subtract tens.

Example
8 – 3 = 5

8 tens – 3 tens = 5 tens
80 – 30 = 50

1 Write the answers.

a) 7 – 2 =
70 – 20 =

b) 5 – 4 =
50 – 40 =

c) 6 – 3 =
60 – 30 =

d) 9 – 2 =
90 – 20 =

e) 3 – 1 =
30 – 10 =

f) 8 – 5 =
80 – 50 =

g) 6 – 2 =
60 – 20 =

h) 4 – 2 =
40 – 20 =

i) 9 – 3 =
90 – 30 =

j) 8 – 6 =
80 – 60 =

k) 7 – 4 =
70 – 40 =

l) 5 – 3 =
50 – 30 =

42

2 Answer these.
Cross out the rods to help you.

a) 80 – 60 =
b) 50 – 20 =
c) 90 – 30 =
d) 70 – 10 =
e) 50 – 30 =
f) 90 – 40 =
g) 80 – 20 =
h) 70 – 50 =

3 Subtract these. Use the number line to help you.

0 10 20 30 40 50 60 70 80 90 100

a) 90 – 40 =
b) 50 – 30 =
c) 90 – 70 =
d) 80 – 20 =
e) 60 – 50 =
f) 70 – 10 =
g) 40 – 30 =
h) 50 – 20 =

Try this

☐ – ☐ = 30

Two numbers have a difference of 30.
If one of the numbers is 40, what could the other number be?

43

Activities

- Write 9 – 6 = on the board. 'What do we add to 6 to make 9? So what is 9 – 6?' Record the answer then repeat with other subtraction facts within 10, e.g. 7 – 2, 5 – 3, 6 – 4, 4 – 3.
- 'If 9 – 6 is 3, what is 90 – 60? How do you know?' Demonstrate using the abacus and record below 9 – 6 = 3 on the board. Draw out that 90 is 9 tens, 60 is 6 tens, so the answer is 3 tens because 9 – 6 = 3. Repeat using the other subtraction facts on the board.
- Look at page 42. Go through the introduction with the class, using the illustrations to reinforce that subtracting tens involves the same facts as subtracting units.
- At the end of the lesson ask questions for pupils to answer orally, e.g. 30 – 10, 50 – 20, 60 – 40, 80 – 30 etc.

Answers

1 a) 5, 50 b) 1, 10 c) 3, 30 d) 7, 70 e) 2, 20
f) 3, 30 g) 4, 40 h) 2, 20 i) 6, 60 j) 2, 20
k) 3, 30 l) 2, 20

2 a) 20 b) 30 c) 60 d) 60 e) 20 f) 50
g) 60 h) 20

3 a) 50 b) 20 c) 20 d) 60 e) 10 f) 60
g) 10 h) 30

Try this

70 or 10

Lesson 3 **Subtracting: TU – U**

Pupil's Book pages 44 and 45 **Oral and mental starter: What's the question?**

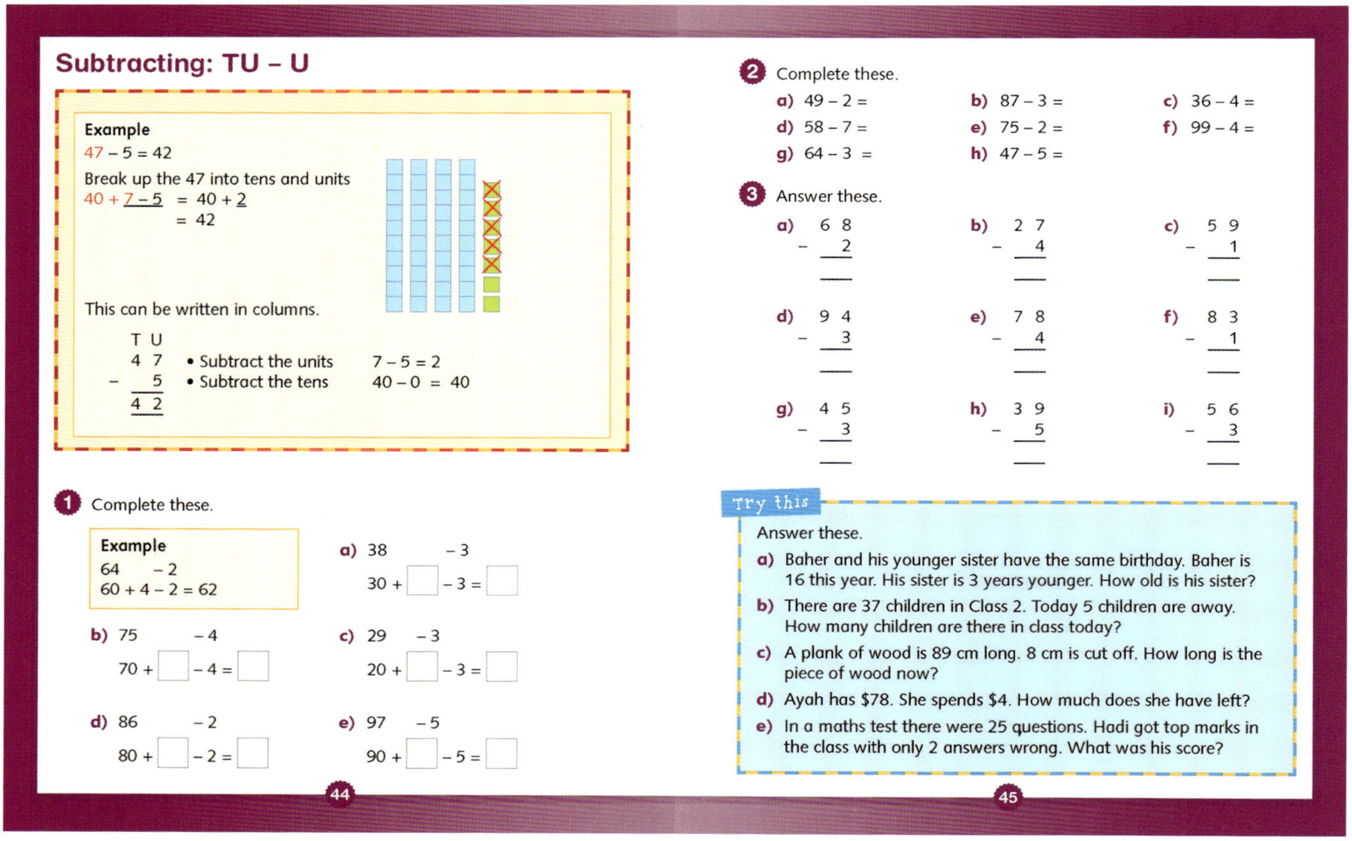

Subtracting: TU – U

Example
47 – 5 = 42
Break up the 47 into tens and units
40 + 7 – 5 = 40 + 2
= 42

This can be written in columns.

T	U		
4	7	• Subtract the units	7 – 5 = 2
–	5	• Subtract the tens	40 – 0 = 40
4	2		

1 Complete these.

Example
64 – 2
60 + 4 – 2 = 62

a) 38 – 3
30 + ☐ – 3 = ☐

b) 75 – 4
70 + ☐ – 4 = ☐

c) 29 – 3
20 + ☐ – 3 = ☐

d) 86 – 2
80 + ☐ – 2 = ☐

e) 97 – 5
90 + ☐ – 5 = ☐

44

2 Complete these.

a) 49 – 2 = **b)** 87 – 3 = **c)** 36 – 4 =
d) 58 – 7 = **e)** 75 – 2 = **f)** 99 – 4 =
g) 64 – 3 = **h)** 47 – 5 =

3 Answer these.

a) 68 – 2 **b)** 27 – 4 **c)** 59 – 1
d) 94 – 3 **e)** 78 – 4 **f)** 83 – 1
g) 45 – 3 **h)** 39 – 5 **i)** 56 – 3

Try this

Answer these.

a) Baher and his younger sister have the same birthday. Baher is 16 this year. His sister is 3 years younger. How old is his sister?
b) There are 37 children in Class 2. Today 5 children are away. How many children are there in class today?
c) A plank of wood is 89 cm long. 8 cm is cut off. How long is the piece of wood now?
d) Ayah has $78. She spends $4. How much does she have left?
e) In a maths test there were 25 questions. Hadi got top marks in the class with only 2 answers wrong. What was his score?

45

Activities

- Ask questions such as 'What is 8 – 3?' Record the subtraction on the board. 'If 8 – 3 is 5, what is 18 – 3?' Record below the first subtraction on the board. Continue in the same way with 28 – 3, 38 – 3, 48 – 3, 78 – 3, 98 – 3. 'What do you notice about each answer?' Draw out that each involves 8 – 3 = 5 and that the tens digit is unchanged. Explain that this always happens when the units digit being subtracted is smaller than the units digit of the larger number. Repeat with other subtractions such as 7 – 5 (17 – 5, 27 – 5, 57 – 5, 87 – 5); 9 – 6 (29 – 6, 49 – 6, 79 – 6).
- Look at page 44. Go through the example with the class, pointing out that subtraction can be written on one line or in columns. Remind them that in question 3 the units must be in line with the units, the tens with the tens.
- Towards the end of the lesson ask pupils who did 'Try this' to give their answers and explain how they worked them out. Ask some TU – U questions for pupils to work out mentally, e.g. 35 – 5, 24 – 2, 59 – 7, 87 – 3 etc.

Answers

1 a) 8, 35 b) 5, 71 c) 9, 26 d) 6, 84 e) 7, 92
2 a) 47 b) 84 c) 32 d) 51 e) 73
f) 95 g) 61 h) 42
3 a) 66 b) 23 c) 58 d) 91 e) 74
f) 82 g) 42 h) 34 i) 53

Try this

a) 13 years old b) 32 c) 81 cm d) $74 e) 23

Lesson 4 **Subtracting: TU and tens**

Pupil's Book pages 46 and 47 **Oral and mental starter: Tell me a story**

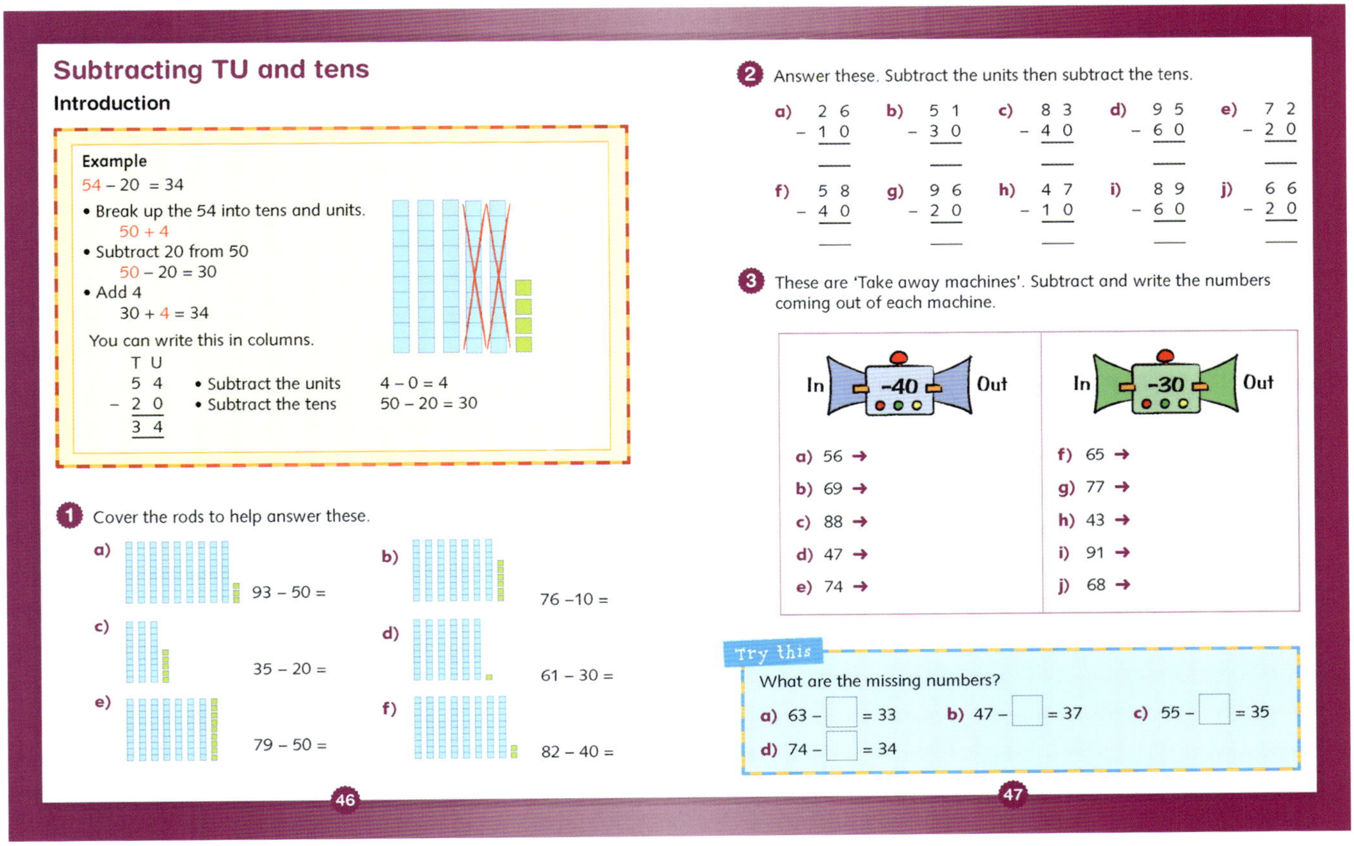

Subtracting TU and tens

Introduction

Example

54 – 20 = 34

- Break up the 54 into tens and units.
  50 + 4
- Subtract 20 from 50
  50 – 20 = 30
- Add 4
  30 + 4 = 34

You can write this in columns.

```
  T U
  5 4     • Subtract the units    4 – 0 = 4
– 2 0     • Subtract the tens     50 – 20 = 30
  3 4
```

1 Cover the rods to help answer these.

a) 93 – 50 =
b) 76 – 10 =
c) 35 – 20 =
d) 61 – 30 =
e) 79 – 50 =
f) 82 – 40 =

2 Answer these. Subtract the units then subtract the tens.

a) 26 – 10 b) 51 – 30 c) 83 – 40 d) 95 – 60 e) 72 – 20
f) 58 – 40 g) 96 – 20 h) 47 – 10 i) 89 – 60 j) 66 – 20

3 These are 'Take away machines'. Subtract and write the numbers coming out of each machine.

In –40 Out

a) 56 →
b) 69 →
c) 88 →
d) 47 →
e) 74 →

In –30 Out

f) 65 →
g) 77 →
h) 43 →
i) 91 →
j) 68 →

Try this

What are the missing numbers?

a) 63 – □ = 33 b) 47 – □ = 37 c) 55 – □ = 35
d) 74 – □ = 34

Activities

- Using ten rods and unit cubes (or an abacus), illustrate a subtraction such as 33 – 10. Record as a horizontal subtraction on the board, pointing out that they know that 30 – 10 = 20, so 33 – 10 is 30 – 10 + 3. Repeat with one or two more subtractions, e.g. 47 – 20, 56 – 30, 84 – 50. Establish that when subtracting a multiple of ten from a 2-digit number the units are unchanged.
- Look at page 46. Go through the introduction with the class. Remind them to align the digits carefully when setting out column subtractions.
- Make sure pupils understand how the function machines work in question 3.
- At the end of the lesson ask questions for pupils to work out mentally such as 90 – 50, 48 – 30, 62 – 20, 75 – 20, 49 – 40 etc.

Answers

1	a) 43	b) 66	c) 15	d) 31	e) 29	f) 42
2	a) 16	b) 21	c) 43	d) 35	e) 52	f) 18
	g) 76	h) 37	i) 29	j) 46		
3	a) 16	b) 29	c) 48	d) 7	e) 34	f) 35
	g) 47	h) 13	i) 61	j) 38		

Try this

a) 30 b) 10 c) 20 d) 40

Lesson 5 **Subtracting 2-digit numbers: no exchange**

Pupil's Book pages 48 and 49 **Oral and mental starter: Name it**

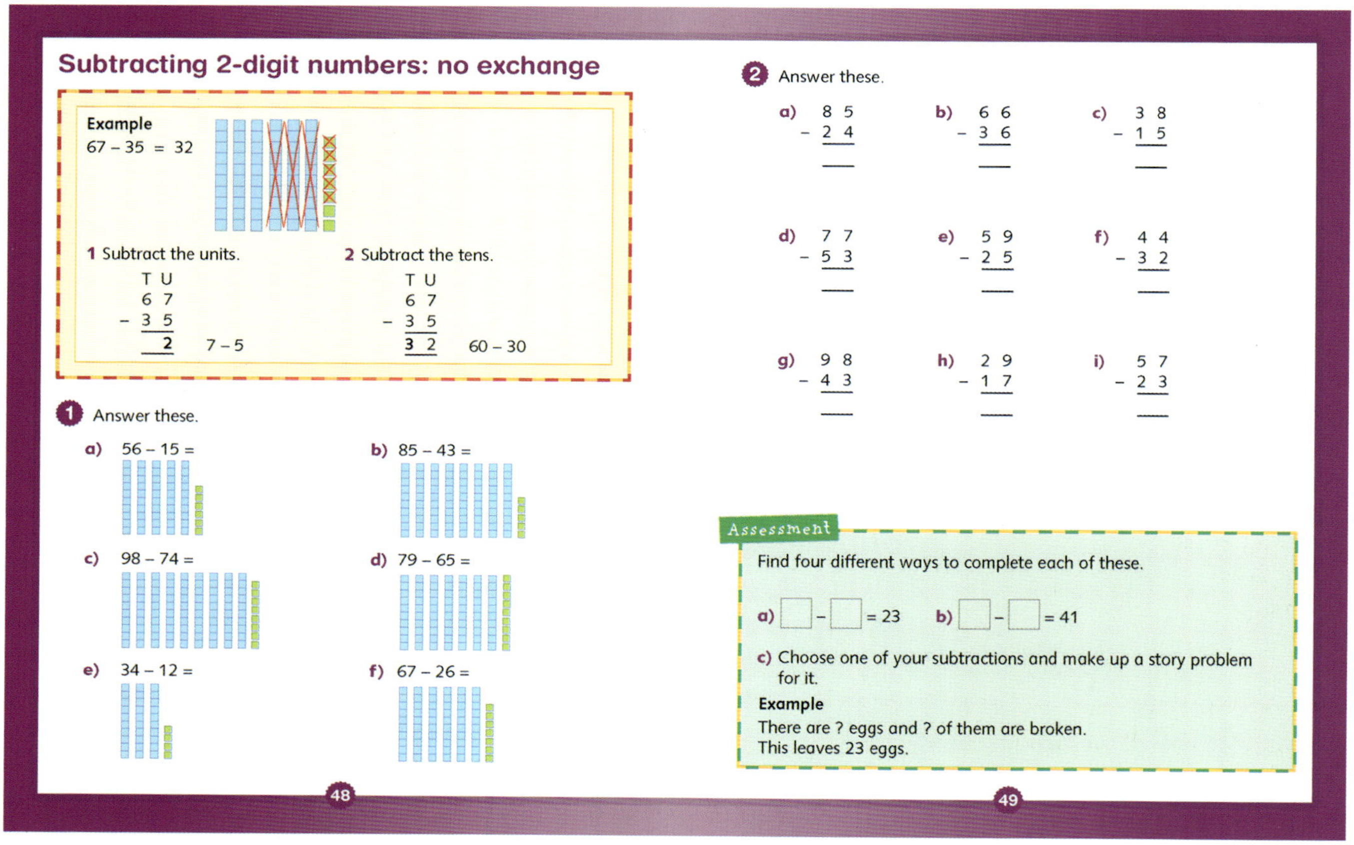

Subtracting 2-digit numbers: no exchange

Example
67 – 35 = 32

1 Subtract the units.

```
  T U
  6 7
– 3 5
    2    7 – 5
```

2 Subtract the tens.

```
  T U
  6 7
– 3 5
  3 2    60 – 30
```

1 Answer these.

a) 56 – 15 =
b) 85 – 43 =
c) 98 – 74 =
d) 79 – 65 =
e) 34 – 12 =
f) 67 – 26 =

48

2 Answer these.

a) 85 – 24
b) 66 – 36
c) 38 – 15
d) 77 – 53
e) 59 – 25
f) 44 – 32
g) 98 – 43
h) 29 – 17
i) 57 – 23

Assessment

Find four different ways to complete each of these.

a) ☐ – ☐ = 23 b) ☐ – ☐ = 41

c) Choose one of your subtractions and make up a story problem for it.

Example
There are ? eggs and ? of them are broken.
This leaves 23 eggs.

49

Activities

- Look at page 48. Go through the example with the class, relating the process to the rods and cubes illustrated. Write another subtraction on the board, e.g. 28 – 12, and work through it with the class, following the instructions given in the example. Repeat with other subtractions, e.g. 36 – 21, 58 – 32, 47 – 25.
- Provide a context for the first subtraction on the board, e.g. 'There are 28 pupils in a class, 12 of them are boys. How many girls are there?' Repeat for the second subtraction, e.g. '36 people walk to work, 21 people go by bus. How many more people walk?' Ask pupils to give contexts for the other subtractions on the board.
- At the end of the lesson ask questions for pupils to work out mentally such as 26 – 14, 39 – 27, 75 – 52, 48 – 34 etc. Each time ask volunteers to explain how they worked it out.

Answers

1	a) 41	b) 42	c) 24	d) 14	e) 22	f) 41
2	a) 61	b) 30	c) 23	d) 24	e) 34	f) 12
	g) 55	h) 12	i) 34			

Unit 6 **Multiplication**

Term 1 Block B **Number operations** Unit 5 Subtraction within 99 **Unit 6 Multiplication** Unit 7 Number facts Unit 8 Assess and review	**Objectives** *At the end of the unit, students should be able to…* Comprehend and identify that multiplication is repeated addition. Understand and state the products of multiplication up to table 9. Understand the concepts of multiplying by 1 and 0. Give numerical examples showing the properties of multiplication up to table 9 without naming the property.
Vocabulary grouping, group, set, repeated addition, multiplying, multiplication, multiplied by, total, double, doubling	**Lessons** 1 Grouping 2 Repeated addition 3 Multiplying 4 Arrays 5 Multiplying by 1 and 0
Oral and mental starters Hands up Pairs for sums Steps Double it Flash facts (multiplication)	**Resources** Counters – 20 per pupil *Pupil's Book pages 50–59*
Prior learning Counting in steps of two, five and ten Addition of 2-digit numbers	**Background notes** This unit develops the link between addition and multiplication, building from previous learning. It introduces the concept of multiplication as repeated addition and the use of the multiplication sign to represent the operation. The commutative nature of multiplication (i.e. that multiplication can be done in any order), is introduced through the use of arrays. Pupils should begin to learn multiplication facts in this unit. Further work on multiplication facts is contained in Unit 7 and Unit 9.
End of unit evaluation Check that pupils are able to: 1 Multiply given numbers using repeated addition. 2 Understand that multiplication can be done in any order. 3 State some of the products of multiplication up to table 9. 4 Multiply by 1 and by 0.	**Supporting the topic** Illustrate situations in which multiplication is used, e.g. 'If there are ten pairs of shoes, how many shoes are there? On four hands how many fingers and thumbs are there?' Develop knowledge and recall of multiplication facts, e.g.: ● Have a 'fact of the day', such as $3 \times 5 = 15$, and display it in the classroom. Every time you speak to a child begin by asking for the answer to the fact. Every time pupils walk through the door they must say $3 \times 5 = 15$. ● Have copies of appropriate multiplication facts in random order, with answers in the same order on a different piece of paper, available for children to 'test' each other at odd moments. Encourage them to record those which they cannot recall quickly and to focus on these for learning (see Unit 7). ● Encourage pupils to learn multiplication facts at home.

Lesson 1 **Grouping**

Pupil's Book pages 50 and 51 **Oral and mental starter: Hands up**

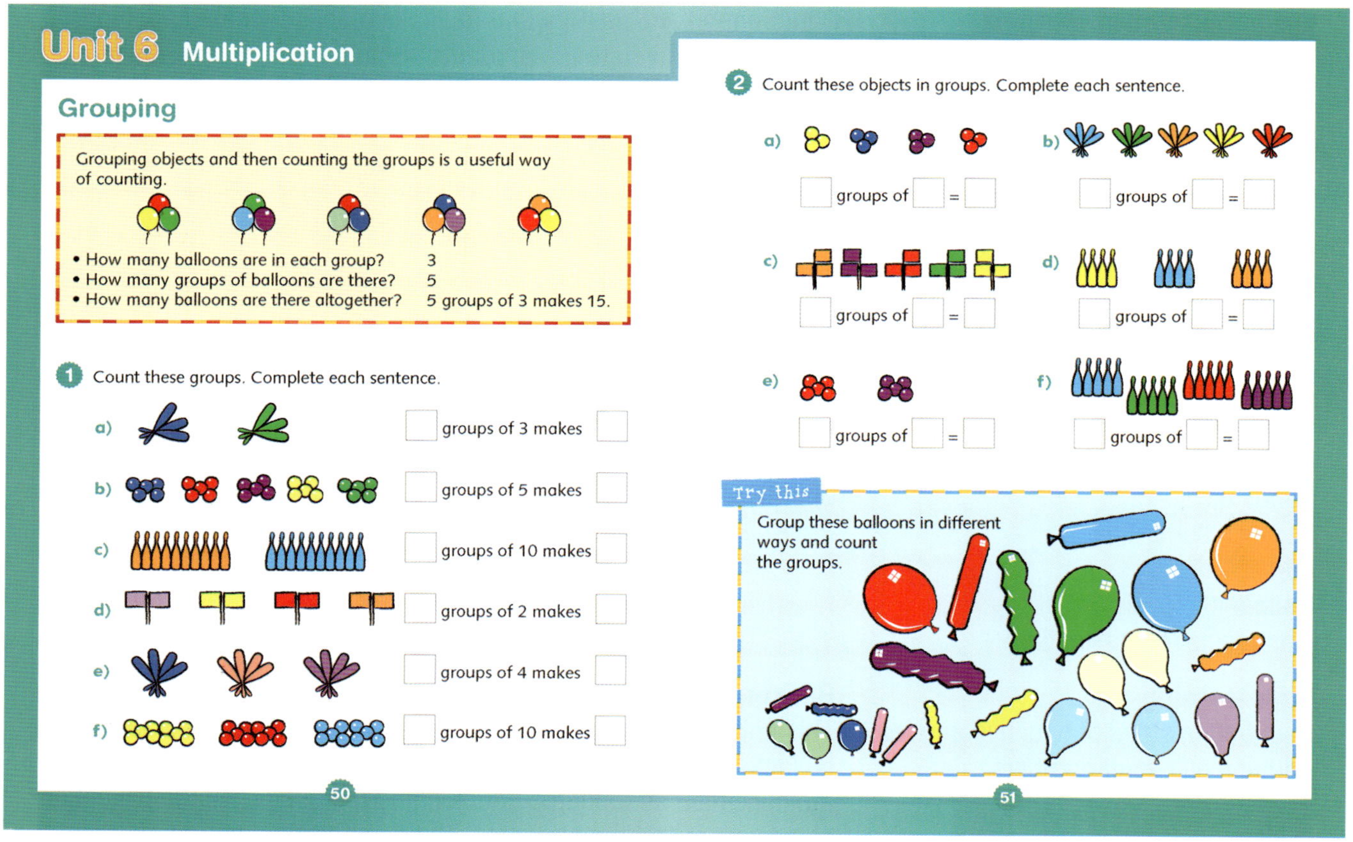

Activities

- Ask an even number of pupils to stand in pairs at the front, e.g. 12 pupils. 'How many pupils in each pair? How many pairs of pupils? How many pupils altogether?' Confirm the answer by counting together in 2s as each pair goes back to their seats in turn. Record on the board, e.g. 6 groups of 2 makes 12 (depending on the number of pairs).
- Look for and discuss any examples of objects in the classroom which can easily be counted in groups, e.g. panes of glass in each window, pupils in each row, books in piles of 5. Each time ask questions such as 'How many books in each pile? How many piles? How many books altogether?' and record, e.g. 4 groups of 5 makes 20.
- Look at page 50. Talk about the balloons in groups and the way in which the total number has been worked out and recorded.

Answers

1 a) 2 groups of 3 makes 6 b) 5 groups of 5 makes 25
c) 2 groups of 10 makes 20 d) 4 groups of 2 makes 8
e) 3 groups of 4 makes 12 f) 3 groups of 10 makes 30

2 a) 4 groups of 3 = 12 b) 5 groups of 4 =20
c) 5 groups of 3 =15 d) 3 groups of 4 = 12
e) 2 groups of 5 =10 f) 4 groups 5 = 20

Try this

There are 24 balloons: 8 large, 8 small, 8 medium; 6 round, 6 curly, 6 long, 6 bulb shaped; 2 red, 2 pale purple, 2 dark purple, 2 cream, 2 pale blue, 2 mid-blue, 2 dark blue, 2 yellow, 2 pale green, 2 dark green, 2 orange, 2 pink.

Lesson 2 **Repeated addition**

Pupil's Book pages 52 and 53 **Oral and mental starter: Pairs for sums**

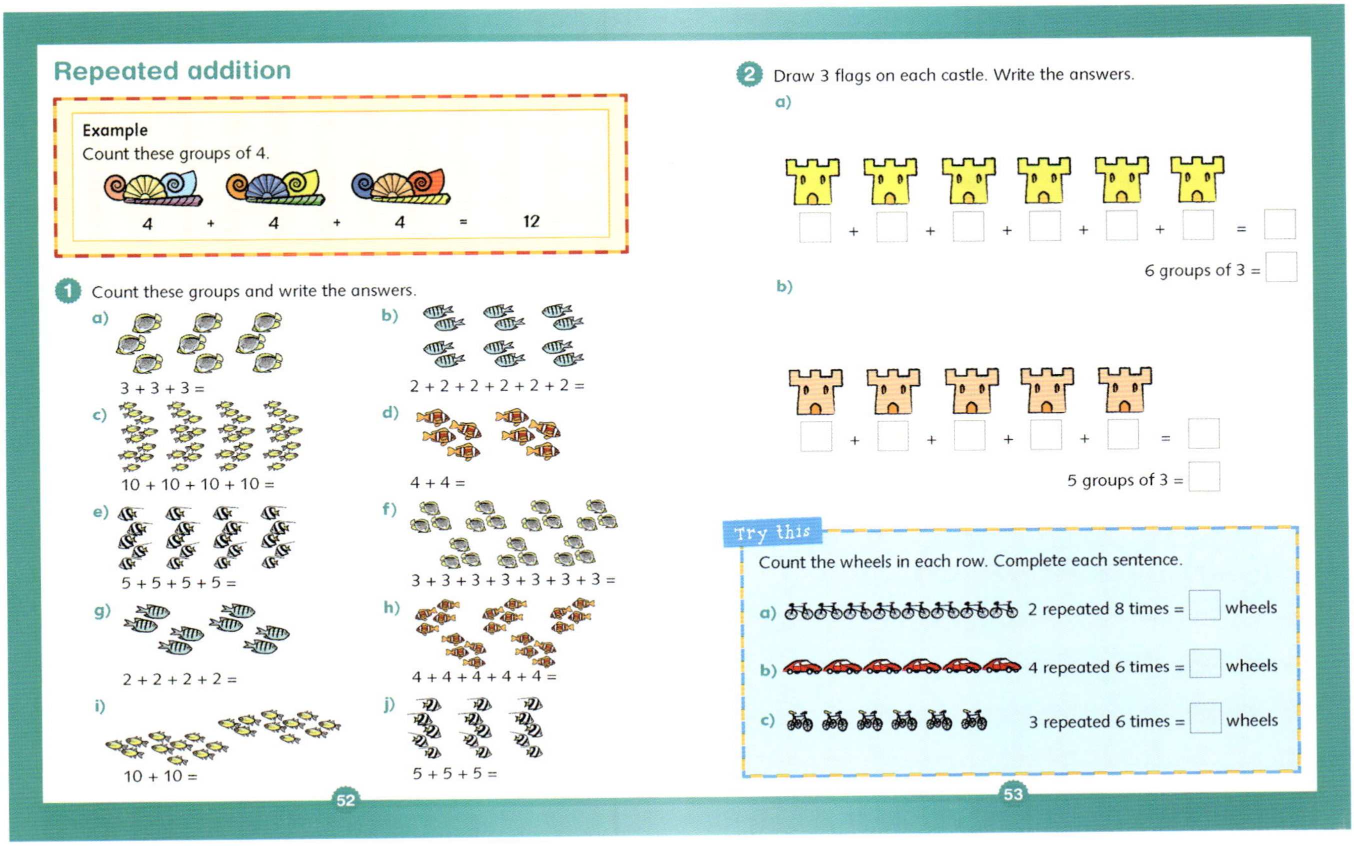
Repeated addition

Example
Count these groups of 4.
4 + 4 + 4 = 12

1 Count these groups and write the answers.

a) 3 + 3 + 3 =
b) 2 + 2 + 2 + 2 + 2 + 2 =
c) 10 + 10 + 10 + 10 =
d) 4 + 4 =
e) 5 + 5 + 5 + 5 =
f) 3 + 3 + 3 + 3 + 3 + 3 + 3 =
g) 2 + 2 + 2 + 2 =
h) 4 + 4 + 4 + 4 + 4 =
i) 10 + 10 =
j) 5 + 5 + 5 =

52

2 Draw 3 flags on each castle. Write the answers.

a) □ + □ + □ + □ + □ + □ = □
6 groups of 3 = □

b) □ + □ + □ + □ + □ = □
5 groups of 3 = □

Try this
Count the wheels in each row. Complete each sentence.
a) 2 repeated 8 times = □ wheels
b) 4 repeated 6 times = □ wheels
c) 3 repeated 6 times = □ wheels

53

Activities

- Ask the class to count in 2s to 20, then in 10s to 100, then in 5s to 50. Ask them to try counting in 3s to 30. Use the classroom 1–100 grid to illustrate one strategy by pointing to each number in turn, but only saying 0, 3, 6, 9 etc. (1, 2 in their heads, 3 out loud, 4, 5 in their heads, 6 out loud etc.) until 30. Count in 3s several times.
- Ask pupils to take 5 pairs of counters and find the total by counting in 2s. Record on the board as 2 + 2 + 2 + 2 + 2 = 10. 'How many 2s are added together?' Draw a number line from 0 to 10 on the board and demonstrate that this is a repeated addition of two 5 times from 0.
- Ask pupils to group 10 counters in 5s. 'How many 5s are there?' Record '5 + 5 = 10' on the board.
- Ask pupils to take any number of their counters, group them in an appropriate way (replacing any which are left over from the grouping), then find the total using repeated addition. Discuss the different groupings chosen and record them on the board as repeated additions.
- Go through the introduction on page 52. Explain that when the same number is added several times it is called repeated addition.

Answers

1 a) 9 b) 12 c) 40 d) 8 e) 20 f) 21
g) 8 h) 20 i) 20 j) 15

2 a) 3 + 3 + 3 + 3 + 3 + 3 = 18, 18
b) 3 + 3 + 3 + 3 + 3 = 15, 15

Try this

a) 16 b) 24 c) 18

Lesson 3 **Multiplying**

Pupil's Book pages 54 and 55 **Oral and mental starter: Steps**

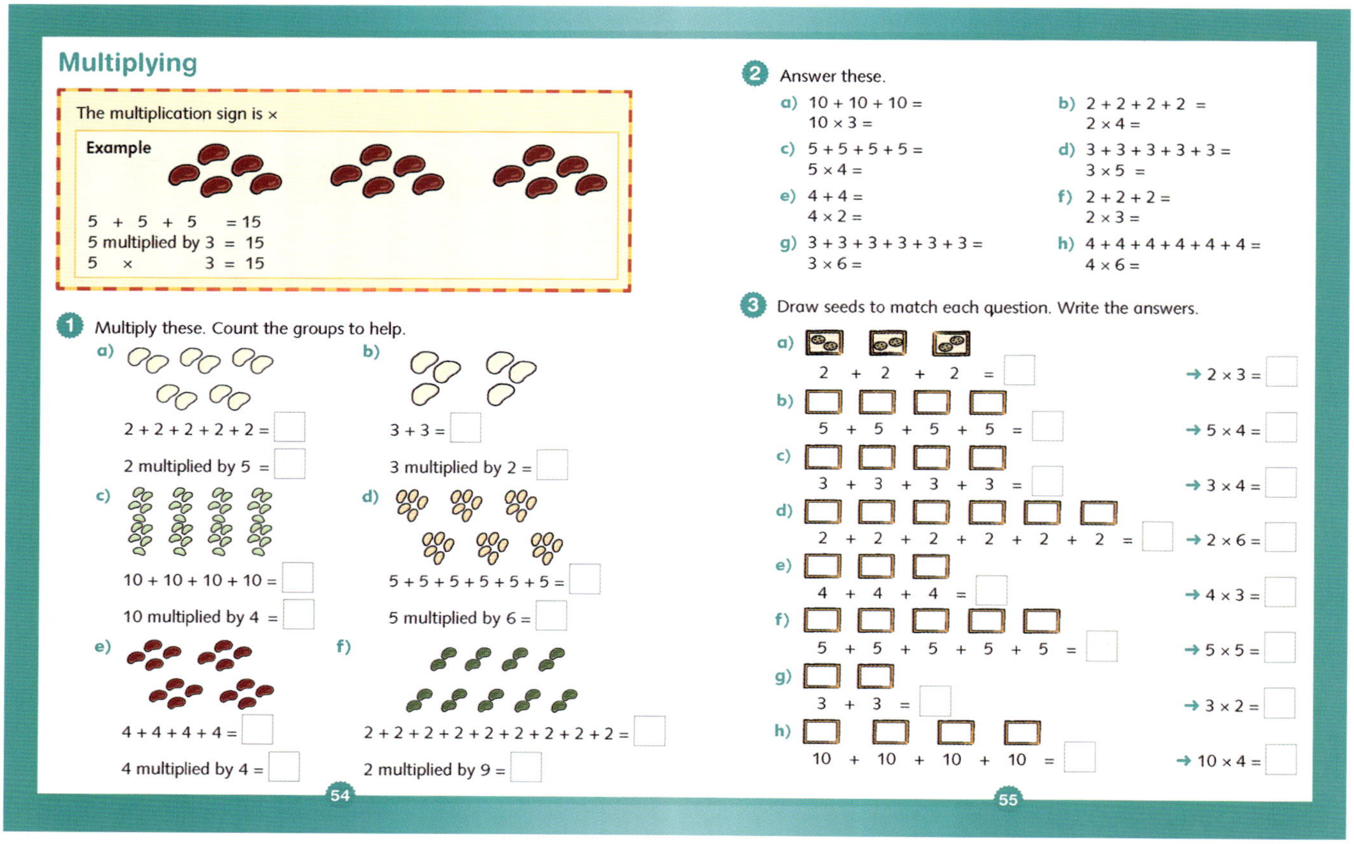

Multiplying

The multiplication sign is ×

Example

5 + 5 + 5 = 15
5 multiplied by 3 = 15
5 × 3 = 15

1 Multiply these. Count the groups to help.

a) 2 + 2 + 2 + 2 + 2 = ☐
2 multiplied by 5 = ☐

b) 3 + 3 = ☐
3 multiplied by 2 = ☐

c) 10 + 10 + 10 + 10 = ☐
10 multiplied by 4 = ☐

d) 5 + 5 + 5 + 5 + 5 + 5 = ☐
5 multiplied by 6 = ☐

e) 4 + 4 + 4 + 4 = ☐
4 multiplied by 4 = ☐

f) 2 + 2 + 2 + 2 + 2 + 2 + 2 + 2 + 2 = ☐
2 multiplied by 9 = ☐

54

2 Answer these.

a) 10 + 10 + 10 =
10 × 3 =

b) 2 + 2 + 2 + 2 =
2 × 4 =

c) 5 + 5 + 5 + 5 =
5 × 4 =

d) 3 + 3 + 3 + 3 + 3 =
3 × 5 =

e) 4 + 4 =
4 × 2 =

f) 2 + 2 + 2 =
2 × 3 =

g) 3 + 3 + 3 + 3 + 3 + 3 =
3 × 6 =

h) 4 + 4 + 4 + 4 + 4 + 4 =
4 × 6 =

3 Draw seeds to match each question. Write the answers.

a) 2 + 2 + 2 = ☐ → 2 × 3 = ☐
b) 5 + 5 + 5 + 5 = ☐ → 5 × 4 = ☐
c) 3 + 3 + 3 + 3 = ☐ → 3 × 4 = ☐
d) 2 + 2 + 2 + 2 + 2 + 2 = ☐ → 2 × 6 = ☐
e) 4 + 4 + 4 = ☐ → 4 × 3 = ☐
f) 5 + 5 + 5 + 5 + 5 = ☐ → 5 × 5 = ☐
g) 3 + 3 = ☐ → 3 × 2 = ☐
h) 10 + 10 + 10 + 10 = ☐ → 10 × 4 = ☐

55

Activities

- Look at the introduction on page 54 and remind the class about the repeated additions they did in lesson 2. Explain that the maths word for repeated addition of the same number is multiplication. Discuss the 3 groups of beans and explain that in maths 5 added 3 times is called 5 multiplied by 3. 'What is the total when 5 is multiplied by 3?' Focus on the multiplication sign as a short way of saying 'multiplied by'.
- Write 3 + 3 + 3 + 3 = on the board and ask pupils to read it as a 'multiplied by' statement (3 multiplied by 4). Ask for the answer and record, then write 3 multiplied by 4 = 12 and 3 × 4 = 12 below it. Repeat with other repeated additions such as 4 + 4 =, 10 + 10 + 10 =, 5 + 5 + 5 + 5 =.
- At the end of the lesson ask 'What is 2 × 2? … 3 × 2? … 4 × 2? … (to 10 × 2?)' Record each fact on the board in a vertical list as the questions are answered with the repeated addition alongside, e.g.
  1 × 2 = 2, 1 + 1 = 2
  2 × 2 = 4, 2 + 2 = 4 etc.
- Explain that any number multiplied by 2 is called doubling the number because it is the same as adding 2 of the same number, double 2 is 4, double 3 is 6 etc. Ask the class to double given numbers, saying the answers together.

Answers

1 a) 10, 10	b) 6, 6	c) 40, 40	d) 30, 30
e) 16, 16	f) 18, 18		
2 a) 30, 30	b) 8, 8	c) 20, 20	d) 15, 15
e) 8, 8	f) 6, 6	g) 18, 18	h) 24, 24
3 a) 6, 6	b) 20, 20	c) 12, 12	d) 12, 12
e) 12, 12	f) 25, 25	g) 6, 6	h) 40, 40

Lesson 4 **Arrays**

Pupil's Book pages 56 and 57 **Oral and mental starter: Double it**

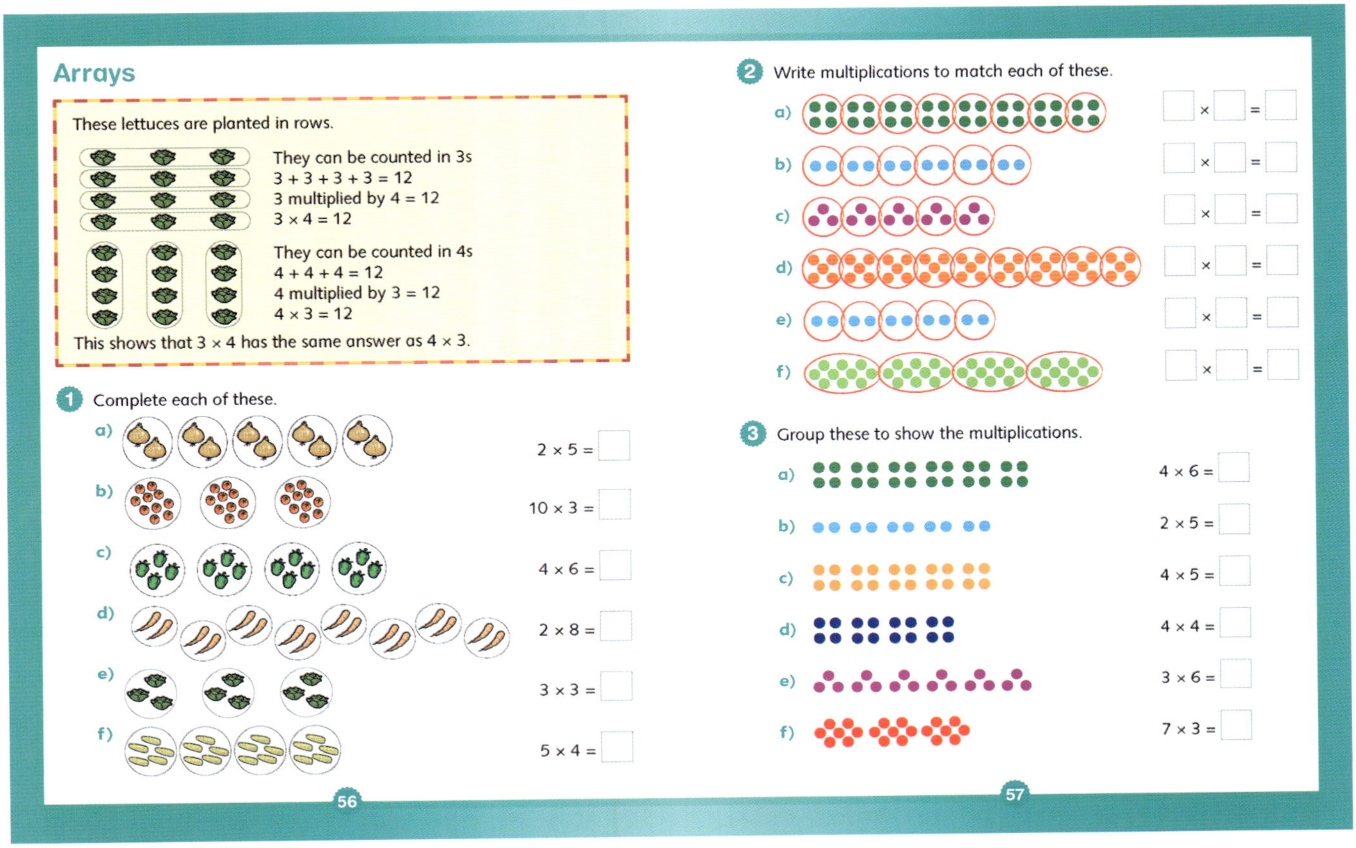

Arrays

These lettuces are planted in rows.

They can be counted in 3s
3 + 3 + 3 + 3 = 12
3 multiplied by 4 = 12
3 × 4 = 12

They can be counted in 4s
4 + 4 + 4 = 12
4 multiplied by 3 = 12
4 × 3 = 12

This shows that 3 × 4 has the same answer as 4 × 3.

1 Complete each of these.

a) 2 × 5 =
b) 10 × 3 =
c) 4 × 6 =
d) 2 × 8 =
e) 3 × 3 =
f) 5 × 4 =

2 Write multiplications to match each of these.

a) ☐ × ☐ = ☐
b) ☐ × ☐ = ☐
c) ☐ × ☐ = ☐
d) ☐ × ☐ = ☐
e) ☐ × ☐ = ☐
f) ☐ × ☐ = ☐

3 Group these to show the multiplications.

a) 4 × 6 =
b) 2 × 5 =
c) 4 × 5 =
d) 4 × 4 =
e) 3 × 6 =
f) 7 × 3 =

56 57

Activities

- Ask 6 pupils to come to the front and stand in 2 rows of 3 so that those in the first row are in line with those in the second row, i.e.
  × × ×
  × × ×
  Explain that there are 2 rows and 3 lines of pupils. 'How many pupils are there in each row? How many rows? How many pupils altogether? How can we write that as a multiplication?' Record 3 × 2 = 6 on the board. 'How many pupils in each line? How many lines? How many pupils altogether? How can we write that as a multiplication?' Record 2 × 3 = 6 on the board. Discuss that 3 × 2 has the same answer as 2 × 3.
- Look at page 56. Go through the introduction with the class, stressing that the illustrations show how 3 × 4 has the same result as 4 × 3 because 3 columns of 4 has the same total as 4 rows of 3.
- Draw an array of crosses or dots on the board, e.g. 4 rows of 2, making sure that the crosses are also aligned in 2 columns. Discuss and record the two ways of counting the array in the same way as illustrated in the introduction. Ask for and record the multiplication fact in each case (2 × 4 = 8, 4 × 2 = 8). Repeat for another multiplication such as 5 × 6.

Answers

1 a) 10 b) 30 c) 24 d) 16 e) 9 f) 20

2 a) 4 × 8 = 32 b) 2 × 6 = 12 c) 3 × 5 = 15
d) 5 × 9 = 45 e) 2 × 5 = 10 f) 10 × 4 = 40

3 a) 24 b) 10 c) 20 d) 16 e) 18 f) 21

Lesson 5 Multiplying by 1 and 0

Pupil's Book pages 58 and 59 **Oral and mental starter: Flash facts (simple multiplication facts)**

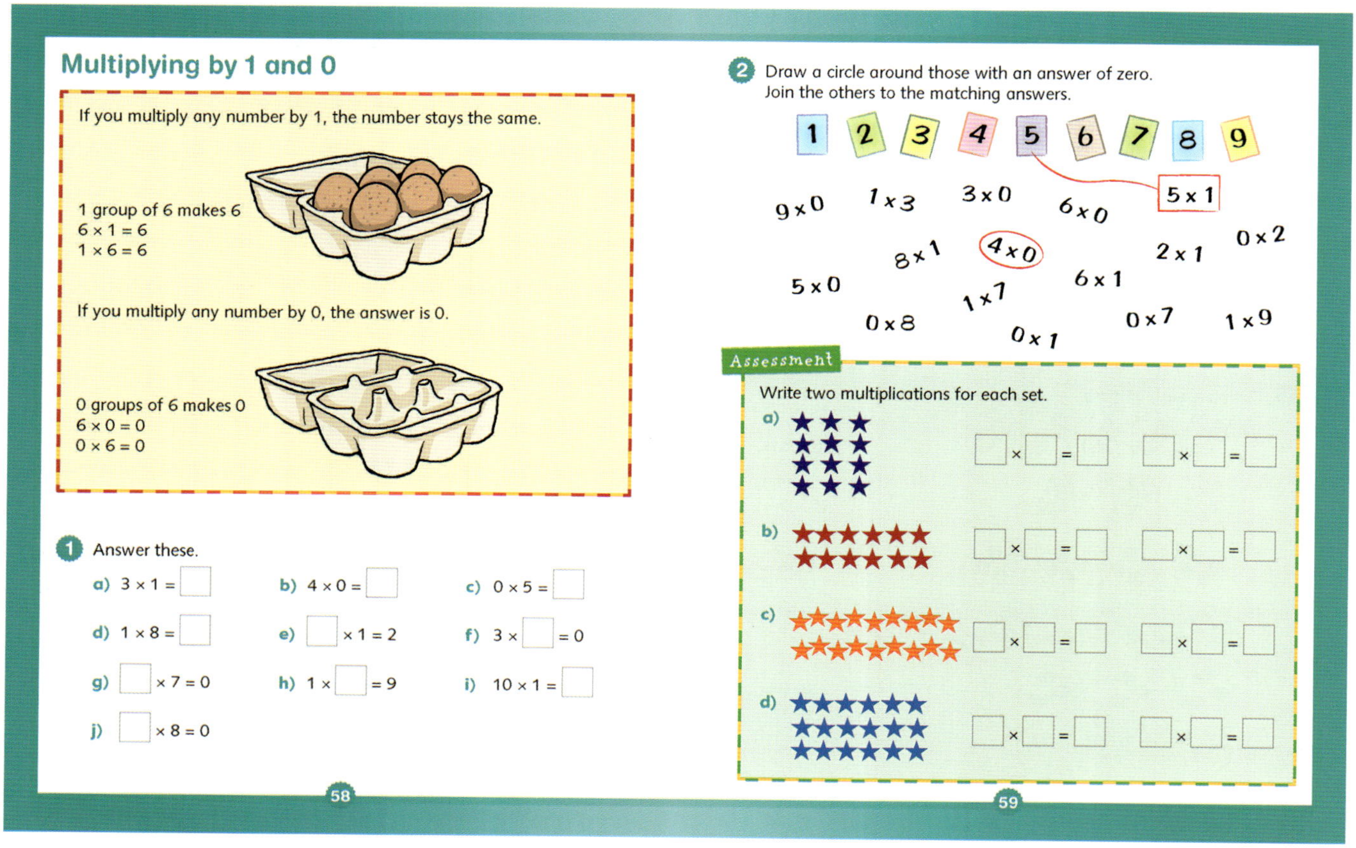

Multiplying by 1 and 0

If you multiply any number by 1, the number stays the same.

1 group of 6 makes 6
6 × 1 = 6
1 × 6 = 6

If you multiply any number by 0, the answer is 0.

0 groups of 6 makes 0
6 × 0 = 0
0 × 6 = 0

1 Answer these.

a) 3 × 1 = ☐ b) 4 × 0 = ☐ c) 0 × 5 = ☐
d) 1 × 8 = ☐ e) ☐ × 1 = 2 f) 3 × ☐ = 0
g) ☐ × 7 = 0 h) 1 × ☐ = 9 i) 10 × 1 = ☐
j) ☐ × 8 = 0

2 Draw a circle around those with an answer of zero.
Join the others to the matching answers.

1 2 3 4 5 6 7 8 9

9 × 0, 1 × 3, 3 × 0, 6 × 0, 5 × 1, 0 × 2, 8 × 1, 4 × 0, 2 × 1, 5 × 0, 1 × 7, 6 × 1, 0 × 8, 0 × 1, 0 × 7, 1 × 9

Assessment

Write two multiplications for each set.

a) ☐ × ☐ = ☐ ☐ × ☐ = ☐
b) ☐ × ☐ = ☐ ☐ × ☐ = ☐
c) ☐ × ☐ = ☐ ☐ × ☐ = ☐
d) ☐ × ☐ = ☐ ☐ × ☐ = ☐

58 59

Activities

- Ask pupils to take one counter in each hand. 'How many counters in 1 hand? How many in 2 hands?' Explain that 1 hand shows 1 group of 1 and 2 hands show 2 groups of 1. Record $1 \times 1 = 1$ and $1 \times 2 = 2$ on the board and remind the class that we use 'multiplied by' in maths for groups of the same number. Ask 'How many counters are there in 3 hands? How can we write that as a multiplication?' Record $1 \times 3 = 3$ on the board. Repeat for 4, 5, 6, 7, 8, 9 and 10 hands. 'What happens when we multiply 1 by any number?' (The number is unchanged.)
- Ask pupils to put their counters down. 'How many counters are there in 1 hand now?' Record $0 \times 1 = 0$ on the board. 'How many in 2 hands?' Record $0 \times 2 = 0$. Repeat for 3, 4, …, 10 hands. 'What happens when we multiply 0 by any number?' (The answer is always 0.)
- Look at page 58. Go through the introduction with the class. Remind them that 6×1 has the same result as 1×6 and 6×0 the same result as 0×6. Reinforce this by checking with the relevant facts on the board. Ask 'What is 8×1? … 3×0? … 10×1? … 5×0?'

Answers

1 a) 3 b) 0 c) 0 d) 8 e) 2 f) 0
g) 0 h) 9 i) 10 j) 0

2 Circle: $9 \times 0, 3 \times 0, 6 \times 0, 5 \times 0, 0 \times 8, 0 \times 1, 0 \times 7, 0 \times 2$;
$1 \times 3 = 3, 8 \times 1 = 8, 1 \times 7 = 7, 6 \times 1 = 6, 2 \times 1 = 2,$
$1 \times 9 = 9$

Assessment

a) $4 \times 3 = 12,\ 3 \times 4 = 12$ b) $2 \times 6 = 12, 6 \times 2 = 12$
c) $2 \times 9 = 18, 9 \times 2 = 18$ d) $3 \times 6 = 18,\ 6 \times 3 = 18$

Unit 7 **Number facts**

Term 1 Block A
Number operations
Unit 5 Subtraction within 99
Unit 6 Multiplication
Unit 7 Number facts
Unit 8 Assess and review

Objectives
At the end of the unit, students should be able to…
Use different and suitable methods for addition, subtraction and/or multiplication, like Mental Maths or use of written methods.
Comprehend that the relation between addition and subtraction is an inverse relation and apply this using shapes and symbols.
Understand and state the products of multiplication up to table 9.
Understand the concepts of multiplying by 1 and 0.
Give numerical examples showing the properties of multiplication up to table 9 without naming the property.

Vocabulary
addition, subtraction, multiplication, facts, total, strategy, double, near doubles, crossing 10, trios, inverse, table, sequence, multiple

Lessons
1 Adding to 20
2 Addition and subtraction trios
3 Multiplication facts for 2 and 4
4 Multiplication facts for 3
5 Multiplying by 5 and 10

Oral and mental starters
Double it
Flash facts (addition)
Steps (10s, 5s, 3s, 2s)
Flash facts (2× and 4×)
Product pairs

Resources
Counters – about 20 per pupil
Classroom 1–100 grid
Pupil's Book pages 60–69

Prior learning
Knowledge of addition facts, using addition facts to find subtraction facts (Grade 1)
Understanding multiplication and familiarity with some of the facts (Grade 2 Unit 6)

Background notes
Many pupils will know addition and subtraction facts to 10.
Discounting adding 2, 1 or 0 to any number, there are nine combinations of numbers with sums up to 10: 3 plus 3, 4, 5, 6 or 7; 4 plus 4, 5, or 6; 5 plus 5.
Pupils should develop their learning to addition facts to 20 when they are confident with all the facts within 10.
Strategies for recalling multiplication facts in tables 2, 3, 4, 5 and 10 are developed in this unit. When these are known the remaining facts up to table 9 are: 6×6, 6×7, 6×8, 7×7, 7×8, 8×8.

End of unit evaluation
Check that pupils are able to:
1 Recall addition and subtraction facts for totals to 11.
2 Use appropriate strategies for finding unknown addition facts quickly.
3 Use addition facts to find related subtraction facts.
4 Recall multiplication facts in tables 2, 3, 4, 5 and 10.
5 Use the commutative property of multiplication.

Supporting the topic
Use opportunities in everyday classroom activities to practise and develop pupils' knowledge of number facts e.g.:

- Have a 'fact of the day', such as $8 + 6 = 14$, and display it with the three related facts ($6 + 8 = 14$, $14 - 6 = 8$, $14 - 8 = 6$). Regularly ask for the answer to one of the four facts. Similarly include multiplication facts, e.g. 3×5 and 5×3.
- Have copies of addition facts and their three related facts, and multiplication facts available for self-testing. Grade the facts into sets appropriate to different pupils' stages of learning. Record those which they cannot recall quickly and learn them.
  - Encourage pupils to learn number facts at home.

Lesson 1 **Adding to 20**

Pupil's Book pages 60 and 61 **Oral and mental starter: One**

Unit 7 Number facts

Adding to 20

Try to learn all the addition facts to 20.
Use different strategies to help learn them.

Near doubles	Counting on	Crossing 10
4 + 4 = 8 4 + 5 is 1 more → 9 6 + 6 = 12 6 + 7 is 1 more → 13	4 + 8 gives the same answer as 8 + 4. Start at 8 and count on. 8 9 10 11 12	Take 2 steps: 8 + 5 = 8 + 2 + 3 = 8 + 2 + 3 = 10 + 3 8 + 5 = 13

1 Use near doubles to help answer these.

a) 3 + 3 =
   3 + 4 =
b) 7 + 7 =
   7 + 8 =
c) 5 + 5 =
   5 + 6 =
d) 8 + 8 =
   8 + 9 =
e) 4 + 4 =
   4 + 5 =
f) 6 + 6 =
   6 + 7 =

2 Choose a method to answer these.

a) 9 + 5 =   b) 7 + 4 =   c) 8 + 3 =
d) 9 + 7 =   e) 7 + 6 =   f) 9 + 4 =
g) 8 + 6 =   h) 5 + 8 =   i) 7 + 5 =
j) 6 + 9 =

3 Write the answers as number words to complete the crossword.

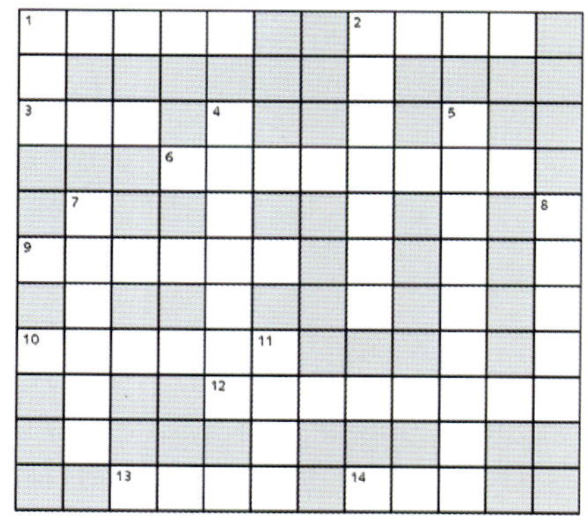

Across
1) 2 + 1 =
2) 2 + 2 =
3) 0 + 1 =
6) 9 + 9 =
9) 10 + 10 =
10) 7 + 4 =
12) 9 + 10 =
13) 3 + 2 =
14) 2 + 8 =

Down
1) 2 + 0 =
2) 7 + 8 =
4) 9 + 7 =
5) 8 + 9 =
7) 7 + 5 =
8) 3 + 4 =
11) 5 + 4 =

Try this

☐ + ☐ = 20

Complete this in different ways.

60   61

Activities

- Ask pupils for two numbers with a sum of 10. Record on the board until all six facts have been recorded (10 + 0, 9 + 1, …, 5 + 5). Remind them that 6 + 4 and 4 + 6 give the same answer.
- 'Which numbers below 20 are very easy to add to another number?' (0, 1, 2, 9 (by adding 10 and subtracting 1), 10, 11). Provide some examples for the class to answer together on your signal, e.g. 3 + 0, 14 + 0; 5 + 1, 18 + 1; 9 + 2, 13 + 2; 6 + 9, 8 + 9; 10 + 3, 10 + 6; 11 + 5, 11 + 7 etc. Increase the pace to encourage quick responses. Encourage confidence, saying how well they know many addition facts.
- Explain that this lesson is about finding ways to learn other addition facts. Emphasise the first statement on page 60 and encourage pupils to practise and learn facts at home. Explain that the strategies make it easy to work out calculations.

Go through the three examples carefully and give further examples using that strategy, e.g. near doubles: 5 + 6, 6 + 7; counting on: 4 + 7, 3 + 8; crossing ten: 7 + 5; 8 + 4.

Answers

1 a) 6, 7   b) 14, 15   c) 10, 11   d) 16, 17
  e) 8, 9   f) 12, 13

2 a) 14   b) 11   c) 11   d) 16   e) 13
  f) 13   g) 14   h) 13   i) 12   j) 15

3
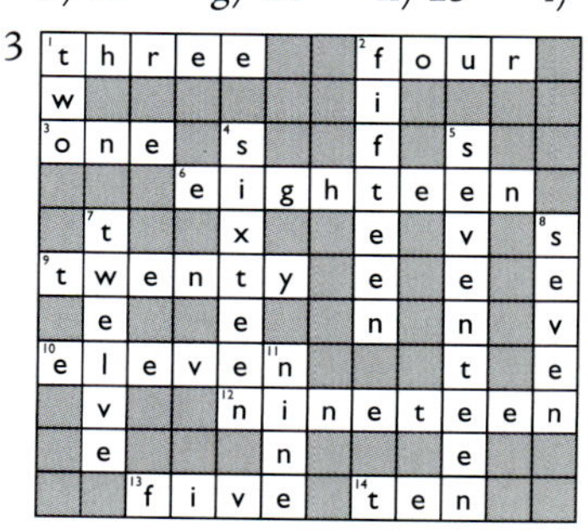

Lesson 2 **Addition and subtraction trios**

Pupil's Book pages 62 and 63 **Oral and mental starter: Flash facts (addition)**

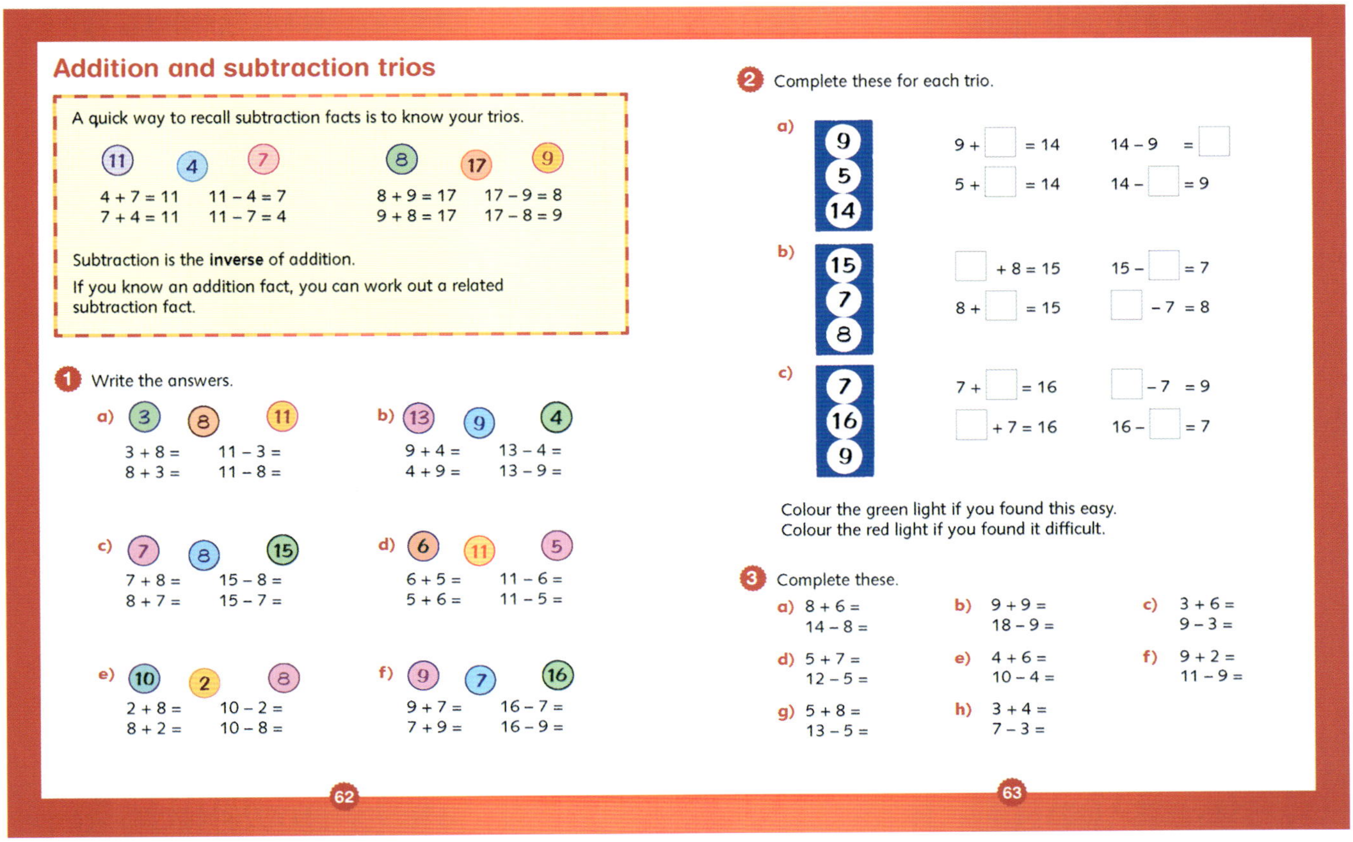
Addition and subtraction trios

A quick way to recall subtraction facts is to know your trios.

(11) (4) (7)
4 + 7 = 11   11 − 4 = 7
7 + 4 = 11   11 − 7 = 4

(8) (17) (9)
8 + 9 = 17   17 − 9 = 8
9 + 8 = 17   17 − 8 = 9

Subtraction is the **inverse** of addition.
If you know an addition fact, you can work out a related subtraction fact.

1 Write the answers.

a) (3) (8) (11)
3 + 8 =   11 − 3 =
8 + 3 =   11 − 8 =

b) (13) (9) (4)
9 + 4 =   13 − 4 =
4 + 9 =   13 − 9 =

c) (7) (8) (15)
7 + 8 =   15 − 8 =
8 + 7 =   15 − 7 =

d) (6) (11) (5)
6 + 5 =   11 − 6 =
5 + 6 =   11 − 5 =

e) (10) (2) (8)
2 + 8 =   10 − 2 =
8 + 2 =   10 − 8 =

f) (9) (7) (16)
9 + 7 =   16 − 7 =
7 + 9 =   16 − 9 =

2 Complete these for each trio.

a) 9, 5, 14
9 + ☐ = 14   14 − 9 = ☐
5 + ☐ = 14   14 − ☐ = 9

b) 15, 7, 8
☐ + 8 = 15   15 − ☐ = 7
8 + ☐ = 15   ☐ − 7 = 8

c) 7, 16, 9
7 + ☐ = 16   ☐ − 7 = 9
☐ + 7 = 16   16 − ☐ = 7

Colour the green light if you found this easy.
Colour the red light if you found it difficult.

3 Complete these.

a) 8 + 6 =
14 − 8 =

b) 9 + 9 =
18 − 9 =

c) 3 + 6 =
9 − 3 =

d) 5 + 7 =
12 − 5 =

e) 4 + 6 =
10 − 4 =

f) 9 + 2 =
11 − 9 =

g) 5 + 8 =
13 − 5 =

h) 3 + 4 =
7 − 3 =

62   63

Activities

- Remind the class that they found two addition and two subtraction facts using the same three numbers in Grade 1. Ask them to take 8 counters and then 6 from their set. Write 8 + 6 = on the board, ask for the answer then record it. 'What other addition fact can we write using 8, 6 and 14?' Record 6 + 8 = 14. 'What is 14 – 6?' Record on the board. 'What other subtraction fact can we make from these numbers?' Record 14 – 8 = 6 on the board.
- Look at page 62. Go through the introduction with the class, stressing the statements at the end. Ask for any addition fact, write it on the board, then ask for a subtraction fact which can be made from it (e.g. 7 + 5 = 12, 12 – 5 = 7) 'What other two facts could we write using these numbers?' (5 + 7 = 12, 12 – 7 = 5). Stress that because the pupils know one addition fact, they also know another addition fact and two subtraction facts.
- At the end of the lesson ask for answers to a few known addition facts, then ask for the other three facts, e.g. 'What is 8 + 4? So what is 4 + 8? … 12 – 4? … 12 – 8?'

Answers

1 a) 3 + 8 = **11**, 11 – 3 = **8**, 8 + 3 = **11**, 11 – 8 = **3**
b) 9 + 4 = **13**, 13 – 4 = **9**, 4 + 9 = **13**, 13 – 9 = **4**
c) 7 + 8 = **15**, 15 – 8 = **7**, 8 + 7 = **15**, 15 – 7 = **8**
d) 6 + 5 = **11**, 11 – 6 = **5**, 5 + 6 = **11**, 11 – 5 = **6**
e) 2 + 8 = **10**, 10 – 2 = **8**, 8 + 2 = **10**, 10 – 8 = **2**
f) 9 + 7 = **16**, 16 – 7 = **9**, 7 + 9 = **16**, 16 – 9 = **7**

2 a) 9 + **5** = 14, 14 – 9 = **5**, 5 + **9** = 14, 14 – **5** = 9
b) **7** + 8 = 15, 15 – **8** = 7, 8 + **7** = 15, **15** – 7 = 8
c) 7 + **9** = 16, **16** – 7 = 9, **9** + 7 = 16, 16 – **9** = 7

3 a) 14, 6 b) 18, 9 c) 9, 6 d) 12, 7 e) 10, 6
f) 11, 2 g) 13, 8 h) 7, 4

Lesson 3 **Multiplication facts for 2 and 4**

Pupil's Book pages 64 and 65 **Oral and mental starter: Steps (10s, 5s, 3s, 2s)**

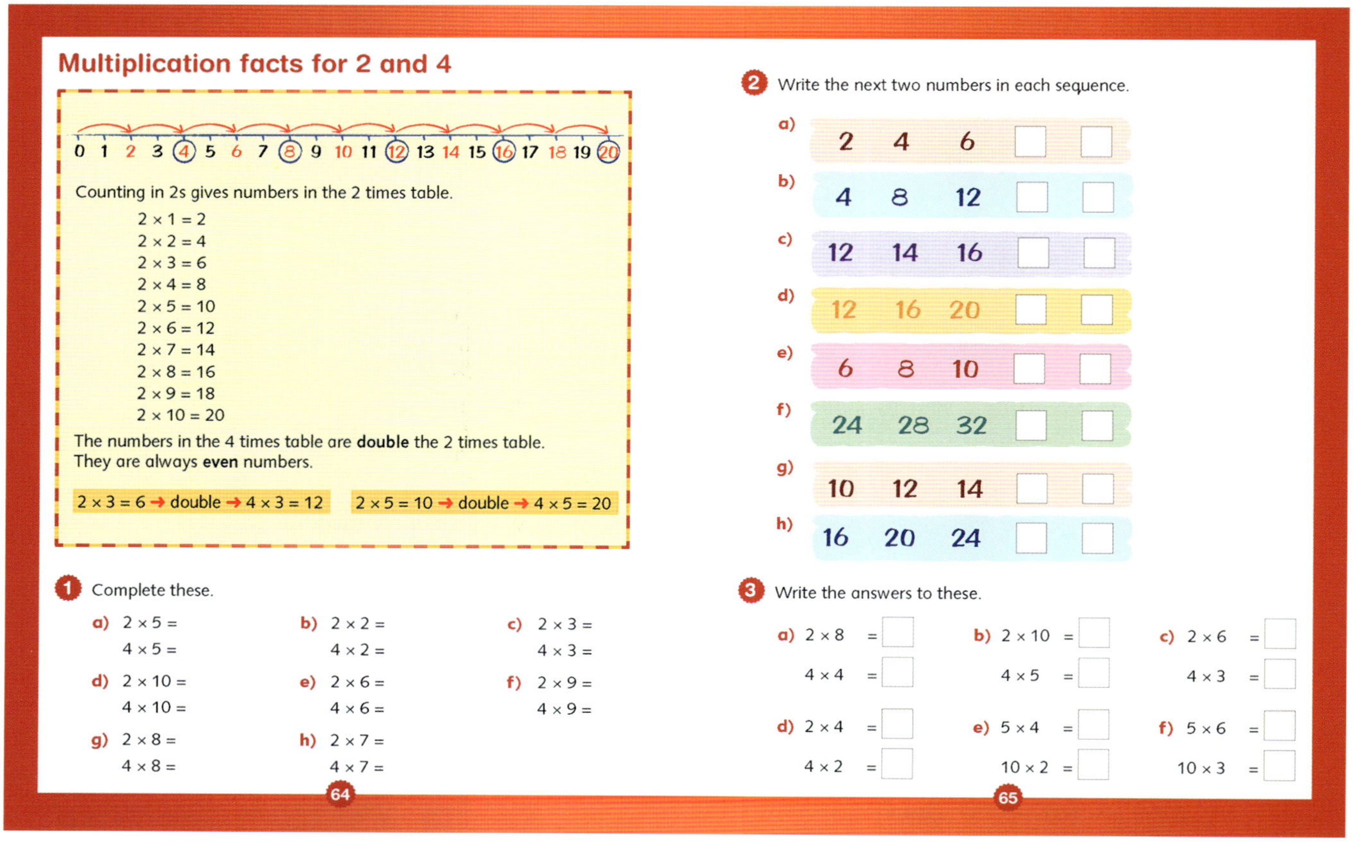

Multiplication facts for 2 and 4

0 1 2 3 4 5 6 7 8 9 10 11 12 13 14 15 16 17 18 19 20

Counting in 2s gives numbers in the 2 times table.

2 × 1 = 2
2 × 2 = 4
2 × 3 = 6
2 × 4 = 8
2 × 5 = 10
2 × 6 = 12
2 × 7 = 14
2 × 8 = 16
2 × 9 = 18
2 × 10 = 20

The numbers in the 4 times table are **double** the 2 times table.
They are always **even** numbers.

2 × 3 = 6 → double → 4 × 3 = 12   2 × 5 = 10 → double → 4 × 5 = 20

1 Complete these.

a) 2 × 5 = 4 × 5 =
b) 2 × 2 = 4 × 2 =
c) 2 × 3 = 4 × 3 =
d) 2 × 10 = 4 × 10 =
e) 2 × 6 = 4 × 6 =
f) 2 × 9 = 4 × 9 =
g) 2 × 8 = 4 × 8 =
h) 2 × 7 = 4 × 7 =

64

2 Write the next two numbers in each sequence.

a) 2 4 6 ☐ ☐
b) 4 8 12 ☐ ☐
c) 12 14 16 ☐ ☐
d) 12 16 20 ☐ ☐
e) 6 8 10 ☐ ☐
f) 24 28 32 ☐ ☐
g) 10 12 14 ☐ ☐
h) 16 20 24 ☐ ☐

3 Write the answers to these.

a) 2 × 8 = ☐ 4 × 4 = ☐
b) 2 × 10 = ☐ 4 × 5 = ☐
c) 2 × 6 = ☐ 4 × 3 = ☐
d) 2 × 4 = ☐ 4 × 2 = ☐
e) 5 × 4 = ☐ 10 × 2 = ☐
f) 5 × 6 = ☐ 10 × 3 = ☐

65

Activities

- Look at page 64. Explain the meaning of '2 times table' with reference to the pattern of 2s on the number line. Ask the class to read the table aloud together. Remind them that multiplying 2 by any number is the same as doubling that number. Ask random 2 times table facts for the class to answer together orally, e.g. 2 × 5, 2 × 8, 2 × 3 etc. Repeat with pupils' books closed.
- Ask the class to count together in 2s from 0 to 40 as you indicate each step of 2 on the class 1–100 grid. Now ask them to count in 4s to 40 as you indicate each step of 4 on the grid. Point out that each step of 4 is the same as 2 steps of 2. Ask them to count in 4s to 40 again, but this time do not indicate the numbers on the grid.
- Look at page 64 again and go through the rest of the introduction about the 4 times table.

Emphasise that multiplying 4 by a number is double multiplying 2 by the same number. Write 4 × 1 =, 4 × 2 =, …, 4 × 10 = in a vertical list on the board. Ask the class to use the facts given in the 2 times table to give the answers. Record them in the table on the board. Ask them to read the table aloud together twice, then remove it from the board as pupils answer the questions in the Pupil's Book.

Answers

1	a) 10, 20	b) 4, 8	c) 6, 12	d) 20, 40
	e) 12, 24	f) 18, 36	g) 16, 32	h) 14, 28
2	a) 8, 10	b) 16, 20	c) 18, 20	d) 24, 28
	e) 12, 14	f) 36, 40	g) 16, 18	h) 28, 32
3	a) 16, 16	b) 20, 20	c) 12, 12	d) 8, 8
	e) 20, 20	f) 30, 30		

Lesson 4 **Multiplication facts for 3**

Pupil's Book pages 66 and 67 **Oral and mental starter: Flash facts (2× and 4×)**

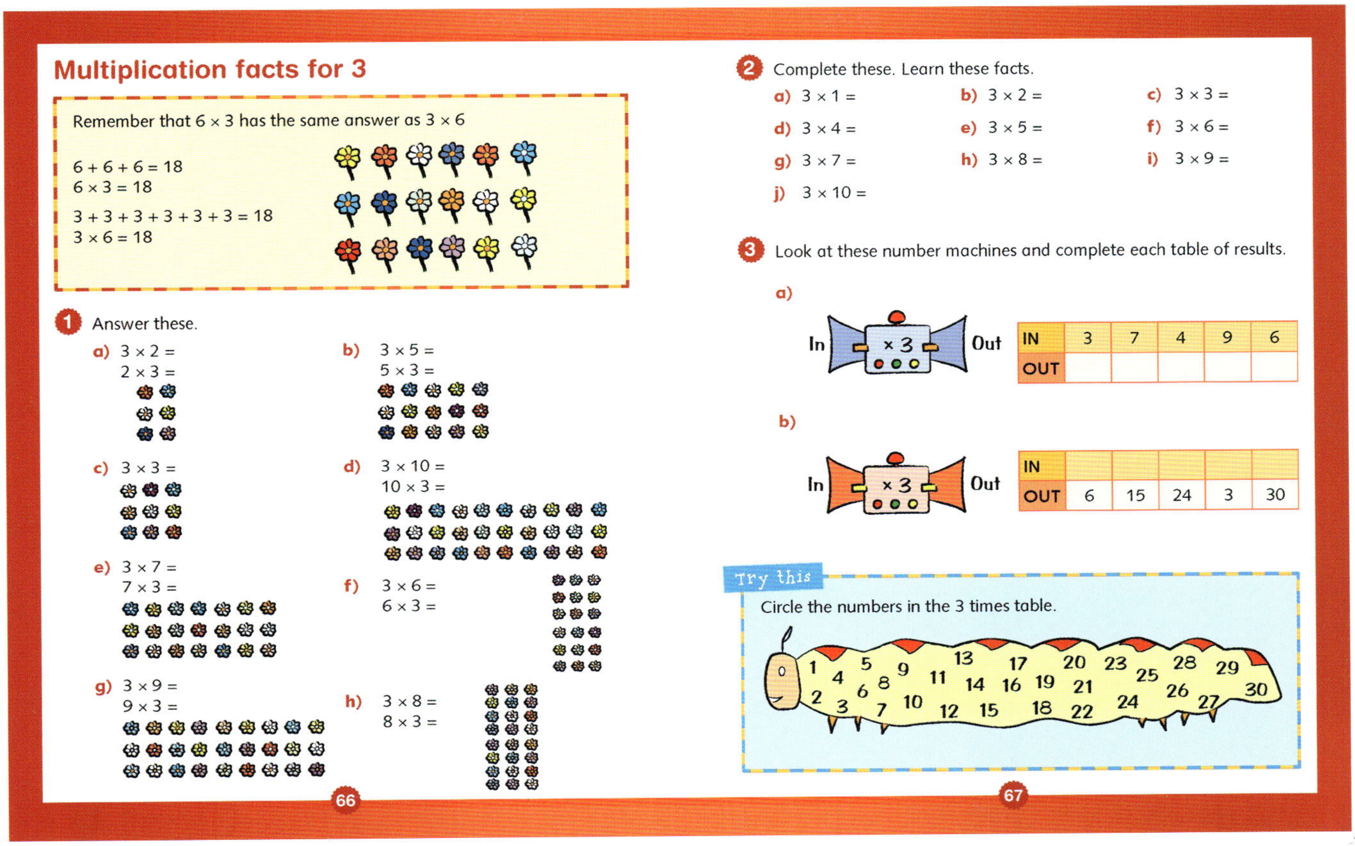

Multiplication facts for 3

Remember that 6 × 3 has the same answer as 3 × 6

6 + 6 + 6 = 18
6 × 3 = 18

3 + 3 + 3 + 3 + 3 + 3 = 18
3 × 6 = 18

1 Answer these.

a) 3 × 2 =
2 × 3 =

b) 3 × 5 =
5 × 3 =

c) 3 × 3 =

d) 3 × 10 =
10 × 3 =

e) 3 × 7 =
7 × 3 =

f) 3 × 6 =
6 × 3 =

g) 3 × 9 =
9 × 3 =

h) 3 × 8 =
8 × 3 =

66

2 Complete these. Learn these facts.

a) 3 × 1 = b) 3 × 2 = c) 3 × 3 =
d) 3 × 4 = e) 3 × 5 = f) 3 × 6 =
g) 3 × 7 = h) 3 × 8 = i) 3 × 9 =
j) 3 × 10 =

3 Look at these number machines and complete each table of results.

a) In × 3 Out

IN	3	7	4	9	6
OUT					

b) In × 3 Out

IN					
OUT	6	15	24	3	30

Try this

Circle the numbers in the 3 times table.

1 2 3 4 5 6 7 8 9 10 11 12 13 14 15 16 17 18 19 20 21 22 23 24 25 26 27 28 29 30

67

Activities

- Ask the class to count together in 3s to 30 as you indicate each step of 3 on the class 1–100 grid. Repeat, but do not indicate the numbers on the grid. Remind them that they worked on the 2 times and 4 times tables yesterday and explain that this lesson is about the 3 times table.
- Write 3 × 1 = on the board, ask for the answer and record. Write 3 × 2 = below 3 × 1 on the board and repeat. Continue until the table is complete to 3 × 10. Point out that each new fact in the table can be found by adding 3 to the previous fact, i.e. 3 × 1 = 3, 3 × 2 = 3 + 3 = 6, 3 × 3 = 6 + 3 = 9, 3 × 4 = 9 + 3 = 12 etc. Ask the class to read the table together twice, then remove it from the board and ask them to say it again.
- Look at page 66. Revise that 6 × 3 is the same as 3 × 6 with reference to the array.
- At the end of the lesson ask the class to say the 3 times table together, then ask facts in random order, e.g. 4 × 3, 7 × 3, 2 × 3, 10 × 3 etc.

Answers

1 a) 6, 6 b) 15, 15 c) 9 d) 30, 30
e) 21, 21 f) 18, 18 g) 27, 27 h) 24, 24

2 a) 3 b) 6 c) 9 d) 12 e) 15 f) 18
g) 21 h) 24 i) 27 j) 30

3 a) 9, 21, 12, 27, 18 b) 2, 5, 8, 1, 10

Try this

3, 6, 9, 12, 15, 18, 21, 24, 27, 30

Lesson 5 **Multiplying by 5 and 10**

Pupil's Book pages 68 and 69 **Oral and mental starter: Product pairs**

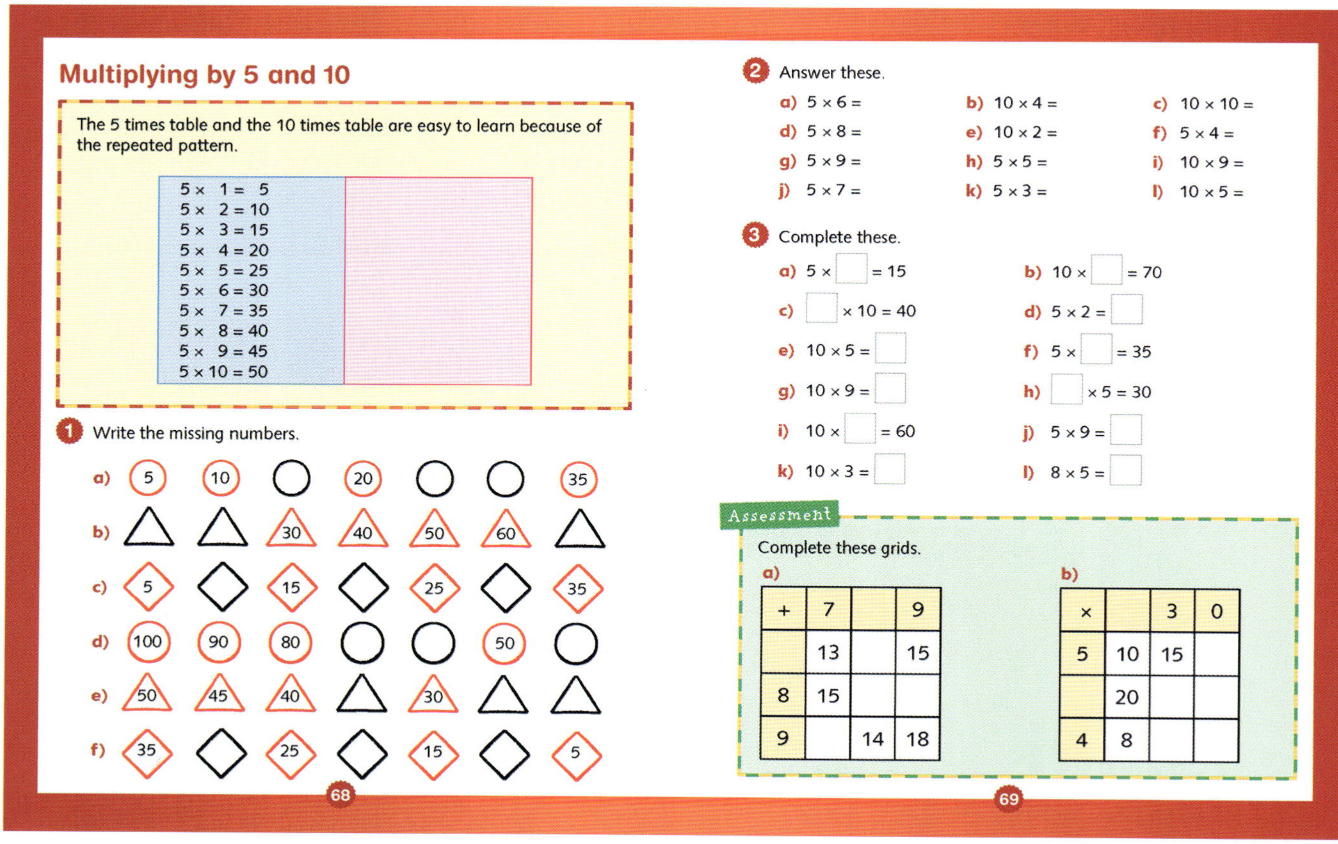

Multiplying by 5 and 10

The 5 times table and the 10 times table are easy to learn because of the repeated pattern.

5 × 1 = 5	
5 × 2 = 10	
5 × 3 = 15	
5 × 4 = 20	
5 × 5 = 25	
5 × 6 = 30	
5 × 7 = 35	
5 × 8 = 40	
5 × 9 = 45	
5 × 10 = 50	

1 Write the missing numbers.

a) 5, 10, ○, 20, ○, ○, 35
b) △, △, 30, 40, 50, 60, △
c) 5, ◇, 15, ◇, 25, ◇, 35
d) 100, 90, 80, ○, ○, 50, ○
e) 50, 45, 40, △, 30, △, △
f) 35, ◇, 25, ◇, 15, ◇, 5

2 Answer these.

a) 5 × 6 = b) 10 × 4 = c) 10 × 10 =
d) 5 × 8 = e) 10 × 2 = f) 5 × 4 =
g) 5 × 9 = h) 5 × 5 = i) 10 × 9 =
j) 5 × 7 = k) 5 × 3 = l) 10 × 5 =

3 Complete these.

a) 5 × ☐ = 15 b) 10 × ☐ = 70
c) ☐ × 10 = 40 d) 5 × 2 = ☐
e) 10 × 5 = ☐ f) 5 × ☐ = 35
g) 10 × 9 = ☐ h) ☐ × 5 = 30
i) 10 × ☐ = 60 j) 5 × 9 = ☐
k) 10 × 3 = ☐ l) 8 × 5 = ☐

Assessment

Complete these grids.

a)

+	7		9
	13		15
8	15		
9		14	18

b)

×		3	0
5	10	15	
	20		
4	8		

68 69

Activities

- Ask the class to count to 50 in 5s as you indicate each number on the class grid. Repeat, counting in 10s to 100.
- Ask questions such as 'What is 5 × 3? ... 5 × 5? ... 10 × 4? ... 10 × 6?' Each time confirm the answer by indicating the appropriate number of steps on the class grid, i.e. for 5 × 3 show 3 steps of 5 on the grid; 4 steps of 10 for 10 × 4 etc.
- Look at page 68. Look at the 5 and 10 times tables and talk about the patterns in the multiples of each. Point out that any multiple of 5 is half the same multiple of 10 (e.g. 5 × 4 is half 10 × 4).
- Explain the assessment activity, e.g. demonstrate a similar grid on the board and show how to complete it. Point out that the first grid on page 69 involves addition, the second multiplication.

Answers

1 a) 15, 25, 30 b) 10, 20, 70 c) 10, 20, 30
d) 70, 60, 40 e) 35, 25, 20 f) 30, 20, 10

2 a) 30 b) 40 c) 100 d) 40 e) 20 f) 20
g) 45 h) 25 i) 90 j) 35 k) 15 l) 50

3 a) 3 b) 7 c) 4 d) 10 e) 50 f) 7
g) 90 h) 6 i) 6 j) 45 k) 30 l) 40

Assessment

+	7	5	9
6	13	11	15
8	15	13	17
9	16	14	18

×	2	3	0
5	10	15	0
10	20	30	0
4	8	12	0

Unit 8 Assess and review

Term 1 Block B
Number operations
Unit 5 Subtraction within 99
Unit 6 Multiplication
Unit 7 Number facts
Unit 8 Assess and review

Final evaluation
Check that pupils are able to:
1 Subtract with 2-digit numbers without renaming.
2 Use appropriate mental and written methods for subtraction.
3 Understand and use the commutative property of multiplication.
4 Multiply by 1 and by 0.
5 Recall addition and subtraction facts with sums less than 11.
6 Use appropriate strategies for finding unknown addition facts.
7 Use addition facts to find related subtraction facts.
8 Recall multiplication facts in tables 2, 3, 4, 5 and 10.

Vocabulary
take away, subtract, difference, count on, digit, tens, units, (place) value, opposite, inverse, grouping, group, set, repeated addition, multiplying, multiplication, multiplied by, total, double, doubling, number facts, strategy, double, near doubles, crossing 10, trios, inverse, table, sequence

Resources
Counters for each child
Classroom 1–100 grid
Pupil's Book pages 70–75

Pupil's Book pages 70–75
1 Ask pupils for different words or phrases for subtraction (e.g. subtract, less than, take away). (page 70)
2 Write any multiple of 10 on the board and ask pupils to give two numbers which have that difference. Record suggestions on the board as subtractions, e.g. 50 – 20 = 30. (page 70)
3 Write 5 + 5 + 5 + 5 = on the board. 'How do we write this as a multiplication?' Record 5 × 4 = on the board, ask for the answer and record. (page 72)
4 'What happens when we multiply any number by 0? … by 1?' (page 73)
5 Remind the class about the ways to work out addition and subtraction facts they don't immediately know (e.g. using known trios, near doubles, counting on from the largest number, crossing 10). (page 74)
6 Explain that pupils should write two addition and two subtraction facts for each trio. (page 74)
7 Explain how the number machines work. (page 75)

Assessment activities
Use these to assess pupils' knowledge and understanding:
What is the difference between 12 and 7? How did you work it out? What is 80 subtract 30? How did you work it out? What is 68 take away 4? How did you work it out? What is 56 take away 30? How did you work it out? Copy and complete these subtractions:

67 – 32 = 86 – 43 = $\begin{array}{r} 79 \\ -\underline{45} \end{array}$ $\begin{array}{r} 58 \\ -\underline{17} \end{array}$

Write this as a multiplication: 3 + 3 + 3 + 3. What is 3 × 4? Answer these: 4 × 2 =, 7 × 1 =, 10 × 6 =.
Give me any two numbers which total 16 when added together. Now two numbers with a difference of 16. Now two numbers with a total of 16 when they are multiplied.
What is 8 plus 6? Which 2 subtraction facts use the same three numbers as 8 + 6 = 14?
Write the answers to these: 7 + 3 =, 10 – 6 =, 5 + 4 =, 12 – 5 =, 14 + 5 =, 18 – 4 =, 13 + 6 =, 3 × 3 =, 8 × 2 =, 5 × 4 =, 7 × 5 =, 10 × 9 =, 7 × 3 =, 4 × 7 =, 19 – 19 =.

Assess and review activities

Use these activities taken from the previous three weeks to monitor, evaluate and consolidate pupils' knowledge and understanding.

- 'What happens when we take away 0 from a number? How do we subtract 1 from a number? What is 8 – 2? How did you work it out?' Establish that subtracting 0 leaves a number unchanged, subtracting 1 is simply 1 less and subtracting 2 is counting back 2 so 0, 1 or 2 can be subtracted from any number very quickly.
- Write 9 – 6 = on the board. 'What do we add to 6 to make 9? So what is 9 – 6? Record the answer then repeat with other subtraction facts within 10, e.g. 7 – 2, 5 – 3, 6 – 4, 4 – 3. 'If 9 – 6 is 3, what is 90 – 60? How do you know?' Repeat using the other subtraction facts on the board.
- Ask questions such as 'What is 8 – 3?' Record the subtraction on the board. 'If 8 – 3 is 5, what is 18 – 3?' Record below the first subtraction on the board. Continue in the same way with 28 – 3, 38 – 3, 48 – 3, 78 – 3, 98 – 3. 'What do you notice about each answer?' Draw out that each involves 8 – 3 = 5 and that the tens digit is unchanged.
- Using ten rods and unit cubes (or an abacus), illustrate a subtraction such as 33 – 10. Record as a horizontal subtraction on the board, pointing out that they know that 30 – 10 = 20, so 33 – 10 is 30 – 10 + 3. Repeat with one or two more subtractions, e.g. 47 – 20, 56 – 30, 84 – 50.
- Ask questions for pupils to answer orally such as 26 – 14, 39 – 27, 75 – 52, 48 – 34 etc.
- Ask pupils to take any number of counters, group them in an appropriate way (discarding any which are left over from the grouping), then find the total using repeated addition. Discuss the different groupings chosen and record them on the board as repeated additions.
- Write 3 + 3 + 3 + 3 = on the board and ask pupils to read it as a 'multiplied by' statement (3 multiplied by 4). Ask for the answer and record, then write 3 multiplied by 4 = 12 and 3 × 4 = 12 below it. Repeat with other repeated additions such as 4 + 4 =, 10 + 10 + 10 =, 5 + 5 + 5 + 5 =.
- Draw an array of crosses or dots on the board, e.g. 4 rows of 2, making sure that the crosses are also aligned in 2 columns. Discuss and record the two ways of counting the array. Ask for and record the multiplication fact in each case. Repeat for another multiplication such as 5 × 6.
- 'Which numbers below 20 are very easy to add to another number?' (0, 1, 2, 9 (by adding 10 and subtracting1), 10, 11). Provide some examples for the class to answer together on your signal, e.g. 3 + 0, 9 + 0, 14 + 0; 5 + 1, 12 + 1, 18 + 1; 6 + 2, 9 + 2, 13 + 2; 6 + 9, 2 + 9, 8 + 9; 10 + 3, 10 + 6, 10 + 9; 11 + 2, 11 + 5, 11 + 7; 17 + 0, 9 + 1, 14 + 2, 7 + 9, 10 + 5, 11 + 6 etc.
- Ask for any addition fact, write it on the board, then ask for a subtraction fact which can be made from it (e.g. 7 + 5 = 12, 12 – 5 = 7). 'What other two facts could we write using these numbers?' (5 + 7 = 12, 12 – 7 = 5).
- Ask the class to count together in 2s to 40 as you indicate each step of 2 on the class 1–100 grid. Now ask them to count in 4s to 40 as you indicate each step of 4 on the grid. Point out that each step of 4 is the same as 2 steps of 2. Ask them to count in 4s to 40 again, but this time do not indicate the numbers on the grid.
- Ask the class to say the 3 times table together, then ask facts in random order, e.g. 4 × 3, 7 × 3, 2 × 3, 10 × 3 etc.
- Ask questions such as 'What is 5 × 3? ... 5 × 5? ... 10 × 4? ... 10 × 6?' Each time confirm the answer by indicating the appropriate number of steps on the class grid, i.e. for 5 × 3 show 3 steps of 5 on the grid; 4 steps of 10 for 10 × 4 etc.

Unit 8 Assess and review

Subtraction within 99

1 Choose pairs of numbers to complete each of these.

a) □ – □ = 40 b) □ – □ = 10 c) □ – □ = 70

d) □ – □ = 30 e) □ – □ = 20 f) □ – □ = 50

2 Answer these.

a) 47 – 2 = ___ b) 59 – 4 = ___ c) 24 – 3 = ___

d) 85 – 3 = ___ e) 68 – 4 = ___ f) 79 – 6 = ___

3 Answer these.

a) What is 37 subtract 24?

b) What is 23 less than 59?

c) What is 56 take away 22?

d) What is the difference between 74 and 41?

e) What is 35 subtracted from 58?

f) What is 94 take away 63?

4 Write the difference between each pair of numbers. One has been done for you.

a)

45	□	20
35		□
10	□	65

b)

55	□	30
□		□
20	□	45

c)

85	□	50
□		□
30	□	75

5 Answer these.

a) 85 – 23 = ___ b) 96 – 71 = ___ c) 59 – 35 = ___

d) 78 – 54 = ___ e) 56 – 34 = ___ f) 79 – 52 = ___

Multiplication

1 Count these groups and write the answers.

a) 
3 + 3 + 3 + 3 =
3 × 4 =

b) 
2 + 2 + 2 =
2 × 3 =

c) 
5 + 5 + 5 + 5 + 5 + 5 =
5 × 6 =

d) 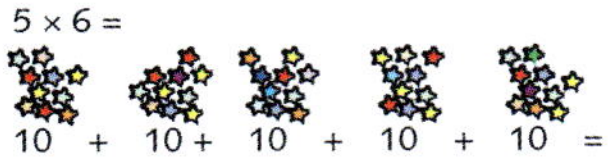
10 + 10 + 10 + 10 + 10 =
10 × 5 =

e) 
4 + 4 + 4 + 4 =
4 × 4 =

f) 
3 + 3 + 3 + 3 + 3 + 3 + 3 + 3 =
3 × 8 =

2 Complete each of these.

a) 3 × 5 = □
5 × 3 = □
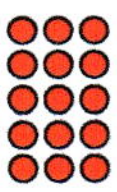

b) 4 × 3 = □
3 × 4 = □
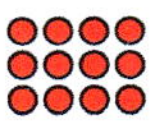

c) 2 × 6 = □
6 × 2 = □
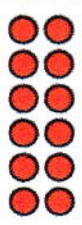

d) 3 × 8 = □
8 × 3 = □

3 Complete these.

a) 4 × □ = 4 b) 6 × □ = 0 c) □ × 5 = 0

d) □ × 2 = 2 e) 10 × □ = 10 f) 2 × □ = 0

4 Find the answers for each multiplication on this word search. Each number word is written across or down. One has been completed for you.

f	o	u	r	s	z	s
t	e	n	f	i	v	e
z	e	r	o	x	p	v
w	f	i	f	t	y	e
f	i	f	t	e	e	n
o	j	d	w	e	x	t
r	t	w	e	n	t	y
t	c	e	l	g	h	t
y	u	k	v	p	m	c
n	i	n	e	j	d	u

10 × 4
2 × 2
5 × 1
4 × 0
3 × 3
10 × 7
3 × 5
5 × 2
4 × 5
3 × 4
10 × 5
4 × 4

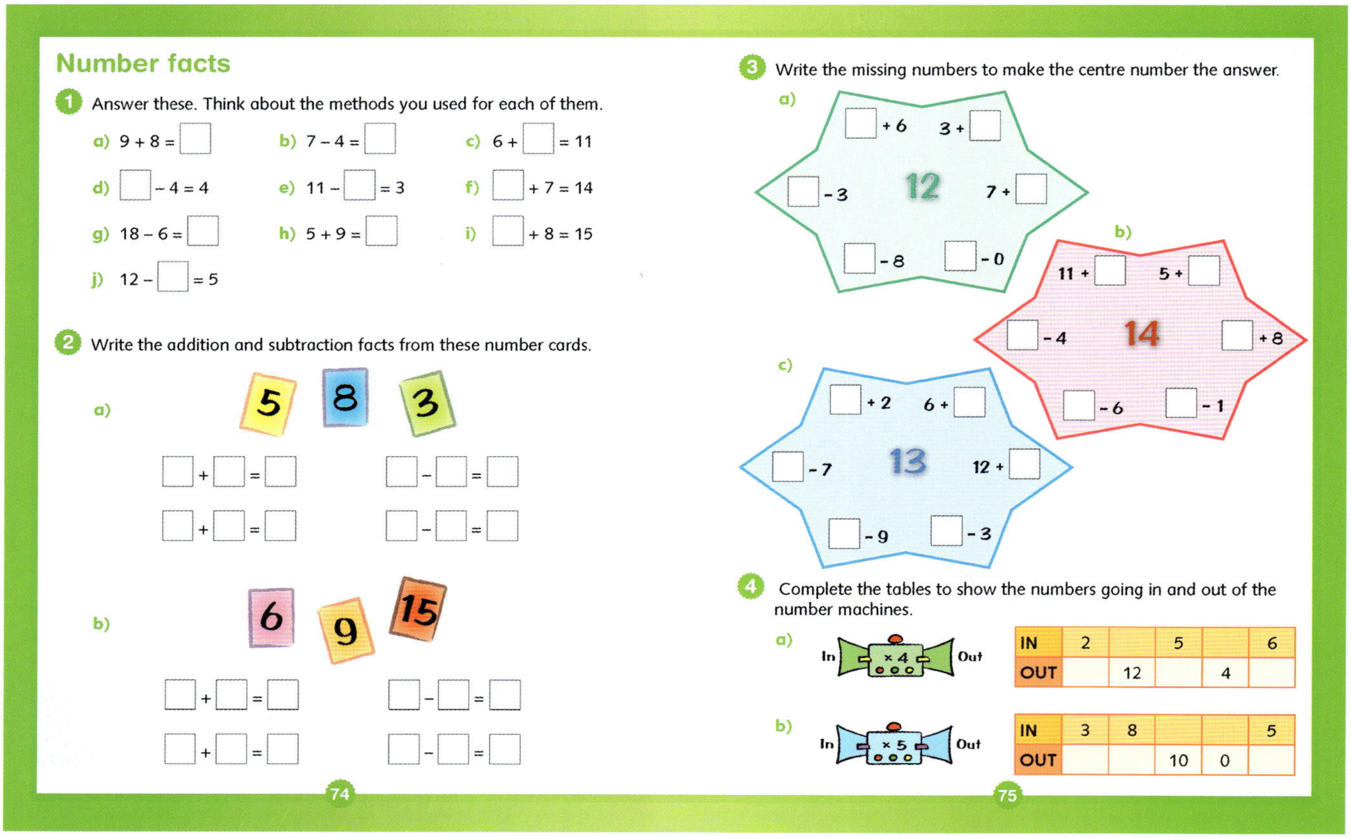

Number facts

1 Answer these. Think about the methods you used for each of them.

a) 9 + 8 = ☐ b) 7 − 4 = ☐ c) 6 + ☐ = 11

d) ☐ − 4 = 4 e) 11 − ☐ = 3 f) ☐ + 7 = 14

g) 18 − 6 = ☐ h) 5 + 9 = ☐ i) ☐ + 8 = 15

j) 12 − ☐ = 5

2 Write the addition and subtraction facts from these number cards.

a) 5 8 3

☐ + ☐ = ☐ ☐ − ☐ = ☐

☐ + ☐ = ☐ ☐ − ☐ = ☐

b) 6 9 15

☐ + ☐ = ☐ ☐ − ☐ = ☐

☐ + ☐ = ☐ ☐ − ☐ = ☐

3 Write the missing numbers to make the centre number the answer.

a) 12: ☐ + 6, 3 + ☐, ☐ − 3, 7 + ☐, ☐ − 8, ☐ − 0

b) 14: 11 + ☐, 5 + ☐, ☐ − 4, ☐ + 8, ☐ − 6, ☐ − 1

c) 13: ☐ + 2, 6 + ☐, ☐ − 7, 12 + ☐, ☐ − 9, ☐ − 3

4 Complete the tables to show the numbers going in and out of the number machines.

a) In × 4 Out

IN	2		5		6
OUT		12		4	

b) In × 5 Out

IN	3	8			5
OUT			10	0	

74 75

Answers pages 70 and 71

2 a) 45 b) 55 c) 21 d) 82 e) 64 f) 73

3 a) 13 b) 36 c) 34 d) 33 e) 23 f) 31

4 a)

45	**25**	20
35		**45**
10	**55**	65

b)

55	**25**	30
35		**15**
20	**25**	45

c)

85	**35**	50
55		**25**
30	**45**	75

5 a) 62 b) 25 c) 24 d) 24 e) 22 f) 27

Answers pages 72 and 73

1 a) 12, 12 b) 6, 6 c) 30, 30 d) 50, 50
e) 16, 16 f) 24, 24

2 a) 15, 15 b) 12, 12 c) 12, 12 d) 24, 24

3 a) 1 b) 0 c) 0 d) 1 e) 1 f) 0

4

f	o	u	r	s	z	s
t	e	n	f	i	v	e
z	e	r	o	x	p	v
w	f	i	f	t	y	e
f	i	f	t	e	e	n
o	j	d	w	e	x	t
r	t	w	e	n	t	y
t	c	e	l	g	h	t
y	u	k	v	p	m	c
n	i	n	e	j	d	u

Answers pages 74 and 75

1 a) 17 b) 3 c) 5 d) 8 e) 8 f) 7
g) 12 h) 14 i) 7 j) 7

2 a) 5 + 3 = 8, 8 − 3 = 5, 3 + 5 = 8, 8 − 5 = 3
b) 6 + 9 = 15, 15 − 6 = 9, 9 + 6 = 15, 15 − 9 = 6

3 a) **6** + 6, 3 + **9**, 7 + **5**, **12** − 0, **20** − 8, **15** − 3
b) 11 + **3**, 5 + **9**, **6** + 8, **15** − 1, **20** − 6, **18** − 4
c) **11** + 2, 6 + **7**, 12 + **1**, **16** − 3, **22** − 9, **20** − 7

4 a)

IN	2	**3**	5	**1**	6
OUT	**8**	12	**20**	4	**24**

b)

IN	3	8	**2**	**0**	5
OUT	**15**	**40**	10	0	**25**

Block C Equations, fractions and time

Maths Topic	National Standards from Government Guidelines	
Unit	*Curriculum area*	*End of year objectives / success criteria*
9 Equations and functions	Use of symbols and shapes to display simple mathematical situations Use of mathematical models to show relations and to analyse change in mathematical and everyday situations	Comprehend that the relation between addition and subtraction is an inverse relation and apply this up to 99 using shapes and symbols. Solve simple open equations containing equalities and inequalities. Give numerical examples showing the properties of multiplication up to table 9 without naming the property. Give real-life models of numerical statements.
10 Fractions	Understanding numerical operations and relations between them	Understand the meaning of simple fractions (third, fifth, sixth, …) as part of a whole using realia or illustrations and displaying them in different methods. Read and write the fractions $\frac{1}{4}, \frac{1}{5}, \frac{1}{6}, \ldots$ and arrange them on a number line.
11 Time	Understanding the properties (features) of measurable items and the units, regulations and operations of measurements Application of appropriate methods, tools and rules of measurement	Identify units of measuring time (hour–minute). Tell the time and approximate time to the nearest hour (half hour, quarter of an hour). Name both the Gregorian and Hijri calendars and order the months correctly.
12 Assess and review	Revision and assessment of previous 3 units – problems, formative and summative assessment. Monitor, assess, evaluate and consolidate pupils' knowledge and understanding.	

During this block of work, pupils will experience:

1. Identifying missing numbers in simple equations (addition and subtraction).
2. Reinforcing knowledge of multiplication facts within tables 2, 3, 4, 5 and 10.
3. Understanding equalities and inequalities and using the symbols =, < and > to identify them.
4. Calculating input and output numbers through simple function machines.
5. Using logical thinking to identify numbers represented by shapes.
6. Revision of halves and quarters as equal parts of wholes.
7. Finding half and then one quarter of different amounts.
8. Understanding and identifying simple unitary fractions of shapes ($\frac{1}{3}, \frac{1}{5}, \frac{1}{6}, \frac{1}{8}$).
9. Identifying $\frac{1}{2}, \frac{1}{3}, \frac{1}{4}, \frac{1}{5}, \frac{1}{6}, \frac{1}{8}$ on number lines.
10. Reading time to the hour, half past, quarter to and quarter past on analogue and digital clocks.
11. Naming and ordering days of the week and months of the year (Gregorian and Hijri).
12. Reading days and dates from a calendar (Gregorian).
13. Solving word problems related to time.

Unit 9 Equations and fractions

Term 1 Block C
Equations, fractions and time
Unit 9 Equations and functions
Unit 10 Fractions
Unit 11 Time
Unit 12 Assess and review

Objectives
At the end of the unit, students should be able to…
Comprehend that the relation between addition and subtraction is an inverse relation and apply this up to 99 using shapes and symbols.
Solve simple open equations containing equalities and inequalities.
Give numerical examples showing the properties of multiplication up to table 9 without naming the property.
Give models stating numerical statements of real-life examples.

Vocabulary
trios, addition, subtraction, add, subtract, multiplication, multiplied by, tables, is equal to, is less than, is greater than, symbol, calculation, function, total, stands for, represents

Lessons
1 Missing numbers: addition and subtraction
2 Multiplication tables
3 Equalities and inequalities
4 Function machines
5 Logic problems

Oral and mental starters
Pairs for sums
Product pairs
What's the order?
Hands up (3-digit numbers)
My way

Resources
Pupil's Book pages 76–85

Prior learning
Using the inverse relationship between addition and subtraction
Understanding multiplication and multiplication facts in tables 2, 3, 4, 5 and 10
Comparing numbers using < and >
Working out numbers represented by shapes or symbols

Background notes
This unit brings together several different areas of previous learning within the framework of understanding and representing mathematical relationships.

End of unit evaluation
Check that pupils are able to:
1 Use the inverse relationship between addition and subtraction.
2 Recall facts within the 2×, 3×, 4×, 5× and 10× tables.
3 Use symbols <, > and = to complete number statements.
4 Understand that a function is a constant relationship and use it to find missing numbers.
5 Find missing numbers represented by symbols such as shapes.

Supporting the topic
Continue to practise and develop pupils' knowledge of number facts (see 'Supporting the topic' in Unit 7). Include the use of inverse operations, e.g. 'I'm thinking of a number. When I add 8 to it the answer is 13. What's my number?'; 'I'm thinking of a number. When I multiply it by 5 the answer is 35. What's my number?' Provide opportunities for pupils to play this game together.
Give 'story problems' and ask pupils to supply the calculation which each involves, e.g. 'There are 58 pages in my book. I have read 36 of them, so I have 22 pages still to read' (58 – 36 = 22). 'I have six 10¢ coins in my purse, which is 60¢ altogether' (10 × 6 = 60).
Provide opportunities for pupils to set such puzzles for each other.

Lesson 1 Missing numbers: addition

Pupil's Book pages 76 and 77 **Oral and mental starter: Pairs for sums**

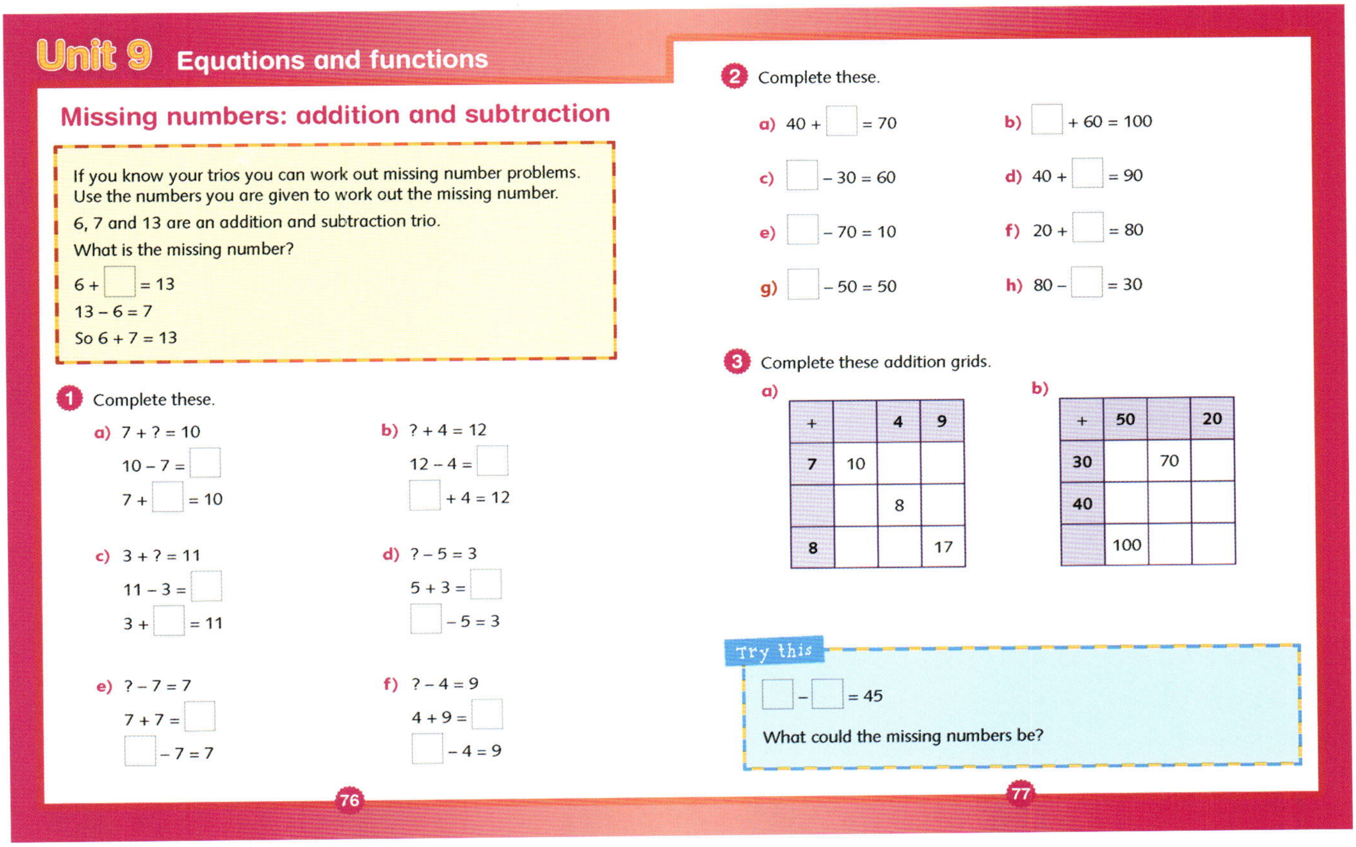

Unit 9 Equations and functions

Missing numbers: addition and subtraction

If you know your trios you can work out missing number problems.
Use the numbers you are given to work out the missing number.
6, 7 and 13 are an addition and subtraction trio.
What is the missing number?

6 + ☐ = 13
13 – 6 = 7
So 6 + 7 = 13

1 Complete these.

a) 7 + ? = 10
10 – 7 = ☐
7 + ☐ = 10

b) ? + 4 = 12
12 – 4 = ☐
☐ + 4 = 12

c) 3 + ? = 11
11 – 3 = ☐
3 + ☐ = 11

d) ? – 5 = 3
5 + 3 = ☐
☐ – 5 = 3

e) ? – 7 = 7
7 + 7 = ☐
☐ – 7 = 7

f) ? – 4 = 9
4 + 9 = ☐
☐ – 4 = 9

76

2 Complete these.

a) 40 + ☐ = 70
b) ☐ + 60 = 100
c) ☐ – 30 = 60
d) 40 + ☐ = 90
e) ☐ – 70 = 10
f) 20 + ☐ = 80
g) ☐ – 50 = 50
h) 80 – ☐ = 30

3 Complete these addition grids.

a)

+		4	9
7	10		
		8	
8			17

b)

+	50		20
30		70	
40			
	100		

Try this

☐ – ☐ = 45

What could the missing numbers be?

77

Activities

- Remind the class that they used trios in previous units to make addition and subtraction facts. Explain that in this lesson they have to work out a number missing from a trio. Write a missing number statement such as 5 + ☐ = 9. Ask 'What do we add to 5 to make 9?' Record 4 in the space.
- Look at page 76. Go through the introduction together. Provide another example such as ☐ – 8 = 11. 'How could we work out the missing number?' Allow time for different suggestions if necessary and stress the use of addition as the inverse of subtraction to solve the problem. Record 8 + 11 = 17 and 17 – 8 = 11 on the board. Repeat with an example such as ☐ + 6 = 13.
- Look at question 3 together and establish how the addition grids work.
- At the end of the lesson ask pupils who did 'Try this' to give some of their answers. Record each one on the board and ask for other suggestions.

Answers

1 a) 3, 3 b) 8, 8 c) 8, 8 d) 8, 8
e) 14, 14 f) 13, 13

2 a) 30 b) 40 c) 90 d) 50
e) 80 f) 60 g) 100 h) 50

3 a)

+	3	4	9
7	10	11	16
4	7	8	13
8	11	12	17

b)

+	50	40	20
30	80	70	50
40	90	80	60
50	100	90	70

Lesson 2 **Multiplication tables**

Pupil's Book pages 78 and 79 **Oral and mental starter: Product pairs**

Multiplication tables

Try to learn these multiplication tables.

×	0	1	2	3	4	5	6	7	8	9	10
2	0	2	4	6	8	10	12	14	16	18	20
3	0	3	6	9	12	15	18	21	24	27	30
4	0	4	8	12	16	20	24	28	32	36	40
5	0	5	10	15	20	25	30	35	40	45	50
10	0	10	20	30	40	50	60	70	80	90	100

Find these.

4 × 5 = 20

5 × 4 = 20

Remember – the order for multiplication does not matter.

1 Answer these.

a) 4 × 4 **b)** 5 × 6 **c)** 2 × 9

d) 3 × 1 **e)** 10 × 7 **f)** 8 × 5

g) 2 × 0 **h)** 4 × 6 **i)** 3 × 3

j) 5 × 2 **k)** 9 × 10 **l)** 4 × 7

78

2 Multiply these.

a) 3 × 5 **b)** 2 × 10 **c)** 7 × 2 **d)** 4 × 9

e) 5 × 7 **f)** 10 × 8 **g)** 2 × 2 **h)** 4 × 0

i) 4 × 5 **j)** 2 × 8 **k)** 5 × 9 **l)** 10 × 4

3 Follow the instructions to complete this number grid.

1	2	3	4	5	6	7	8	9	10
11	12	13	14	15	16	17	18	19	20
21	22	23	24	25	26	27	28	29	30

Colour all the numbers in the 2 times table yellow.
Circle all the numbers in the 3 times table.
Cross through all the numbers in the 5 times table.
What patterns do you notice?

Try this

Complete these by writing the missing numbers.

a) 5 × ☐ = 50 **b)** ☐ × 2 = 6 **c)** 1 × ☐ = 4

d) ☐ × 3 = 15 **e)** 6 × ☐ = 12 **f)** ☐ × 4 = 32

g) 3 × ☐ = 27 **h)** 5 × ☐ = 0

79

Activities

- Look at page 78. Ask pupils to explain how the multiplication grid works. Establish that the number at the beginning of each row is the multiplication table number and the number at the top of each column is the number which the multiplication table number is multiplied by. Ask the class to look for the pattern in each row, then ask volunteers to explain each one.
- Ask the class to say the 2× table using the grid to help if needed. Ask them to begin with 2 × 0 = 0. Repeat for each table.
- Ask pupils to find the answer to 4 × 3 from the grid by going along the 4 row with a finger from their left hand and down the 3 column with a finger from their right hand until the two meet. Repeat with another multiplication such as 3 × 6. Check that all pupils are confident in using the grid and provide further help if needed.

Answers

1 a) 16 b) 30 c) 18 d) 3 e) 70 f) 40
g) 0 h) 24 i) 9 j) 10 k) 90 l) 28

2 a) 15 b) 20 c) 14 d) 36 e) 35 f) 80
g) 4 h) 0 i) 20 j) 16 k) 45 l) 40

3 2 times table: 2, 4, 6, 8, 10, 12, 14, 16, 18, 20, 22, 24, 26, 28, 30
3 times table: 3, 6, 9, 12, 15, 18, 21, 24, 27, 30
5 times table: 5, 10, 15, 20, 25, 30

Try this

a) 10 b) 3 c) 4 d) 5
e) 2 f) 8 g) 9 h) 0

Lesson 3 **Equalities and inequalities**

Pupil's Book pages 80 and 81 **Oral and mental starter: What's the order? (to 999)**

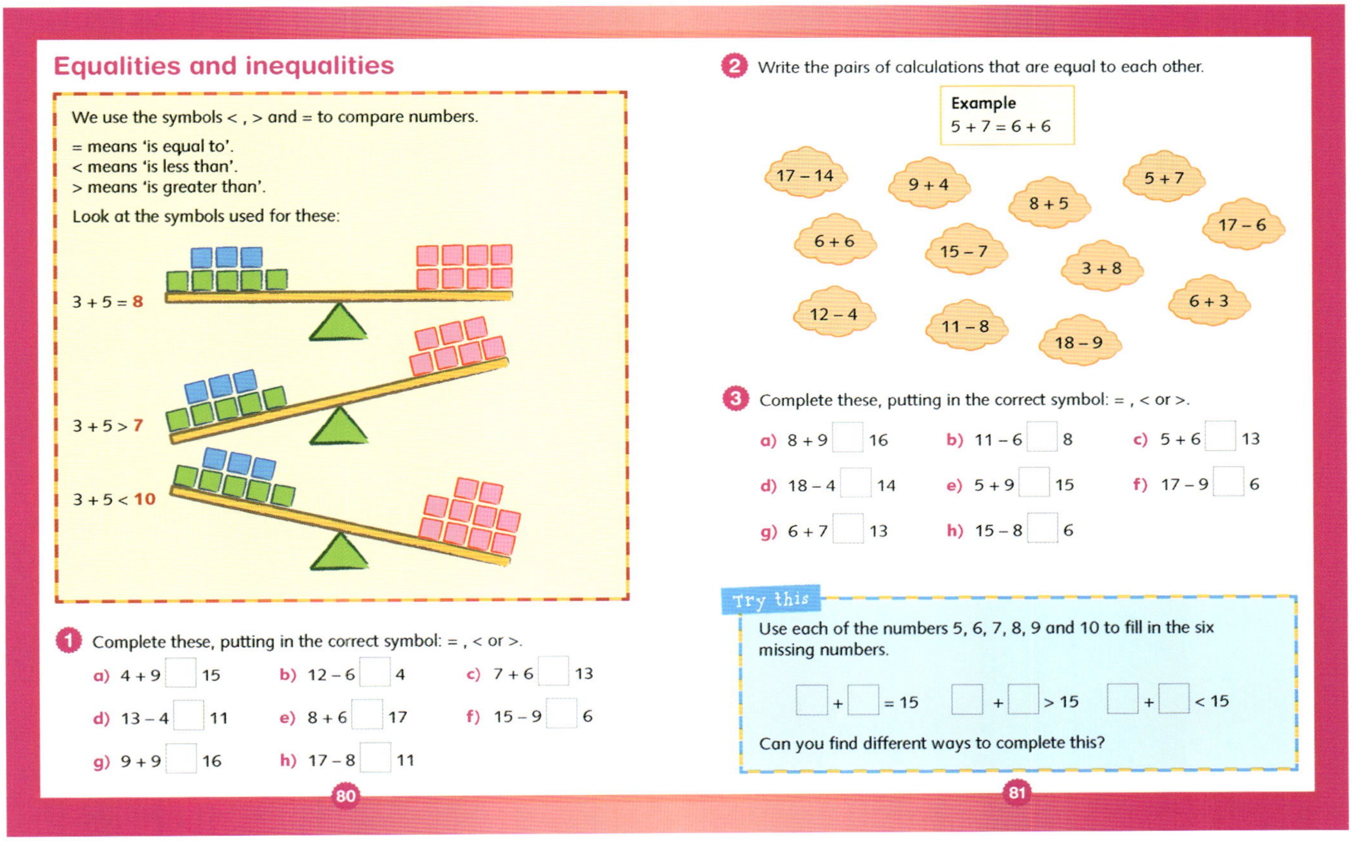

Equalities and inequalities

We use the symbols < , > and = to compare numbers.

= means 'is equal to'.
< means 'is less than'.
> means 'is greater than'.

Look at the symbols used for these:

3 + 5 = 8

3 + 5 > 7

3 + 5 < 10

1 Complete these, putting in the correct symbol: = , < or >.

a) 4 + 9 □ 15 b) 12 − 6 □ 4 c) 7 + 6 □ 13
d) 13 − 4 □ 11 e) 8 + 6 □ 17 f) 15 − 9 □ 6
g) 9 + 9 □ 16 h) 17 − 8 □ 11

80

2 Write the pairs of calculations that are equal to each other.

Example
5 + 7 = 6 + 6

17 − 14, 9 + 4, 8 + 5, 5 + 7, 17 − 6, 6 + 6, 15 − 7, 3 + 8, 6 + 3, 12 − 4, 11 − 8, 18 − 9

3 Complete these, putting in the correct symbol: = , < or >.

a) 8 + 9 □ 16 b) 11 − 6 □ 8 c) 5 + 6 □ 13
d) 18 − 4 □ 14 e) 5 + 9 □ 15 f) 17 − 9 □ 6
g) 6 + 7 □ 13 h) 15 − 8 □ 6

Try this

Use each of the numbers 5, 6, 7, 8, 9 and 10 to fill in the six missing numbers.

□ + □ = 15 □ + □ > 15 □ + □ < 15

Can you find different ways to complete this?

81

Activities

- Look at page 80 and go through the introduction with the class. Emphasise how the illustrations demonstrate the number statements.
- Write 6 + 4 __ 12 on the board. 'What is 6 + 4? Is 10 equal to 12? Is it greater than 12? Is it less than 12?' Record < in the space. Repeat with further examples such as 13 − 9__4; 8 + 7__13; 3 × 2__9; 9 + 8__17.
- At the end of the lesson ask pupils who did 'Try this' to share their results with the class. Record all the answers for each open statement on the board and ask whether there are any other possibilities.

Answers

1 a) < b) > c) = d) <
e) < f) = g) > h) <

2 17 − 14 = 11 − 8, 9 + 4 = 8 + 5, 5 + 7 = 6 + 6
17 − 6 = 3 + 8, 18 − 9 = 6 + 3, 12 − 4 = 15 − 7

3 a) > b) < c) < d) =
e) < f) > g) = h) >

Lesson 4 **Function machines**

Pupil's Book pages 82 and 83 **Oral and mental starter: Hands up**

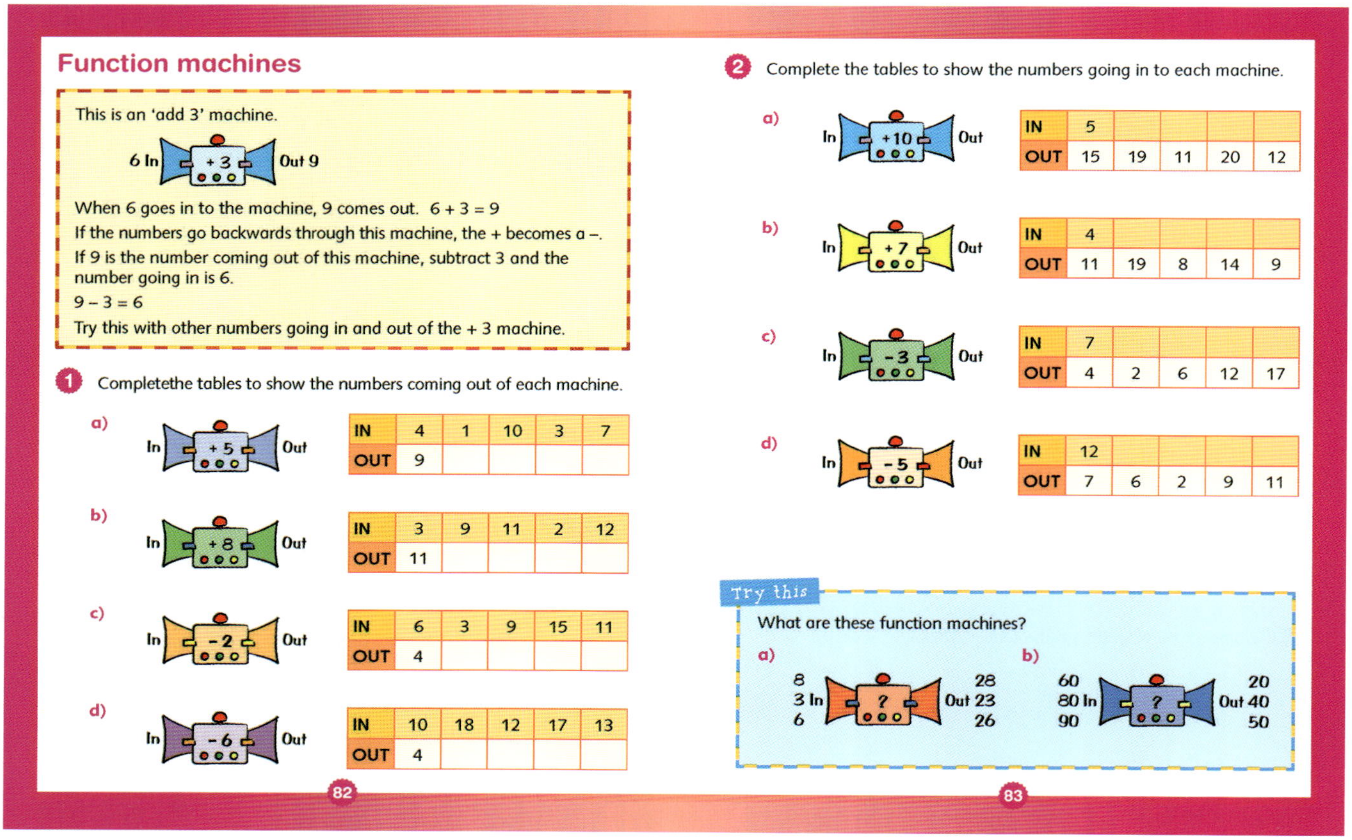

Function machines

This is an 'add 3' machine.

6 In [+ 3] Out 9

When 6 goes in to the machine, 9 comes out. 6 + 3 = 9
If the numbers go backwards through this machine, the + becomes a –.
If 9 is the number coming out of this machine, subtract 3 and the number going in is 6.
9 – 3 = 6
Try this with other numbers going in and out of the + 3 machine.

1 Completethe tables to show the numbers coming out of each machine.

a) In [+ 5] Out

IN	4	1	10	3	7
OUT	9				

b) In [+ 8] Out

IN	3	9	11	2	12
OUT	11				

c) In [– 2] Out

IN	6	3	9	15	11
OUT	4				

d) In [– 6] Out

IN	10	18	12	17	13
OUT	4				

2 Complete the tables to show the numbers going in to each machine.

a) In [+10] Out

IN	5				
OUT	15	19	11	20	12

b) In [+ 7] Out

IN	4				
OUT	11	19	8	14	9

c) In [– 3] Out

IN	7				
OUT	4	2	6	12	17

d) In [– 5] Out

IN	12				
OUT	7	6	2	9	11

Try this

What are these function machines?

a) 8, 3, 6 In [?] Out 28, 23, 26

b) 60, 80, 90 In [?] Out 20, 40, 50

82 83

Activities

- Write + 6 on the board with the numbers 1 to 10 in row above and to the right of it. Explain to the class that they are going to add 6 to each number. Ask for the result for each number and record them in another row below the first thus:

	1	2	3	4	5	6	7	8	9	10
+ 6										
	7	8	9	10	11	12	13	14	15	16

  Explain that + 6 is called a function when it is used on each number in one set to give a corresponding number in another set.
- Look at page 82 and go through the introduction carefully with the class. Provide a further example in which the function involves subtraction, e.g. – 3, with random 'in' numbers such as 7, 10, 3, 20, 15 and ask pupils to give the 'out' numbers in turn. Repeat with a function such as + 2 with 'out' numbers given, e.g. 8, 15, 28, 46, 90 for pupils to supply the 'in' numbers.
- At the end of the lesson ask pupils who did 'Try this' to explain what they did to the class.

Answers

1 a) 6 15 8 12 b) 17 19 10 20
c) 1 7 13 9 d) 12 6 11 7
2 a) 9 1 10 2 b) 12 1 7 2
c) 5 9 15 20 d) 11 7 14 16

Try this

a) + 20 b) – 40

Lesson 5 **Logic problems**

Pupil's Book pages 84 and 85 **Oral and mental starter: My way**

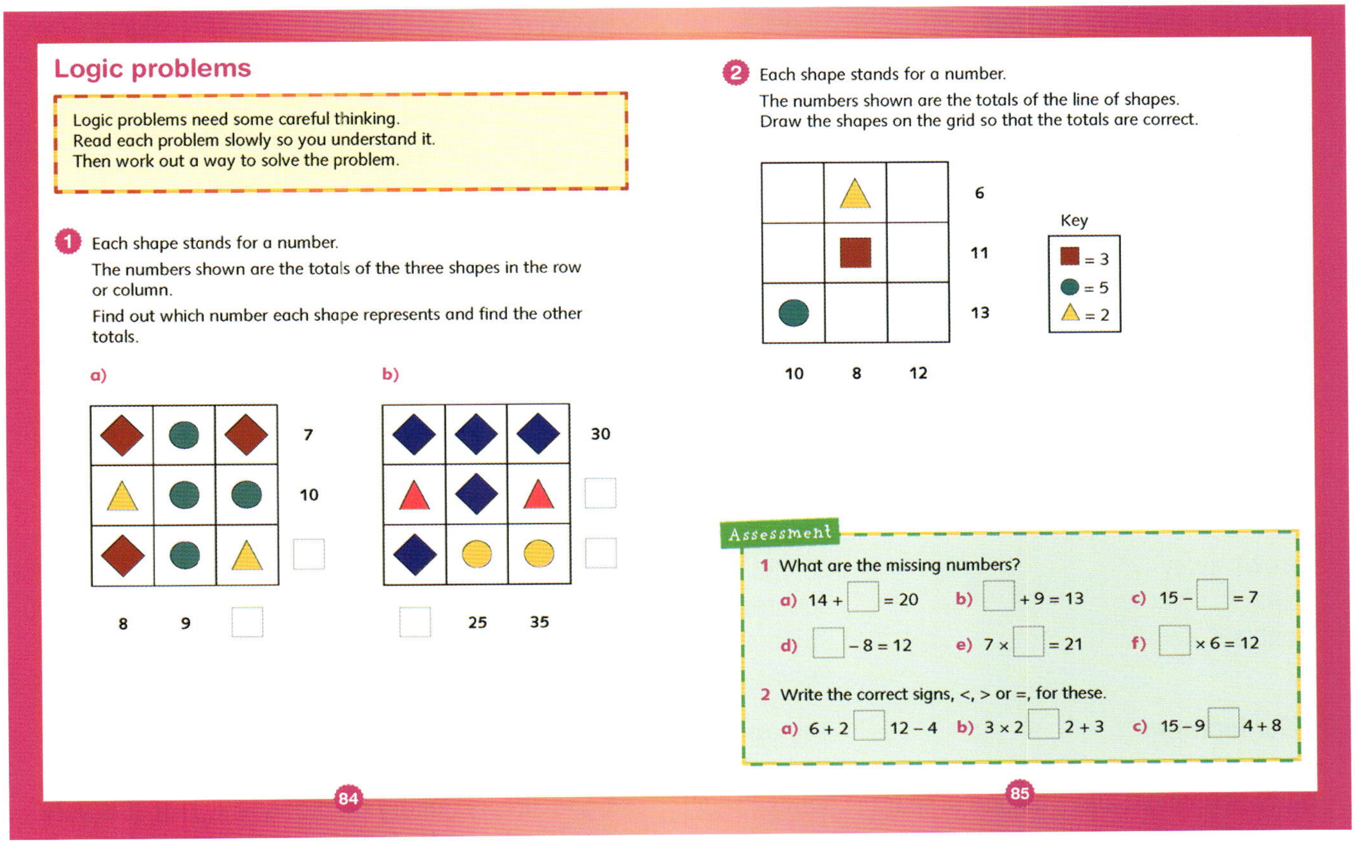
Logic problems

Logic problems need some careful thinking.
Read each problem slowly so you understand it.
Then work out a way to solve the problem.

1 Each shape stands for a number.
The numbers shown are the totals of the three shapes in the row or column.
Find out which number each shape represents and find the other totals.

a) 7, 10, ☐; 8, 9, ☐

b) 30, ☐, ☐; ☐, 25, 35

2 Each shape stands for a number.
The numbers shown are the totals of the line of shapes.
Draw the shapes on the grid so that the totals are correct.

6, 11, 13; 10, 8, 12

Key: square = 3, circle = 5, triangle = 2

Assessment

1 What are the missing numbers?

a) 14 + ☐ = 20 b) ☐ + 9 = 13 c) 15 − ☐ = 7
d) ☐ − 8 = 12 e) 7 × ☐ = 21 f) ☐ × 6 = 12

2 Write the correct signs, <, > or =, for these.

a) 6 + 2 ☐ 12 − 4 b) 3 × 2 ☐ 2 + 3 c) 15 − 9 ☐ 4 + 8

84 85

Activities

- Put three identical small squares on the board in a row with 6 at the end. Explain that each square represents the same number and the sum of the numbers is 6. 'Which number do the squares stand for? How do you know?' Repeat with two triangles and a square which have a sum of 12. 'We know that the square represents 2, so what does a triangle stand for?' Repeat with a square, a circle and a triangle which have a sum of 10. 'What number does the circle represent? How do you know?' Reinforce for any pupils who are unsure by recording 2 + 5 + ? = 10 and talking through the process.
- Look at page 84. Read through the introduction and the first part of question 1 with the class.

Answers

1 a) square = 2, triangle = 4, circle = 3; 9, 9
b) square = 10, triangle = 20, circle = 5; 50, 20, 40

2 

Assessment

1 a) 6 b) 4 c) 8 d) 20 e) 3 f) 2
2 a) = b) > c) <

Unit 10 **Fractions**

Term 1 Block C
Equations, fractions and time
Unit 9 Equations and functions
Unit 10 Fractions
Unit 11 Time
Unit 12 Assess and review

Objectives
At the end of the unit, students should be able to…
Understand the meaning of simple fractions (third, fifth, sixth, …) as part of a whole using realia or illustrations and displaying them in different methods.
Read and write the fractions $\frac{1}{4}$, $\frac{1}{5}$, $\frac{1}{6}$, … and arrange them on a number line.

Vocabulary
fraction, equal parts; one: whole, half, quarter, third, fifth, sixth, eighth

Lessons
1 Halves and quarters
2 Halves of amounts
3 One-quarter of amounts
4 Fractions of shapes
5 Fractions on a number track

Oral and mental starters
Hold up
Start here
Arrows away
Name it
Double it

Resources
Arrow cards to 999
Large paper rectangle, e.g. A4
Counters for each pupil
Squared paper for each pupil
Strips of paper for each child (for folding into thirds)
Pupil's Book pages 86–95

Prior learning
Understanding $\frac{1}{2}$ as one of two equal parts of a whole and $\frac{1}{4}$ as one of four equal parts of a whole

Background notes
This unit provides revision of halves and quarters and develops pupils' understanding to simple unitary fractions ($\frac{1}{3}$, $\frac{1}{5}$, $\frac{1}{6}$, $\frac{1}{8}$). It is very important that pupils understand the following concepts:
- A unitary fraction is one of equal parts of a whole.
- Fractions of shapes can be represented in different ways, e.g. a square can be halved by a diagonal line, a vertical line or a horizontal line.
- The higher the denominator in a unitary fraction, the smaller the fraction.

End of unit evaluation
Check that pupils are able to:
1 Find $\frac{1}{2}$ and $\frac{1}{4}$ of given amounts.
2 Identify $\frac{1}{2}$, $\frac{1}{3}$, $\frac{1}{4}$, $\frac{1}{5}$, $\frac{1}{6}$ and $\frac{1}{8}$ of given shapes.
3 Identify $\frac{1}{2}$, $\frac{1}{3}$, $\frac{1}{4}$, $\frac{1}{5}$, $\frac{1}{6}$ and $\frac{1}{8}$ on a number track.

Supporting the topic
Discuss examples of unitary fractions in everyday life, e.g. 'A chocolate bar divided into segments, what fraction of the whole bar is each segment? A bag of 8 sweets shared between 8 people, what fraction of the whole bag of sweets does each person receive?'

Lesson 1 **Halves and quarters**

Pupil's Book pages 86 and 87 **Oral and mental starter: Hold up**

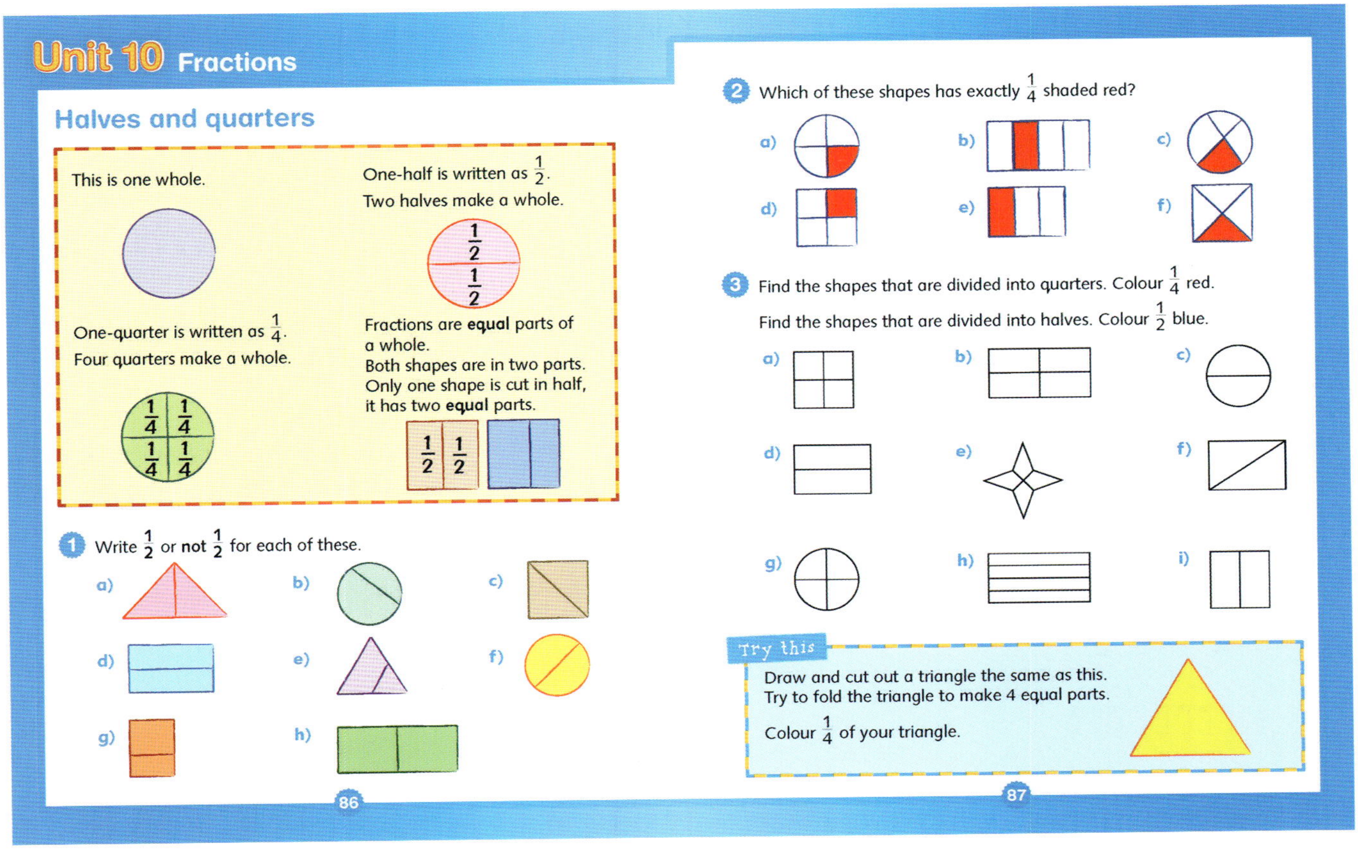

Unit 10 Fractions

Halves and quarters

This is one whole.

One-half is written as $\frac{1}{2}$.
Two halves make a whole.

One-quarter is written as $\frac{1}{4}$.
Four quarters make a whole.

Fractions are **equal** parts of a whole.
Both shapes are in two parts.
Only one shape is cut in half, it has two **equal** parts.

1 Write $\frac{1}{2}$ or **not** $\frac{1}{2}$ for each of these.

a) b) c) d) e) f) g) h)

86

2 Which of these shapes has exactly $\frac{1}{4}$ shaded red?

a) b) c) d) e) f)

3 Find the shapes that are divided into quarters. Colour $\frac{1}{4}$ red.
Find the shapes that are divided into halves. Colour $\frac{1}{2}$ blue.

a) b) c) d) e) f) g) h) i)

Try this

Draw and cut out a triangle the same as this.
Try to fold the triangle to make 4 equal parts.
Colour $\frac{1}{4}$ of your triangle.

87

Activities

- Remind the class that they learned about halves and quarters in Grade 1. Hold up a large paper rectangle and ask pupils to suggest how it could be folded in half. Fold it carefully and ask 'Is this folded exactly in half? How could we check?' Establish that one half must be exactly the same size as the other, so they must match exactly when the rectangle is folded. Repeat for quarters.
- Ask 'How many halves are there in one whole rectangle? How many quarters?'
- Look at page 86. Talk about the circles showing one whole, halves and quarters and stress the statement about equal parts. Discuss the squares. 'Which square has two halves? How do you know? How could you describe the parts of the other square?' (e.g. One is bigger than the other.)
- At the end of the lesson discuss the shapes in question 2 to reinforce the concept of equal parts.

Answers

1 a) $\frac{1}{2}$ b) not $\frac{1}{2}$ c) $\frac{1}{2}$ d) $\frac{1}{2}$
e) not $\frac{1}{2}$ f) $\frac{1}{2}$ g) not $\frac{1}{2}$ h) $\frac{1}{2}$

2 a, b, d and f

3 a) $\frac{1}{4}$ red b) $\frac{1}{4}$ red c) $\frac{1}{2}$ blue d) $\frac{1}{2}$ blue e) $\frac{1}{4}$ red
f) $\frac{1}{2}$ blue g) $\frac{1}{4}$ red h) $\frac{1}{4}$ red i) $\frac{1}{2}$ blue

Try this

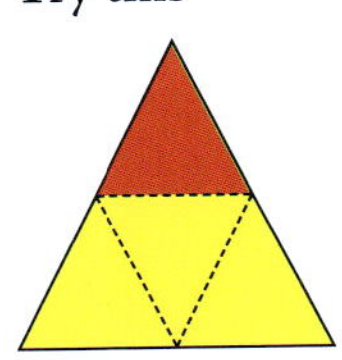

Lesson 2 Halves of amounts

Pupil's Book pages 88 and 89 **Oral and mental starter: Start here**

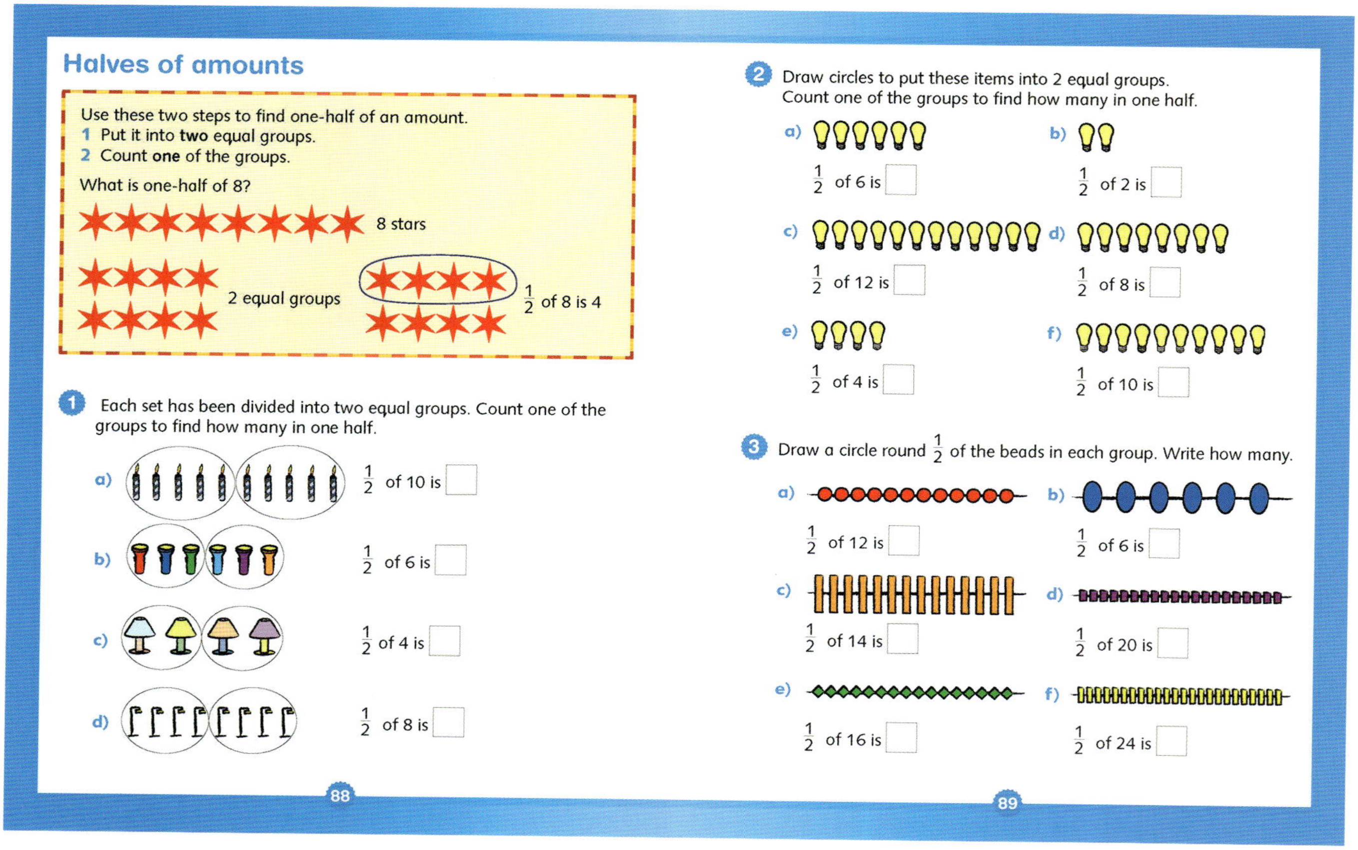

Halves of amounts

Use these two steps to find one-half of an amount.
1 Put it into **two** equal groups.
2 Count **one** of the groups.

What is one-half of 8?

8 stars

2 equal groups

$\frac{1}{2}$ of 8 is 4

1 Each set has been divided into two equal groups. Count one of the groups to find how many in one half.

a) $\frac{1}{2}$ of 10 is ☐

b) $\frac{1}{2}$ of 6 is ☐

c) $\frac{1}{2}$ of 4 is ☐

d) $\frac{1}{2}$ of 8 is ☐

88

2 Draw circles to put these items into 2 equal groups. Count one of the groups to find how many in one half.

a) $\frac{1}{2}$ of 6 is ☐

b) $\frac{1}{2}$ of 2 is ☐

c) $\frac{1}{2}$ of 12 is ☐

d) $\frac{1}{2}$ of 8 is ☐

e) $\frac{1}{2}$ of 4 is ☐

f) $\frac{1}{2}$ of 10 is ☐

3 Draw a circle round $\frac{1}{2}$ of the beads in each group. Write how many.

a) $\frac{1}{2}$ of 12 is ☐

b) $\frac{1}{2}$ of 6 is ☐

c) $\frac{1}{2}$ of 14 is ☐

d) $\frac{1}{2}$ of 20 is ☐

e) $\frac{1}{2}$ of 16 is ☐

f) $\frac{1}{2}$ of 24 is ☐

89

Activities

- Look at page 88. Go through the instructions for finding half of an amount with the class and discuss how they relate to finding half of 8 stars.
- Ask pupils to take 6 of their counters and follow the instructions for finding half of them. 'What is half of 6? How did you work it out?' Repeat with 4, 10 and 14 counters.
- At the end of the lesson ask pupils to look at the illustrations of stars in the introduction. Ask 'What is double 4? What is half of 8?' Ask them to look at the illustrations in question 1 and ask 'What is half of 10? … double 5? … half of 6? … double 3? … half of 4? ... double 2? Can you see a connection between halving and doubling?' Establish that halving is the opposite (inverse) of doubling.

Answers

1 a) 5	b) 3	c) 2	d) 4		
2 a) 3	b) 1	c) 6	d) 4	e) 2	f) 5
3 a) 6	b) 3	c) 7	d) 10	e) 8	f) 12

Lesson 3 **One-quarter of amounts**

Pupil's Book pages 90 and 91 **Oral and mental starter: Arrows away**

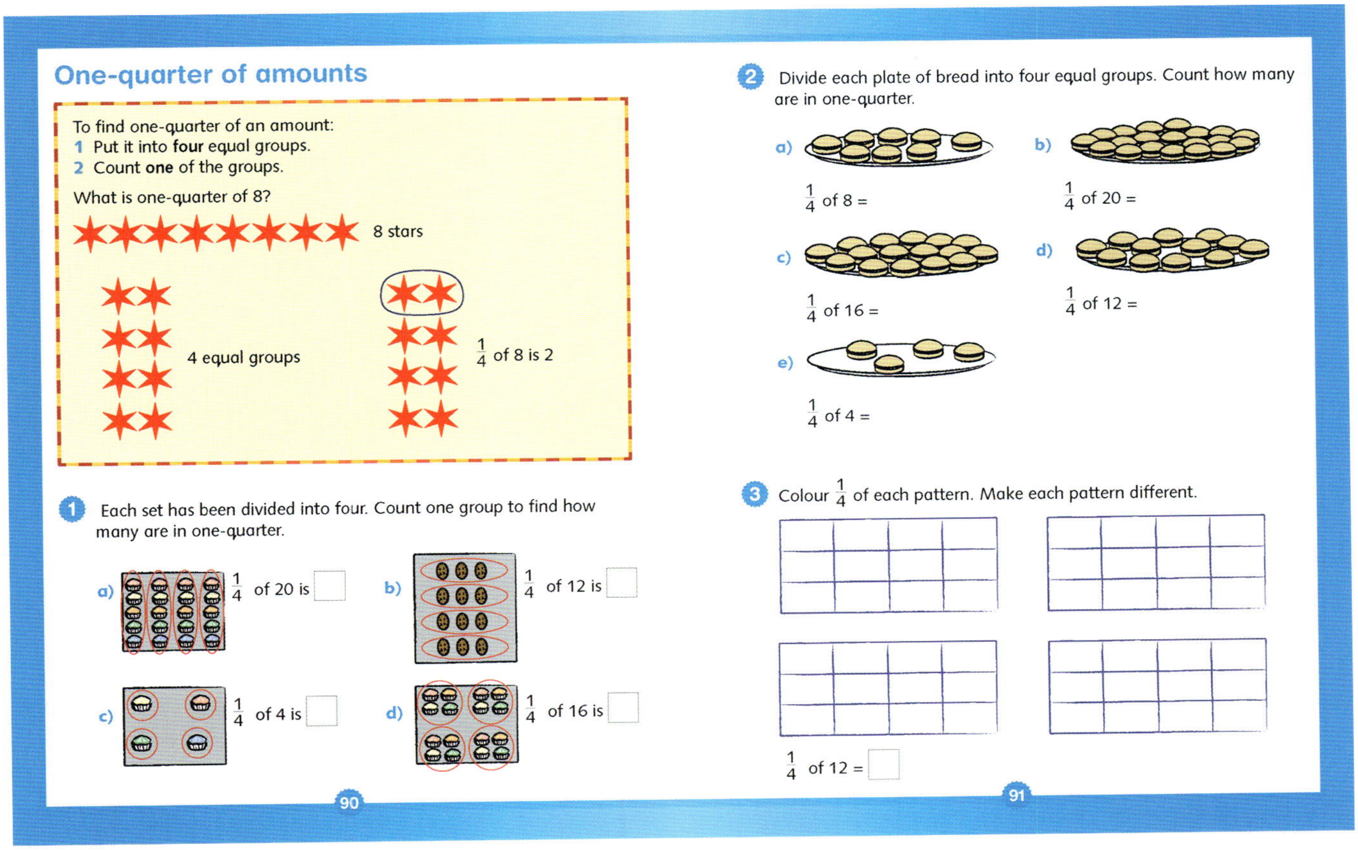

One-quarter of amounts

To find one-quarter of an amount:
1 Put it into **four** equal groups.
2 Count **one** of the groups.

What is one-quarter of 8?

8 stars

4 equal groups

$\frac{1}{4}$ of 8 is 2

1 Each set has been divided into four. Count one group to find how many are in one-quarter.

a) $\frac{1}{4}$ of 20 is ☐

b) $\frac{1}{4}$ of 12 is ☐

c) $\frac{1}{4}$ of 4 is ☐

d) $\frac{1}{4}$ of 16 is ☐

2 Divide each plate of bread into four equal groups. Count how many are in one-quarter.

a) $\frac{1}{4}$ of 8 =

b) $\frac{1}{4}$ of 20 =

c) $\frac{1}{4}$ of 16 =

d) $\frac{1}{4}$ of 12 =

e) $\frac{1}{4}$ of 4 =

3 Colour $\frac{1}{4}$ of each pattern. Make each pattern different.

$\frac{1}{4}$ of 12 = ☐

90 91

Activities

- Give each pupil a piece of squared paper. Ask them to draw round a 4 × 4 square. 'How many small squares are there on your square?' Ask them to draw along lines of the paper to divide the square into quarters. 'How have you divided your square? Did anyone do it a different way?' Draw three squares on the board and demonstrate three different ways of quartering them: one along vertical lines, one along horizontal lines, and one with a vertical and a horizontal line intersecting in the middle.
- Draw another square on the board. 'Can anyone see another way to show quarters if we didn't use the lines on your paper?' Draw intersecting diagonal lines and discuss how each resulting triangle is $\frac{1}{4}$ of the square.
- Ask pupils to look at their squares again and ask 'How many quarters are there? How many squares in each quarter? What is $\frac{1}{4}$ of 16?' Repeat with a 3 × 4 rectangle.
- Look at page 90. Go through the instructions for finding $\frac{1}{4}$ of an amount with the class and relate to the illustrations of stars.

Answers

1 a) 5 b) 3 c) 1 d) 4
2 a) 2 b) 5 c) 4 d) 3 e) 1
3 3

Lesson 4 **Fractions of shapes**

Pupil's Book pages 92 and 93 **Oral and mental starter: Name it**

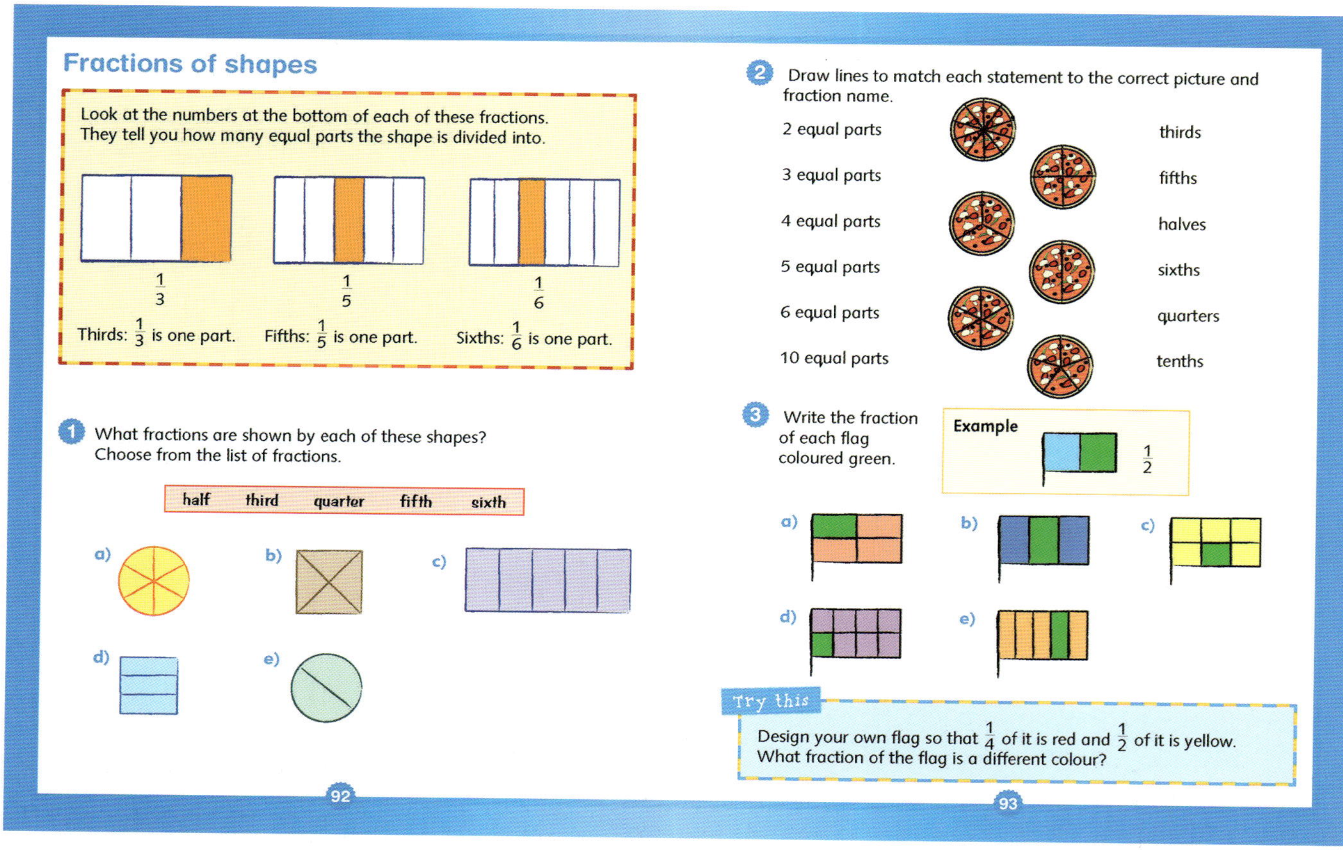

Fractions of shapes

Look at the numbers at the bottom of each of these fractions. They tell you how many equal parts the shape is divided into.

$\frac{1}{3}$ $\frac{1}{5}$ $\frac{1}{6}$

Thirds: $\frac{1}{3}$ is one part. Fifths: $\frac{1}{5}$ is one part. Sixths: $\frac{1}{6}$ is one part.

1 What fractions are shown by each of these shapes? Choose from the list of fractions.

half third quarter fifth sixth

a) b) c) d) e)

2 Draw lines to match each statement to the correct picture and fraction name.

2 equal parts — thirds
3 equal parts — fifths
4 equal parts — halves
5 equal parts — sixths
6 equal parts — quarters
10 equal parts — tenths

3 Write the fraction of each flag coloured green.

Example $\frac{1}{2}$

a) b) c) d) e)

Try this

Design your own flag so that $\frac{1}{4}$ of it is red and $\frac{1}{2}$ of it is yellow. What fraction of the flag is a different colour?

92 93

Activities

- Draw a rectangle on the board with a line dividing it in half accurately. Ask 'What are these fractions of the rectangle called? How many equal parts are there?' Write '$\frac{1}{2}$ = 1 of 2 equal parts'. Ask 'If I divided it into quarters, how many equal parts would there be?' Write '$\frac{1}{4}$ = 1 of 4 equal parts'.
- Introduce thirds. Draw another rectangle divided into thirds. Explain that when a whole is divided into 3 equal parts each fraction is called one-third. Write '$\frac{1}{3}$ = 1 of 3 equal parts'. 'What do you notice about the bottom numbers of the fractions?' Establish that in each case it shows the number of equal parts.
- Give a strip of paper to each pupil. Ask them to fold it into 3 equal parts. Ask a neighbour to check that it is folded accurately and write $\frac{1}{3}$ on each fraction on the strip. Reinforce that fractions must be equal parts of the whole.
- Go through the introduction on page 92. For each illustration ask 'How many equal parts are there in the rectangle? What fraction of the whole is each part?' Record '$\frac{1}{5}$ = 1 of 5 equal parts' and '$\frac{1}{6}$ = 1 of 6 equal parts' below the other three statements on the board. Ask 'If there were 8 equal parts, what fraction would each part be? Record '$\frac{1}{8}$ = 1 of 8 equal parts' on the board.

Answers

1 a) sixth b) quarter c) fifth d) third e) half

2 1st pizza, 10 equal parts, tenths;
2nd pizza, 4 equal parts, quarters;
3rd pizza, 3 equal parts, thirds;
4th pizza, 2 equal parts, halves;
5th pizza, 6 equal parts, sixths;
6th pizza, 5 equal parts, fifths

3 a) $\frac{1}{4}$ b) $\frac{1}{3}$ c) $\frac{1}{6}$ d) $\frac{1}{8}$ e) $\frac{1}{5}$

Try this

$\frac{1}{4}$

Lesson 5 **Fractions on a number track**

Pupil's Book pages 94 and 95 **Oral and mental starter: Double it**

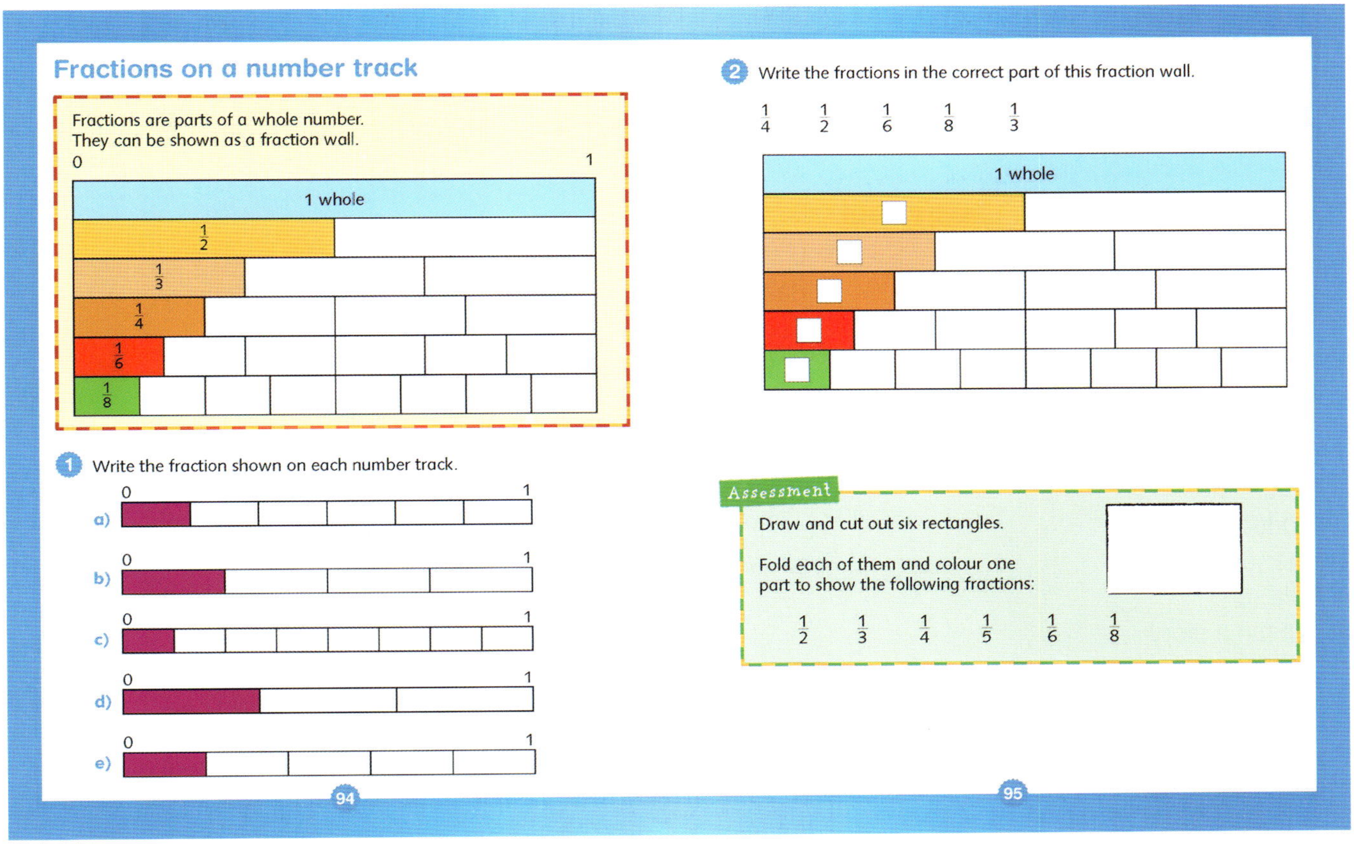

Fractions on a number track

Fractions are parts of a whole number.
They can be shown as a fraction wall.

0 1

1 whole

$\frac{1}{2}$ $\frac{1}{3}$ $\frac{1}{4}$ $\frac{1}{6}$ $\frac{1}{8}$

1 Write the fraction shown on each number track.

a) 0 1

b) 0 1

c) 0 1

d) 0 1

e) 0 1

94

2 Write the fractions in the correct part of this fraction wall.

$\frac{1}{4}$ $\frac{1}{2}$ $\frac{1}{6}$ $\frac{1}{8}$ $\frac{1}{3}$

1 whole

Assessment

Draw and cut out six rectangles.

Fold each of them and colour one part to show the following fractions:

$\frac{1}{2}$ $\frac{1}{3}$ $\frac{1}{4}$ $\frac{1}{5}$ $\frac{1}{6}$ $\frac{1}{8}$

95

Activities

- Look at page 94 and discuss the fraction wall in the introduction. Stress that the top strip represents one whole. Talk about the relative size of each fraction, e.g. 'Which is the largest fraction? How many halves are there?' Repeat for other fractions shown. 'What do you notice about the size of the fractions and the bottom numbers?' Establish that the larger the number the smaller the fraction.
- Ask questions such as 'Which fraction is larger than $\frac{1}{4}$ but smaller than $\frac{1}{2}$? … between $\frac{1}{6}$ and $\frac{1}{3}$?' etc. 'Which would you prefer, $\frac{1}{2}$ of a bar of chocolate or $\frac{1}{6}$ of it? Why?'
- Explain the assessment activity and remind pupils to fold their rectangles as accurately as possible.

Answers

1 a) $\frac{1}{6}$ b) $\frac{1}{4}$ c) $\frac{1}{8}$ d) $\frac{1}{3}$ e) $\frac{1}{5}$

2 $\frac{1}{2}$, $\frac{1}{3}$, $\frac{1}{4}$, $\frac{1}{6}$, $\frac{1}{8}$

Unit 11 **Equations, fractions and time**

Term 1 Block C **Equations, fractions and time** Unit 9 Equations and functions Unit 10 Fractions **Unit 11 Time** Unit 12 Assess and review	**Objectives** *At the end of the unit, students should be able to…* Identify units of measuring time (hour–minute). Tell the time and approximate time to the nearest hour (half hour, quarter of an hour). Name both the Gregorian and Hijri calendars and order the months correctly.
Vocabulary hour, minute, o'clock, half past, quarter past, quarter to, digital, names of days of the week and months of the year (both Gregorian and Hijri), calendar	**Lessons** 1 O'clock 2 Half past 3 Quarter to/past 4 Days and months 5 Time problems
Oral and mental starters Language Product pairs Quarter it Hold up Tell me a story	**Resources** Working analogue and digital clocks Teaching clock with large face and moveable hands *Pupil's Book pages 96–105*
Prior learning No previous work on telling the time Names and order of days of the week (Grade 1)	**Background notes** The most effective way to teach pupils to read the time on an analogue clock is to have a working clock as a permanent classroom fixture and to refer to it at different times throughout the day, every day. A wall clock is ideal, but any working clock that can be held up for all pupils to see will do. Time on a digital clock is relatively easy to read.
End of unit evaluation Check that pupils are able to: 1 Say the time shown on a clock (o'clock, half past, quarter past and quarter to). 2 Write times shown on clocks (as above) in digital form and in words. 3 Name and order days of the week and months of the year (Gregorian and Hijri). 4 Solve word problems in the context of time.	**Supporting the topic** Ask pupils to read the time from the classroom clock when it shows o'clock, half past, quarter to and quarter past times. Talk about significant times and amounts of time at school and in everyday life, e.g. start and finish times of school/lessons/breaks, bedtimes, mealtimes; number of hours spent at school, asleep, awake etc.

Lesson 1 O'clock

Pupil's Book pages 96 and 97 **Oral and mental starter: Language**

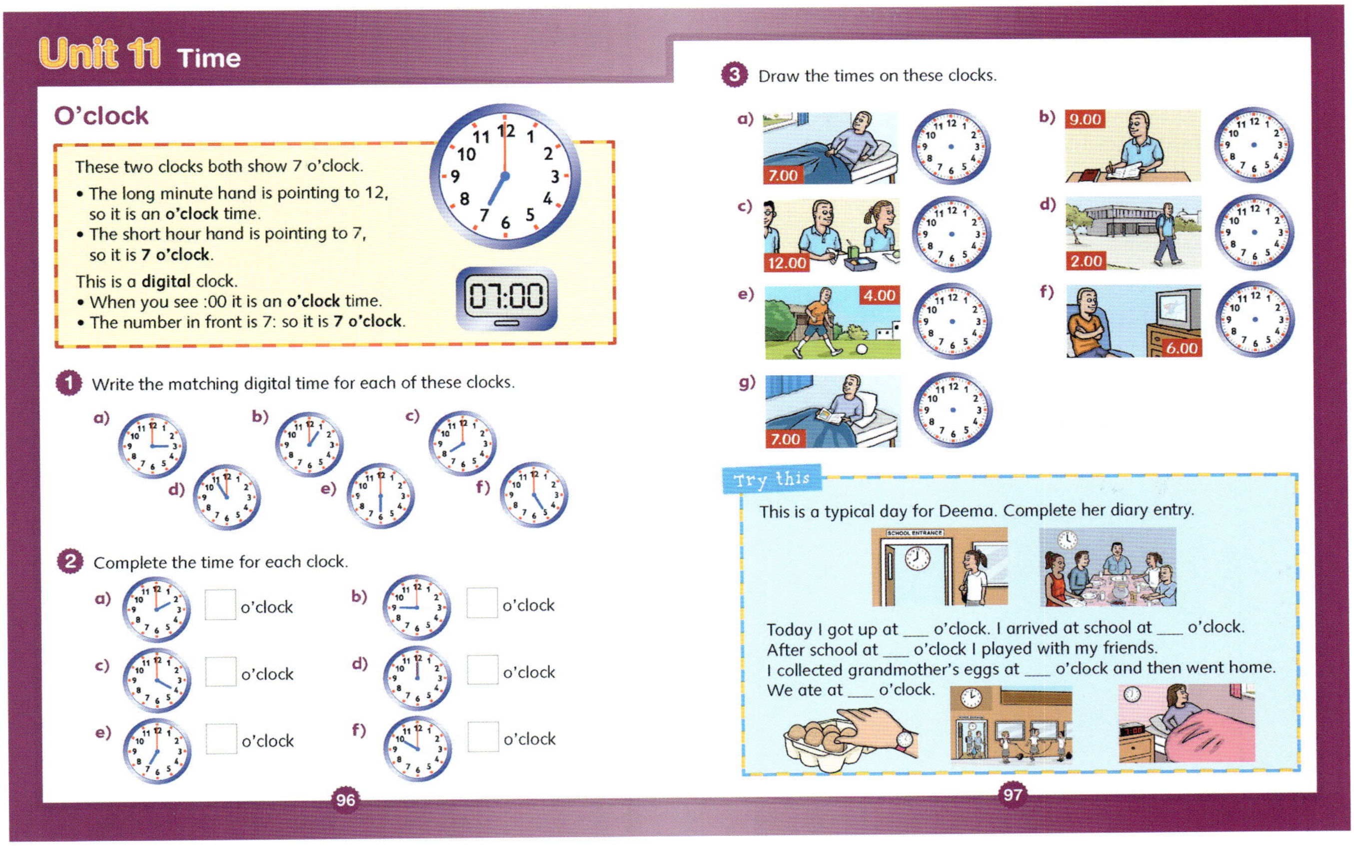

Unit 11 Time

O'clock

These two clocks both show 7 o'clock.
- The long minute hand is pointing to 12, so it is an **o'clock** time.
- The short hour hand is pointing to 7, so it is **7 o'clock**.

This is a **digital** clock.
- When you see :00 it is an **o'clock** time.
- The number in front is 7: so it is **7 o'clock**.

07:00

1 Write the matching digital time for each of these clocks.

a) b) c) d) e) f)

2 Complete the time for each clock.

a) o'clock b) o'clock
c) o'clock d) o'clock
e) o'clock f) o'clock

3 Draw the times on these clocks.

a) 7.00 b) 9.00
c) 12.00 d) 2.00
e) 4.00 f) 6.00
g) 7.00

Try this

This is a typical day for Deema. Complete her diary entry.

Today I got up at ___ o'clock. I arrived at school at ___ o'clock.
After school at ___ o'clock I played with my friends.
I collected grandmother's eggs at ___ o'clock and then went home.
We ate at ___ o'clock.

96 97

Activities

- Look at page 96. Talk about the times on the clocks, emphasising that the short hand points to the hour, the long hand to the minutes, and that when it is something o'clock the long hand points to 12.
- Use an analogue teaching clock or pictures drawn on the board. Show a variety of o'clock times for the children to identify. Each time emphasise that the short hour hand points to the number of hours, the long minute hand to 12. Record each time on the board, e.g. 6 o'clock. Ask for the digital representation and record this alongside.
- Explain that as the hands move round the clock, the long hand passes all the minutes and the short hand goes from one number to the next. In 1 hour the short hour hand moves to the next number, the long minute hand moves all the way round. Demonstrate this on the teaching clock if possible. Set the clock to 1 o'clock. 'What time is 1 hour after 1 o'clock? … after 2 o'clock? … after 3 o'clock?' 'What time is 2 hours after 3 o'clock?' etc.
- Ask a volunteer who did 'Try this' to read out their 'diary'. Ask the class to check whether each time is reasonable.

Answers

1 a) 3:00 b) 1:00 c) 8:00 d) 11:00 e) 6:00 f) 5:00

2 a) 2 o'clock b) 9 o'clock c) 4 o'clock
d) 12 o'clock e) 7 o'clock f) 10 o'clock

3 a)  b) 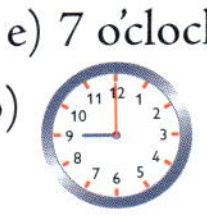 c) 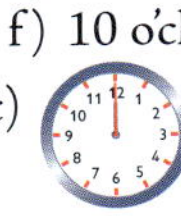 d) 
e)  f)  g) 

Try this

Today I got up at **7** o'clock. I arrived at school at **8** o'clock. After school at **2** o'clock I played with my friends. I collected grandmother's eggs at **3** o'clock and then went home. We ate at **4** o'clock.

Lesson 2 **Half past**

Pupil's Book pages 98 and 99 **Oral and mental starter: Product pairs**

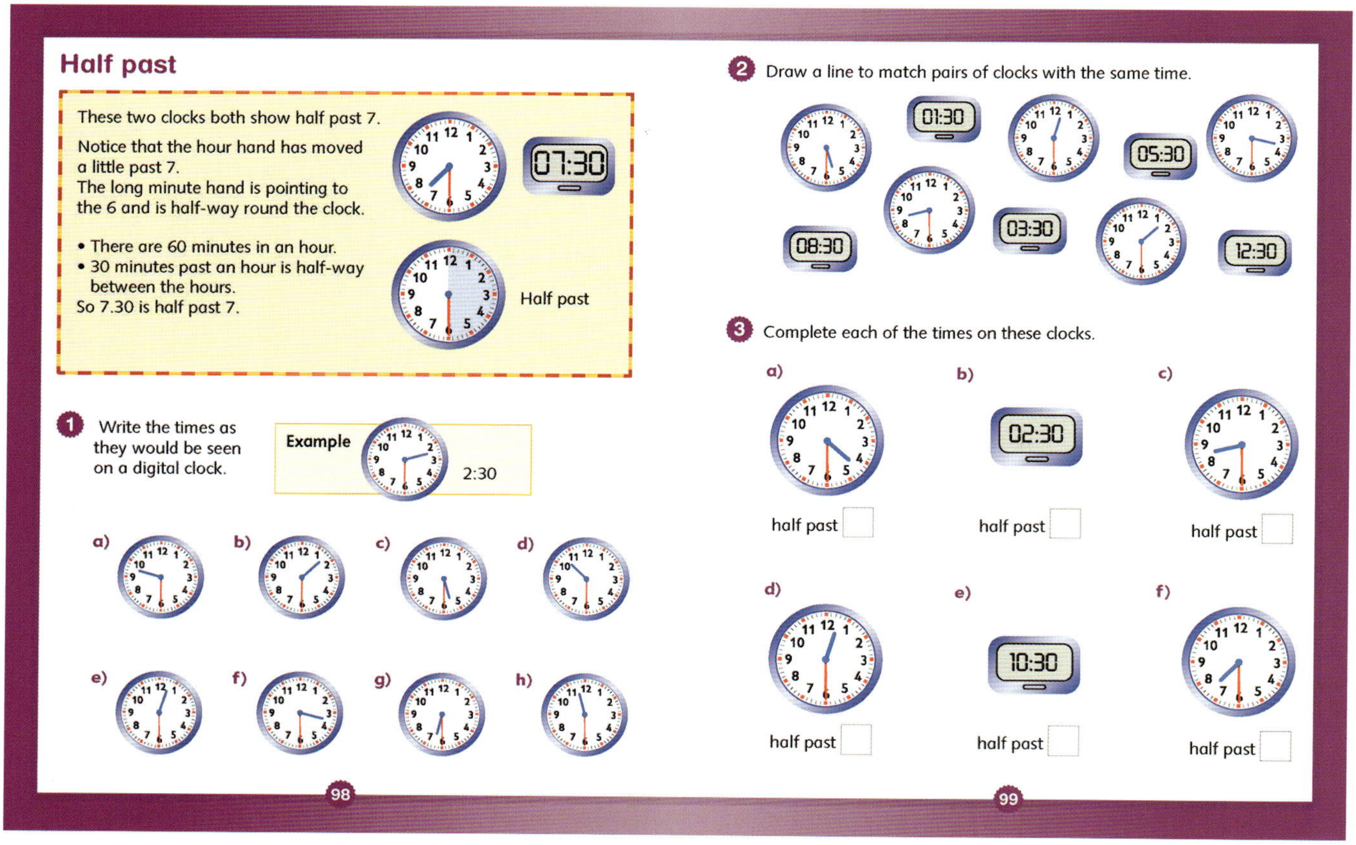

Half past

These two clocks both show half past 7.

Notice that the hour hand has moved a little past 7.
The long minute hand is pointing to the 6 and is half-way round the clock.

- There are 60 minutes in an hour.
- 30 minutes past an hour is half-way between the hours.

So 7.30 is half past 7.

07:30

Half past

1 Write the times as they would be seen on a digital clock.

Example 2:30

a) b) c) d)

e) f) g) h)

2 Draw a line to match pairs of clocks with the same time.

01:30 05:30 08:30 03:30 12:30

3 Complete each of the times on these clocks.

a) half past
b) 02:30 half past
c) half past
d) half past
e) 10:30 half past
f) half past

98 99

Activities

- Look at page 98. Discuss and compare the first two clocks in the introduction with the class. Explain that 'seven thirty' is the same time as half past seven. Stress that the short hour hand is half way between two hours when the analogue clock shows half past. Discuss the shaded clock and the statements next to it. Stress that the long minute hand points to the six at half past times.
- Show a variety of half past times for the children to identify on an analogue teaching clock (or pictures on the board). Each time emphasise that the hour hand is between the relevant hour and the next hour. Record each time, e.g. half past 3, on the board. Ask for the digital representation for each time and record it with the analogue recording.
- At the end of the lesson say different half past times and ask for another way of saying them, e.g. 'half past four' (four thirty); 'eight thirty' (half past eight).

Answers

1 a) 9:30 b) 1:30 c) 5:30 d) 10:30
e) 12:30 f) 3:30 g) 6:30 h) 11:30

2 If top row is A B C D E and bottom row is U V X Y Z, join A → D, B → Y, C → Z, E → X, U → V

3 a) half past 4 b) half past 2 c) half past 8
d) half past 12 e) half past 10 f) half past 7

Lesson 3 Quarter to/past

Pupil's Book pages 100 and 101 **Oral and mental starter: Quarter it**

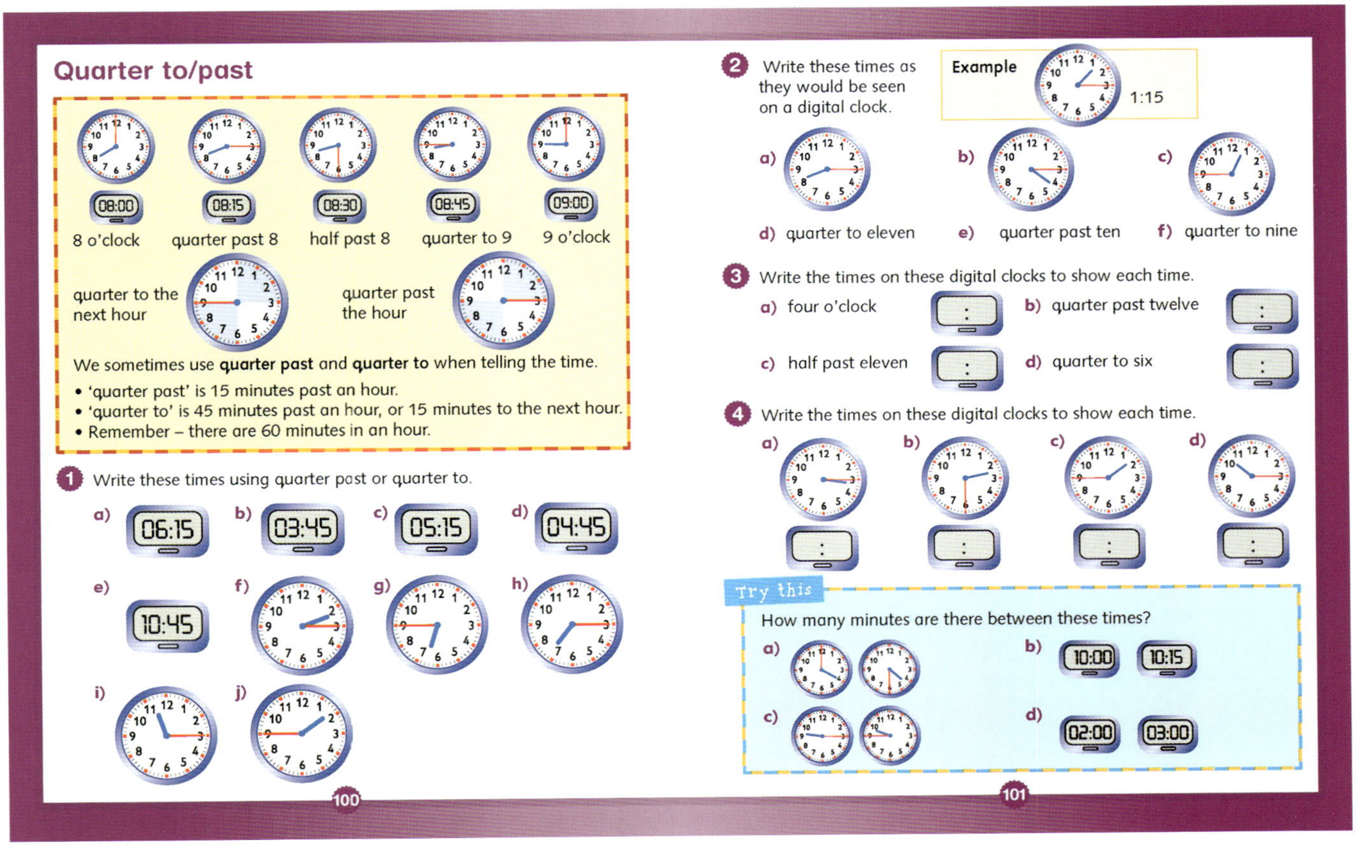

Activities

- Look at page 100. Go through the introduction with the class. Point out that the hour hand points a little past the hour when the analogue clock shows quarter past and almost to the next hour when it shows quarter to. Stress that 15 minutes is one quarter of an hour, so when it is 15 minutes past, that is one quarter of an hour past the o'clock time, and when it is 15 minutes before the next hour, that is one quarter of an hour before or to the next hour.
- Show a variety of quarter past and quarter to times for the children to identify on an analogue teaching clock (or pictures on the board). Each time emphasise the position of the hour hand. Record each time, e.g. quarter past 3, on the board. Ask for the digital representation for each time and record it with the analogue recording.
- At the end of the lesson show different o'clock times, half past times, quarter past and quarter to times for pupils to identify and to give the digital representation.

Answers

1 a) quarter past 6 b) quarter to 4 c) quarter past 5
d) quarter to 5 e) quarter to 11 f) quarter past 2
g) quarter to 7 h) quarter past 7 i) quarter past 11
j) quarter to 2

2 a) 8:15 b) 4:15 c) 12:45
d) 10:45 e) 10:15 f) 8:45

3 a) 4:00 b) 12:15 c) 11:30 d) 5:45

4 a) 3:15 b) 2:30 c) 1:45 d) 10:15

Try this

a) 30 minute b) 15 minutes c) 30 minute
d) 60 minutes

Lesson 4 **Days and months**

Pupil's Book pages 102 and 103 **Oral and mental starter: Hold up**

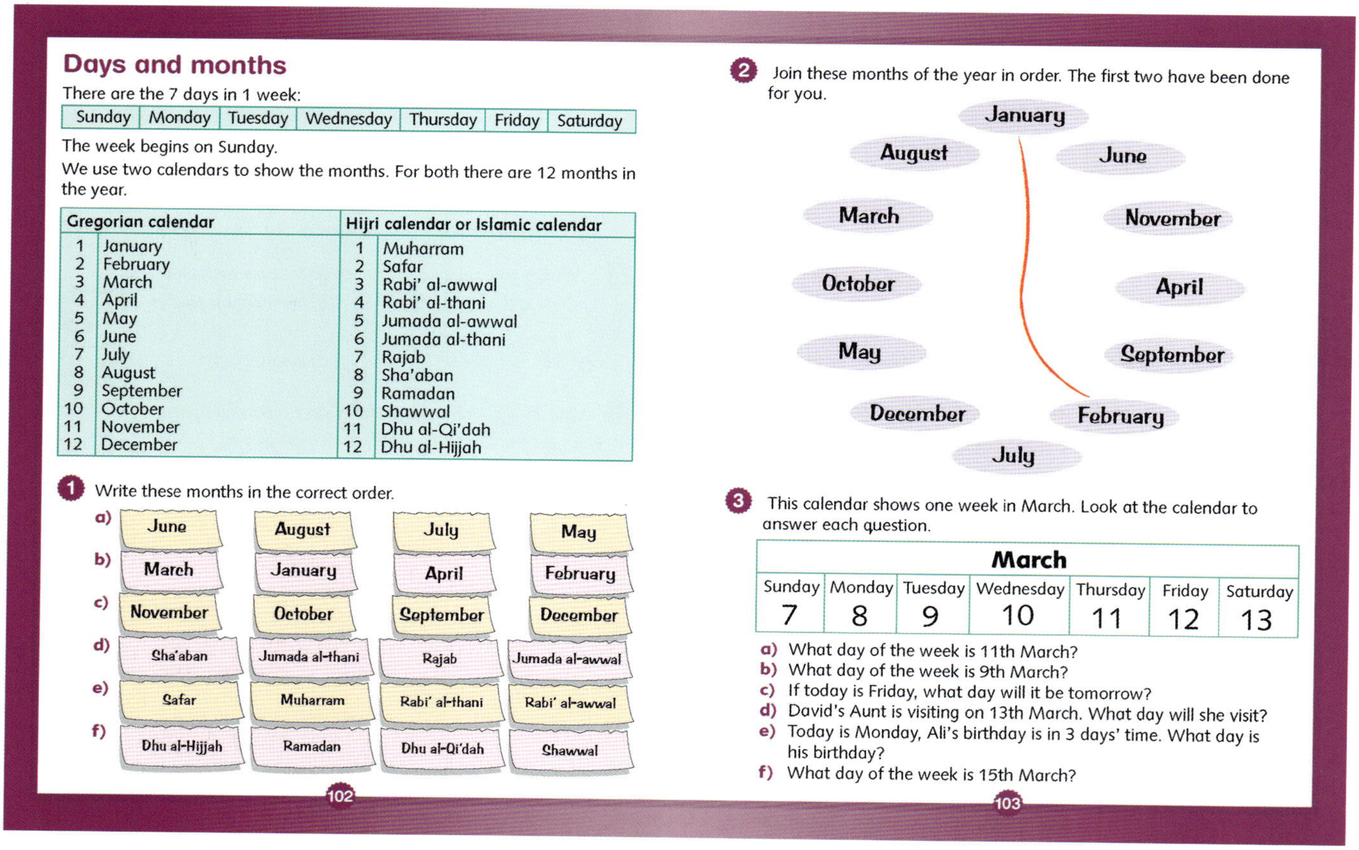

Days and months

There are the 7 days in 1 week:

Sunday	Monday	Tuesday	Wednesday	Thursday	Friday	Saturday

The week begins on Sunday.

We use two calendars to show the months. For both there are 12 months in the year.

Gregorian calendar		Hijri calendar or Islamic calendar	
1	January	1	Muharram
2	February	2	Safar
3	March	3	Rabi' al-awwal
4	April	4	Rabi' al-thani
5	May	5	Jumada al-awwal
6	June	6	Jumada al-thani
7	July	7	Rajab
8	August	8	Sha'aban
9	September	9	Ramadan
10	October	10	Shawwal
11	November	11	Dhu al-Qi'dah
12	December	12	Dhu al-Hijjah

1 Write these months in the correct order.

a) June, August, July, May

b) March, January, April, February

c) November, October, September, December

d) Sha'aban, Jumada al-thani, Rajab, Jumada al-awwal

e) Safar, Muharram, Rabi' al-thani, Rabi' al-awwal

f) Dhu al-Hijjah, Ramadan, Dhu al-Qi'dah, Shawwal

102

2 Join these months of the year in order. The first two have been done for you.

3 This calendar shows one week in March. Look at the calendar to answer each question.

March						
Sunday	Monday	Tuesday	Wednesday	Thursday	Friday	Saturday
7	8	9	10	11	12	13

a) What day of the week is 11th March?

b) What day of the week is 9th March?

c) If today is Friday, what day will it be tomorrow?

d) David's Aunt is visiting on 13th March. What day will she visit?

e) Today is Monday, Ali's birthday is in 3 days' time. What day is his birthday?

f) What day of the week is 15th March?

103

Activities

- Talk about days of the week, e.g. 'What day is it today? What day was it yesterday? What day will it be tomorrow? On which days do we not come to school?' etc. Ask the class to say the names of the days in order, starting with Sunday.
- Look at page 102. Ask pupils to touch the name of different days of the week as you say them in random order. Ask them to answer together questions such as 'Which day comes after Friday? ... before Wednesday? ... two days after Tuesday? ... after Sunday? ... two days before Monday?'
- Look at the two lists of months. Explain that they show the twelve months of the year in order, the first using the Gregorian calendar, the second using the Hijri calendar. Ask the class to read the names in order on both calendars. Point out that the numbering of the months is the same for each list, so the fourth month is April or Rabi' al-thani etc. Ask questions such as 'What is the Hijri name for March? ... September? What is the Gregorian name for ... Rajab? ... Shawwal?'
- Make sure that pupils understand the extract from a calendar in question 3.

Answers

1 a) May, June, July, August
  b) January, February, March, April
  c) September, October, November, December
  d) Jumada al-awwal, Jumada al-thani, Rajab, Sha'aban
  e) Muharram, Safar, Rabi' al-awwal, Rabi' al-thani
  f) Ramadan, Shawwal, Dhu al-Qi'dah, Dhu al-Hijjah

2 January, February, March, April, May, June, July, August, September, October, November, December

3 a) Thursday b) Tuesday c) Saturday
  d) Saturday e) Thursday f) Monday

Lesson 5 Time problems

Pupil's Book pages 104 and 105 **Oral and mental starter: Tell me a story**

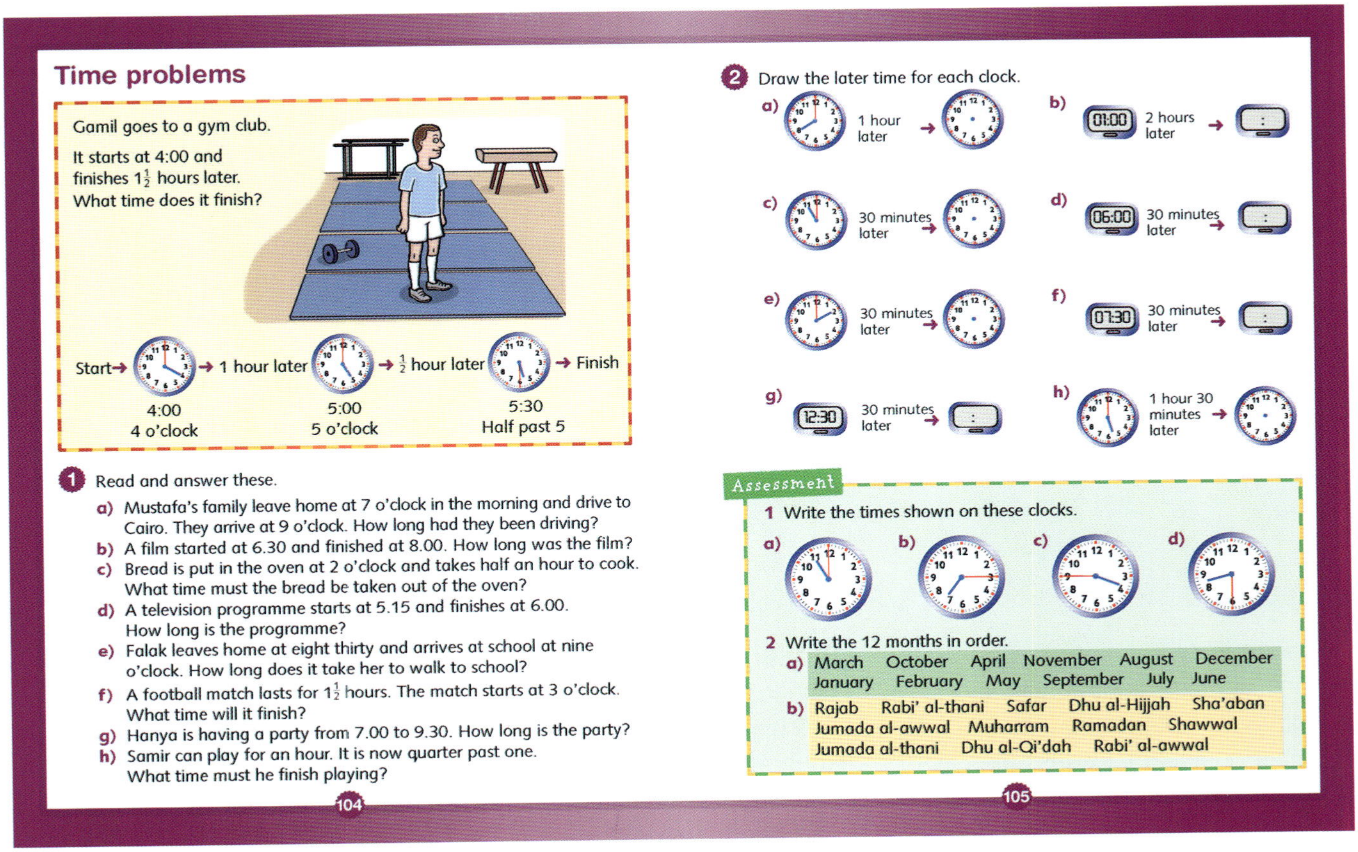

Time problems

Gamil goes to a gym club.

It starts at 4:00 and finishes $1\frac{1}{2}$ hours later. What time does it finish?

Start → 4:00 4 o'clock → 1 hour later → 5:00 5 o'clock → $\frac{1}{2}$ hour later → 5:30 Half past 5 → Finish

1 Read and answer these.

a) Mustafa's family leave home at 7 o'clock in the morning and drive to Cairo. They arrive at 9 o'clock. How long had they been driving?
b) A film started at 6.30 and finished at 8.00. How long was the film?
c) Bread is put in the oven at 2 o'clock and takes half an hour to cook. What time must the bread be taken out of the oven?
d) A television programme starts at 5.15 and finishes at 6.00. How long is the programme?
e) Falak leaves home at eight thirty and arrives at school at nine o'clock. How long does it take her to walk to school?
f) A football match lasts for $1\frac{1}{2}$ hours. The match starts at 3 o'clock. What time will it finish?
g) Hanya is having a party from 7.00 to 9.30. How long is the party?
h) Samir can play for an hour. It is now quarter past one. What time must he finish playing?

2 Draw the later time for each clock.

a) 1 hour later →
b) 01:00 2 hours later →
c) 30 minutes later →
d) 06:00 30 minutes later →
e) 30 minutes later →
f) 07:30 30 minutes later →
g) 12:30 30 minutes later →
h) 1 hour 30 minutes later →

Assessment

1 Write the times shown on these clocks.

a) b) c) d)

2 Write the 12 months in order.

a) March October April November August December January February May September July June

b) Rajab Rabi' al-thani Safar Dhu al-Hijjah Sha'aban Jumada al-awwal Muharram Ramadan Shawwal Jumada al-thani Dhu al-Qi'dah Rabi' al-awwal

104 105

Activities

- Use the teaching clock to revise that there are 60 minutes in 1 hour, 30 in half an hour and 15 in a quarter of an hour. Show times and ask questions, e.g. show quarter past 4: 'What time is this? How many minutes have gone since 4 o'clock? How many minutes are there before half past 4? What time will it be in 1 hour?' Show 6 o'clock: 'What time is this? What time will it be in 45 minutes? What time was it 2 hours earlier? etc. Use the clock to demonstrate answers.
- Go through the introduction on page 104. Emphasise that the problem can be solved in two stages. Demonstrate by finding the answer to another problem, e.g. 'I leave school at 2 o'clock, walk home in 15 minutes, spend 1 hour doing chores, then prepare my meal. At what time do I start preparing the meal?'

Answers

1 a) 2 hours b) 1 hour 30 minutes or 90 minutes
c) 2.30 or half past 2 d) 45 minutes
e) 30 minutes or half an hour f) 4.30 or half past 4
g) 2 hours 30 minutes or $2\frac{1}{2}$ hours h) quarter past 2 or 2.15

2 a) 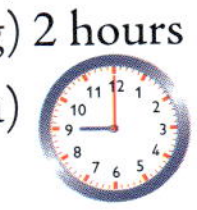 b) 3:00 c) 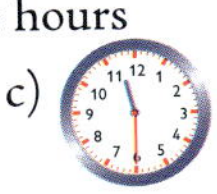 d) 6:30

e)  f) 8:00 g) 1:00 g) 

Assessment

1 a) 11 o'clock or 11:00 b) quarter past 7 or 7:15
c) quarter to 4 or 3:45 d) half past 8 or 8:30

2 a) January, February, March, April, May, June, July, August, September, October, November, December

b) Muharram, Safar, Rabi' al-awwal, Rabi' al-thani, Jumada al-awwal, Jumada al-thani, Rajab, Sha'aban, Ramadan, Shawwal, Dhu al-Qi'dah, Dhu al-Hijjah

Unit 12 **Assess and review**

Term 1 Block C
Equations, fractions and time
Unit 9 Equations and functions
Unit 10 Fractions
Unit 11 Time
Unit 12 Assess and review

Final evaluation
Check that pupils are able to:

1. Use the inverse relationship between addition and subtraction, e.g. trios.
2. Recall facts within the 2×, 3×, 4×, 5× and 10× tables.
3. Use symbols <, > and = to complete number statements.
4. Understand that a function is a constant relationship and use it to find missing numbers, e.g. in a function machine.
5. Find missing numbers represented by symbols such as shapes.
6. Understand unitary fractions, e.g. that $\frac{1}{5}$ is one of 5 equal parts of a whole.
7. Calculate $\frac{1}{2}$ and $\frac{1}{4}$ of amounts.
8. Order unitary fractions ($\frac{1}{2}, \frac{1}{3}, \frac{1}{4}, \frac{1}{5}, \frac{1}{6}, \frac{1}{8}$).
9. Say the time shown on a clock (o'clock, half past, quarter past and quarter to).
10. Write times shown on clocks in digital form and in words.
11. Name and order days of the week and months of the year (Gregorian and Hijri).
12. Solve word problems in the context of time.

Vocabulary
trios, addition, subtraction, add, subtract, multiplication, multiplied by, tables, is equal to, is less than, is greater than, symbol, calculation, function, total, stands for, represents, fraction, equal parts; one: whole, half, quarter, third, fifth, sixth, eighth; hour, minute, o'clock, half past, quarter past, quarter to, digital; names of days of the week and months of the year (both Gregorian and Hijri), calendar

Resources
Working analogue and digital clocks
Teaching clock with large face and moveable hands
Squared paper for each pupil
Counters for each pupil
Classroom 1–100 grid
Pupil's Book pages 106–111

Pupil's Book pages 106–111

1. Write __ + 4 = 10 on the board then ask 'I'm thinking of a number. When I add 4 to it the answer is 10. What is my number?' How did you work it out?' Repeat with 16 – __ = 8. (page 106)
2. Write × 2 on the board and numbers 0–10 in random order. Explain that × 2 is the function. Point to each number in turn (but not in numerical order) and ask the class to say the answer together. (page 106)
3. Write 3 + 5 __10 on the board and the symbols =, > and <. Ask the following as you point to each symbol in turn: 'Is 3 + 5 equal to 10? Is it greater than 10? Is it less than 10?' Record < in the space. (page 107)
4. Ask pupils to take 12 counters each and put them into 2 equal groups. Ask 'What fraction of the counters is each group? What is $\frac{1}{2}$ of 12?' Repeat with 4 equal groups, asking for $\frac{1}{4}$ of 12. (page 108)
5. Ask 'Which fraction is one of 2 equal parts of a whole? If a shape is divided into 5 equal parts, what fraction of the whole shape is one of those parts? Which fraction is the larger, $\frac{1}{5}$ or $\frac{1}{3}$?' (page 109)
6. Ask questions such as 'What is one hour later than 12 o'clock? … half past 3? (page 110)
7. Ask questions such as 'How many minutes are there between quarter to 4 and 4 o'clock? How long is it from 3 o'clock to half past 4?' Record the answer on the board, e.g. 15 minutes … 1 hour and 30 minutes. (page 111)

Assessment activities

Use these to assess pupils' knowledge and understanding:

Which number is added to 14 to make 20? Which number is subtracted from 17 to leave 12?

Here are two sets of numbers

3	5	8	14	20	30
6	8	11	17	23	33

What has been done to each number in the top row to give the number below it?

Use a card with 7 + 5 on it. Give me a number that is equal to 7 + 5 ... greater than 7 + 5 ... less than 7 + 5.

Draw lines on this rectangle to divide it into six equal parts. What fraction of the rectangle is this part?

What is $\frac{1}{2}$ of 8? … $\frac{1}{4}$ of 8?

Write these fractions in order starting with the smallest ($\frac{1}{3}$, $\frac{1}{6}$, $\frac{1}{2}$, $\frac{1}{5}$, $\frac{1}{4}$).

What time does it say on this (analogue) clock? Can you write that time in two different ways? Repeat for o'clock, half past, quarter past and quarter to times.

How many minutes are there in 1 hour? … half an hour? … a quarter of an hour?

How long is it from 1:15 to 2:00? … 1:30 to 3:00?

This lesson began at (e.g. 9 o'clock). It ends at (e.g. quarter to 10). How long does the lesson last?

Say the days of the week and the Gregorian and Hijri months of the year in order.

Assess and review activities

Use these activities taken from the previous three weeks to monitor, evaluate and consolidate pupils' knowledge and understanding.

- Write 6 + 4 __ 12 on the board. 'What is 6 + 4? Is 10 equal to 12? Is it greater than 12? Is it less than 12?' Record < in the space. Repeat with further examples such as 13 – 9__4; 8 + 7__13; 3 × 2__9; 9 + 8__17.
- Write + 6 on the board with the numbers 1 to 10 in row above and to the right of it. Explain to the class that they are going to add 6 to each number. Ask for the result for each number and record them in another row below the first thus:

	1	2	3	4	5	6	7	8	9	10
+ 6										
	7	8	9	10	11	12	13	14	15	16

  Explain that + 6 is called a function when it is used on each number in one set to give a corresponding number in another set.
- Ask pupils to take 6 of their counters and divide them in half. 'What is half of 6? How did you work it out?' Repeat with 4, 10 and 14 counters.
- Ask pupils to draw a 4 × 4 square. 'How many small squares are there?' Ask them to draw lines to make quarters. 'How many quarters are there? How many squares in each quarter? What is $\frac{1}{4}$ of 16?' Repeat with a 3 × 4 rectangle.
- Draw a rectangle on the board with a line dividing it in half accurately. Ask 'What are these fractions called? How many equal parts are there?' Write '$\frac{1}{2}$ = 1 of 2 equal parts' on the board. 'If I divided it into quarters, how many equal parts would there be?' Write '$\frac{1}{4}$ = 1 of 4 equal parts'. Introduce thirds to the class. Draw another rectangle divided into thirds. Explain that when a whole is divided into 3 equal parts each fraction is called one-third. Write '$\frac{1}{3}$ = 1 of 3 equal parts'. 'What do you notice about the bottom number of the fractions? Establish that in each case it shows the number of equal parts.
- Look at page 94 and discuss the fraction wall in the introduction. Stress that the top strip represents one whole. Talk about the relative size of each fraction, e.g. 'Which is the largest fraction? How many halves are there?' Repeat for other fractions shown. 'What do you notice about the size of the fractions and the bottom numbers?' Establish that the larger the number the smaller the fraction.
- Using the teaching clock (or pictures on the board), show different o'clock times, half past times, quarter past and quarter to times for pupils to identify and to give the digital representation.
- Ask the class to answer together questions such as 'Which day comes after Friday? … before Wednesday? … two days after Tuesday?'

- Ask the class to say the names in order on both calendars. Point out that the numbering of the months is the same for each, so the fourth month is April or Rabi' al-thani etc. Ask questions such as 'What is the Hijri name for March? … September? What is the Gregorian name for … Rajab? … Shawwal?'
- Use the teaching clock to revise that there are 60 minutes in 1 hour, 30 minutes in half an hour and 15 in a quarter of an hour. Show different times and ask questions, e.g. show quarter past 4: 'What time is this? How many minutes have gone since 4 o'clock? How many minutes are there before half past 4? What time will it be in one and a half hours?' etc. Use the clock to show the answers to support pupils who are less confident.

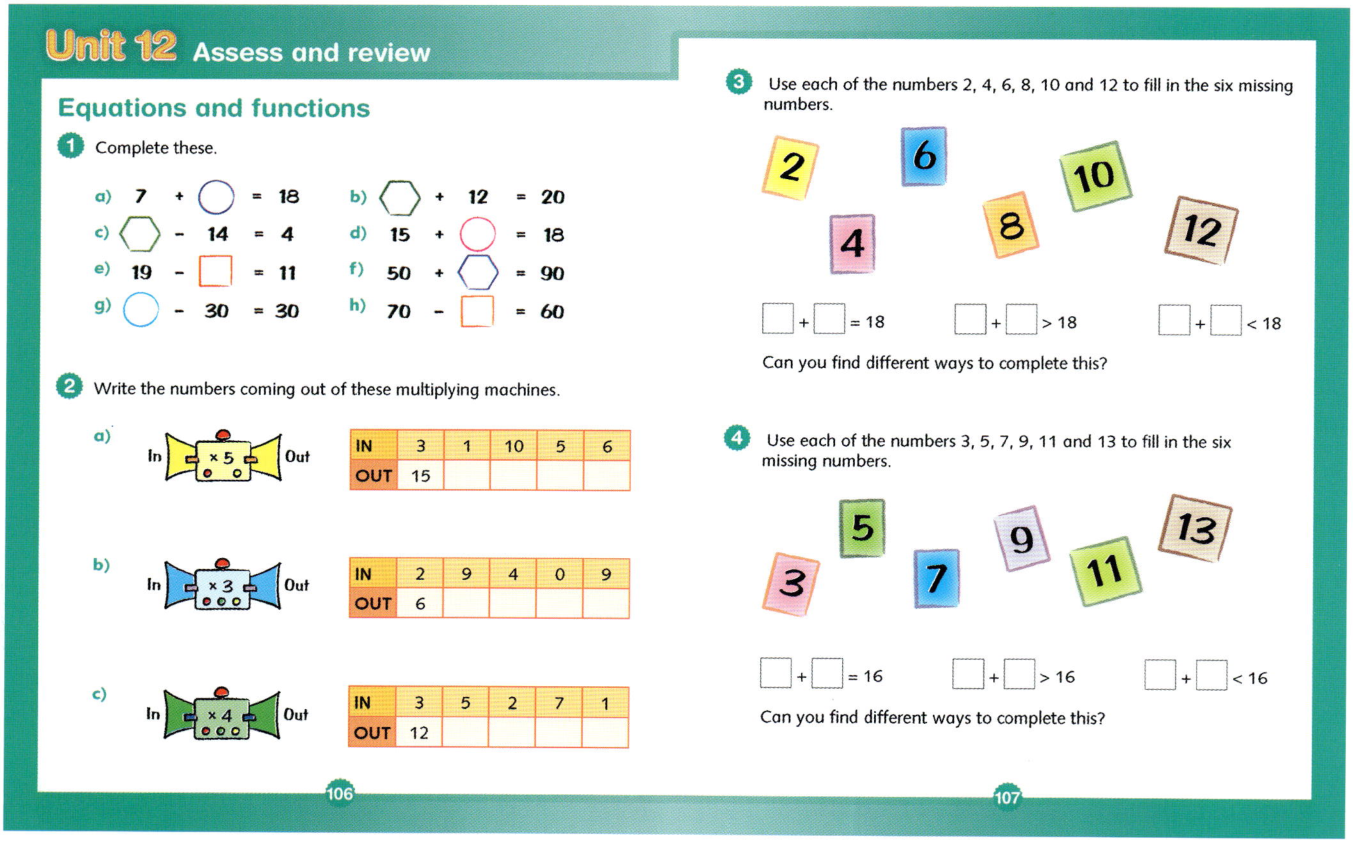

Unit 12 Assess and review

Equations and functions

1 Complete these.

a) 7 + ◯ = 18 b) ⬡ + 12 = 20
c) ⬡ − 14 = 4 d) 15 + ◯ = 18
e) 19 − □ = 11 f) 50 + ⬡ = 90
g) ◯ − 30 = 30 h) 70 − □ = 60

2 Write the numbers coming out of these multiplying machines.

a) In → × 5 → Out

IN	3	1	10	5	6
OUT	15				

b) In → × 3 → Out

IN	2	9	4	0	9
OUT	6				

c) In → × 4 → Out

IN	3	5	2	7	1
OUT	12				

3 Use each of the numbers 2, 4, 6, 8, 10 and 12 to fill in the six missing numbers.

2 6 10 4 8 12

□ + □ = 18 □ + □ > 18 □ + □ < 18

Can you find different ways to complete this?

4 Use each of the numbers 3, 5, 7, 9, 11 and 13 to fill in the six missing numbers.

5 9 13 3 7 11

□ + □ = 16 □ + □ > 16 □ + □ < 16

Can you find different ways to complete this?

106 107

Answers pages 106 and 107

1 a) 11 b) 8 c) 18 d) 3
e) 8 f) 40 g) 60 h) 10

2 a) 5 50 25 30 b) 27 12 0 27 c) 20 8 28 4

Answers pages 108 and 109

1 a) 6 b) 3 c) 4

2 a) 3 b) 4 c) 5 d) 7 e) 2

3 a) third b) quarter c) fifth d) half e) third

4 1st shape, $\frac{1}{3}$, one-third; 2nd shape, $\frac{1}{5}$, one-fifth;
3rd shape, $\frac{1}{4}$, one-quarter; 4th shape, $\frac{1}{6}$, one-sixth;
5th shape, $\frac{1}{2}$, one-half

5 a) $\frac{1}{4}$ b) $\frac{1}{3}$ c) $\frac{1}{2}$

Answers pages 110 and 111

1

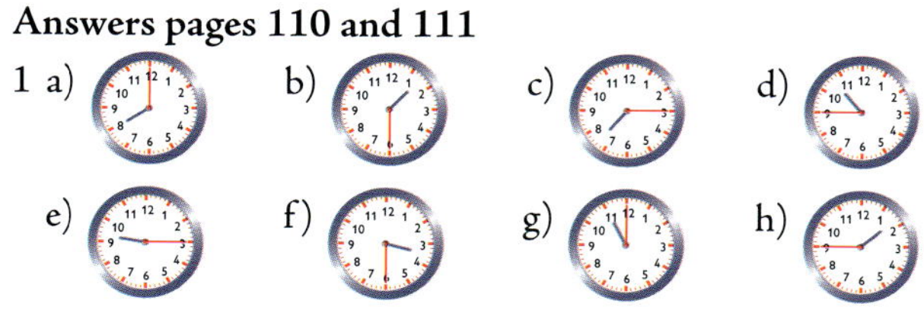

2 a) 3.00 b) 9.00 c) 11.00
d) 4.30 e) 6.30 f) 1.30

3 a) 45 minutes b) 30 minutes c) 45 minutes
d) 1 hour e) 45 minutes f) 1 hour 30 minutes

4 a) January, February, March, April, May, June
b) Rajab, Sha'aban, Ramadan, Shawwal, Dhu al-Qi'dah, Dhu al-Hijjah

Fractions

1 Cut out a grid of 12 squares from squared paper.

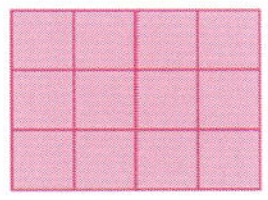

a) Fold the grid in half and count the squares in one-half.

$\frac{1}{2}$ of 12 = ☐

b) Open the grid out. Fold it in quarters and count the squares in one-quarter.

$\frac{1}{4}$ of 12 = ☐

c) Open the grid out. Fold it in thirds and count the squares in one-third.

$\frac{1}{3}$ of 12 = ☐

2 Divide each bowl of fruit into equal groups. Count how many are in one-half or one-quarter.

a) 

$\frac{1}{2}$ of 6 = ☐

b) 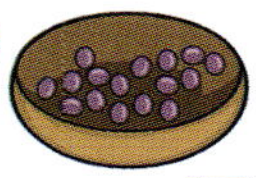

$\frac{1}{4}$ of 16 = ☐

c) 

$\frac{1}{4}$ of 20 = ☐

d) 

$\frac{1}{2}$ of 14 = ☐

e) 

$\frac{1}{4}$ of 8 = ☐

3 What fractions are shown by each of these shapes?
Choose from the list of fractions.

half	third	quarter	fifth	sixth

a) 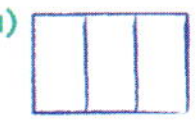

b) 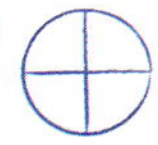

c) 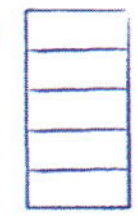

d) 

e) 

4 Look at the fractions shaded in each shape. Draw a line to join each shape to the matching fraction and fraction word.

$\frac{1}{4}$ one-sixth

$\frac{1}{2}$ one-third

$\frac{1}{3}$ one-quarter

$\frac{1}{6}$ one-half

$\frac{1}{5}$ one-fifth

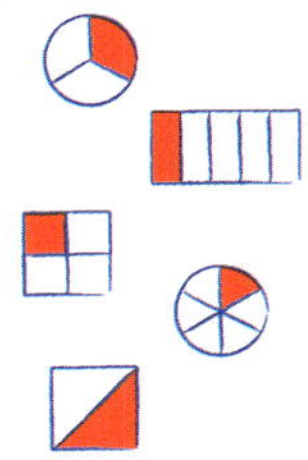

5 What fractions are shown on this number line?

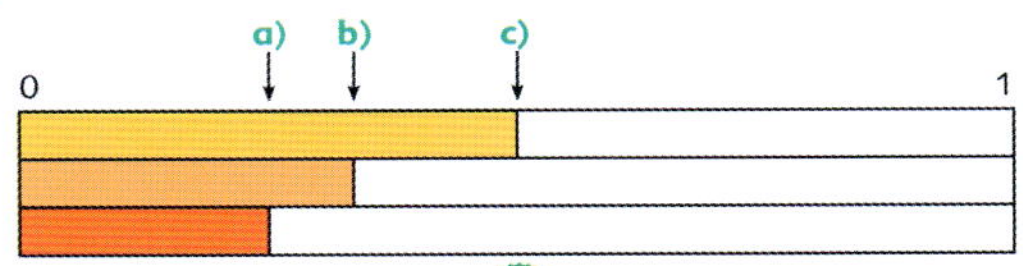

Time

1 Draw hands on these clocks to show these times.
Remember to draw the hour hand shorter than the minute hand.

a) 8.00 

b) 1.30 

c) 7.15 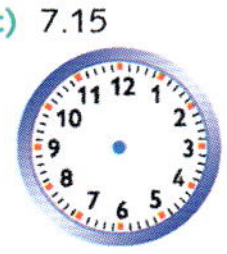

d) 10.45 

e) quarter past nine 

f) half past three 

g) eleven o'clock 

h) quarter to two 

2 What is the time one hour later than each of these?

a) 

One hour later is ☐

b) 

One hour later is ☐

c) 

One hour later is ☐

d) 

One hour later is ☐

e) 

One hour later is ☐

f) 

One hour later is ☐

3 These are from a school timetable.
Write the time taken for each of these.

a) English lessons start at 9.00 and finish at 9.45.

b) Maths lessons start at 9.45 and finish at 10.15.

c) Science lessons start at half past 10 and finish at quarter past 11.

d) Art classes are from 11.15 to 12.15.

e) Lunch is between quarter past 12 and 1 o'clock.

f) Sport is from one o'clock to half past two.

4 Write these months in order.

a) March April June January February May

b) Dhu al-Qi'dah Ramadan Dhu al-Hijjah Rajab Sha'aban Shawwal

Try this

Make a list of all the birthday months of your friends and family.
Which is the most popular month? Are there any months with no birthdays?

Pupil's Book 2B

Block D Addition and subtraction to 999

Maths Topic	**National Standards from Government Guidelines**	
Unit	*Curriculum area*	*End of year objectives / success criteria*
13 Numbers and number patterns	Understanding numbers, methods of displaying them and the relations between them Understand and identify numerical patterns relations and functions	Develop a primary understanding of counting in tens and place value up to 999. Read and write numbers to 999 in figures and words. Arrange a set of 3-digit numbers and compare them. Identify and complete simple numerical patterns. Build up new patterns of their own.
14 Addition and subtraction to 999	Understanding numerical operations and the relations between them Calculate skilfully and make reasonable assessments	Add 2 or 3 numbers whose sum does not exceed 99, with or without renaming. Add and subtract hundreds on the number line. Add and subtract two 3-digit numbers without renaming. Choose the operation needed to solve mathematical or word problems. Check the results of any addition or subtraction problem. Use mental and written methods of calculation. Use approximation in solving addition and subtraction. Use the properties of addition and subtraction.
15 Money	Understanding the properties of measurable items and the units and operations of measurement Application of appropriate methods, tools and rules of measurement Understanding numerical operations and the relations between them	Identify money (types of money). Do simple addition and subtraction problems related to money. Solve simple everyday problems (word problems) that include units of measurement (time, money). Choose the basic operation (addition – subtraction – multiplication) needed to solve mathematical or everyday problems (word problems). Check the results of any addition, subtraction or multiplication problem.
16 Assess and review	Revision and assessment of previous 3 units – problems, formative and summative assessment. Monitor, assess, evaluate and consolidate pupils' knowledge and understanding.	

During this block of work, pupils will experience:

1 Identifying odd and even numbers.
2 Identifying and completing number patterns.
3 Comparing and ordering numbers to 999.
4 Approximating numbers to the nearest ten.
5 Adding 2-digit numbers with exchange.
6 Adding and subtracting 3-digit numbers (no exchange).
7 Recognising and ordering coins and notes.
8 Finding totals of money and giving change from $1.
9 Solving word problems related to money.

Unit 13 **Numbers and number patterns**

Term 2 Block D **Addition and subtraction to 999** **Unit 13 Numbers and number patterns** Unit 14 Addition and subtraction to 999 Unit 15 Money Unit 16 Assess and review	**Objectives** *At the end of the unit, students should be able to…* Develop a primary understanding of counting in tens and place value up to 999. Read and write numbers composed of units, tens and hundreds in both number (figure) and letter form. Arrange a set of 3-digit numbers and compare between them. Identify simple numerical patterns and complete them by adding new numbers that follow the same pattern. Build up new patterns of their own.
Vocabulary odd, even, digit, hundreds, tens, units, abacus, grid, pattern, multiple, sequence, compare, greater, greatest, smaller, smallest, order	**Lessons** 1 Odd and even numbers 2 Patterns on grids 3 Number patterns 4 Comparing numbers to 999 5 Ordering numbers to 999
Oral and mental starter Halve it Steps Flash facts What's the question? Start here	**Resources** Counters for each pupil Classroom 1–100 grid Squared paper for each pupil *Pupil's Book pages 4–13*
Prior learning Reading, writing, ordering numbers to 999 Understanding place value in numbers to 999 Counting in tens to 90 and hundreds to 900 Beginning to recognise odd and even numbers	**Background notes** In this unit confidence and understanding of numbers which pupils encountered in previous units are developed through patterns, sequences and properties of numbers.
End of unit evaluation Check that pupils are able to: 1 Read and write numbers to 999. 2 Identify the place value of numbers to 999. 3 Compare and order numbers to 999. 4 Identify and complete number patterns and sequences.	**Supporting the topic** Discuss real-life examples of number patterns, sequences, odd/even numbers, multiples of 10 and 100, e.g. sequence of house/flat numbering, properties of personal numbers such as age, birthday dates, own house numbers etc.

Lesson 1 **Odd and even numbers**

Pupil's Book pages 4 and 5 **Oral and mental starter: Halve it**

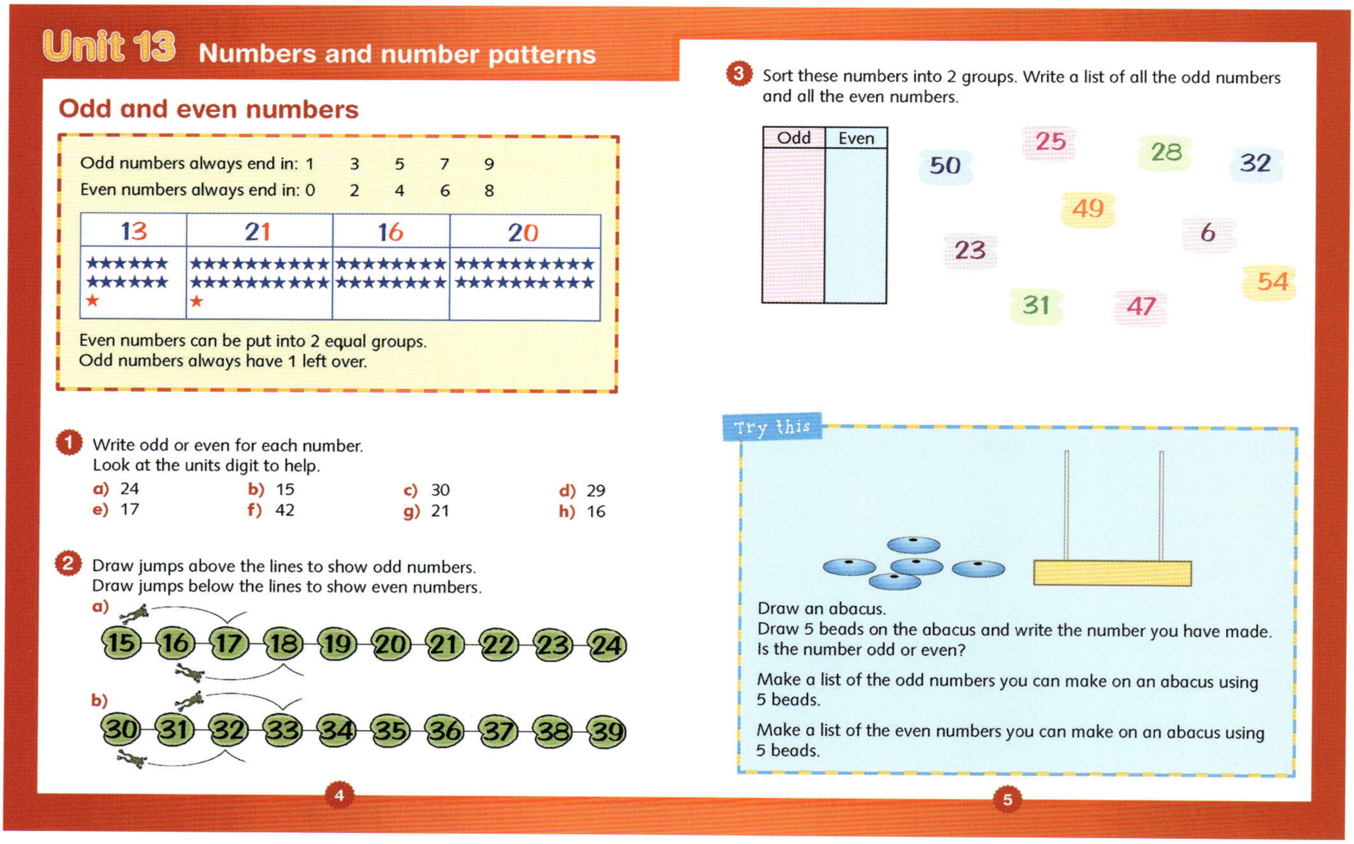

Unit 13 Numbers and number patterns

Odd and even numbers

Odd numbers always end in: 1 3 5 7 9
Even numbers always end in: 0 2 4 6 8

13	21	16	20
★★★★★★ ★★★★★★ ★	★★★★★★★★★★ ★★★★★★★★★★ ★	★★★★★★★★ ★★★★★★★★	★★★★★★★★★★ ★★★★★★★★★★

Even numbers can be put into 2 equal groups.
Odd numbers always have 1 left over.

1 Write odd or even for each number.
Look at the units digit to help.

a) 24 b) 15 c) 30 d) 29
e) 17 f) 42 g) 21 h) 16

2 Draw jumps above the lines to show odd numbers.
Draw jumps below the lines to show even numbers.

a) 15 16 17 18 19 20 21 22 23 24

b) 30 31 32 33 34 35 36 37 38 39

3 Sort these numbers into 2 groups. Write a list of all the odd numbers and all the even numbers.

Odd	Even

50 25 28 32 49 23 6 54 31 47

Try this

Draw an abacus.
Draw 5 beads on the abacus and write the number you have made.
Is the number odd or even?

Make a list of the odd numbers you can make on an abacus using 5 beads.

Make a list of the even numbers you can make on an abacus using 5 beads.

4 5

Activities

- Remind the class that they learned about odd and even numbers in Grade 1. 'Can anyone remember how we decide whether a number is odd or even?' Discuss all suggestions.
- Look at page 4 and go through the introduction with the class, linking the explanation to relevant suggestions pupils made above. Emphasise that even numbers of things can be divided into two equal groups, odd numbers of things always have an 'odd' one left over. Remind pupils about the mental starter activity. 'Can we halve an odd number of objects? Why?'
- Ask pupils to each take a handful of counters, count them, then try to halve them to see whether they have an even number or an odd number. When this has been done ask individual pupils how many counters they had and whether that is an odd or even number. Record the numbers in two lists on the board, one headed 'odd' the other 'even'. Confirm that the odd numbers end in 1, 3, 5, 7 or 9 and the even numbers in 0, 2, 4, 6 or 8.
- Give a few 2-digit numbers, e.g. 83, 74, 20, 99, 56 and ask pupils to say whether they are odd or even. Add them to the lists on the board.
- Look again at pages 4 and 5 and ask pupils to complete them.

Answers

1 a) even b) odd c) even d) odd
e) odd f) even g) odd h) even

3 Odd: 25, 49, 23, 31, 47; even: 50, 28, 32, 6, 54

Try this

Odd: 5, 41, 23; even: 50, 14, 32

Lesson 2 Patterns on grids

Pupil's Book pages 6 and 7 **Oral and mental starter: Steps**

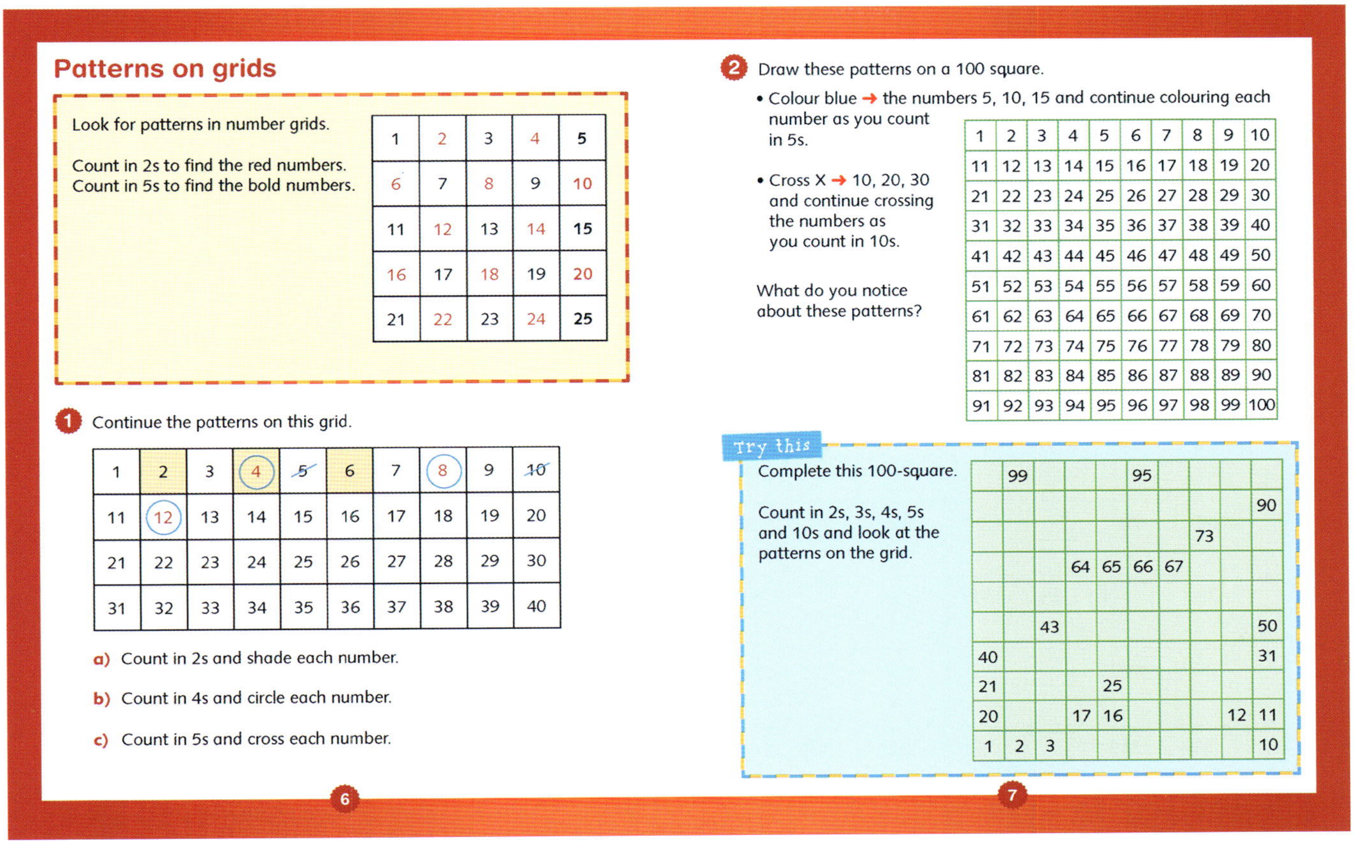

Patterns on grids

Look for patterns in number grids.

Count in 2s to find the red numbers.
Count in 5s to find the bold numbers.

1	2	3	4	**5**
6	7	8	9	**10**
11	12	13	14	**15**
16	17	18	19	**20**
21	22	23	24	**25**

1 Continue the patterns on this grid.

1	2	3	4	5	6	7	8	9	10
11	12	13	14	15	16	17	18	19	20
21	22	23	24	25	26	27	28	29	30
31	32	33	34	35	36	37	38	39	40

a) Count in 2s and shade each number.

b) Count in 4s and circle each number.

c) Count in 5s and cross each number.

2 Draw these patterns on a 100 square.

- Colour blue → the numbers 5, 10, 15 and continue colouring each number as you count in 5s.
- Cross X → 10, 20, 30 and continue crossing the numbers as you count in 10s.

What do you notice about these patterns?

1	2	3	4	5	6	7	8	9	10
11	12	13	14	15	16	17	18	19	20
21	22	23	24	25	26	27	28	29	30
31	32	33	34	35	36	37	38	39	40
41	42	43	44	45	46	47	48	49	50
51	52	53	54	55	56	57	58	59	60
61	62	63	64	65	66	67	68	69	70
71	72	73	74	75	76	77	78	79	80
81	82	83	84	85	86	87	88	89	90
91	92	93	94	95	96	97	98	99	100

Try this

Complete this 100-square.

Count in 2s, 3s, 4s, 5s and 10s and look at the patterns on the grid.

	99				95				
									90
							73		
			64	65	66	67			
		43							50
40									31
21				25					
20			17	16				12	11
1	2	3							10

6 7

Activities

- Using the classroom 1–100 grid ask pupils to comment on any patterns they can see, e.g. consecutive numbers along the rows; multiples of 10 down the right-hand column; all columns have the same units digits; every other number along the rows is odd/even; the numbers down the columns increase by 10.
- Look at the introduction on page 6. 'How is the grid different from the classroom grid?' Discuss a variety of suggestions. Ask pupils to count in 2s as they touch each highlighted multiple of 2 on the grid. Explain that every number they touched is called a multiple of 2 like the answers in the 2× table. Repeat, asking them to count in 5s. 'Which numbers are multiples of both 2 and 5?'
- Towards the end of the lesson ask questions about the patterns of the multiples in question 1, e.g. 'What sort of pattern do the multiples of 10 make? What about the multiples of 2? … the multiples of 4?'

Answers

1 Even numbers: 2, 4, 6, 8, 10, 12, 14, 16, 18, 20, 22, 24, 26, 28, 30, 32, 34, 36, 38, 40; Multiples of 4: 4, 8, 12, 16, 20, 24, 28, 32, 36, 40; Multiples of 5: 5, 10, 15, 20, 25, 30, 35, 40

2 Multiples of 5: 5, 10, 15, 20, 25, 30, 35, 40, 45, 50, 55, 60, 65, 70, 75, 80, 85, 90, 95, 100; Multiples of 10: 10, 20, 30, 40, 50, 60, 70, 80, 90, 100

Try this

100	99	98	97	96	95	94	93	92	91
81	82	83	84	85	86	87	88	89	90
80	79	78	77	76	75	74	73	72	71
61	62	63	64	65	66	67	68	69	70
60	59	58	57	56	55	54	53	52	51
41	42	43	44	45	46	47	48	49	50
40	39	38	37	36	35	34	33	32	31
21	22	23	24	25	26	27	28	29	30
20	19	18	17	16	15	14	13	12	11
1	2	3	4	5	6	7	8	9	10

Lesson 3 **Number patterns**

Pupil's Book pages 8 and 9 **Oral and mental starter: Flash facts**

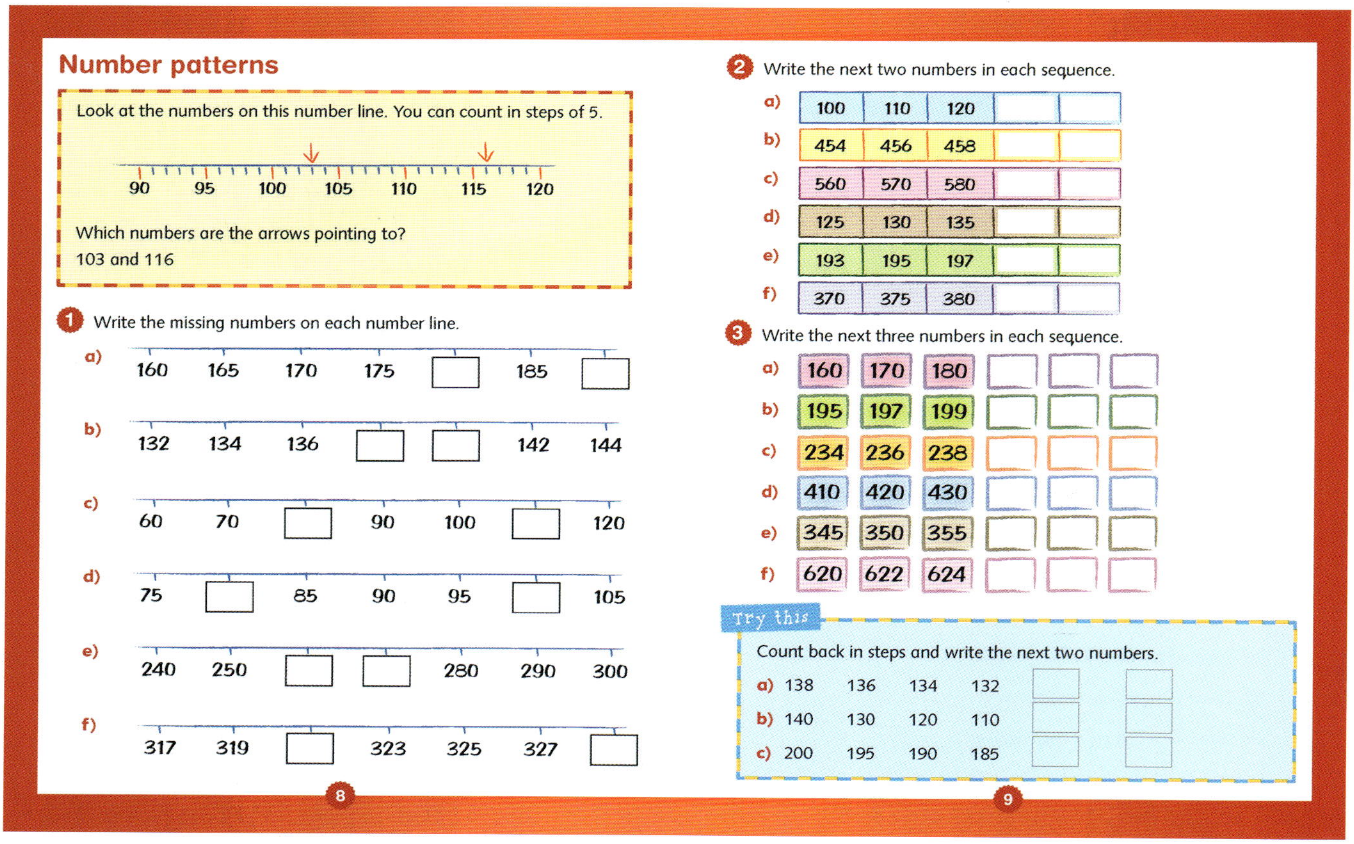

Number patterns

Look at the numbers on this number line. You can count in steps of 5.

90 95 100 105 110 115 120

Which numbers are the arrows pointing to?
103 and 116

1 Write the missing numbers on each number line.

a) 160 165 170 175 ☐ 185 ☐

b) 132 134 136 ☐ ☐ 142 144

c) 60 70 ☐ 90 100 ☐ 120

d) 75 ☐ 85 90 95 ☐ 105

e) 240 250 ☐ ☐ 280 290 300

f) 317 319 ☐ 323 325 327 ☐

8

2 Write the next two numbers in each sequence.

a) 100 110 120 ☐ ☐

b) 454 456 458 ☐ ☐

c) 560 570 580 ☐ ☐

d) 125 130 135 ☐ ☐

e) 193 195 197 ☐ ☐

f) 370 375 380 ☐ ☐

3 Write the next three numbers in each sequence.

a) 160 170 180 ☐ ☐ ☐

b) 195 197 199 ☐ ☐ ☐

c) 234 236 238 ☐ ☐ ☐

d) 410 420 430 ☐ ☐ ☐

e) 345 350 355 ☐ ☐ ☐

f) 620 622 624 ☐ ☐ ☐

Try this

Count back in steps and write the next two numbers.

a) 138 136 134 132 ☐ ☐

b) 140 130 120 110 ☐ ☐

c) 200 195 190 185 ☐ ☐

9

Activities

- Ask the class to count on in 10s from 0 to 100 and then back; from 12 to 92 and back; in 100s from 100 to 900 and back; in 100s from 130 to 930 and back; in 2s from 100 to 120 and back; in 5s from 0 to 50 and back; in 5s from 100 to 150 and back.
- Write a sequence such as 315, 415, 515, 615 on the board. 'What sort of count is shown in this sequence?' Establish that it is counting on in 100s. 'What are the next two numbers? Which number comes before 315?' Repeat using other sequences such as 126, 128, 130, 132; 67, 65, 63, 61; 470, 460, 450, 440; 215, 225, 235, 245. Each time ask for the counting pattern shown, the next two or three numbers and the number before the first number.
- Look at page 8. Go through the introduction with the class. Ask for the next few numbers in the sequence. Ask for the numbers indicated by the arrows. Ask pupils to suggest where other numbers would be on the line, e.g. 101, 98, 113.

Answers

1 a) 180, 190 b) 138, 140 c) 80, 110
d) 80, 100 e) 260, 270 f) 321, 329

2 a) 130, 140 b) 460, 462 c) 590, 600
d) 140, 145 e) 199, 201 f) 385, 390

3 a) 190, 200, 210 b) 201, 203, 205 c) 240, 242, 244
d) 440, 450, 460 e) 360, 365, 370 f) 626, 628, 630

Try this

a) 130, 128 b) 100, 90 c) 180, 175

Lesson 4 **Comparing numbers to 999**

Pupil's Book pages 10 and 11 **Oral and mental starter: What's the question?**

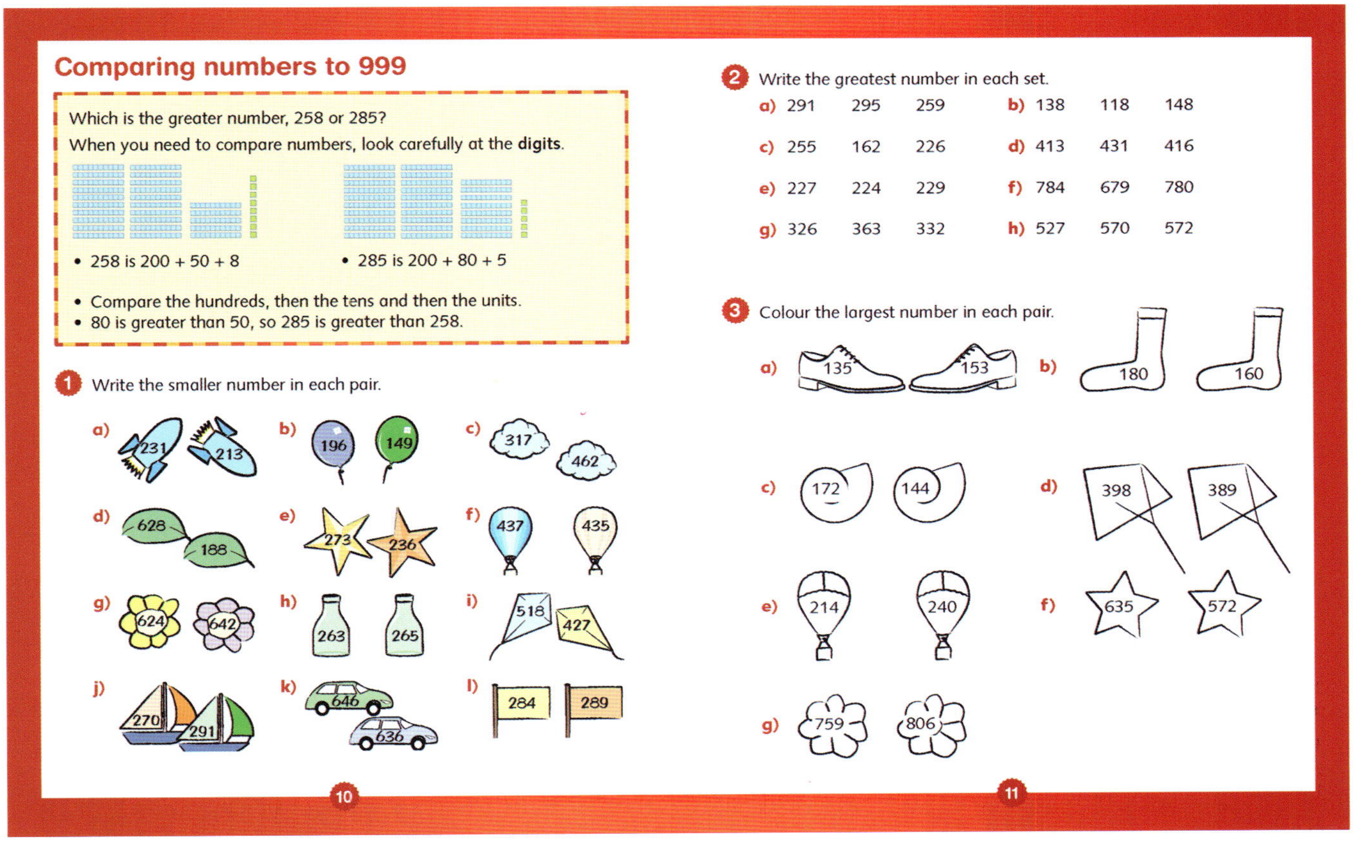

Comparing numbers to 999

Which is the greater number, 258 or 285?
When you need to compare numbers, look carefully at the **digits**.

- 258 is 200 + 50 + 8
- 285 is 200 + 80 + 5

- Compare the hundreds, then the tens and then the units.
- 80 is greater than 50, so 285 is greater than 258.

1 Write the smaller number in each pair.

a) 231 213 **b)** 196 149 **c)** 317 462
d) 628 188 **e)** 273 236 **f)** 437 435
g) 624 642 **h)** 263 265 **i)** 518 427
j) 270 291 **k)** 646 636 **l)** 284 289

2 Write the greatest number in each set.

a) 291 295 259 **b)** 138 118 148
c) 255 162 226 **d)** 413 431 416
e) 227 224 229 **f)** 784 679 780
g) 326 363 332 **h)** 527 570 572

3 Colour the largest number in each pair.

a) 135 153 **b)** 180 160
c) 172 144 **d)** 398 389
e) 214 240 **f)** 635 572
g) 759 806

10 11

Activities

- Write 367 and 478 on the board. Ask 'Which is the larger number? How do you know?' Repeat with other pairs of numbers such as 387 and 198; 564 and 620; 426 and 501; 630 and 603.
- Look at page 10 and go through the introduction with the class. Discuss how 258 and 285 are represented by the blocks, rods and cubes. Emphasise that the tens are the most important digits when comparing two numbers with the same hundreds digits.
- Write pairs of numbers on the board such as 167 and 176; 431 and 428; 348 and 384; 360 and 300. Ask pupils to compare the two numbers each time and say which is the smaller.
- Write sets of three numbers on the board such as 157, 171, 148; 842, 815, 854; 629, 614, 651. Ask pupils to compare the three numbers each time and say which is the greatest.

Answers

1	a) 213	b) 149	c) 317	d) 188	e) 236	f) 435
	g) 624	h) 263	i) 427	j) 270	k) 636	l) 284
2	a) 295	b) 148	c) 255	d) 431	e) 229	f) 784
	g) 363	h) 572				
3	a) 153	b) 180	c) 172	d) 398	e) 240	
	f) 635	g) 806				

Lesson 5 **Ordering numbers to 999**

Pupil's Book pages 12 and 13 **Oral and mental starter: Start here**

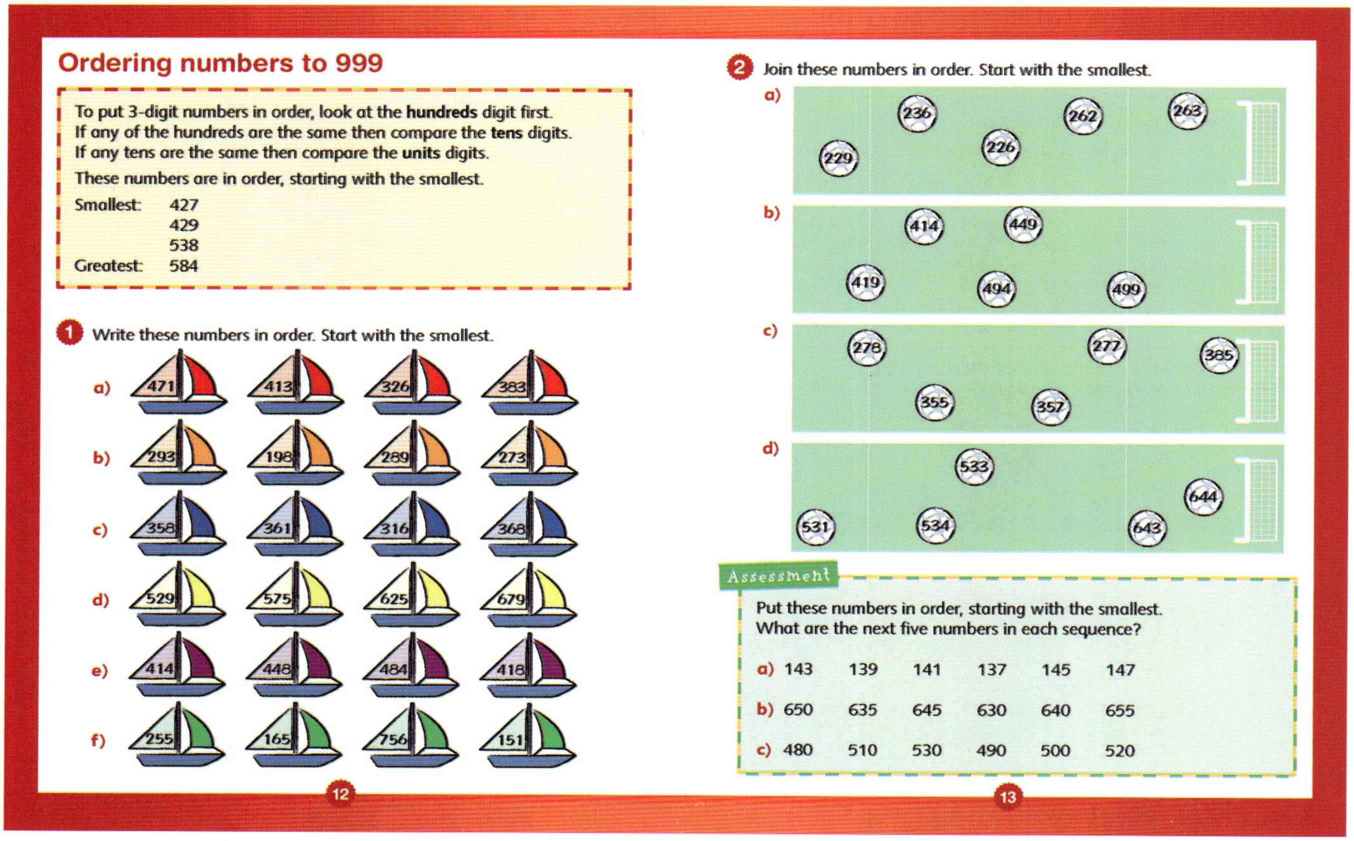

Ordering numbers to 999

To put 3-digit numbers in order, look at the **hundreds** digit first.
If any of the hundreds are the same then compare the **tens** digits.
If any tens are the same then compare the **units** digits.

These numbers are in order, starting with the smallest.

Smallest: 427
429
538
Greatest: 584

1 Write these numbers in order. Start with the smallest.

a) 471 413 326 383
b) 293 198 289 273
c) 358 361 316 368
d) 529 575 625 679
e) 414 448 484 418
f) 255 165 756 151

12

2 Join these numbers in order. Start with the smallest.

a) 236 262 263 229 226
b) 414 449 419 494 499
c) 278 277 385 355 357
d) 533 644 531 534 643

Assessment

Put these numbers in order, starting with the smallest.
What are the next five numbers in each sequence?

a) 143 139 141 137 145 147
b) 650 635 645 630 640 655
c) 480 510 530 490 500 520

13

Activities

- Ask questions such as: 'Which number is 1 more than 236? … 1 less than 385? … 10 more than 520? … 2 less than 416? … between 665 and 667? … between 844 and 842? What are the next three numbers after 352? … the two numbers before 199?'
- 'Does anyone know the number which is 1 more than 999?'
- Ask five pupils to each give a 3-digit number and record them on the board. 'Which is the smallest number? How do you know?' Underline the smallest number. 'Which is the largest? How do you know?' Put a ring round the largest number. Repeat with another set of numbers chosen by pupils.
- Look at page 12. Go through the introduction with the class, emphasising the instructions for ordering numbers. Write another set of numbers on the board such as 830, 652, 237, 678, 838. Ask pupils to find the smallest number, compare the tens to find the next number, compare the units in numbers with the same hundreds and tens value. Repeat for another set of numbers such as 291, 440, 296, 196, 432.

Answers

1 a) 326, 383, 413, 471 b) 198, 273, 289, 293
c) 316, 358, 361, 368 d) 529, 575, 625, 679
e) 414, 418, 448, 484 f) 151, 165, 255, 756

2 a) 226, 229, 236, 262, 263 b) 414, 419, 449, 494, 499
c) 277, 278, 355, 357, 385 d) 531, 533, 534, 643, 644

Assessment

a) 137, 139, 141, 143, 145, 147 → 149, 151, 153, 155, 157
b) 630, 635, 640, 645, 650, 655 → 660, 665, 670, 675, 680
c) 480, 490, 500, 510, 520, 530 → 540, 550, 560, 570, 580

Unit 14 Addition and subtraction to 999

Term 2 Block D
Addition and subtraction to 999

Objectives

At the end of the unit, students should be able to…

Understand the meaning of adding two or three numbers whose sum does not exceed 99, with or without renaming.
Add and subtract hundreds and display this on the number line.
Add and subtract two 3-digit numbers without renaming.
Choose the basic operation needed to solve mathematical or everyday problems (word problems).
Check the results of any addition or subtraction problem.
Use different and suitable methods for addition and subtraction like Mental Math or use of pencil and paper (written).
Use approximation in solving addition and subtraction of numbers.
Identify numerical examples showing the properties of addition and subtraction up to 999, without explicitly naming them.

Vocabulary

rounding, round up/down, nearest ten, approximate, approximately, addition, add, subtraction, subtract, digit, hundreds, tens, units, column

Lessons

1 Rounding to the nearest 10
2 Adding 2-digit numbers: short method
3 Adding and subtracting hundreds
4 Adding 3-digit numbers: no exchange
5 Subtracting 3-digit numbers: no exchange

Oral and mental starters

Arrows away
Flash facts (addition/subtraction)
Pairs for sums
My way
What's the question?

Resources

Large set of arrow cards (to 999)
Abacus
Pupil's Book pages 14–23

Prior learning

Adding and subtracting 2-digit numbers
Reading, writing, comparing and ordering numbers to 999
Understanding place value in 3-digit numbers

Background notes

Encourage pupils to:

- Learn addition/subtraction facts.
- Count on from the largest number when adding numbers.
- Use known addition and subtraction facts in written methods.
- Align the digits correctly in column calculations.
- Check the results of calculations using approximation.

Pupils who understand the written method but can work out a calculation mentally should be encouraged to do so. They should only use a written method when a calculation is beyond their mental ability.

End of unit evaluation

Check that pupils are able to:

1 Approximate answers before carrying out a written calculation.
2 Add and subtract multiples of 100 mentally.
3 Add and subtract 3-digit numbers (without exchange).

Supporting the topic

Continue to encourage pupils to have instant recall of addition/subtraction facts within 20. Talk about situations in everyday life where 3-digit numbers are added or subtracted, e.g. the total weight of cooking ingredients in grams; the amount remaining in the packet when, e.g. 350 grams are removed.

Lesson 1 Rounding to the nearest 10

Pupil's Book pages 14 and 15 **Oral and mental starter: Arrows away**

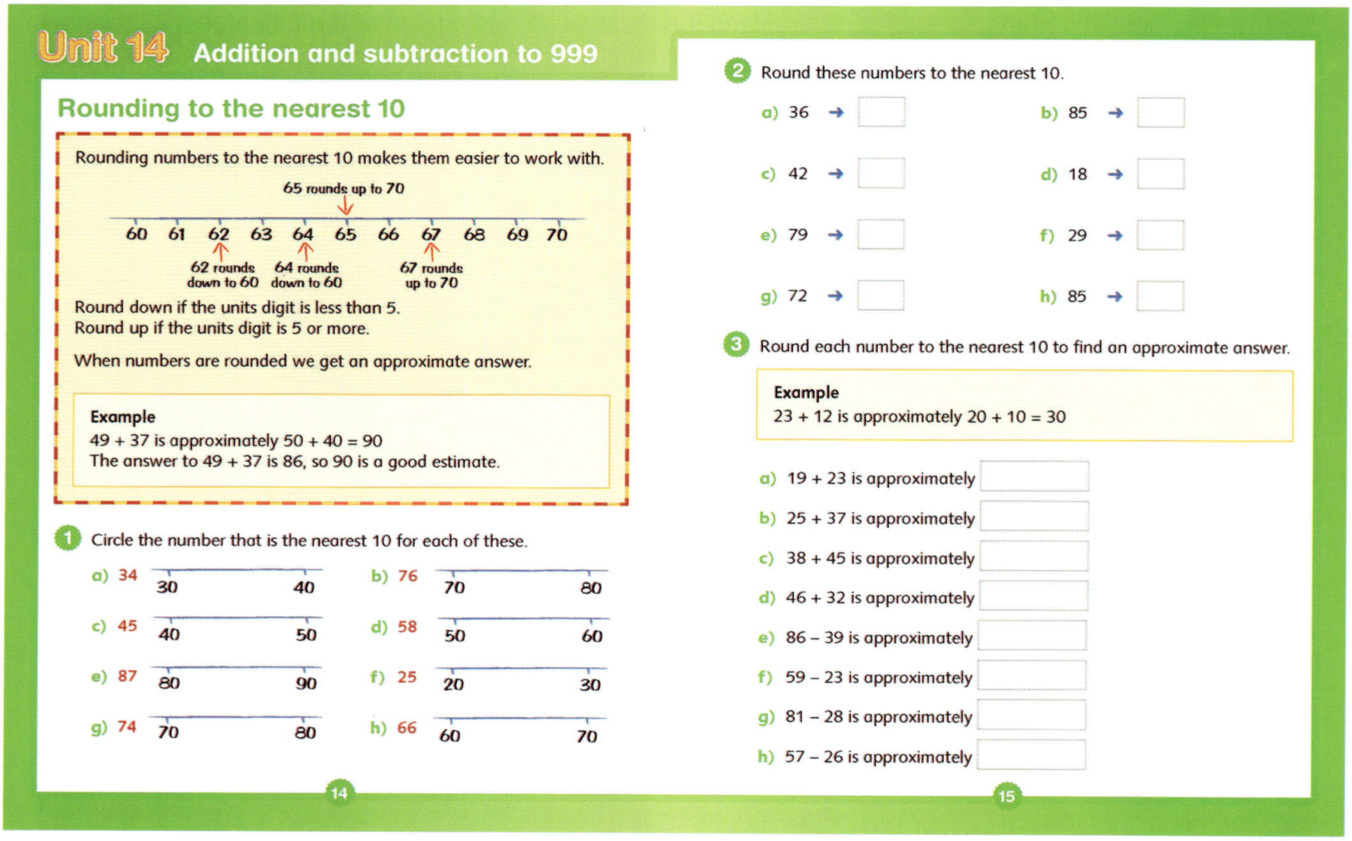

Unit 14 Addition and subtraction to 999

Rounding to the nearest 10

Rounding numbers to the nearest 10 makes them easier to work with.

65 rounds up to 70

60 61 62 63 64 65 66 67 68 69 70

62 rounds down to 60   64 rounds down to 60   67 rounds up to 70

Round down if the units digit is less than 5.
Round up if the units digit is 5 or more.

When numbers are rounded we get an approximate answer.

Example
49 + 37 is approximately 50 + 40 = 90
The answer to 49 + 37 is 86, so 90 is a good estimate.

1 Circle the number that is the nearest 10 for each of these.

a) 34   30 — 40   b) 76   70 — 80
c) 45   40 — 50   d) 58   50 — 60
e) 87   80 — 90   f) 25   20 — 30
g) 74   70 — 80   h) 66   60 — 70

14

2 Round these numbers to the nearest 10.

a) 36 → ☐   b) 85 → ☐
c) 42 → ☐   d) 18 → ☐
e) 79 → ☐   f) 29 → ☐
g) 72 → ☐   h) 85 → ☐

3 Round each number to the nearest 10 to find an approximate answer.

Example
23 + 12 is approximately 20 + 10 = 30

a) 19 + 23 is approximately ☐
b) 25 + 37 is approximately ☐
c) 38 + 45 is approximately ☐
d) 46 + 32 is approximately ☐
e) 86 – 39 is approximately ☐
f) 59 – 23 is approximately ☐
g) 81 – 28 is approximately ☐
h) 57 – 26 is approximately ☐

15

Activities

- Look at page 14. Go through the introduction with the class. Emphasise that when the units digits are less than 5 the number is rounded down and when they are 5 or more the number is rounded up to the next ten. Explain that rounding is used in this way to give an approximate answer to a calculation. 'Why do you think it is useful to work out an approximate answer?' Establish that the approximation can be used to check the result of a precise calculation.
- Provide several 2-digit numbers for pupils to round to the nearest 10, e.g. 37, 51, 64, 75, 46, 13, 28.
- Provide 2-digit additions and subtractions for pupils to approximate the result by rounding then adding or subtracting tens, e.g. 54 + 27, 67 – 25, 48 + 33, 83 – 26.

Answers

1 a) 30   b) 80   c) 50   d) 60
   e) 90   f) 30   g) 70   h) 70

2 a) 40   b) 90   c) 40   d) 20
   e) 80   f) 30   g) 70   h) 90

3 a) 20 + 20 = 40   b) 30 + 40 = 70   c) 40 + 50 = 90
   d) 50 + 30 = 80   e) 90 – 40 = 50   f) 60 – 20 = 40
   g) 80 – 30 = 50   h) 60 – 30 = 30

Lesson 2 **Adding 2-digit numbers: short method**

Pupil's Book pages 16 and 17 **Oral and mental starter: Flash facts (addition/subtraction)**

Adding 2-digit numbers: short method

When you add numbers, always work out an approximate answer in your head.

Example

34 + 48 Approximate answer: 30 + 50 = 80

Step 1 Add the units

```
   T U
   ¹3 4
 + 4 8
 -----
     2
```

4 add 8 is 12. Write the 2 units and write 1 ten in the tens column.

Step 2 Add the tens

```
   T U
   ¹3 4
 + 4 8
 -----
   8 2
```

Add together 3 tens, 4 tens and 1 ten and write 8 tens.

1 Answer these.

a) 38 + 23 b) 48 + 24 c) 43 + 38

d) 26 + 47 e) 59 + 29 f) 16 + 68

16

2 Add these. Use the space to work them out.

a) 44 + 48 = ☐ b) 22 + 39 = ☐

c) 67 + 14 = ☐ d) 35 + 37 = ☐

e) 13 + 28 = ☐ f) 69 + 29 = ☐

g) 36 + 47 = ☐ h) 17 + 38 = ☐

i) 39 + 54 = ☐ j) 25 + 26 = ☐

Try this

Choose pairs of numbers from the grid which total 52.
Write five addition sums.

25	43	36	38
14	16	9	45
19	7	33	27

☐ + ☐ = 52
☐ + ☐ = 52
☐ + ☐ = 52
☐ + ☐ = 52
☐ + ☐ = 52

17

Activities

- Look at page 16 and go through the introduction with the class to revise addition of 2-digit numbers with exchange. Emphasise that the approximation should be carried out before using the written method. Discuss how the answer relates to the approximation and that this is an indication that the addition is correct.
- Provide a few additions for pupils to approximate, e.g. 65 + 32, 28 + 47, 54 + 18. Each time, ask for the approximation, then go through the rounding up or down and adding tens; write out the addition in columns, go through the written method as shown in the introduction and record the answer; discuss how this relates to the approximation and whether the answer looks correct. (It would be useful to have an incorrect answer so that the use of the approximation for fault finding could be demonstrated.)
- At the end of the lesson ask whether anyone discovered that their answer to the column sum looked incorrect when compared with their approximation. Ask whether they discovered a mistake and if so how it had been made. If necessary check with the pupil's work and demonstrate fault finding on the board.

Answers

1 a) 61 b) 72 c) 81 d) 73 e) 88 f) 84
2 a) 92 b) 61 c) 81 d) 72 e) 41
f) 98 g) 83 h) 55 i) 93 j) 51

Lesson 3 Adding and subtracting hundreds

Pupil's Book pages 18 and 19 **Oral and mental starter: Pairs for sums**

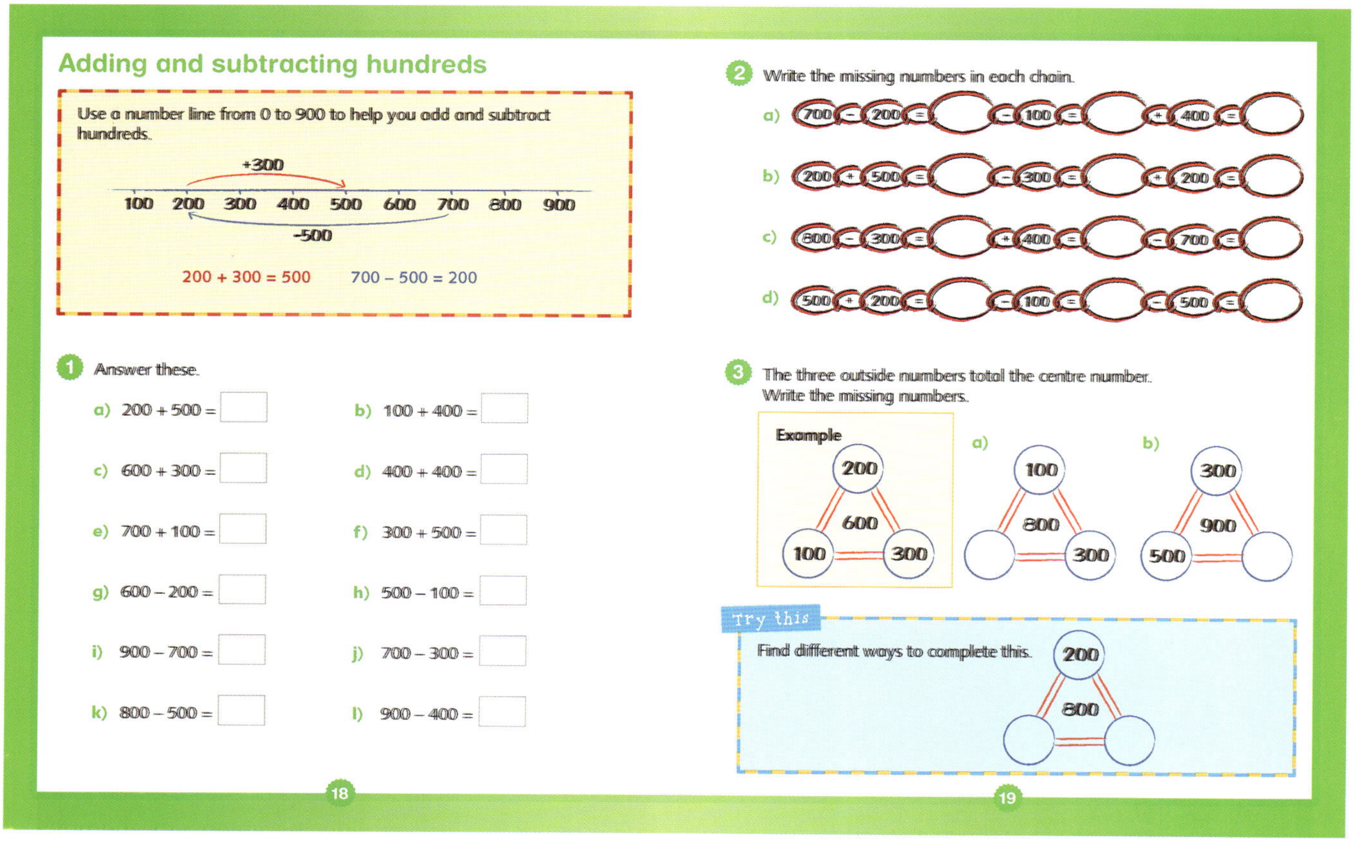

Adding and subtracting hundreds

Use a number line from 0 to 900 to help you add and subtract hundreds.

200 + 300 = 500   700 − 500 = 200

1 Answer these.

a) 200 + 500 = ☐   b) 100 + 400 = ☐

c) 600 + 300 = ☐   d) 400 + 400 = ☐

e) 700 + 100 = ☐   f) 300 + 500 = ☐

g) 600 − 200 = ☐   h) 500 − 100 = ☐

i) 900 − 700 = ☐   j) 700 − 300 = ☐

k) 800 − 500 = ☐   l) 900 − 400 = ☐

2 Write the missing numbers in each chain.

a) 700 − 200 = ◯ − 100 = ◯ + 400 = ◯

b) 200 + 500 = ◯ − 300 = ◯ + 200 = ◯

c) 800 − 300 = ◯ + 400 = ◯ − 700 = ◯

d) 500 + 200 = ◯ − 100 = ◯ − 500 = ◯

3 The three outside numbers total the centre number. Write the missing numbers.

Try this

Find different ways to complete this.

Activities

- Ask the class to count in hundreds to 900 and back. Ask them to start at 200 and count in 200s to 800, then from 100 to 900 (in 200s).
- Look at page 18 and go through the introduction with the class. Ask pupils to use the number line to add and subtract hundreds, e.g. 200 + 300, 600 − 400, 700 − 200, 400 + 500. Ask 'Can anyone answer 300 + 300 without using the number line? What about 800 − 200? How did you do it?' Establish that number facts such as 3 + 3 and 8 − 2 can be used, remembering that the value of the answer is hundreds.
- Go through the example in question 3 with the class.
- At the and of the lesson ask for all the possible ways of completing 'Try this' and record them on the board.

Answers

1 a) 700 b) 500 c) 900 d) 800 e) 800 f) 800
g) 400 h) 400 i) 200 j) 400 k) 300 l) 500

2 a) 500, 400, 800 b) 700, 400, 600
c) 500, 900, 200 d) 700, 600, 100

3 a) 400 b) 100

Lesson 4 Adding 3-digit numbers: no exchange

Pupil's Book pages 20 and 21 **Oral and mental starter: My way**

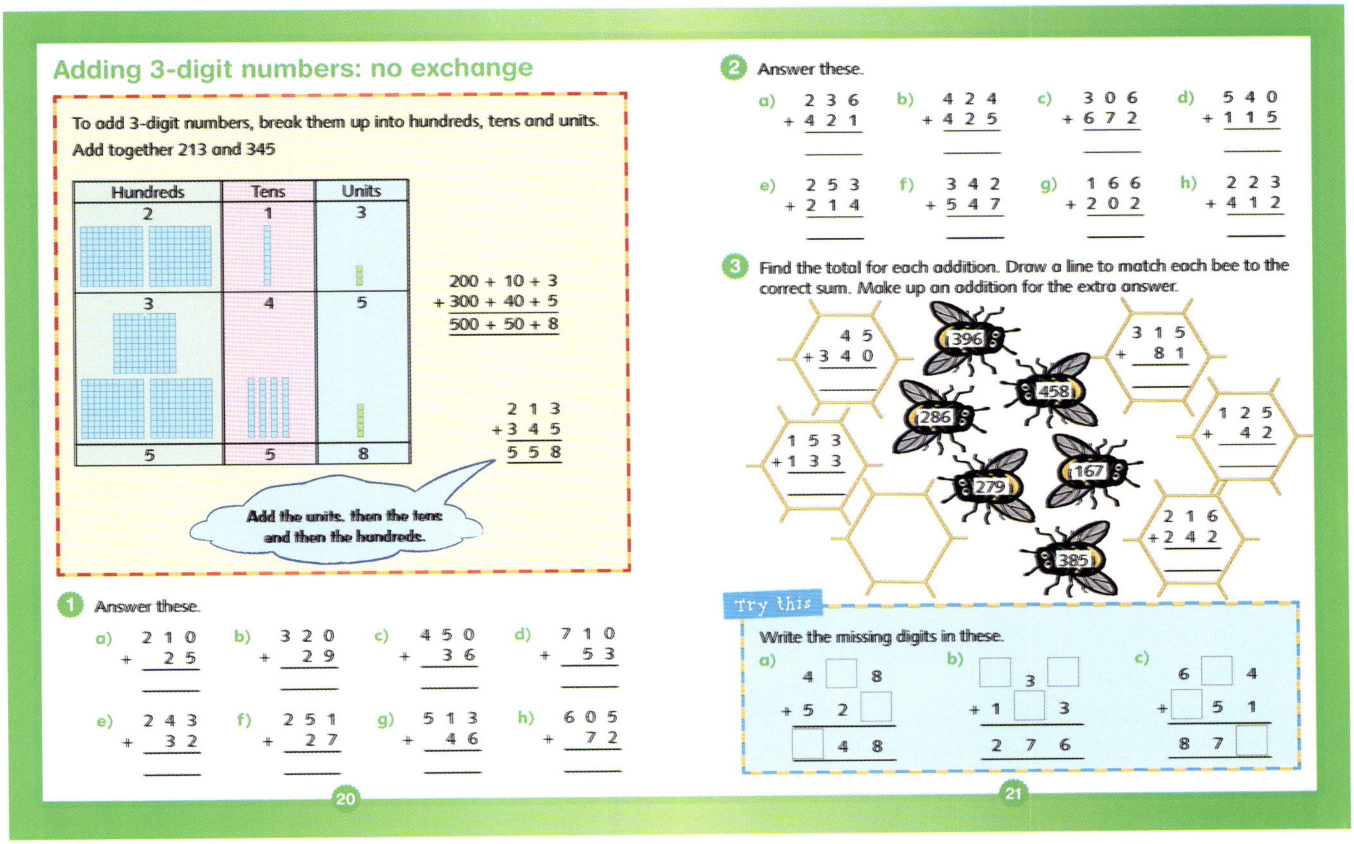
Adding 3-digit numbers: no exchange

To add 3-digit numbers, break them up into hundreds, tens and units.
Add together 213 and 345

Hundreds	Tens	Units
2	1	3
3	4	5
5	5	8

200 + 10 + 3
+ 300 + 40 + 5
500 + 50 + 8

213
+ 345
558

Add the units, then the tens and then the hundreds.

1 Answer these.

a) 210 + 25 b) 320 + 29 c) 450 + 36 d) 710 + 53
e) 243 + 32 f) 251 + 27 g) 513 + 46 h) 605 + 72

20

2 Answer these.

a) 236 + 421 b) 424 + 425 c) 306 + 672 d) 540 + 115
e) 253 + 214 f) 342 + 547 g) 166 + 202 h) 223 + 412

3 Find the total for each addition. Draw a line to match each bee to the correct sum. Make up an addition for the extra answer.

45 + 340, 315 + 81, 125 + 42, 153 + 133, 216 + 242

396, 458, 286, 279, 167, 385

Try this

Write the missing digits in these.

a) 4 □ 8 + 5 2 □ = □ 4 8
b) □ 3 □ + 1 □ 3 = 2 7 6
c) 6 □ 4 + □ 5 1 = 8 7 □

21

Activities

- Ask a pupil to place any 3-digit number on the abacus. Ask another pupil to say the number. Record it on the board, revise the place value of each digit and relate to the place value of the spikes (or loops) on the abacus. Write a sum such as 342 + 253. 'How could we work this out on the abacus?' Ask a pupil to say the answer from the abacus beads and record it on the board.
- Look at page 20. Go through the introduction with the class, reminding them that each ten rod is equivalent to 10 units and each hundred block is equivalent to 10 ten rods or 100 units. Emphasise how the sums in expanded notation reflect the apparatus in the illustrations and that those in the normal notation are how numbers appear on the abacus.
- Record a sum such as 342 + 43 in columns on the board and ask pupils to instruct you as you complete it. Point out the importance of aligning the digits correctly and demonstrate the possible outcome of aligning 43 wrongly. Repeat.
- Check that pupils are aligning the digits correctly.
- Ask for some of the results in 'Try this'. Ask pupils to explain how they worked them out.

Answers

1 a) 235 b) 349 c) 486 d) 763
e) 275 f) 278 g) 559 h) 677

2 a) 657 b) 849 c) 978 d) 655
e) 467 f) 889 g) 368 h) 635

3 45 + 340 = 385, 153 + 133 = 286, 315 + 81 = 396,
125 + 42 = 167, 216 + 242 = 458

Try this

a) 2, 0, 9 b) 1, 3, 4 c) 2, 2, 5

Lesson 5 **Subtracting 3-digit numbers: no exchange**

Pupil's Book pages 22 and 23 **Oral and mental starter: What's the question?**

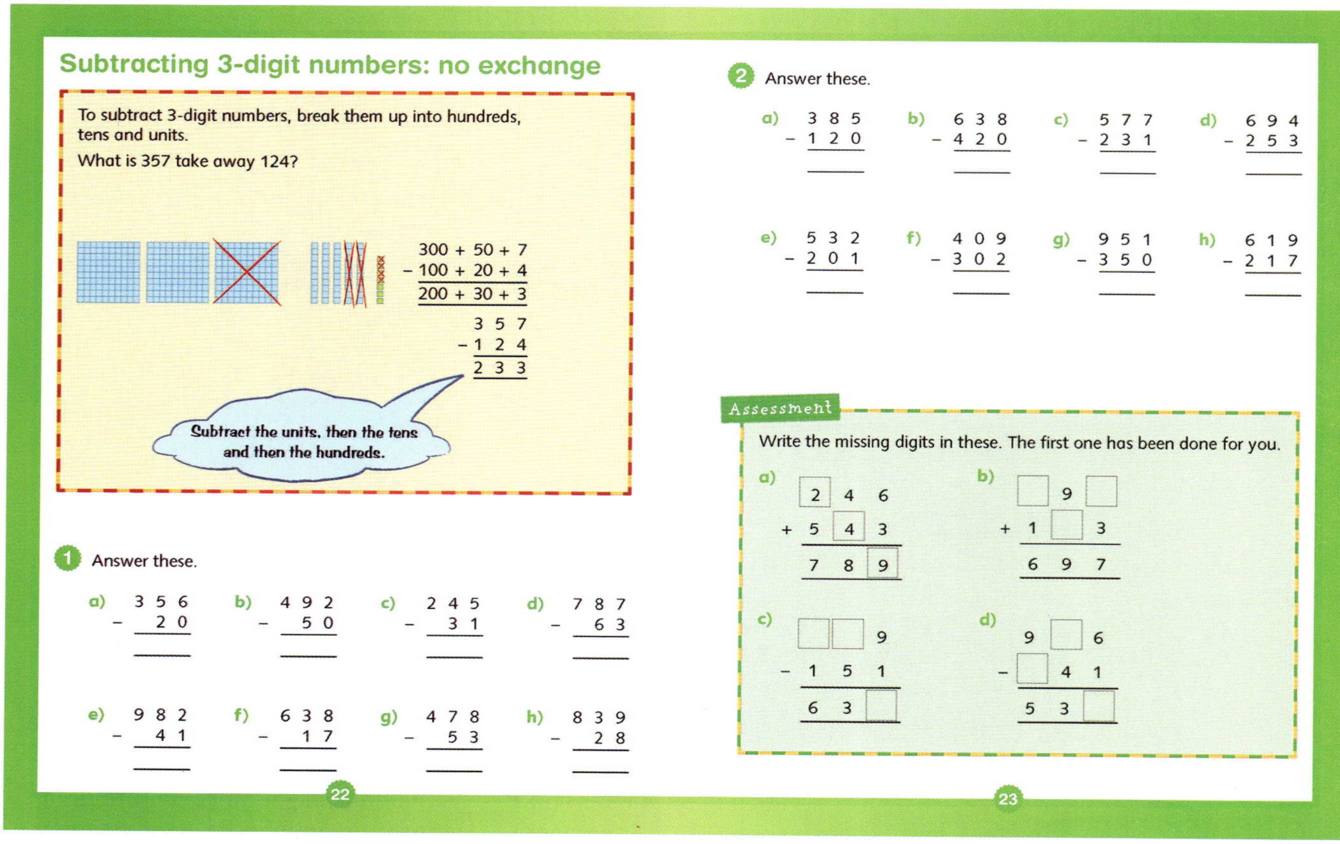

Subtracting 3-digit numbers: no exchange

To subtract 3-digit numbers, break them up into hundreds, tens and units.

What is 357 take away 124?

$$\begin{array}{r} 300 + 50 + 7 \\ -\ 100 + 20 + 4 \\ \hline 200 + 30 + 3 \end{array}$$

$$\begin{array}{r} 357 \\ -124 \\ \hline 233 \end{array}$$

Subtract the units, then the tens and then the hundreds.

1 Answer these.

a) 356 − 20 b) 492 − 50 c) 245 − 31 d) 787 − 63

e) 982 − 41 f) 638 − 17 g) 478 − 53 h) 839 − 28

22

2 Answer these.

a) 385 − 120 b) 638 − 420 c) 577 − 231 d) 694 − 253

e) 532 − 201 f) 409 − 302 g) 951 − 350 h) 619 − 217

Assessment

Write the missing digits in these. The first one has been done for you.

a) [2] 4 6 + 5 [4] 3 = 7 8 [9]

b) [ ] 9 [ ] + 1 [ ] 3 = 6 9 7

c) [ ] [ ] 9 − 1 5 1 = 6 3 [ ]

d) 9 [ ] 6 − [ ] 4 1 = 5 3 [ ]

23

Activities

- Ask a pupil to show 457 on the abacus. Ask another pupil to subtract 234 from it on the abacus. 'How many are left? How can we write that as a subtraction calculation?' Record 457 – 234 = 223 on the board. Repeat with another subtraction, e.g. 358 – 103.
- Look at page 22 and go through the introduction with the class. Emphasise that the expanded notation reflects the illustration of hundreds, tens and units materials, the normal notation reflects the abacus calculation and the way we usually record subtractions.
- Write a subtraction such as 748 – 35 vertically on the board. Work though it with the class and emphasise the importance of aligning the digits correctly. Ask 'How could we check that this is correct?' Consider all suggestions and then demonstrate using the inverse operation, i.e. adding the answer to the number which has been subtracted to give the number it was subtracted from (713 + 35 = 748). Repeat with a subtraction such as 658 – 203.
- Check that pupils are aligning the digits correctly as they work.

Answers

1	a) 336	b) 442	c) 214	d) 724
	e) 941	f) 621	g) 425	h) 811
2	a) 265	b) 218	c) 346	d) 441
	e) 331	f) 107	g) 601	h) 402

Assessment

b) 5, 0, 4 c) 7, 8, 8 d) 7, 4, 5

Unit 15 **Money**

Term 2 Block D **Addition and subtraction to 999** Unit 13 Numbers and number patterns Unit 14 Addition and subtraction to 999 **Unit 15 Money** Unit 16 Assess and review	**Objectives** *At the end of the unit, students should be able to…* Identify money (types of money). Do simple addition and subtraction problems related to money. Solve simple everyday problems (word problems) that include units of measurement (time, money). Choose the basic operation (addition – subtraction – multiplication) needed to solve a mathematical or everyday problem (word problems). Check the results of any addition, subtraction or multiplication problem.
Vocabulary coins, notes, dollar, cents, price, worth, value, cost, total, altogether, change, reduced	**Lessons** 1 Coins and notes 2 Equivalence 3 Making totals 4 Giving change 5 Money problems
Oral and mental starters Steps What's the order? Product pairs Double it Tell me a story	**Resources** Collection of coins and notes (1¢, 5¢, 10¢, 25¢, 50¢ coins; $1, $5 notes); shopping area with items labelled with their prices and money for transactions. *Pupil's Book pages 24–33*
Prior learning Recognising coins and notes Ordering coins according to their value Finding simple total costs	**Background notes** Working with money, prices and total costs is one of the most important applications of number skills in everyday life. In this unit pupils will revise and develop learning that began in Grade 1. Giving change is taught using the counting on method to find the difference between the price and the amount given. The notes and coins given as examples here are dollars and cents, as these are widely used. Other currency can be used as examples as appropriate.
End of unit evaluation Check that pupils are able to: 1 Recognise the value of coins and notes and find equivalent values. 2 Find simple totals of money. 3 Work out change from $1. 4 Solve problems involving costs using addition, subtraction and multiplication.	**Supporting the topic** Provide opportunities for pupils in small groups to buy and sell items in the shopping corner, including calculating total costs and giving change. Discuss shopping situations with which pupils are likely to be familiar in everyday life.

Lesson 1 **Coins and notes**

Pupil's Book pages 24 and 25 **Oral and mental starter: Steps**

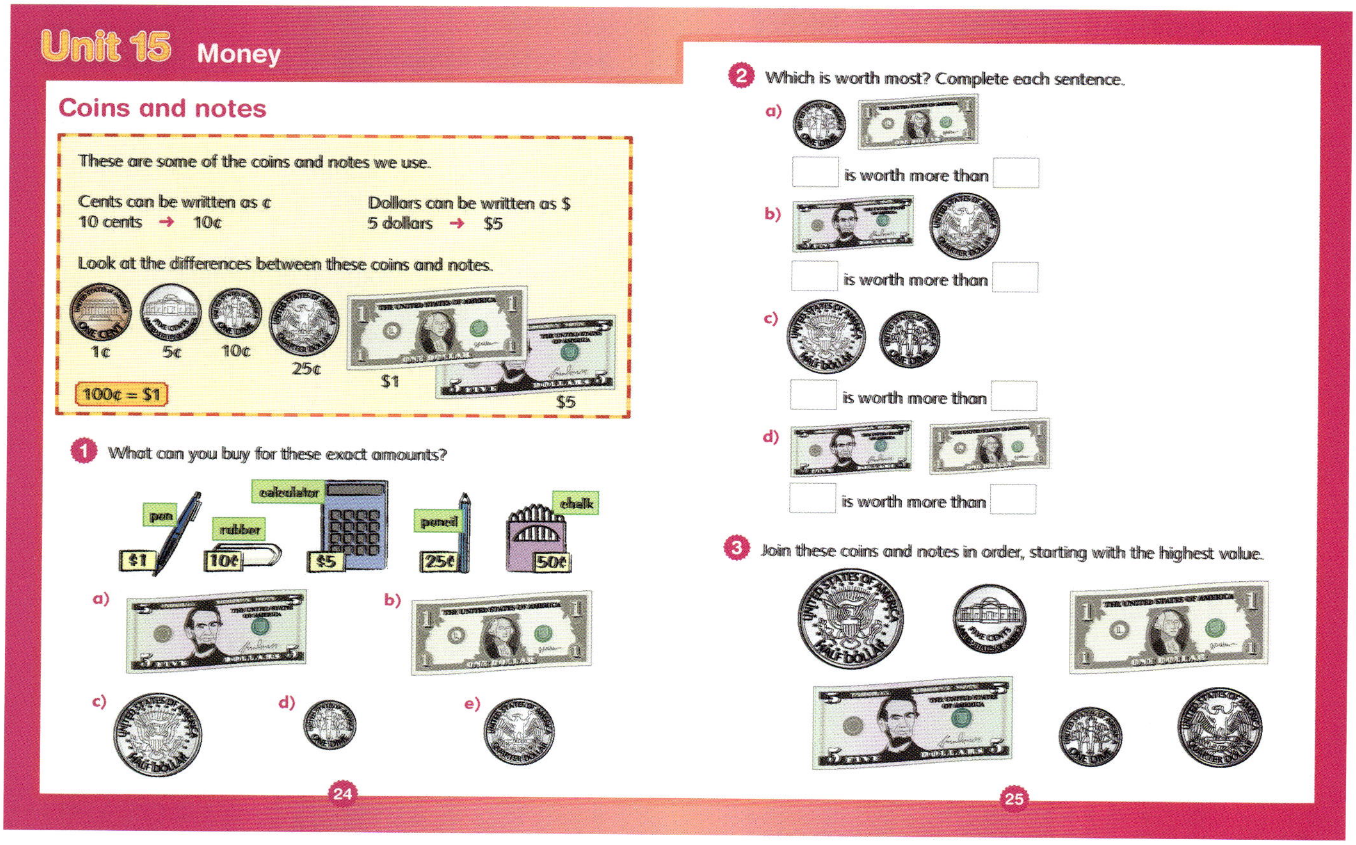

Activities

- Talk about the money we use. Ask pupils to name all the coins and notes they know.
- Pass round, or show to small groups, examples of each coin: 1¢, 5¢, 10¢, 25¢, and each note: $1 and $5 (or similar examples of your currency). Talk about the shape, distinguishing features and relative sizes of the coins and notes. Ask questions such as 'Why do the coins and notes have numbers on them? Which coin has the greatest value? Which note is worth the most? Which can you buy more with, 50¢ or $1? How many cents are there in 1 dollar?'
- Hold up different items from the shopping area which can be bought with one coin or one note. Ask pupils to suggest which coin or note they would use to pay for each item.
- Look at page 24 and go through the introduction with the class. Focus on the name of each coin and note and the way it is abbreviated. Ask pupils to put their fingers on particular coins and notes which you name. Explain that in question 1 pupils should choose one item for each coin or note.

Answers

1 a) calculator b) pen c) chalk
d) rubber e) pencil

2 a) $1 is worth more than 10¢
b) $5 is worth more than 25¢
c) 50¢ is worth more than 10¢
d) $5 is worth more than $1

3 $5 → $1 → 50¢ → 25¢ → 10¢ → 5¢

Lesson 2 **Equivalence**

Pupil's Book pages 26 and 27 **Oral and mental starter: What's the order?**

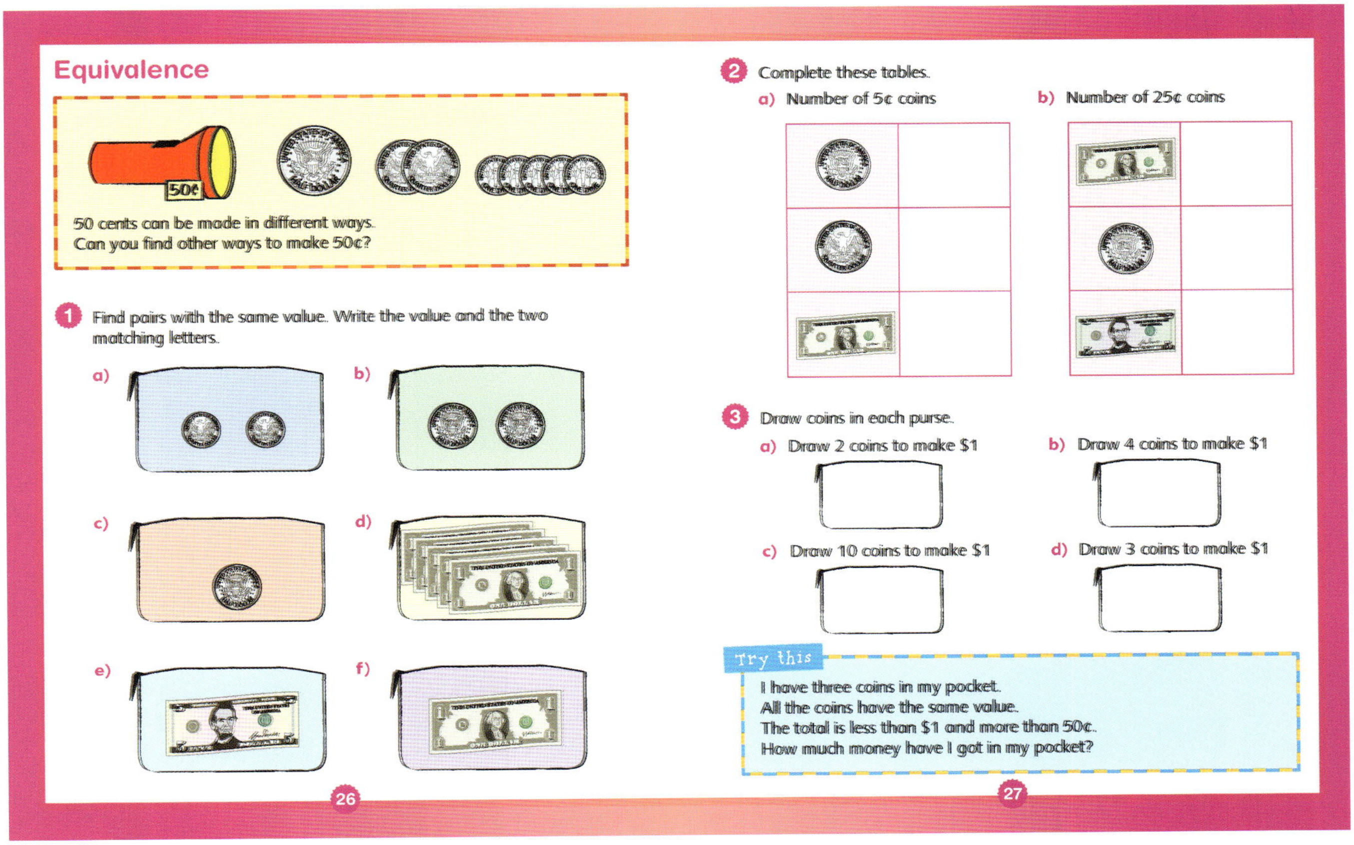

Activities

- Hold up an item from the shopping area with a 20¢ label. Ask 'How many 10¢ coins would I need to buy this? How many 5¢ coins would I need? If I had one 10¢ coin, how many 5¢ coins would I need?' Record the equivalent values on the board, e.g. 20¢ = 10¢ × 2   20¢ = 5¢ × 4
  20¢ = 10¢ + 5¢ + 5¢
- Hold up an item with a 40¢ label and ask pupils to suggest different ways of paying for it. Record each on the board as above. Repeat with other items of different values.
- Look at page 26 and go through the introduction with the class.
- Towards the end of the lesson ask pupils who did 'Try this' to explain how they worked out their results.

Answers

1 a) 25¢ and 25¢ = c) 50¢
  b) 50¢ and 50¢ = f) $1
  d) $1, $1, $1, $1 and $1 = e) $5

2 a) 10, 5, 20   b) 4, 2, 20

3 For example:
  a) 50¢, 50¢ coins
  b) 25¢, 25¢, 25¢, 25¢ coins
  c) 10¢, 10¢, 10¢, 10¢, 10¢, 10¢, 10¢, 10¢, 10¢, 10¢ coins
  d) 50¢, 25¢, 25¢ coins

Try this

75¢

Lesson 3 **Making totals**

Pupil's Book pages 28 and 29 **Oral and mental starter: Product pairs**

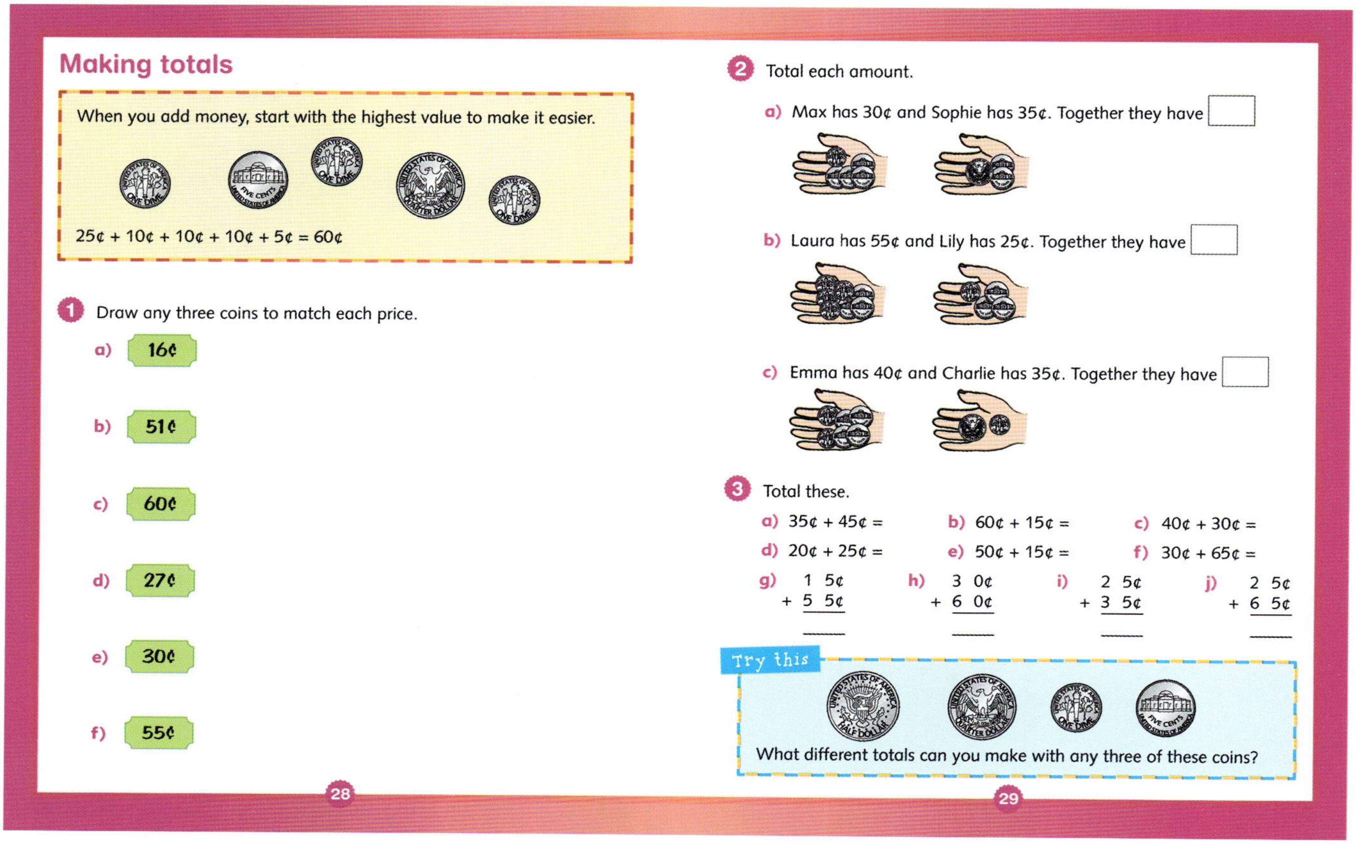
Making totals

When you add money, start with the highest value to make it easier.

25¢ + 10¢ + 10¢ + 10¢ + 5¢ = 60¢

1. Draw any three coins to match each price.
   a) 16¢
   b) 51¢
   c) 60¢
   d) 27¢
   e) 30¢
   f) 55¢

2. Total each amount.
   a) Max has 30¢ and Sophie has 35¢. Together they have
   b) Laura has 55¢ and Lily has 25¢. Together they have
   c) Emma has 40¢ and Charlie has 35¢. Together they have

3. Total these.
   a) 35¢ + 45¢ = b) 60¢ + 15¢ = c) 40¢ + 30¢ =
   d) 20¢ + 25¢ = e) 50¢ + 15¢ = f) 30¢ + 65¢ =
   g) 15¢ + 55¢ h) 30¢ + 60¢ i) 25¢ + 35¢ j) 25¢ + 65¢

Try this

What different totals can you make with any three of these coins?

28 29

Activities

- Look at page 28. Go over the first part of the introduction with the class, emphasising that starting with the highest value coin makes it easier to find the total. Model the totalling process with the children, e.g.'25¢ and 10¢ makes ...? 35¢ plus 10¢ makes ...? 45¢ plus 10¢ makes ...? and 5¢ makes ...? So there is 60¢ altogether.'
- Ask pupils to work in small groups. Give each group a set of coins and ask them to find the total. (The total should be less than $1.) Ask a group to tell you which coins they had and record the values on the board. Ask a member of the group to explain how they worked out the total. Repeat with other groups.
- Look at pages 28 and 29. Ask pupils to look at question 3 and discuss finding totals by using a horizontal written calculation or by using a vertical written calculation. Remind the class that when writing sums in columns they must align the digits correctly.

Answers

1 For example:
a) 10¢, 5¢, 1¢ b) 25¢, 25¢, 1¢ c) 25¢, 25¢, 10¢
d) 25¢, 1¢, 1¢ e) 10¢, 10¢, 10¢ f) 25¢, 25¢, 5¢

2 a) 65¢ b) 80¢ c) 75¢

3 a) 80¢ b) 75¢ c) 70¢ d) 45¢ e) 65¢
f) 95¢ g) 70¢ h) 90¢ i) 60¢ j) 90¢

Try this

50¢ + 25¢ + 10¢ = 85¢, 25¢ + 10¢ + 5¢ = 40¢,
50¢ + 10¢ + 5¢ = 65¢, 50¢ + 25¢ + 5¢ = 80¢

Lesson 4 **Giving change**

Pupil's Book pages 30 and 31 **Oral and mental starter: Double it**

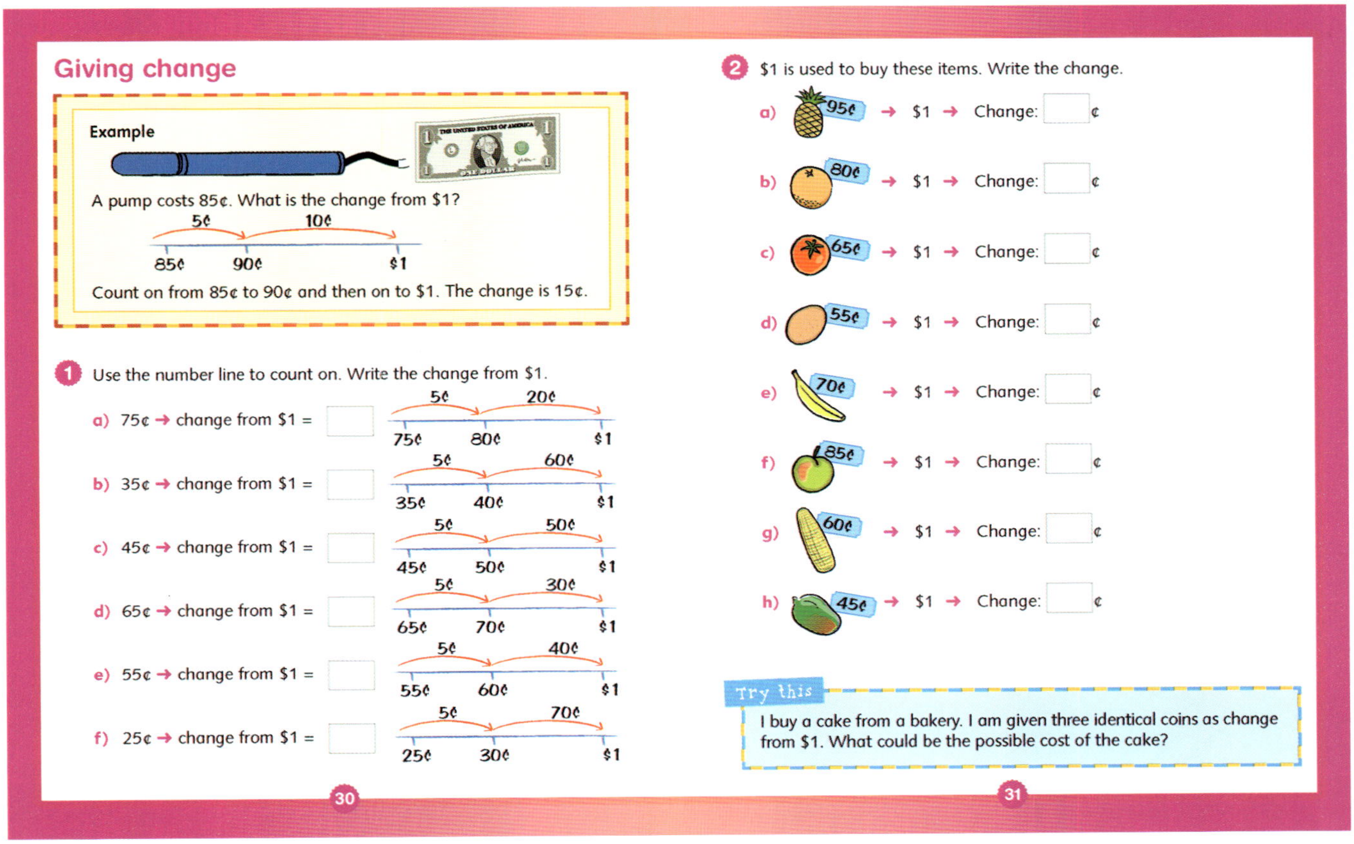

Giving change

Example

A pump costs 85¢. What is the change from $1?

5¢ 10¢

85¢ 90¢ $1

Count on from 85¢ to 90¢ and then on to $1. The change is 15¢.

1 Use the number line to count on. Write the change from $1.

a) 75¢ → change from $1 = ☐ (5¢, 20¢; 75¢, 80¢, $1)

b) 35¢ → change from $1 = ☐ (5¢, 60¢; 35¢, 40¢, $1)

c) 45¢ → change from $1 = ☐ (5¢, 50¢; 45¢, 50¢, $1)

d) 65¢ → change from $1 = ☐ (5¢, 30¢; 65¢, 70¢, $1)

e) 55¢ → change from $1 = ☐ (5¢, 40¢; 55¢, 60¢, $1)

f) 25¢ → change from $1 = ☐ (5¢, 70¢; 25¢, 30¢, $1)

2 $1 is used to buy these items. Write the change.

a) 95¢ → $1 → Change: ☐ ¢

b) 80¢ → $1 → Change: ☐ ¢

c) 65¢ → $1 → Change: ☐ ¢

d) 55¢ → $1 → Change: ☐ ¢

e) 70¢ → $1 → Change: ☐ ¢

f) 85¢ → $1 → Change: ☐ ¢

g) 60¢ → $1 → Change: ☐ ¢

h) 45¢ → $1 → Change: ☐ ¢

Try this

I buy a cake from a bakery. I am given three identical coins as change from $1. What could be the possible cost of the cake?

30 31

Activities

- Talk about shopping and giving change, e.g. 'What happens when we go shopping and we don't have exactly the right coins to give to the shopkeeper/stallholder?' Establish that coins to a higher value than the cost are presented then change is given.
- Ask 'If I bought something which cost 90¢ and gave the shopkeeper $1, how much change would I get? How did you work that out?' Demonstrate counting on by asking a pupil to give you $1 for a 90¢ item from the class shop. Emphasise that the pupil has an item worth 90¢, so needs 10¢ more to make up the value of the $1 given to you. Stress that 90¢ + 10¢ = $1. Provide a few more simple examples, e.g. cost 30¢, change from 50¢; cost 60¢, change from 75¢; cost 20¢, change from 25¢. Each time emphasise that the cost and the change must total the amount given.
- Look at page 30. Talk through the example and how the change is modelled by counting on from the price on the number line, i.e. finding the difference between the cost and the amount given to the shopkeeper. Emphasise that the price label is the starting point of the line and that the steps taken to the next 10, then to the coin given, represent the change.
- At the end of the lesson ask for all the possibilities pupils found in 'Try this'.

Answers

1 a) 25¢ b) 65¢ c) 55¢ d) 35¢ e) 45¢ f) 75¢

2 a) 5¢ b) 20¢ c) 35¢ d) 45¢
e) 30¢ f) 15¢ g) 40¢ h) 55¢

Try this

97¢, 85¢, 70¢ or 25¢

Lesson 5 **Money problems**

Pupil's Book pages 32 and 33 **Oral and mental starter: Tell me a story**

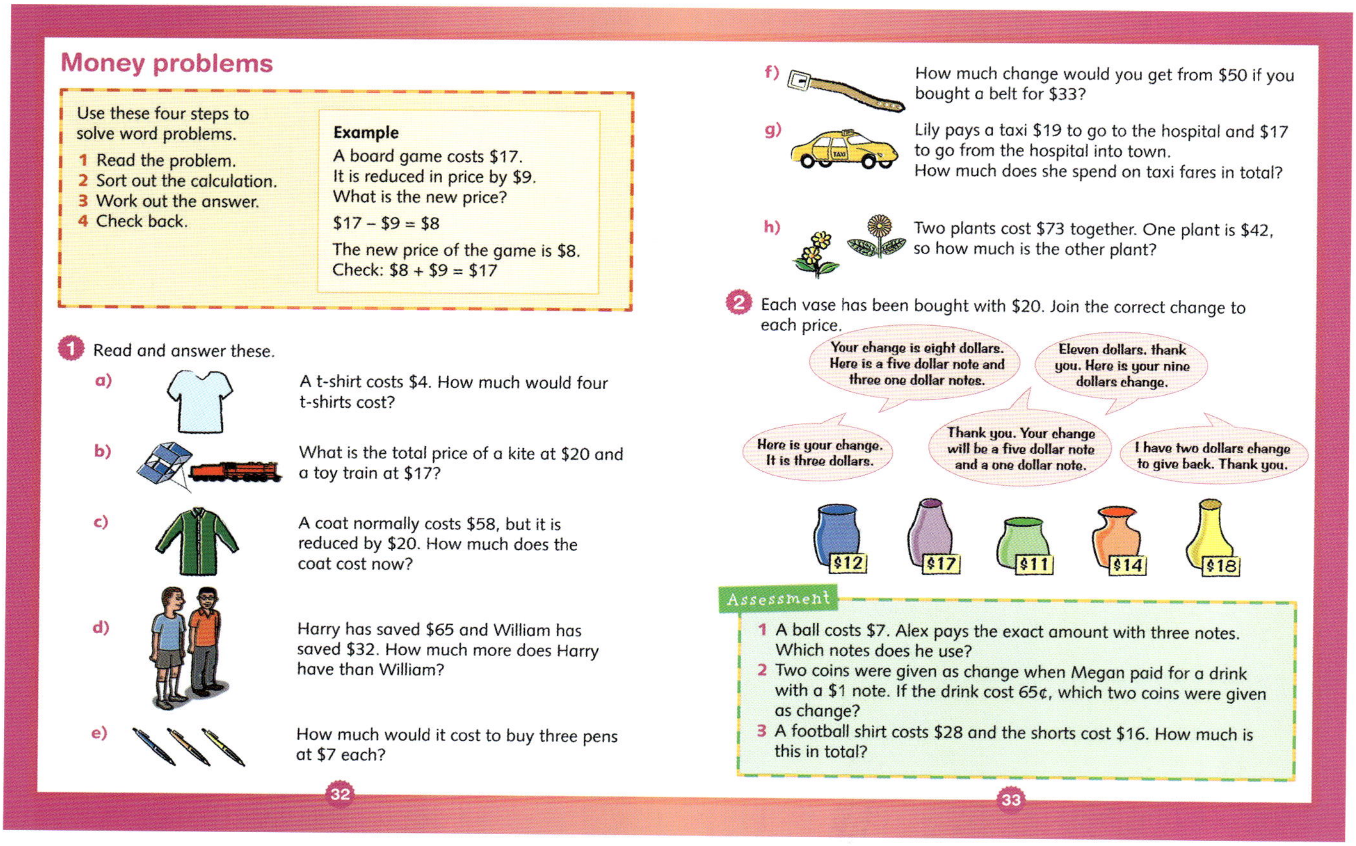

Money problems

Use these four steps to solve word problems.

1 Read the problem.
2 Sort out the calculation.
3 Work out the answer.
4 Check back.

Example
A board game costs $17.
It is reduced in price by $9.
What is the new price?
$17 – $9 = $8
The new price of the game is $8.
Check: $8 + $9 = $17

1 Read and answer these.

a) A t-shirt costs $4. How much would four t-shirts cost?

b) What is the total price of a kite at $20 and a toy train at $17?

c) A coat normally costs $58, but it is reduced by $20. How much does the coat cost now?

d) Harry has saved $65 and William has saved $32. How much more does Harry have than William?

e) How much would it cost to buy three pens at $7 each?

32

f) How much change would you get from $50 if you bought a belt for $33?

g) Lily pays a taxi $19 to go to the hospital and $17 to go from the hospital into town. How much does she spend on taxi fares in total?

h) Two plants cost $73 together. One plant is $42, so how much is the other plant?

2 Each vase has been bought with $20. Join the correct change to each price.

Your change is eight dollars. Here is a five dollar note and three one dollar notes.
Eleven dollars, thank you. Here is your nine dollars change.
Here is your change. It is three dollars.
Thank you. Your change will be a five dollar note and a one dollar note.
I have two dollars change to give back. Thank you.

$12 $17 $11 $14 $18

Assessment

1 A ball costs $7. Alex pays the exact amount with three notes. Which notes does he use?
2 Two coins were given as change when Megan paid for a drink with a $1 note. If the drink cost 65¢, which two coins were given as change?
3 A football shirt costs $28 and the shorts cost $16. How much is this in total?

33

Activities

- Write a word problem on the board and ask pupils to think about how they would work it out, e.g. 'A woman bought 5 oranges which cost 20¢ each. What was the total price?' After a few moments ask volunteers to give their ideas. Establish that the answer could be found by adding five 20ps together, but a quicker way is to use multiplication. Record the calculations on the board and ask pupils to give an answer to the word problem. Record a full answer on the board, e.g. The oranges cost $1 altogether.
- Repeat the process above using a problem which involves subtraction, e.g. choose two items from the class shop, give their prices and ask how much more one costs than the other.
- Look at page 32 and go through the introduction with the class. Emphasise the four steps then discuss the problem, the calculation, how to check the result and how the word problem is answered in a sentence. Stress that when answering word problems the number should be set in context.

Answers

1 a) $16 b) $37 c) $38 d) $33
e) $21 f) $17 g) $36 h) $31

2 A → U, B → X, C → V, D → Y, E → Z

Assessment

1 $5, $1, $1

2 25¢, 10¢

3 $44

Unit 16 **Assess and review**

Term 2 Block D
Addition and subtraction to 999

Final evaluation

Check that pupils are able to:

1. Read and write numbers to 999.
2. Identify place value in numbers to 999.
3. Compare and order numbers to 999.
4. Identify and complete simple number patterns and sequences.
5. Approximate answers before carrying out a written calculation.
6. Add and subtract multiples of 100 mentally.
7. Add and subtract 3-digit numbers (without exchange).
8. Recognise the value of coins and notes and find equivalent values.
9. Find simple totals of money.
10. Work out change from $1.
11. Solve problems involving costs using addition, subtraction and multiplication.

Vocabulary

odd, even, digit, hundreds, tens, units, abacus, grid, pattern, multiple, sequence, compare, greater, greatest, smaller, smallest, order, rounding, round up/down, nearest ten, approximate, approximately, addition, add, subtraction, subtract, column, coins, notes, cents, dollars, price, worth, value, cost, total, altogether, change, reduced

Resources

Abacus
Collection of all types of coins and notes
Shopping area with items labelled with their prices and money for transactions
Pupil's Book pages 34–39

Pupil's Book pages 34–39

1. Ask the class to count in 2s from 164 to 180; 10s from 500 to 600; 5s from 180 to 220. (page 34)
2. Write 371, 463, 327 and 470 on the board. Ask 'Which is the smallest number? How do you know? Which is the next smallest? Which comes next? How do you know? Which is the largest?' (page 35)
3. Revise rounding numbers up or down to work out an approximate answer. (page 36)
4. Remind pupils how the adding (function) machines work. (page 36)
5. Remind pupils how to complete an addition wall. (page 37)
6. Ask 'How much change would I get from 50p if I bought something which cost 30p? How did you work it out? How much change would I get if I gave the shopkeeper $1? How did you work it out?' (page 38)

Assessment activities

Use these to assess pupils' knowledge and understanding:

Look at these numbers (e.g. 657 and 675). Which is the largest number? How do you know?
What are the missing numbers in this sequence? How do you know?
Put this set of numbers in order (e.g. number cards for 253, 367, 229, 40). How did you work it out?
Read this (3-digit) number (written in words). Can you write it as a 3-digit number?
What is the value of the 7 in this number? (673) What about the 6? How many units are there?
What is 74 to the nearest ten? What about 75? What is the approximate answer to 43 + 65?
What is: 300 + 200, 800 – 400?

Write the answers to these:

$$\begin{array}{r} 563 \\ +\ \underline{214} \end{array} \qquad \begin{array}{r} 648 \\ -\ \underline{306} \end{array}$$

What is the value of each of these coins and notes? How many 5¢ coins are worth the same as a 50¢ coin?
How many cents make $1?
What is the total value of this money?
How much change should I get from $1 if I buy this item from the shop? How much would it cost to buy three of these items?

Assess and review activities

Use these activities taken from the previous three weeks to monitor, evaluate and consolidate pupils' knowledge and understanding.

- Ask pupils to each take a handful of counters, count them, then try to halve them to see whether they have an even number or an odd number. Ask individual pupils how many counters they had and whether that is an odd or even number. Record the numbers in two lists on the board, headed 'odd' and 'even'. Confirm that the odd numbers end in 1, 3, 5, 7 or 9 and the even numbers in 0, 2, 4, 6 or 8.
- Using the classroom 1–100 grid ask pupils to comment on any patterns they can see, e.g. consecutive numbers along the rows; multiples of 10 down the right-hand column; all columns have the same units digits; every other number along the rows is odd/even.
- Write a sequence such as 315, 415, 515, 615 on the board. 'What sort of count is shown in this sequence?' Establish that it is counting on in 100s. 'What are the next two numbers? Which number comes before 315?' Repeat using other sequences.
- Write pairs of numbers on the board such as 167 and 176; 431 and 428; 360 and 300. Ask pupils to compare each pair and say which is the smaller.
- Write a set of numbers on the board such as 830, 652, 237, 678, 838. Ask pupils to find the smallest, compare the tens to find the next number, compare the units in numbers with the same hundreds and tens value. Repeat for another set of numbers such as 291, 440, 296, 196, 432.
- Provide 2-digit additions and subtractions for pupils to approximate the result by rounding then adding or subtracting tens, e.g. 54 + 27, 67 – 25, 48 + 33, 83 – 26.
- Ask the class to count in hundreds to 900 and back. Ask them to start at 200 and count in 200s to 800, then from 100 to 900 (in 200s).
- Write a sum such as 342 + 253 on the board. 'How could we work this out on the abacus?' Follow a sensible instruction, ask a pupil to say the answer from the abacus beads and record it.
- Write a subtraction such as 748 – 35 vertically on the board. Work though it and emphasise the importance of aligning the digits correctly. Repeat with a subtraction such as 658 – 203.
- Hold up different items from the shopping area which can be bought with one coin or one note. Ask pupils to suggest which coin or note they would use to pay for each item.
- Hold up an item with a 40¢ label and ask pupils to suggest different ways of paying for it. Record each on the board. Repeat.
- Ask pupils to work in small groups. Give each group a set of coins and ask them to find the total. Ask a group to tell you which coins they had and record the values on the board. Ask how they worked out the total. Repeat with other groups.
- 'If I bought something which cost 90¢ and gave the shopkeeper $1, how much change would I get? How did you work that out?' Provide a few more simple examples, e.g. cost 30¢, change from 50¢; cost 60¢, change from 75¢; cost 20¢, change from 25¢. Each time emphasise that the cost and the change must total the amount given.
- Write a word problem on the board and ask pupils to think about how they would work it out. Ask for their ideas and record the calculation(s). Record a full answer to the word problem.

Unit 16 Assess and review

Numbers and number patterns

1 Write the missing numbers in these sequences.

a)	45	47	49			55	
b)	96				104	106	108
c)	230	240		260	270		
d)	350	355			370	375	
e)	410	412			418		422
f)	297	299		303	305		

2 Complete this 100-square.

Count in 2s, 3s, 4s, 5s and 10s and look at the patterns on the grid.

1	2	3						9	10
			14						20
21				25					
			34	35	36				
		53							60
61						67			70
71									
								89	
			94						

3 Look at these price labels.
Compare them and write the highest price.

a) \$79 \$74 b) \$102 \$111 c) \$192 \$197

d) \$141 \$139 e) \$203 \$199 f) \$311 \$309

4 Look at these numbers.

a) Which is the smallest number?
b) Which is the largest number?
c) Which numbers are greater than 500?
d) Write the numbers in order, starting with the smallest.

Try this

Use the digits 3, 4 and 5.

Make as many different 1-digit, 2-digit and 3-digit numbers as you can.
Write them in order, starting with the smallest.

Addition and subtraction to 999

1 These are adding machines. What numbers will come out of each machine?

Write an approximate answer first and then work out the answer.

a)

In	Approximate answer	Answer
28		
39		
15		
26		
37		

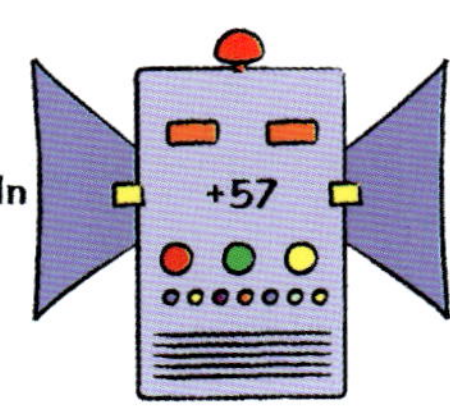

b)

In	Approximate answer	Answer
55		
27		
49		
38		
46		

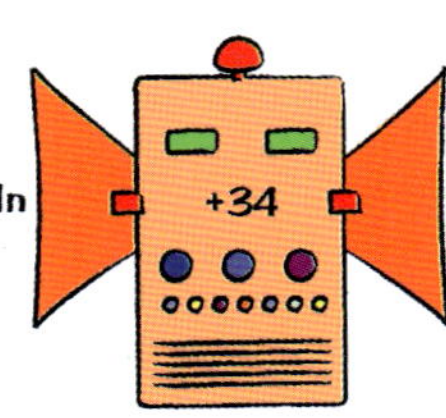

2 Complete these addition walls.

a)

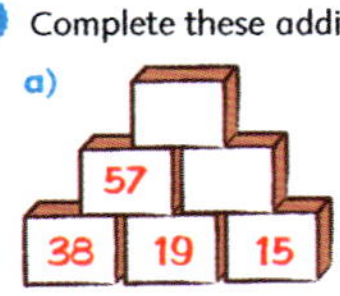

b)

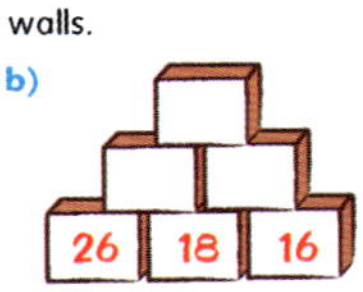

c)

3 Answer these.

a) 152 + 720
b) 631 + 247
c) 146 + 343
d) 835 − 420
e) 518 − 307
f) 946 − 134

4 Complete these.

a) □36 + 52□ = 7□6
b) □3□ + 4□7 = 549
c) 345 + □4□ = 6□9
d) 93□ − □21 = 6□7
e) 85□ − 1□3 = □16
f) 7□6 − □52 = 53□

Try this

Find five different ways to complete each of these.

□ + □ = 750 □ − □ = 250

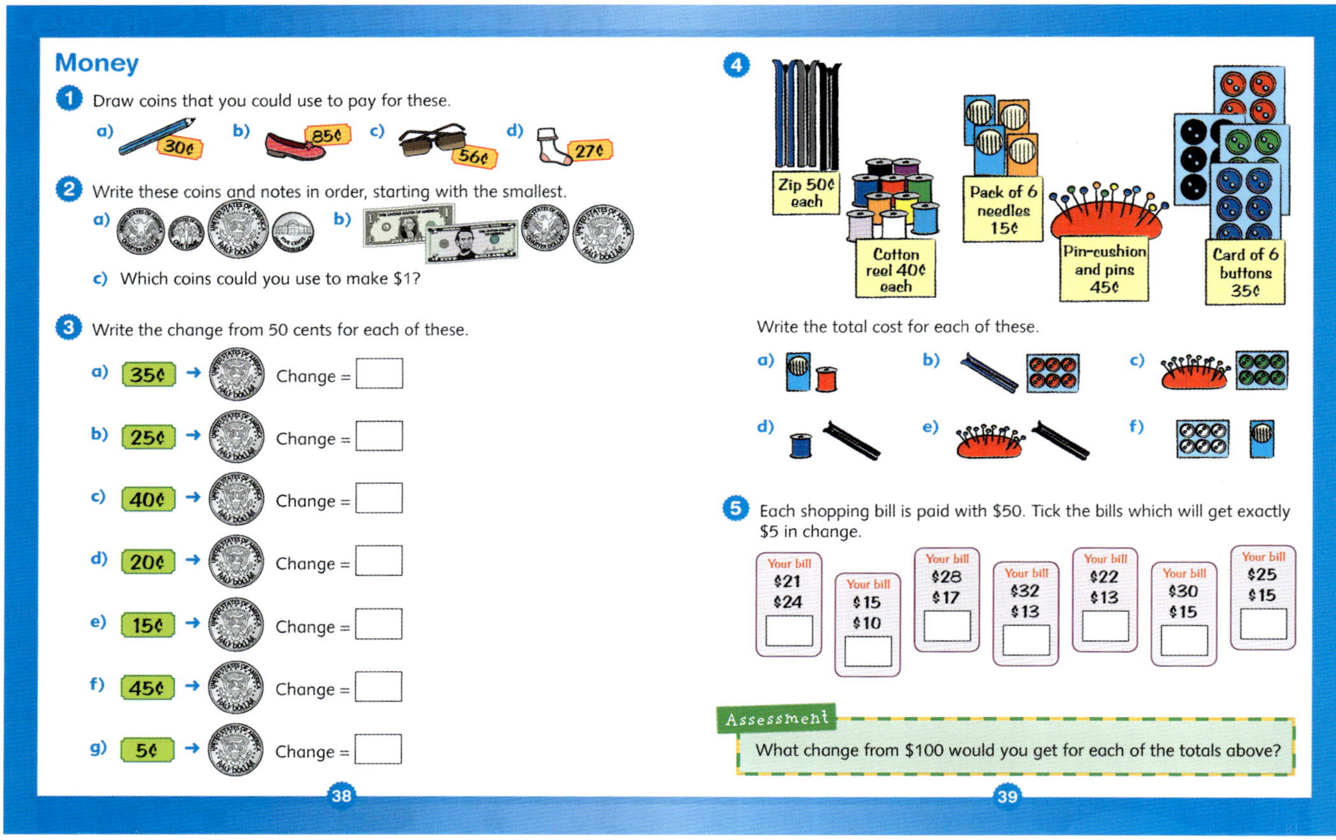

Money

1 Draw coins that you could use to pay for these.

a) 30¢ b) 85¢ c) 56¢ d) 27¢

2 Write these coins and notes in order, starting with the smallest.

a) b)

c) Which coins could you use to make $1?

3 Write the change from 50 cents for each of these.

a) 35¢ → Change =
b) 25¢ → Change =
c) 40¢ → Change =
d) 20¢ → Change =
e) 15¢ → Change =
f) 45¢ → Change =
g) 5¢ → Change =

4 Zip 50¢ each; Cotton reel 40¢ each; Pack of 6 needles 15¢; Pin-cushion and pins 45¢; Card of 6 buttons 35¢

Write the total cost for each of these.

a) b) c) d) e) f)

5 Each shopping bill is paid with $50. Tick the bills which will get exactly $5 in change.

Your bill $21 $24; Your bill $15 $10; Your bill $28 $17; Your bill $32 $13; Your bill $22 $13; Your bill $30 $15; Your bill $25 $15

Assessment

What change from $100 would you get for each of the totals above?

38 39

Answers pages 34 and 35

1 a) 51, 53, 57 b) 98, 100, 102 c) 250, 280, 290
d) 360, 365, 380 e) 414, 416, 420 f) 301, 307, 309

2

1	2	3	4	5	6	7	8	9	10
11	12	13	14	15	16	17	18	19	20
21	22	23	24	25	26	27	28	29	30
31	32	33	34	35	36	37	38	39	40
41	42	43	44	45	46	47	48	49	50
51	52	53	54	55	56	57	58	59	60
61	62	63	64	65	66	67	68	69	70
71	72	73	74	75	76	77	78	79	80
81	82	83	84	85	86	87	88	89	90
91	92	93	94	95	96	97	98	99	100

3 a) $79 b) $111 c) $197
d) $141 e) $203 f) $311

4 a) 218 b) 637 c) 502, 610, 637
d) 218, 229, 440, 449, 502, 610, 637

Try this

3, 4, 5, 34, 35, 43, 45, 53, 54, 345, 354, 435, 453, 534, 543

Answers pages 36 and 37

1 a) 90, 85; 100, 96; 80, 72; 90, 83; 100, 94
b) 90, 89; 60, 61; 80, 83; 70, 72; 80, 80

2 a) 91, 34 b) 78, 44, 34 c) 94, 46, 48

3 a) 872 b) 878 c) 489 d) 415 e) 211 f) 812

4 a) **236** + 520 = **756** b) **132** + 417 = 549
c) 345 + **344** = 689 d) 938 – **321** = 617
e) **859** – 143 = 716 f) 786 – **252** = 534

Answers pages 38 and 39

2 a) 5¢, 10¢, 25¢, 50¢ b) 25¢, 50¢, $1, $5

3 a) 15¢ b) 25¢ c) 10¢ d) 30¢
e) 35¢ f) 5¢ g) 45¢

4 a) 55¢ b) 85¢ c) 80¢ d) 90¢ e) 95¢ f) 50¢

5 $21 & $24, $28 & $17, $32 & $13, $30 & $15

Assessment

$55, $75, $55, $55, $65, $55, $60

Block E Geometry

Maths Topic	National Standards from Government Guidelines	
Unit	*Curriculum area*	*End of year objectives / success criteria*
17 Flat and solid shapes	Analyse the characteristics of 3-, 2- and 1-dimensional geometrical shapes, and identify the relations between them Solve Mathematical and everyday Problems using sense of place and geometric modelling	Differentiate between and draw a closed curve and an open curve. Name (State) the segments that compose a shape. Name some properties of solids. Spot geometric shapes in solids. Form and differentiate mental images of familiar geometric shapes depending on spatial memory and perception of things.
18 Lines and shapes	Analyse the characteristics of 3-, 2- and 1-dimensional geometrical shapes, and identify the relation between them Solve Mathematical and everyday Problems using sense of place and geometric modelling	Differentiate between straight line, segment and ray. Demonstrate the relation between a given point and a closed curve, polygon or straight line. Identify a polygon. Name (State) the segments that compose a shape. Use squared or graph paper to draw a polygon. Identify symmetrical and non-symmetrical shapes. Determine the line of symmetry in a shape. Form and differentiate mental images of familiar geometric shapes.
19 Area of shapes	Analyse the characteristics of 3-, 2- and 1-dimensional geometrical shapes, and identify the relation between them Solve Mathematical and everyday Problems using sense of place and geometric modelling	Understand the meaning of congruency. Identify two congruent shapes. Use congruency in simple everyday situations. Use squared or graph paper to draw a polygon. Use shape cards to form defined flat areas. Practically arrange some simple geometric shapes so that they occupy the least space possible. Dissect simple shapes (flat or solid) into parts and reassemble them to form the same shape or a new one.
20 Assess and review	Revision and assessment of previous 3 units – problems, formative and summative assessment. Monitor, assess, evaluate and consolidate pupils' knowledge and understanding.	

During this block of work, pupils will experience:

1. Comparing: open and closed shapes; flat shapes; solid shapes; cubes and cuboids.
2. Identifying properties of solid shapes.
3. Distinguishing between lines, segments and rays using their definitions.
4. Using line segments to construct polygons.
5. Using the properties of triangles, squares and rectangles.
6. Identifying symmetrical shapes.
7. Identifying lines of symmetry.
8. Finding the area of shapes.
9. Identifying and drawing congruent shapes in different orientations.
10. Making tiling patterns from congruent shapes.
11. Dissecting shapes and rearranging the parts to make other shapes.

Unit 17 Flat and solid shapes

Term 2 Block E **Geometry** **Unit 17 Flat and solid shapes** Unit 18 Lines and shapes Unit 19 Area of shapes Unit 20 Assess and review	**Objectives** *At the end of the unit, students should be able to…* Differentiate between and draw a closed curve and an open curve. Name (State) the segments that compose a shape. Name some properties of solids. Spot geometric shapes in solids. Form and differentiate mental images of familiar geometric shapes depending on spatial memory and perception of things.
Vocabulary open shape, closed shape, square, rectangle, triangle, circle, cube, cuboid, cylinder, sphere, pyramid, faces, face, edge, vertex, properties	**Lessons** 1 Open and closed shapes 2 Comparing flat shapes 3 Comparing solid shapes 4 Cubes and cuboids 5 Properties of solid shapes
Oral and mental starters Hidden fingers Quarter it Tell me a story Product pairs Hold up	**Resources** Sets of solid shapes: cubes, cuboids, cylinders, spheres and pyramids Sets of flat shapes including different types of triangle, different sizes of squares, rectangles and circles A large display chart of shapes in different sizes and positions Strips of card (4 per pupil, lesson 1 'Try this') *Pupil's Book pages 40–49*
Prior learning Identifying and naming squares, rectangles, triangles, circles, cubes, cuboids, cylinders, spheres, pyramids and cones Distinguishing between squares and rectangles Understanding the term 'face'	**Background notes** This unit revises and develops the learning begun in Grade 1 to include further properties of 2-D and 3-D shapes.
End of unit evaluation Check that pupils are able to: 1 Distinguish between open and closed lines, including curves. 2 Name squares, rectangles, circles, triangles, cubes, cuboids, spheres, cylinders and pyramids. 3 Name properties of shapes, e.g. How many curved or straight sides? Number and shape of faces, number of vertices and edges. 4 Explain the differences and similarities between cubes and cuboids. 5 Name shapes from a description.	**Supporting the topic** Provide opportunities for pupils to use the collection of shapes, e.g. choose a shape and describe it to a partner who names the shape from its description. Draw and paint shape patterns and pictures in art. Identify, describe and discuss shapes seen in and around the school and at home.

Lesson 1 Open and closed shapes

Pupil's Book pages 40 and 41 **Oral and mental starter: Hidden fingers**

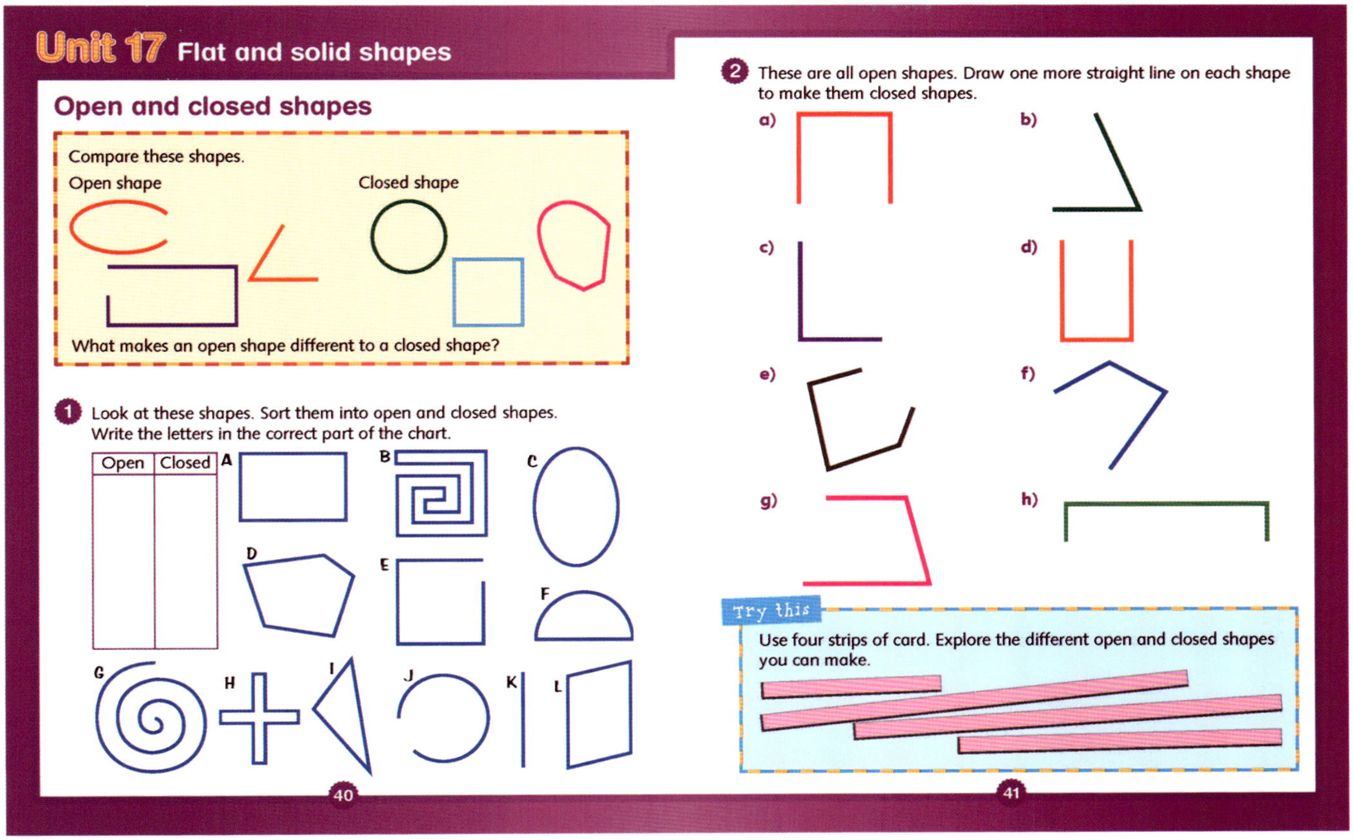

Activities

- Write the letters U, O, A, S, B, C, L, D on the board. Ask the class to pick out the letter you are describing, e.g. 'This letter looks like an open triangle with a line across the middle making a small triangle.' Repeat for another letter, then ask pupils in pairs to each describe one of the other shapes for their partner to identify.
- Ask 'Which letters are open curves? Which have closed curves? Which have straight lines? Which have vertices?'
- Look at page 40 and go through the introduction with the class. Ask 'Which closed shapes can you see in the classroom? Can you see any open shapes? Can you think of any open or closed shapes at home?'
- At the end of the lesson draw some of the shapes pupils made in 'Try this' on the board. Point to each in turn and ask the class to say 'open' or 'closed'.

Answers

1 Open: E, G, J, K; closed: A, B, C, D, F, H, I, L

2 a) rectangle b) triangle c) triangle
d) rectangle e) pentagon f) quadrilateral
g) trapezium h) rectangle

Lesson 2 **Comparing flat shapes**

Pupil's Book pages 42 and 43 **Oral and mental starter: Quarter it**

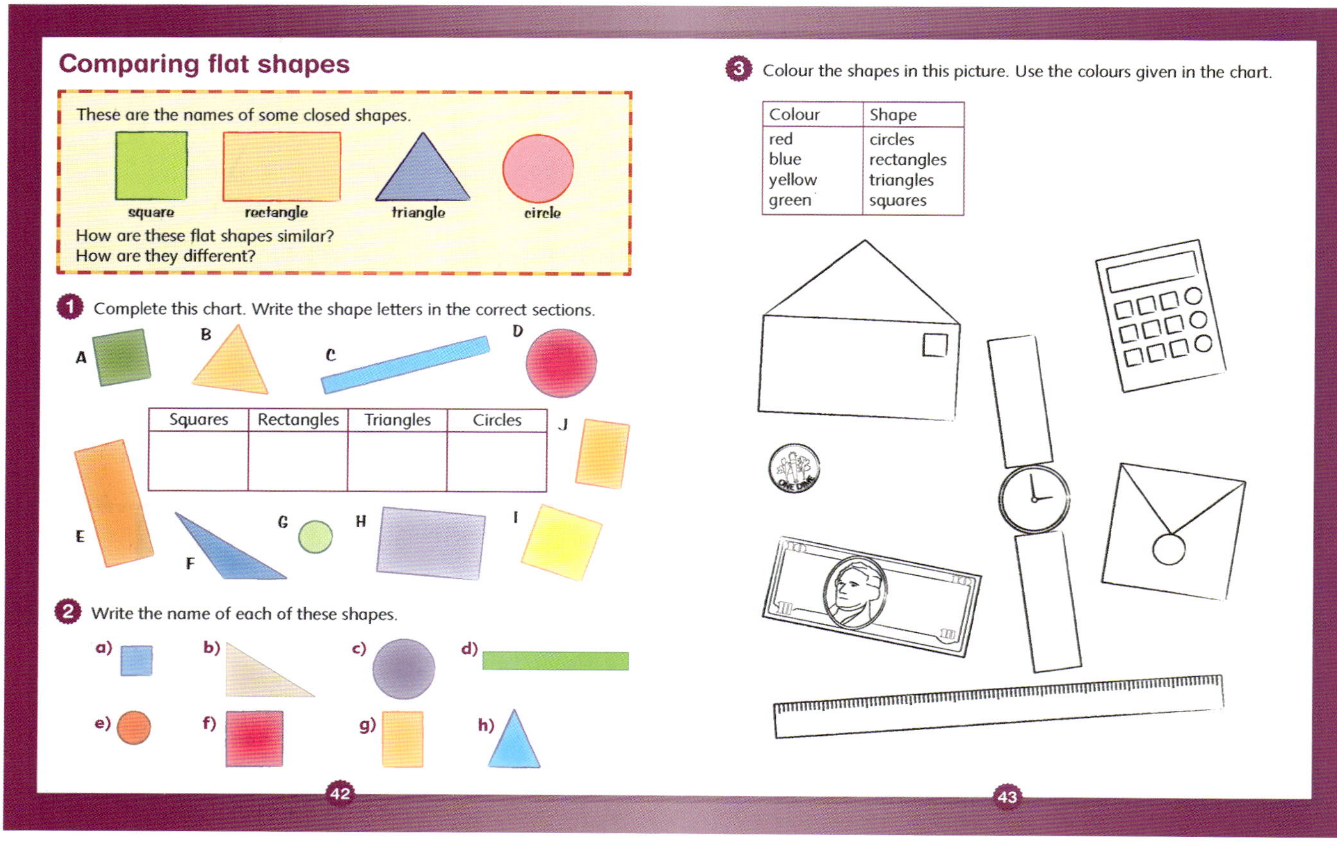

Comparing flat shapes

These are the names of some closed shapes.

square rectangle triangle circle

How are these flat shapes similar?
How are they different?

1 Complete this chart. Write the shape letters in the correct sections.

Squares	Rectangles	Triangles	Circles

A B C D E F G H I J

2 Write the name of each of these shapes.

a) b) c) d) e) f) g) h)

42

3 Colour the shapes in this picture. Use the colours given in the chart.

Colour	Shape
red blue yellow green	circles rectangles triangles squares

43

Activities

- Ask a pupil to select a solid shape from the classroom collection which has a square face and hold it up to show the class. Ask other pupils to do the same for shapes with a rectangular face, a triangular face and a circular face.
- Look at page 42. Talk about the names of the shapes, then discuss how they are similar and how they are different. Look at the classroom chart of shapes. Point to circles, squares, rectangles and triangles, one at a time, and ask the class to say their names together.
- Ask pupils to answer the two questions at the end of the introduction.
- Ask pupils to close their eyes as you describe each of the four shapes in random order. Ask them to raise their hands when they know which shape it is. Repeat the description if necessary. When most of the hands are raised ask the class to name the shape together.
- At the end of the lesson ask pupils to point to a square which they can see in the classroom. Repeat for the other three shapes.

Answers

1 Squares: A, I; rectangles: C, E, H, J; triangles: B, F; circles: D, G

2 a) square b) triangle c) circle d) rectangle
e) circle f) square g) rectangle h) triangle

Lesson 3 **Comparing solid shapes**

Pupil's Book pages 44 and 45 **Oral and mental starter: Tell me a story**

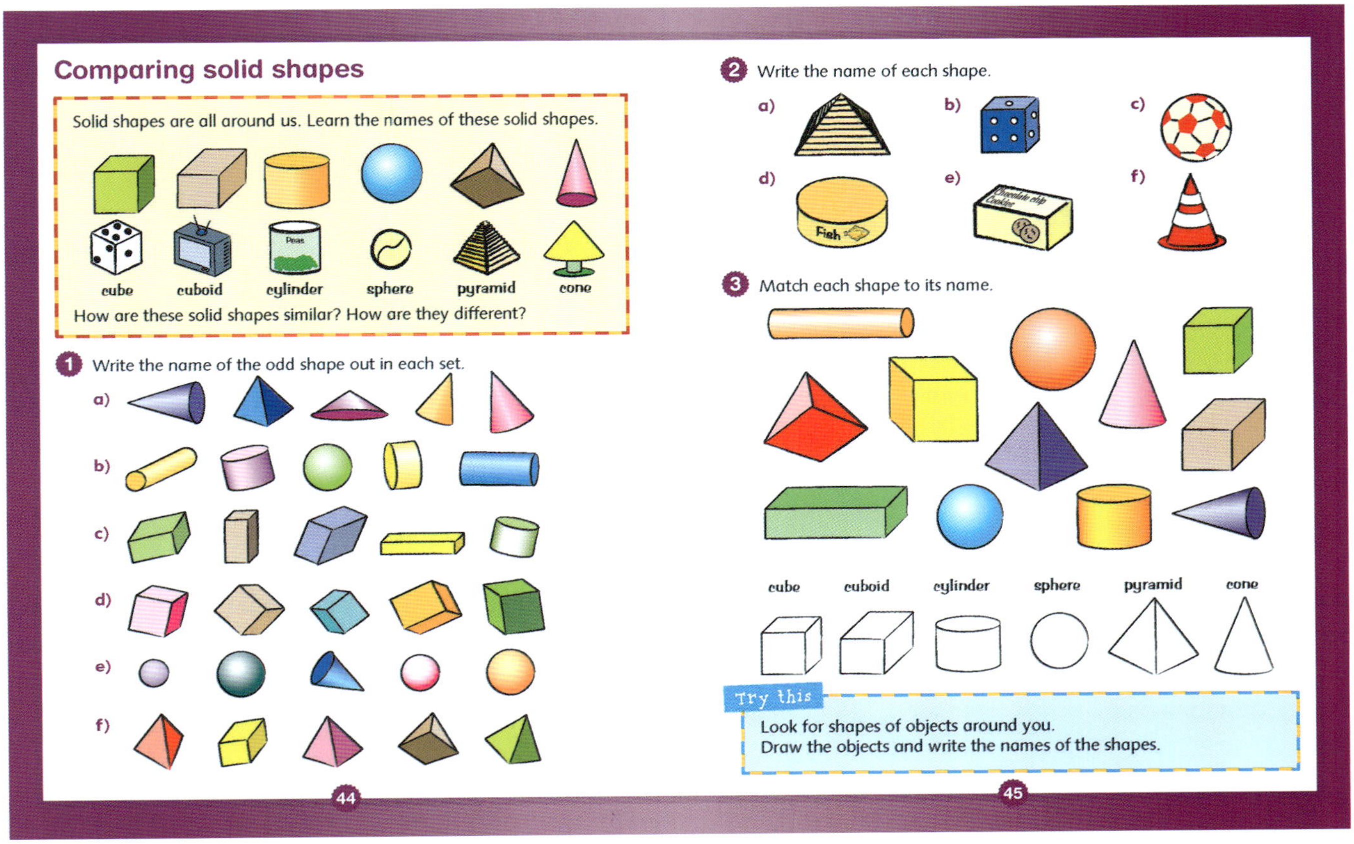

Comparing solid shapes

Solid shapes are all around us. Learn the names of these solid shapes.

cube cuboid cylinder sphere pyramid cone

How are these solid shapes similar? How are they different?

1 Write the name of the odd shape out in each set.

a) b) c) d) e) f)

44

2 Write the name of each shape.

a) b) c) d) e) f)

3 Match each shape to its name.

cube cuboid cylinder sphere pyramid cone

Try this

Look for shapes of objects around you.
Draw the objects and write the names of the shapes.

45

Activities

- Look at page 44. Say the name of each shape in the introduction together. Ask pupils to put a finger on each shape as you name them in random order. Compare the shapes by responses to the two questions in the introduction.
- Hold up different examples of each shape from the classroom collection. Ask the class to identify each one by comparing it with the illustrations and to name it together on your signal.
- Ask for examples of each shape that they can see in the classroom, through the window, or can think of at home, e.g. cuboid – desk top, cube – dice, cylinder – pole, sphere – globe, pyramid – tent.
- Ask pupils to close their eyes as you describe each of the shapes in random order. Ask them to raise their hands when they know which shape it is. Repeat the description if necessary. When most of the hands are raised ask the class to name the shape together.
- At the end of the lesson ask pupils who did 'Try this' to say what they have drawn and point it out in the classroom. Ask other pupils to name the shape.

Answers

1 a) pyramid b) sphere c) cylinder d) cuboid
e) cone f) cuboid

2 a) pyramid b) cube c) sphere d) cylinder
e) cuboid f) cone

3 2 cubes, 2 cuboids, 2 cylinders, 2 spheres, 2 pyramids, 2 cones

Lesson 4 **Cubes and cuboids**

Pupil's Book pages 46 and 47 **Oral and mental starter: Product pairs**

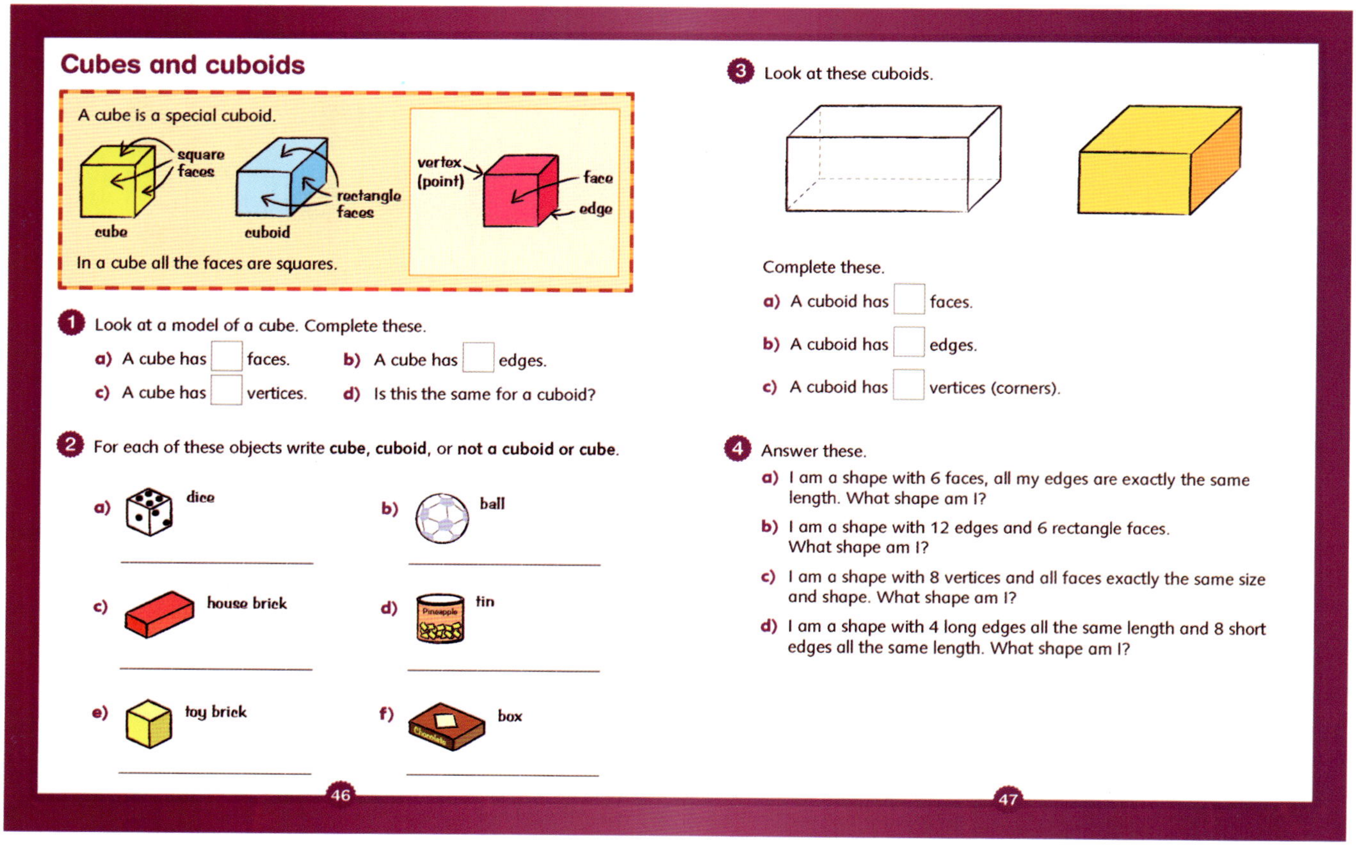

Cubes and cuboids

A cube is a special cuboid.

square faces, cube, rectangle faces, cuboid, vertex (point), face, edge

In a cube all the faces are squares.

1 Look at a model of a cube. Complete these.

a) A cube has ☐ faces. **b)** A cube has ☐ edges.

c) A cube has ☐ vertices. **d)** Is this the same for a cuboid?

2 For each of these objects write **cube**, **cuboid**, or **not a cuboid or cube**.

a) dice ______ **b)** ball ______

c) house brick ______ **d)** tin ______

e) toy brick ______ **f)** box ______

46

3 Look at these cuboids.

Complete these.

a) A cuboid has ☐ faces.

b) A cuboid has ☐ edges.

c) A cuboid has ☐ vertices (corners).

4 Answer these.

a) I am a shape with 6 faces, all my edges are exactly the same length. What shape am I?

b) I am a shape with 12 edges and 6 rectangle faces. What shape am I?

c) I am a shape with 8 vertices and all faces exactly the same size and shape. What shape am I?

d) I am a shape with 4 long edges all the same length and 8 short edges all the same length. What shape am I?

47

Activities

- Give a cube and a cuboid to small groups of pupils. Look at page 46 and revise the terms 'face', 'edge' and 'vertex (vertices)'. Ask pupils to touch a face, an edge and a vertex on one of the shapes. Ask them to count the number of faces, edges and vertices (points) on each of the shapes.
- Compare the two shapes, e.g. 'What is the same about a cube and a cuboid? What is different? Why is a cube a special type of cuboid?' (It is a cuboid with all faces square.)
- Look at the instructions for question 2. Hold up different 3-D shapes from the classroom collection and ask the class to say 'cube', 'cuboid' or 'not a cuboid or cube' together as appropriate for each shape.

Answers

1 a) 6 faces b) 12 edges c) 8 vertices d) yes

2 a) cube b) not a cuboid or cube
c) cuboid d) not a cuboid or a cube
e) cube f) cuboid

3 a) 6 faces b) 12 edges c) 8 vertices

4 a) cube b) cuboid c) cube d) cuboid

Lesson 5 **Properties of solid shapes**

Pupil's Book pages 48 and 49 **Oral and mental starter: Hold up**

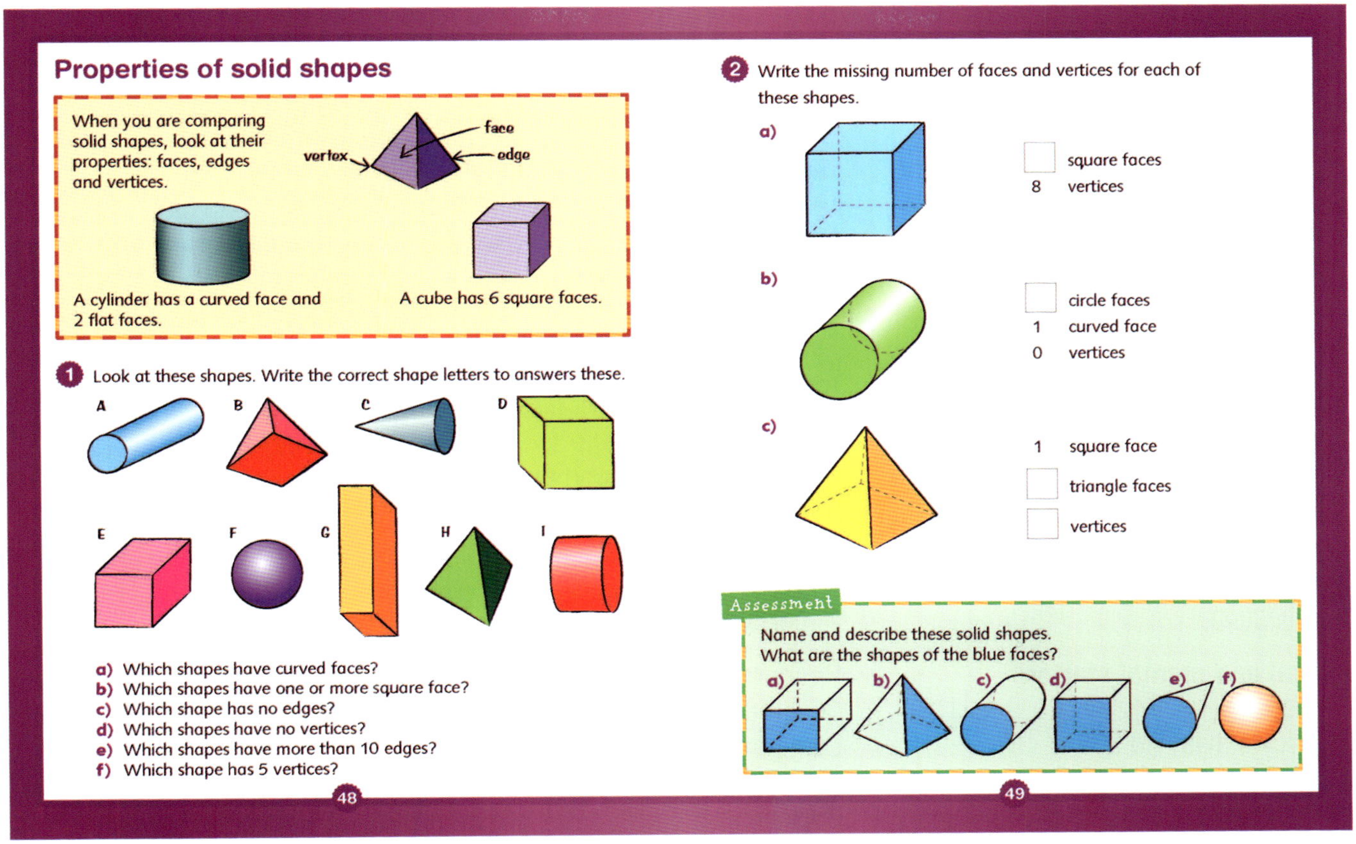

Properties of solid shapes

When you are comparing solid shapes, look at their properties: faces, edges and vertices.

A cylinder has a curved face and 2 flat faces.

A cube has 6 square faces.

1 Look at these shapes. Write the correct shape letters to answers these.

a) Which shapes have curved faces?
b) Which shapes have one or more square face?
c) Which shape has no edges?
d) Which shapes have no vertices?
e) Which shapes have more than 10 edges?
f) Which shape has 5 vertices?

48

2 Write the missing number of faces and vertices for each of these shapes.

a) ☐ square faces
8 vertices

b) ☐ circle faces
1 curved face
0 vertices

c) 1 square face
☐ triangle faces
☐ vertices

Assessment

Name and describe these solid shapes.
What are the shapes of the blue faces?

49

Activities

- Give out a selection of solid shapes: cubes, cuboids, cylinders, spheres and pyramids to small groups of pupils so that each pupil has one shape but can see the others.
- Look at page 48 and go through the introduction with the class. Ask pupils to hold up their shape and point to one of its faces, then one of its edges (if it has one), then one of its vertices (if it has one).
- Ask pupils to hold up their shape if it has: six faces; a curved face; one square face; two square faces; six square faces; triangular faces; rectangular faces; circular faces; twelve edges; eight edges; two edges; no edges; eight vertices; five vertices; no vertices.
- Ask 'What would happen if your desk was a sphere? … wheels were cubes? … chair seats were pyramids? … dice were cylinders? … the world was a cuboid?'
- Explain that pupils can look at the shapes in their group if they need to when doing question 1.

Answers

1 a) A, C, F, I b) B, D, E c) F
d) A, F, I e) D, E, G f) B

2 a) 6 square faces b) 2 circle faces
c) 4 triangle faces, 5 vertices

Assessment

a) Cuboid, 6 faces, 12 edges, 8 vertices – the blue face is a rectangle.
b) Pyramid, 5 faces, 8 edges, 5 vertices – the blue face is a triangle.
c) Cylinder, curved and flat faces – the blue face is a circle.
d) Cube, 6 identical size faces, 12 edges, 8 vertices – the blue face is a square.
e) Cone, 1 curved and 1 flat face – the blue face is a circle.
f) Sphere, no vertices or edges, 1 curved face.

Unit 18 **Lines and shapes**

Term 2 Block E **Geometry** Unit 17 Flat and solid shapes **Unit 18 Lines and shapes** Unit 19 Area of shapes Unit 20 Assess and review	**Objectives** *At the end of the unit, students should be able to…* Differentiate between a straight line, a segment and a ray. Demonstrate the relation between a given point and a closed curve, polygon or straight line. Identify a polygon. Name (State) the segments that compose a shape. Use squared or graph paper to draw a polygon. Identify symmetrical and non-symmetrical shapes through art activities. Determine the line of symmetry in a shape. Form and differentiate mental images of familiar geometric shapes depending on spatial memory and perception of things.
Vocabulary line, segment, ray, point, polygon, triangle, square, rectangle, pentagon, hexagon, quadrilateral, symmetrical, fold line, line of symmetry, mirror line, reflection	**Lessons** 1 Lines, segments and rays 2 Introducing polygons 3 Squares and rectangles 4 Symmetrical shapes 5 Lines of symmetry
Oral and mental starters Steps Arrows away (to 999) What's the order? (within 999) Double it My way	**Resources** Squared paper, rulers, coloured pencils, scissors Large paper isosceles triangle Paint or ink and plain paper (lesson 4 'Try this') Books containing pictures of symmetrical objects or living things Paper squares, rectangles, equilateral triangles and circles sufficient for one shape per pupil *Pupil's Book pages 50–59*
Prior learning Names and properties of 2-D and 3-D shapes Comparing similarities and differences between squares and rectangles	**Background notes** Most of the content of this unit is new learning. The terms 'segment', 'ray' (lesson 1), 'polygon' (lesson 2), 'symmetrical' (lesson 4) and 'line of symmetry' (lesson 5)' are introduced and defined.
End of unit evaluation Check that pupils are able to: 1 Identify lines, segments and rays. 2 Identify and draw polygons. 3 Identify symmetrical and non-symmetrical shapes and lines of symmetry. 4 Visualise and name shapes from their description.	**Supporting the topic** Discuss examples of polygons (triangles, quadrilaterals, pentagons, hexagons) and symmetrical shapes seen in the environment or which occur in nature and are pictured in books. Provide opportunities for pupils to look through the books to find examples of symmetry. Include drawing/painting symmetrical and non-symmetrical pictures in art lessons.

Lesson 1 **Lines, segments and rays**

Pupil's Book pages 50 and 51 **Oral and mental starter: Steps**

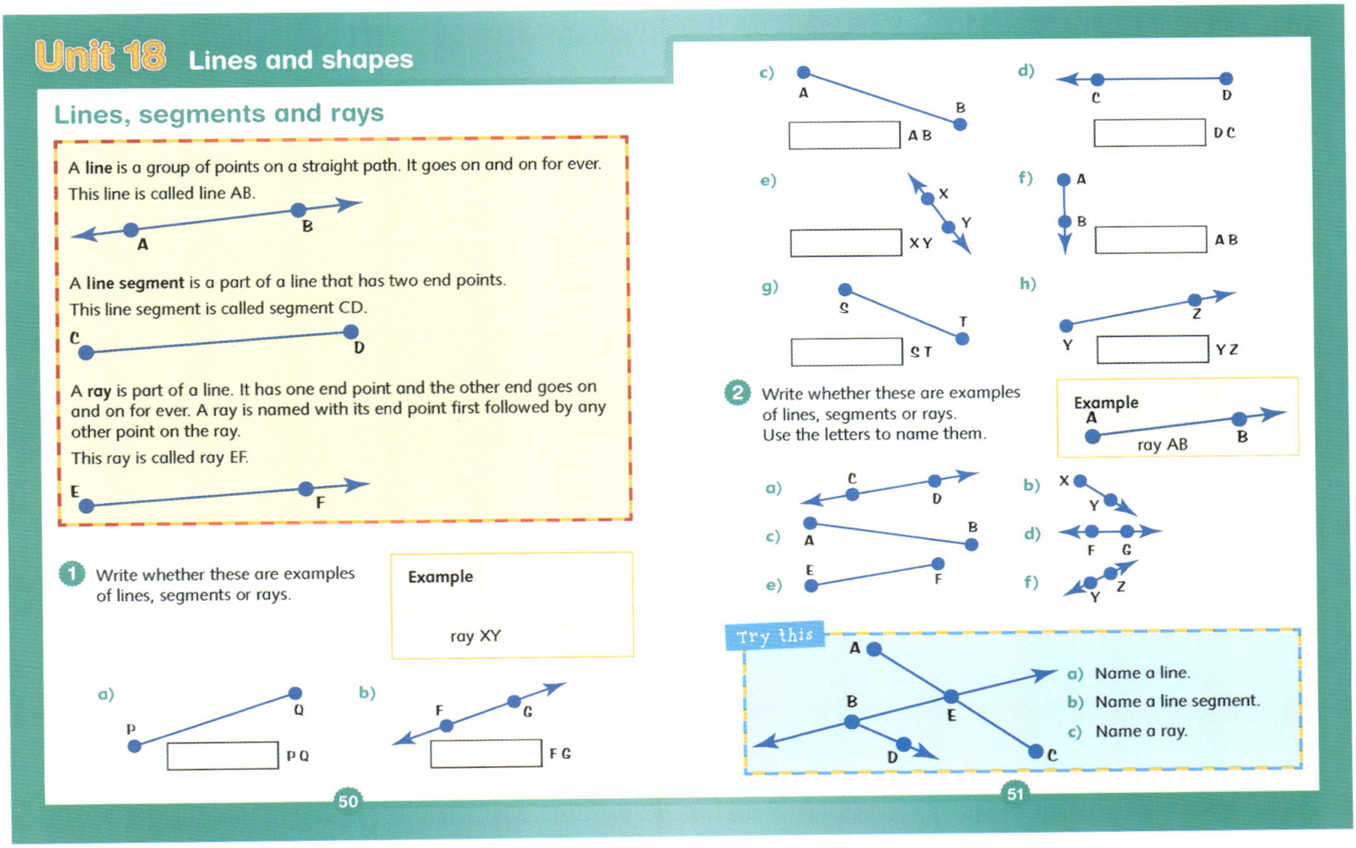

Unit 18 Lines and shapes

Lines, segments and rays

A **line** is a group of points on a straight path. It goes on and on for ever.
This line is called line AB.

A **line segment** is a part of a line that has two end points.
This line segment is called segment CD.

A **ray** is part of a line. It has one end point and the other end goes on and on for ever. A ray is named with its end point first followed by any other point on the ray.
This ray is called ray EF.

1 Write whether these are examples of lines, segments or rays.

Example: ray XY

a) PQ b) FG c) AB d) DC e) XY f) AB g) ST h) YZ

2 Write whether these are examples of lines, segments or rays. Use the letters to name them.

Example: ray AB

a) b) c) d) e) f)

Try this

a) Name a line.
b) Name a line segment.
c) Name a ray.

50 51

Activities

- Look at page 50. Go through the introduction very carefully with the class. Draw a set of points on a straight path and join them to form a straight line on the board. Explain how the lettering on the segment and ray are used to identify them.
- Draw two different examples of lines, two of segments and two of rays on the board. Letter the segments and rays at each end and mark two lettered points on each line, different pairs of letters for each. Give the letters of each one in turn and ask the class to say 'line', 'segment' or 'ray' together. Each time ask 'How do you know?'
- Ask pupils to draw a line with two points on it lettered A and B, a segment lettered C and D and a ray lettered E and F in their books using rulers. Remind them to put arrows on each end of the line, points on each end of the segment and a point and an arrow on the ends of the ray.
- At the end of the lesson ask for the results in 'Try this'.

Answers

1 a) segment PQ b) line FG c) segment AB
d) ray DC e) line XY f) ray AB
g) segment ST h) ray YZ

2 a) line CD b) ray XY c) segment AB
d) line FG e) segment EF f) line YZ

Try this

a) line BE b) segment AC c) ray BD

Lesson 2 **Introducing polygons**

Pupil's Book pages 52 and 53 **Oral and mental starter: Arrows away**

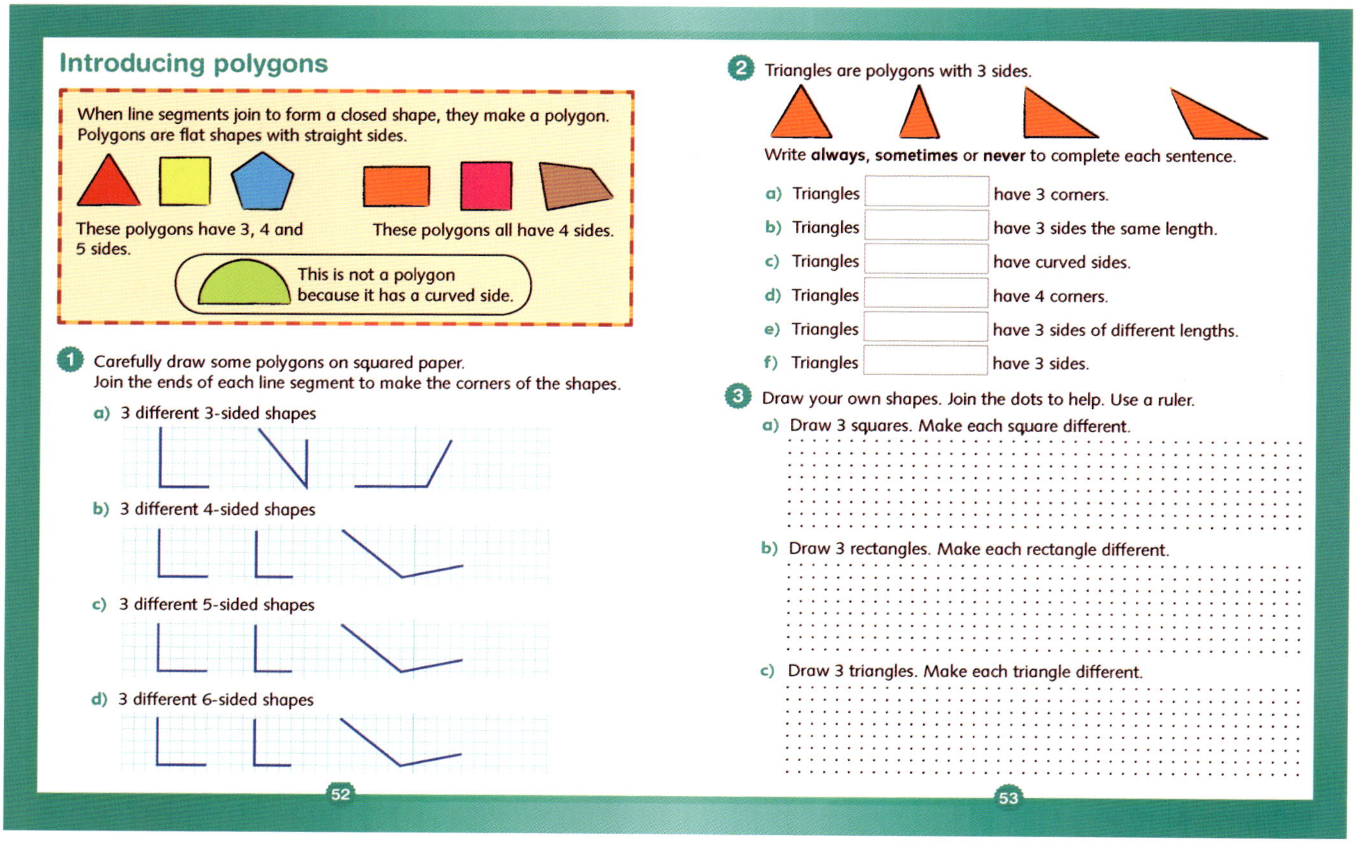

Introducing polygons

When line segments join to form a closed shape, they make a polygon.
Polygons are flat shapes with straight sides.

These polygons have 3, 4 and 5 sides.

These polygons all have 4 sides.

This is not a polygon because it has a curved side.

1 Carefully draw some polygons on squared paper.
Join the ends of each line segment to make the corners of the shapes.

a) 3 different 3-sided shapes

b) 3 different 4-sided shapes

c) 3 different 5-sided shapes

d) 3 different 6-sided shapes

52

2 Triangles are polygons with 3 sides.

Write **always**, **sometimes** or **never** to complete each sentence.

a) Triangles ______ have 3 corners.

b) Triangles ______ have 3 sides the same length.

c) Triangles ______ have curved sides.

d) Triangles ______ have 4 corners.

e) Triangles ______ have 3 sides of different lengths.

f) Triangles ______ have 3 sides.

3 Draw your own shapes. Join the dots to help. Use a ruler.

a) Draw 3 squares. Make each square different.

b) Draw 3 rectangles. Make each rectangle different.

c) Draw 3 triangles. Make each triangle different.

53

Activities

- Before the lesson draw a triangle, a rectangle, a quadrilateral with no equal sides, a pentagon and a hexagon on the board.
- Look at page 52 and go through the introduction with the class.
- Look at the polygons on the board. Ask 'Are these shapes all polygons? How do you know?' Ask a volunteer to come out and point to the square. Write 'square' inside or beneath it. Repeat with the triangle.
- Point to the quadrilateral and explain that it is called a quadrilateral because it has 4 sides. 'Which other shapes do you know which have four sides?' Discuss responses and explain that squares and rectangles (and any other quadrilaterals suggested which have special names) are special types of quadrilaterals because they have special properties, but the one on the board does not so it is just called a quadrilateral. Write its name inside or below it.
- Ask whether anyone knows the names of the other shapes in turn, if not give the names and record them as before. Explain that any shape with five straight sides is a pentagon and any shape with six sides is a hexagon.
- Ask a volunteer to come out and draw a different triangle on the board. Repeat with each of the other shapes.
- Towards the end of the lesson ask 'What do we call a polygon with 3 sides? … 4 sides? … 5 sides? … 6 sides?'

Answers

2 a) always	b) sometimes	c) never
d) never	e) sometimes	f) always

Lesson 3 Squares and rectangles

Pupil's Book pages 54 and 55 **Oral and mental starter: What's the order?**

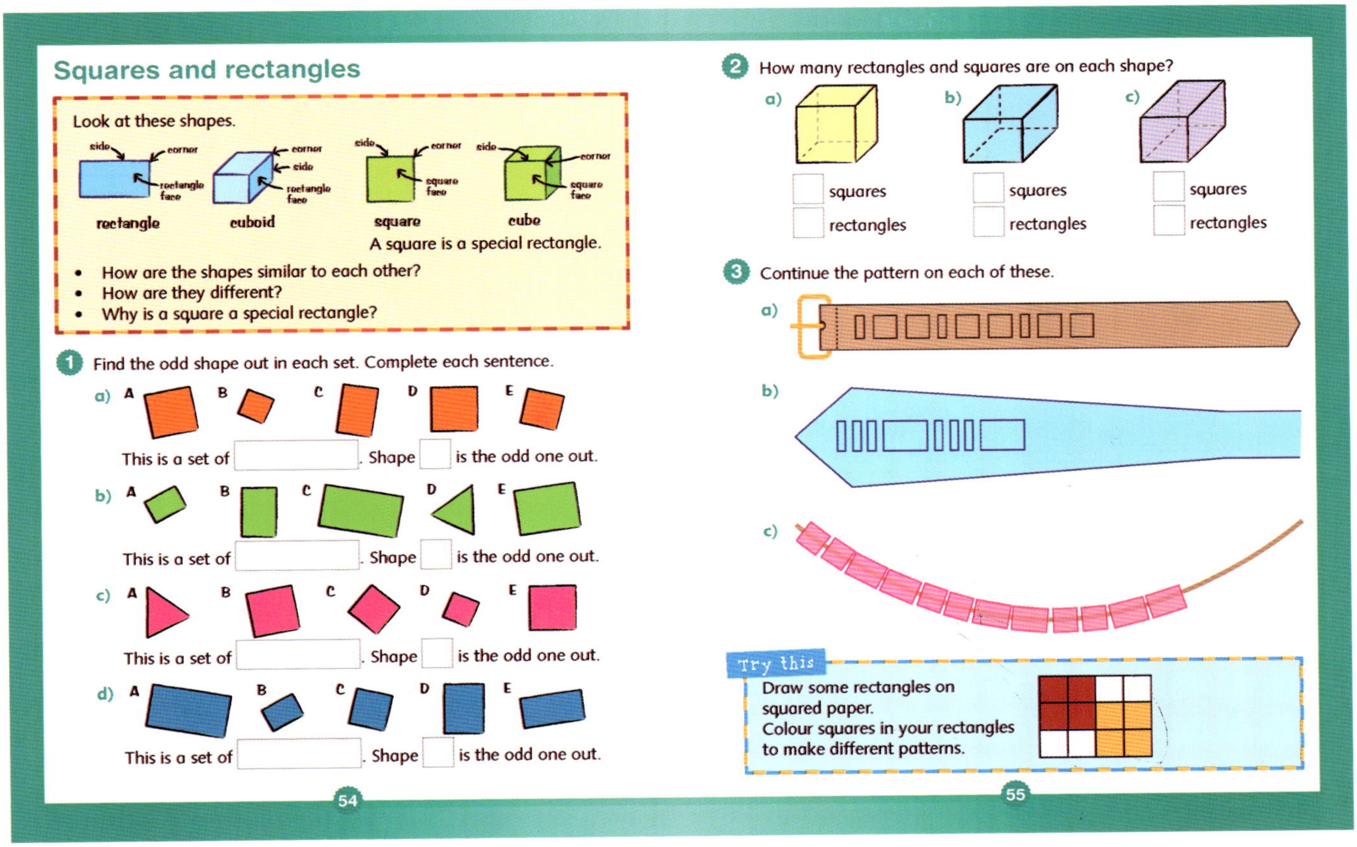
Squares and rectangles

Look at these shapes.

side, corner, rectangle face — **rectangle**
corner, side, rectangle face — **cuboid**
side, corner, square face — **square**
side, corner, square face — **cube**

A square is a special rectangle.

- How are the shapes similar to each other?
- How are they different?
- Why is a square a special rectangle?

1 Find the odd shape out in each set. Complete each sentence.

a) A B C D E
This is a set of ______. Shape ___ is the odd one out.

b) A B C D E
This is a set of ______. Shape ___ is the odd one out.

c) A B C D E
This is a set of ______. Shape ___ is the odd one out.

d) A B C D E
This is a set of ______. Shape ___ is the odd one out.

54

2 How many rectangles and squares are on each shape?

a) ___ squares ___ rectangles
b) ___ squares ___ rectangles
c) ___ squares ___ rectangles

3 Continue the pattern on each of these.

a)

b)

c)

Try this

Draw some rectangles on squared paper.
Colour squares in your rectangles to make different patterns.

55

Activities

- Look at page 54. Remind the class that in the previous unit they compared a cube and a cuboid and found out that a cube is a cuboid with all faces square. Ask pupils to look carefully at the rectangle and square. Discuss the number of sides and vertices, similarities and differences as pupils respond to the questions. Encourage them to make general statements in response to the third question (e.g. a square is a rectangle with equal sides).
- Ask pupils to use a ruler and pencil and to draw a rectangle and then a square as accurately as they can. Ask them to discuss whether each of their shapes is accurate with a partner. Ask a few volunteers to explain why their shapes are not accurate. Ask one or two volunteers who think their shapes are accurate to explain how they drew them.

Answers

1 a) This is a set of squares. Shape C is the odd one out.
b) This is a set of rectangles. Shape D is the odd one out.
c) This is a set of squares. Shape A is the odd one out.
d) This is a set of rectangles. Shape C is the odd one out.

2 a) 6 squares, 0 rectangles
b) 0 squares, 6 rectangles
c) 2 squares, 4 rectangles

3 a) 1 rectangle and 2 squares
b) 3 upright rectangles and 1 large rectangle
c) 2 squares and 2 rectangles

Lesson 4 Symmetrical shapes

Pupil's Book pages 56 and 57 **Oral and mental starter: Double it**

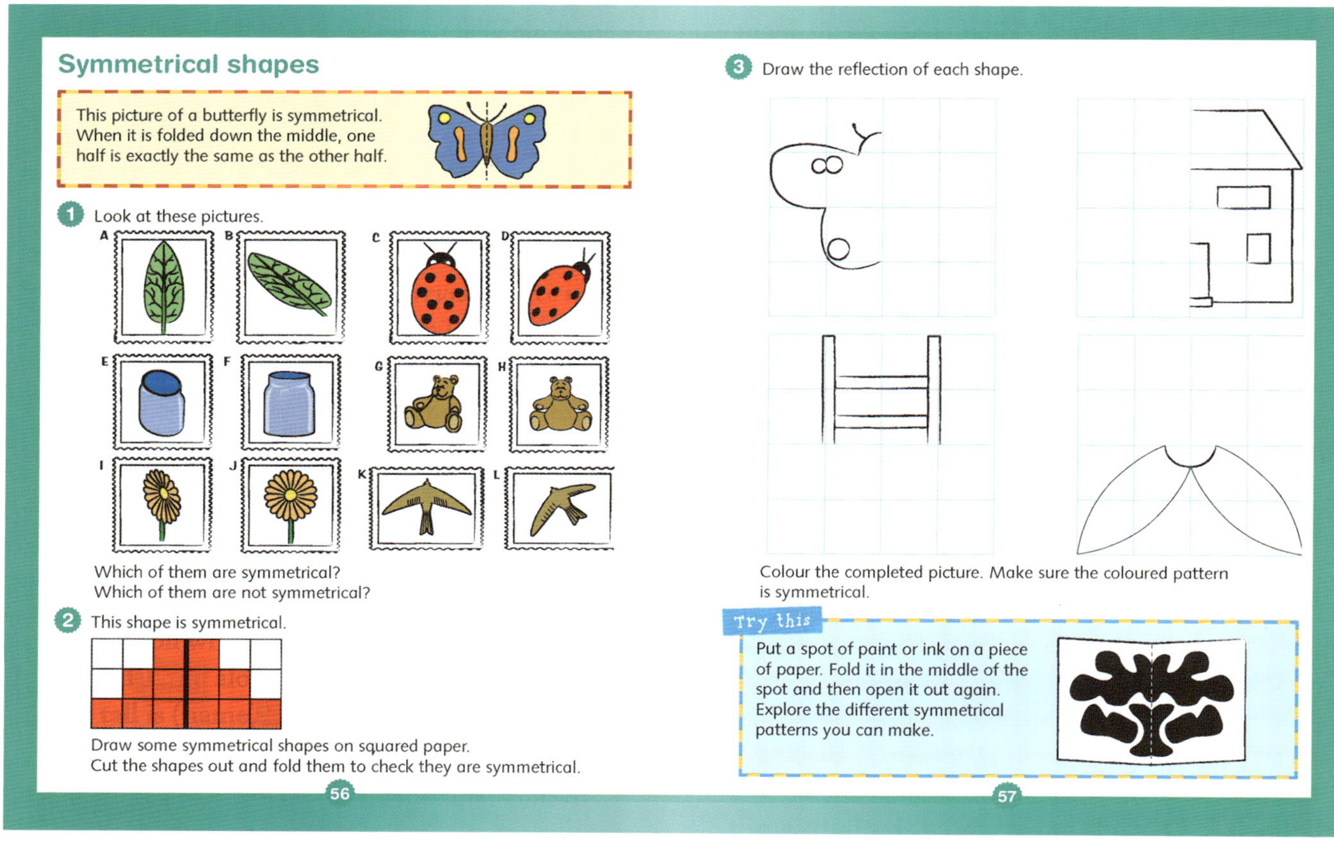

Symmetrical shapes

This picture of a butterfly is symmetrical. When it is folded down the middle, one half is exactly the same as the other half.

1 Look at these pictures.

A B C D E F G H I J K L

Which of them are symmetrical?
Which of them are not symmetrical?

2 This shape is symmetrical.

Draw some symmetrical shapes on squared paper.
Cut the shapes out and fold them to check they are symmetrical.

56

3 Draw the reflection of each shape.

Colour the completed picture. Make sure the coloured pattern is symmetrical.

Try this

Put a spot of paint or ink on a piece of paper. Fold it in the middle of the spot and then open it out again. Explore the different symmetrical patterns you can make.

57

Activities

- Fold a large isosceles triangle down the middle vertically then open it out. Explain that one side of the fold matches the other side exactly when folded over. Fold it over to demonstrate, going round the class for all pupils to see clearly.
- Explain that the triangle is 'symmetrical' because one half matches the other half exactly when folded over.
- Look at page 56 and discuss the introduction with the class. Ask them to imagine folding the butterfly picture along the middle line and to see in their minds that the two sides would fit over each other exactly. Explain that one side is a 'reflection' of the other side.
- Ask pupils to stand up and spread both arms out to the side and imagine a line running down the middle of their bodies. 'Are you symmetrical? How do you know?' Allow different responses. 'Can you see or think of anything else which is symmetrical?' Discuss suggestions and show some pictures from books showing symmetrical things. Each time ask pupils to imagine a line which divides them symmetrically.
- At the end of the lesson ask pupils to share their shapes on squared paper with a partner and discuss whether they are symmetrical. (These shapes and the paint spot patterns from 'Try this' would be useful to display in the classroom.)

Answers

1 Symmetrical: A, C, F, H, J, K; not symmetrical: B, D, E, G, I, L

Lesson 5 **Lines of symmetry**

Pupil's Book pages 58 and 59 **Oral and mental starter: My way**

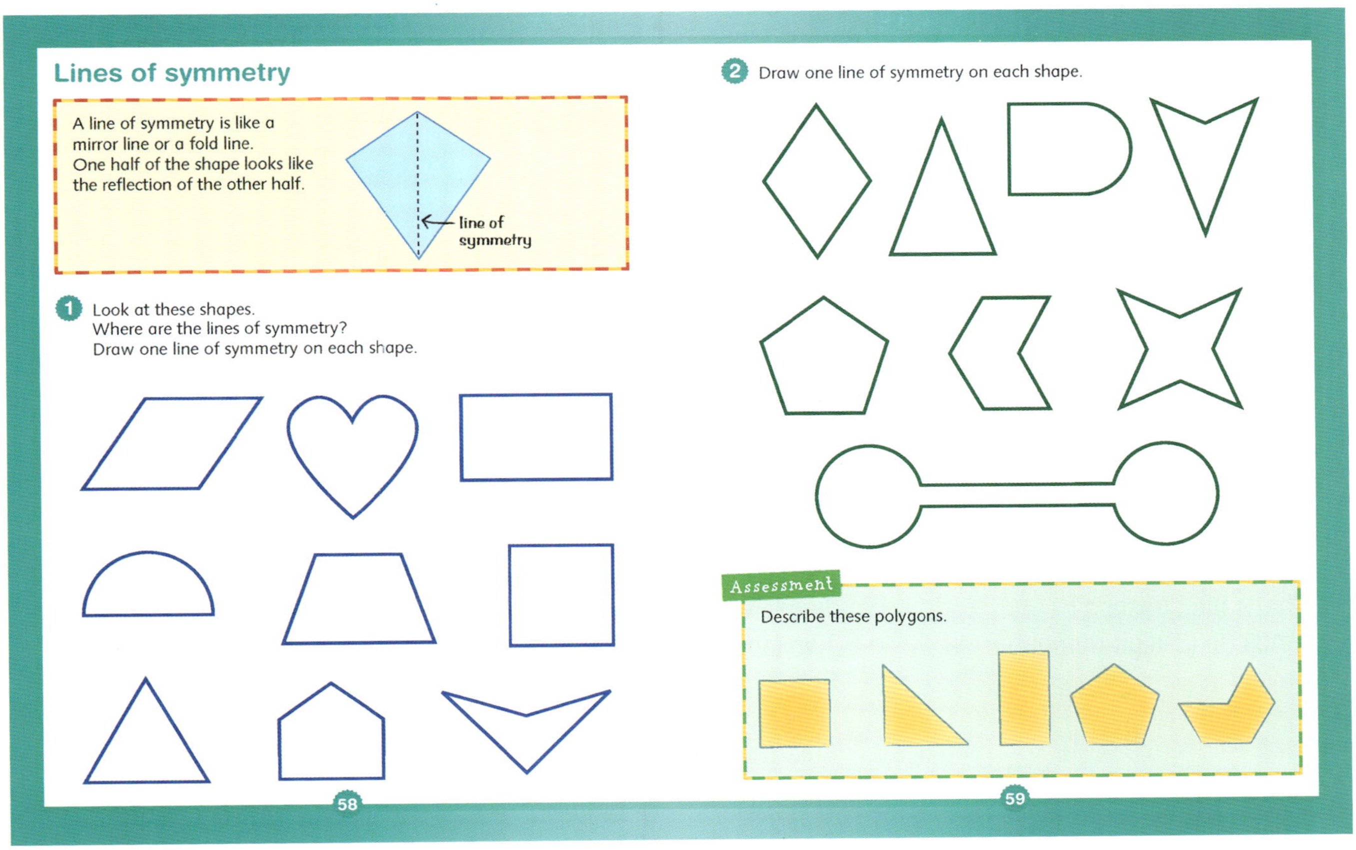

Activities

- Remind the class about the previous lesson. 'How did you check to see whether your shapes on the squared paper were symmetrical?' Explain that the fold line is called a line of symmetry because it divides the shape into two symmetrical parts.
- Look at page 58 and go through the introduction with the class. Give paper squares, rectangles, equilateral triangles and circles out to small groups of pupils, sufficient for one shape per pupil. Ask them to choose a shape and fold it to make a line of symmetry, then to look at all the shapes in the group and check that they have been folded correctly.
- Draw a square on the board and ask a pupil to come out and show where a line of symmetry could be drawn. Ask pupils who found a different line of symmetry on their squares to come and demonstrate. Draw all the lines on the square and discuss why each is a line of symmetry.
- Emphasise that pupils should draw just one line of symmetry on the shapes in questions 1 and 2.

Answers

Assessment

square – symmetrical closed 4-sided shape
triangle – symmetrical closed 3-sided shape
rectangle – symmetrical closed 4-sided shape
symmetrical closed 5-sided shape
symmetrical closed 6-sided shape

Unit 19 **Area of shapes**

Term 2 Block E
Geometry
Unit 17 Flat and solid shapes
Unit 18 Lines and shapes
Unit 19 Area of shapes
Unit 20 Assess and review

Objectives
At the end of the unit, students should be able to…
Understand the term congruent. Identify congruent shapes.
Use the concept of congruency in simple everyday situations.
Use squared or graph paper to draw a polygon.
Use square, triangular or rectangular cards to form defined flat areas.
Arrange geometric shapes to fit the least space.
Dissect shapes into parts and reassemble to form new shapes.

Vocabulary
distance, area, space, congruent, tiling pattern

Lessons
1 Area: counting squares
2 Comparing areas
3 Congruent shapes
4 Tiling patterns
5 Shape puzzle

Oral and mental starter
Start here (within 999)
Flash facts (multiplication)
What's the question?
Hands up (3-digit numbers)
Halve it

Resources
Squared paper (lessons 1, 3 and 5)
Card for pupils to each cut out 6 shapes (lesson 4)
Two large card squares in different colours, 1 larger than the other
Two large card congruent triangles
Sets of squares and rectangles of different areas cut from squared paper, one set per group so that each pupil has one shape
Rulers and scissors
Pupil's Book pages 60–69

Prior learning
Identifying names and properties of 2-D shapes

Background notes
Area, congruence and tiling (tessellation) are introduced in this unit. Pupils often confuse area and perimeter, particularly if the perimeter of a shape is found by counting the edges of cm squares around an edge. It is important to establish the concepts separately and provide tangible examples of each to firmly establish the difference between them. Perimeter is introduced in Unit 21.

End of unit evaluation
Check that pupils are able to:
1 Understand the concept of area.
2 Find areas of shapes on squared paper by counting whole squares.
3 Draw polygons on squared paper.
4 Understand congruence.
5 Identify congruent shapes.
6 Arrange shapes to cover the least possible space.
7 Cut shapes into parts and rearrange them to make a new shape.

Supporting the topic
Identify and compare surfaces in the classroom and discuss how they might be measured, e.g. the number of books / hands / large sheets of paper which cover them. Identify congruent shapes in the classroom, e.g. window panes, desk tops, chair seats. Provide opportunities in art lessons for pupils to make tiling patterns using geometric shapes.

Lesson 1 **Area: counting squares**

Pupil's Book pages 60 and 61 **Oral and mental starter: Start here (within 999)**

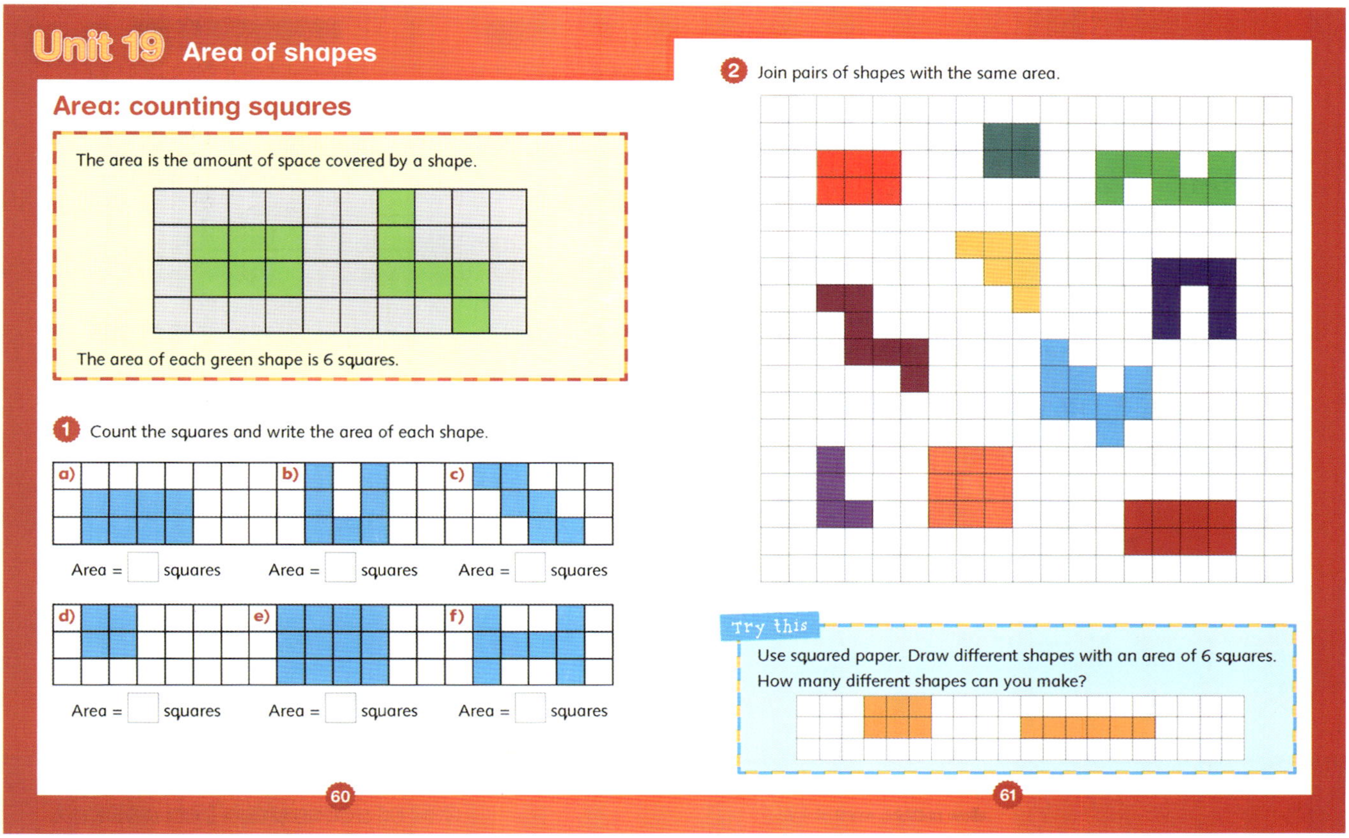
Unit 19 Area of shapes

Area: counting squares

The area is the amount of space covered by a shape.

The area of each green shape is 6 squares.

1 Count the squares and write the area of each shape.

a) Area = ☐ squares b) Area = ☐ squares c) Area = ☐ squares

d) Area = ☐ squares e) Area = ☐ squares f) Area = ☐ squares

2 Join pairs of shapes with the same area.

Try this

Use squared paper. Draw different shapes with an area of 6 squares. How many different shapes can you make?

60 61

Activities

- Ask if any of the class know the meaning of area. They may use the word in general to describe a space or place, or have examples where they have heard the word used. Explain that in mathematics the word 'area' is used to describe the amount of space a shape covers.
- Ask the class to look at their table tops. Ask them how many maths books they think could be laid on a table to cover it. Ask a group or child to demonstrate and then record: 'Area of table is about __ books'. Repeat this in groups to work out the area of other surfaces of objects in the classroom – your table, chair seat, door, board etc.
- Ask the class if they think books are useful for finding areas. Explain that we often use squares to work out the area of different shapes. Draw two shapes on the board with areas of 8 squares and 5 squares. Record under each 'Area of shape = 8 squares' and 'Area of shape = 5 squares'.
- Look at page 60 and go through the introduction with the class. Explain that the two green shapes have the same area, even though their shapes are different, because they both cover 6 squares.
- Towards the end of the lesson ask pupils who did 'Try this' to describe some of the shapes they made to the class.

Answers

1 a) 8 squares b) 7 squares c) 6 squares
d) 4 squares e) 12 squares f) 8 squares

2 A → D, B → H, C → J, E → F, G → I

Lesson 2 Comparing areas

Pupil's Book pages 62 and 63 **Oral and mental starter: Flash facts (multiplication)**

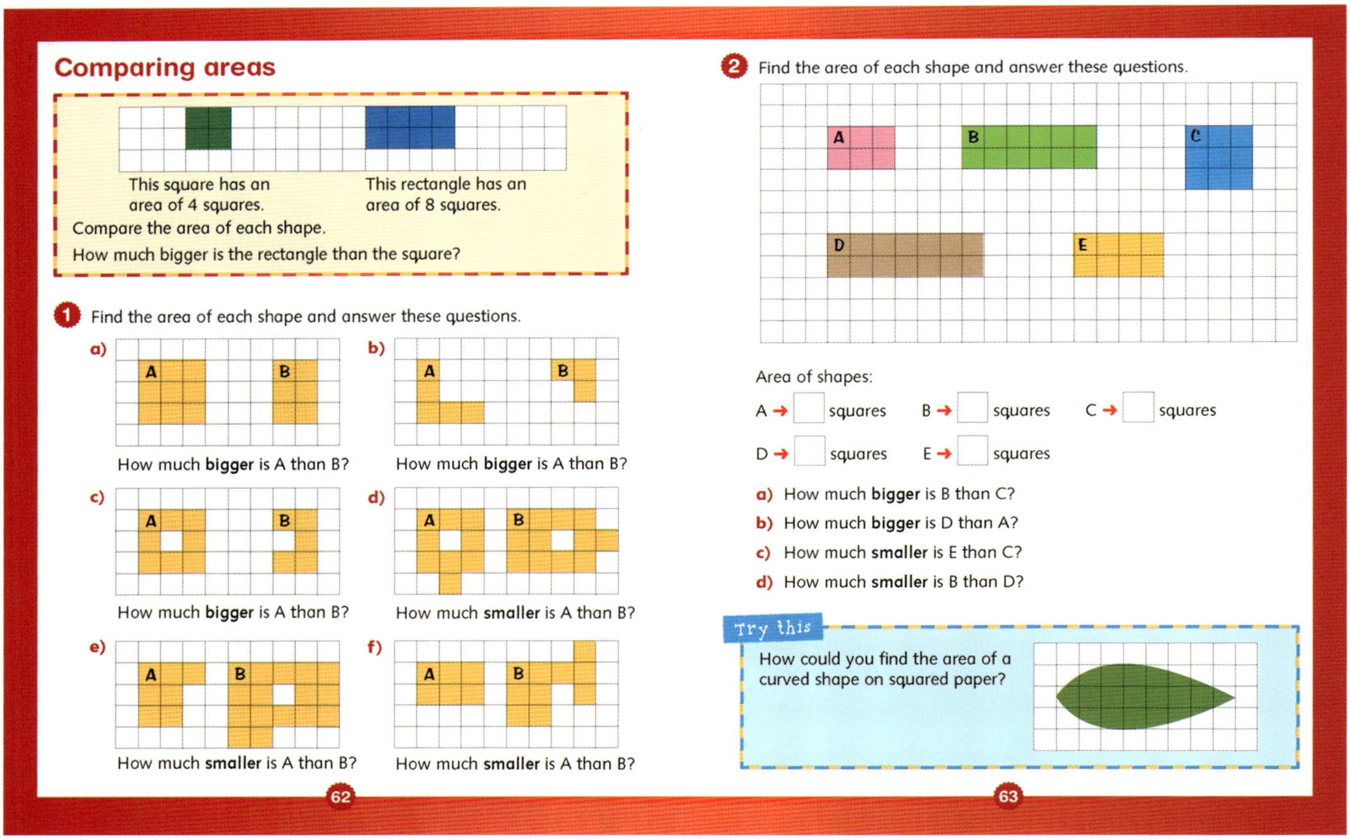
Comparing areas

This square has an area of 4 squares.

This rectangle has an area of 8 squares.

Compare the area of each shape.

How much bigger is the rectangle than the square?

1 Find the area of each shape and answer these questions.

a) How much **bigger** is A than B?

b) How much **bigger** is A than B?

c) How much **bigger** is A than B?

d) How much **smaller** is A than B?

e) How much **smaller** is A than B?

f) How much **smaller** is A than B?

2 Find the area of each shape and answer these questions.

Area of shapes:

A → ☐ squares B → ☐ squares C → ☐ squares

D → ☐ squares E → ☐ squares

a) How much **bigger** is B than C?

b) How much **bigger** is D than A?

c) How much **smaller** is E than C?

d) How much **smaller** is B than D?

Try this

How could you find the area of a curved shape on squared paper?

62

63

Activities

- Show a smaller square in the centre of a larger square. Ask 'Which square is the smaller? How do you know?' When we are comparing the size of two shapes we compare the amount of space they cover. Indicate the space of a square by wiping over the whole surface with your fingers.
- Ask pupils to wipe over the surface of their desks, their chair seats, the front of their Pupil's Books etc. Explain that the surface of a shape is all the space within its sides and is called the 'area' of the shape.
- Give a set of squares and rectangles cut from squared paper to each group. Ask each pupil to take one of the shapes. Ask 'How could you use the squares on your shape to work out the area of the shape?' Establish that the number of squares could be counted. Ask pupils to count the squares, write the number on the shape, then work with their groups to put the shapes in order of size, starting with the smallest area. Discuss the results, e.g. 'What is the area of your largest shape? How many squares larger is it than the next largest?' etc.
- Go through the introduction on page 62.
- Ask pupils who did 'Try this' to suggest how the area could be found. Draw out that only squares which are more than half covered by the shape should be counted.

Answers

1 a) 3 b) 2 c) 3 d) 3 e) 9 f) 4

2 A 6, B 12, C 9, D 14, E 8

a) 3 b) 8 c) 1 d) 2

Try this

Count all whole squares and match parts to make approximate whole squares **or** count all whole squares and count any half or over-half squares. Area will always be approximate for curved shapes.

Lesson 3 **Congruent shapes**

Pupil's Book pages 64 and 65 **Oral and mental starter: What's the question?**

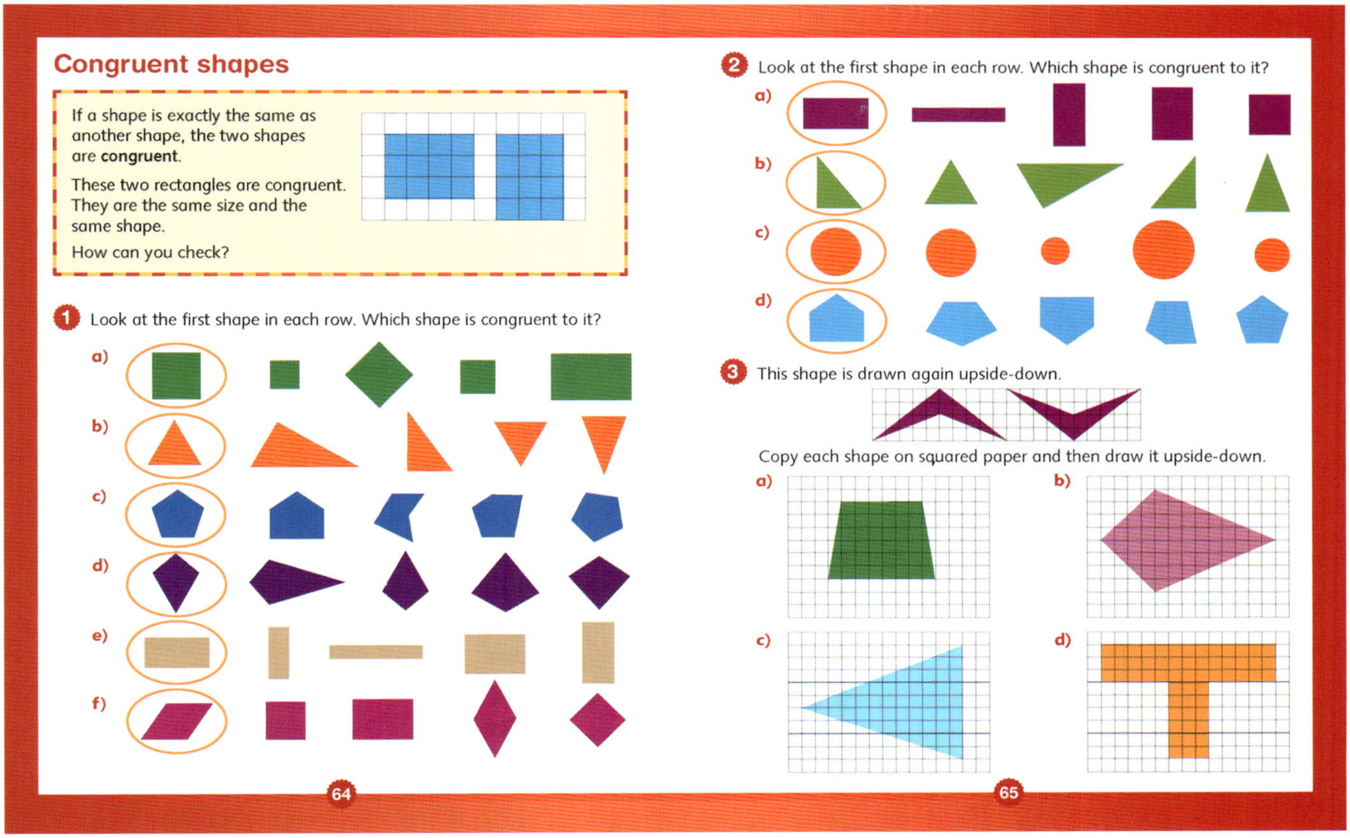

Activities

- Look at page 64 and go through the introduction with the class. Discuss that the rectangles are exactly the same size and shape, but they are in different positions. Emphasise that congruent shapes are exactly the same as each other in size and shape, but need not be in the same position.
- Hold up the two coloured card squares. Explain that they are both squares because they both have all four sides of equal length, but they are not congruent because one is larger than the other. Hold up the two congruent triangles, one with an angle at the top, one with a side at the top. Ask 'Are these triangles congruent? How do you know?' Turn one of them so that it is in the same orientation as the other, then place it on top of the other to show that they are exactly the same size and shape.
- Ask pupils to identify any congruent shapes they can see in the classroom, e.g. window panes, desk tops, front of Pupil's Books etc.
- Look at question 1 on page 64 and ask pupils to name the shapes illustrated ('quadrilateral' is sufficient for the kite and the rhombus).

Answers

1 a) 2nd shape b) 3rd shape c) 4th shape
d) 2nd shape e) 4th shape f) 3rd shape

2 a) 2nd shape b) 3rd shape c) 1st shape
d) 2nd shape

Lesson 4 **Tiling patterns**

Pupil's Book pages 66 and 67 **Oral and mental starter: Hands up (3-digit numbers)**

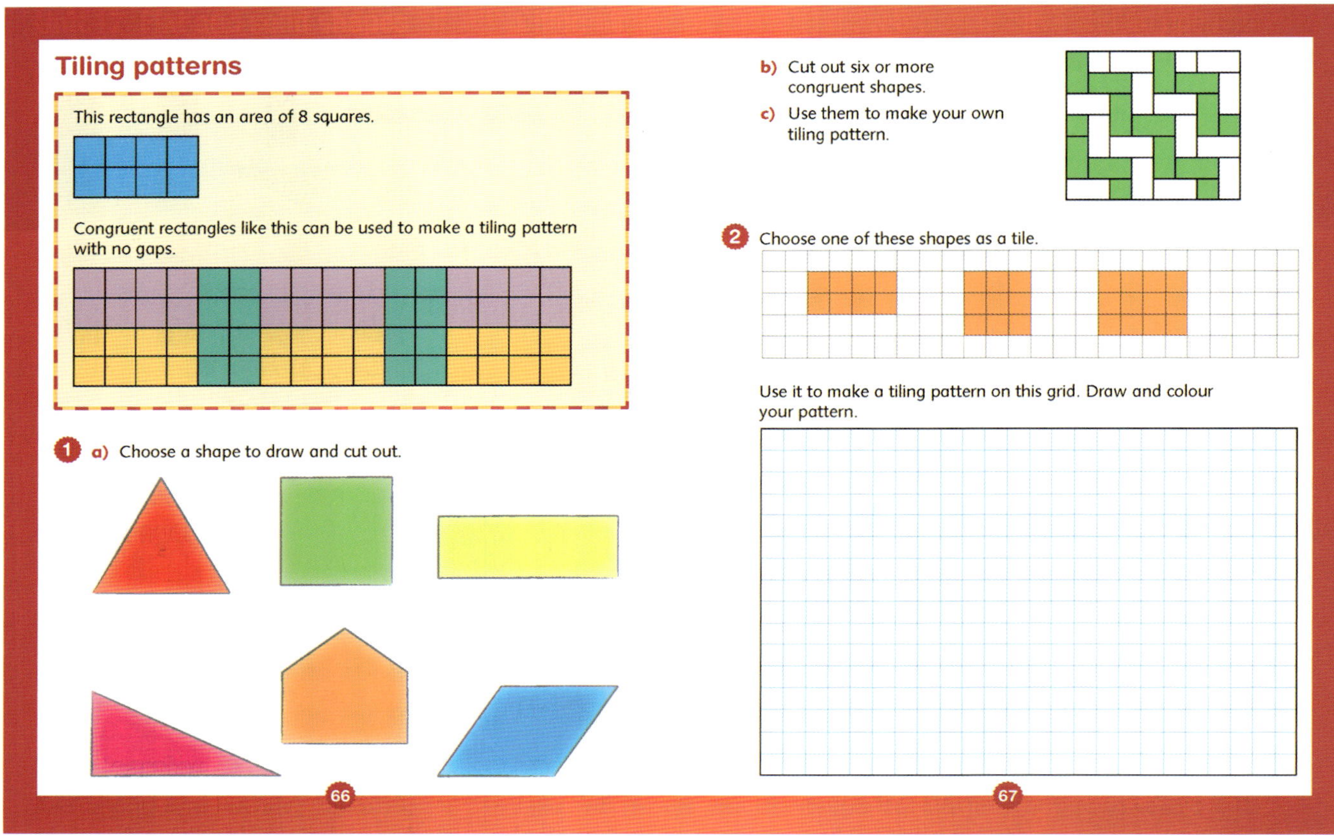

Tiling patterns

This rectangle has an area of 8 squares.

Congruent rectangles like this can be used to make a tiling pattern with no gaps.

1. a) Choose a shape to draw and cut out.

b) Cut out six or more congruent shapes.

c) Use them to make your own tiling pattern.

2. Choose one of these shapes as a tile.

Use it to make a tiling pattern on this grid. Draw and colour your pattern.

66

67

Activities

- Look at page 66 and go through the introduction with the class. Discuss that tiles on a wall or floor fit together without any gaps between them.
- Explain that pupils need to cut out the shapes very carefully for the activity in question 1 so that they are all congruent.
- At the end of the lesson ask 'What would happen if you made circular tiles?' Establish that there would be spaces between them because there are no vertices to fit together. 'Can you think of any other shapes which would not fit together without leaving gaps?' e.g. semi-circles, ovals. (The only regular polygons which tessellate are those whose angle is a factor of 360, but pupils are unlikely to realise that unless they experiment with different polygons.)

N.B. It would be useful to extend the tiling pattern activity in an art lesson, pupils perhaps drawing carefully round shapes and colouring tiles to form a repeating or symmetrical pattern.

Lesson 5 **Shape puzzle**

Pupil's Book pages 68 and 69 **Oral and mental starter: Halve it**

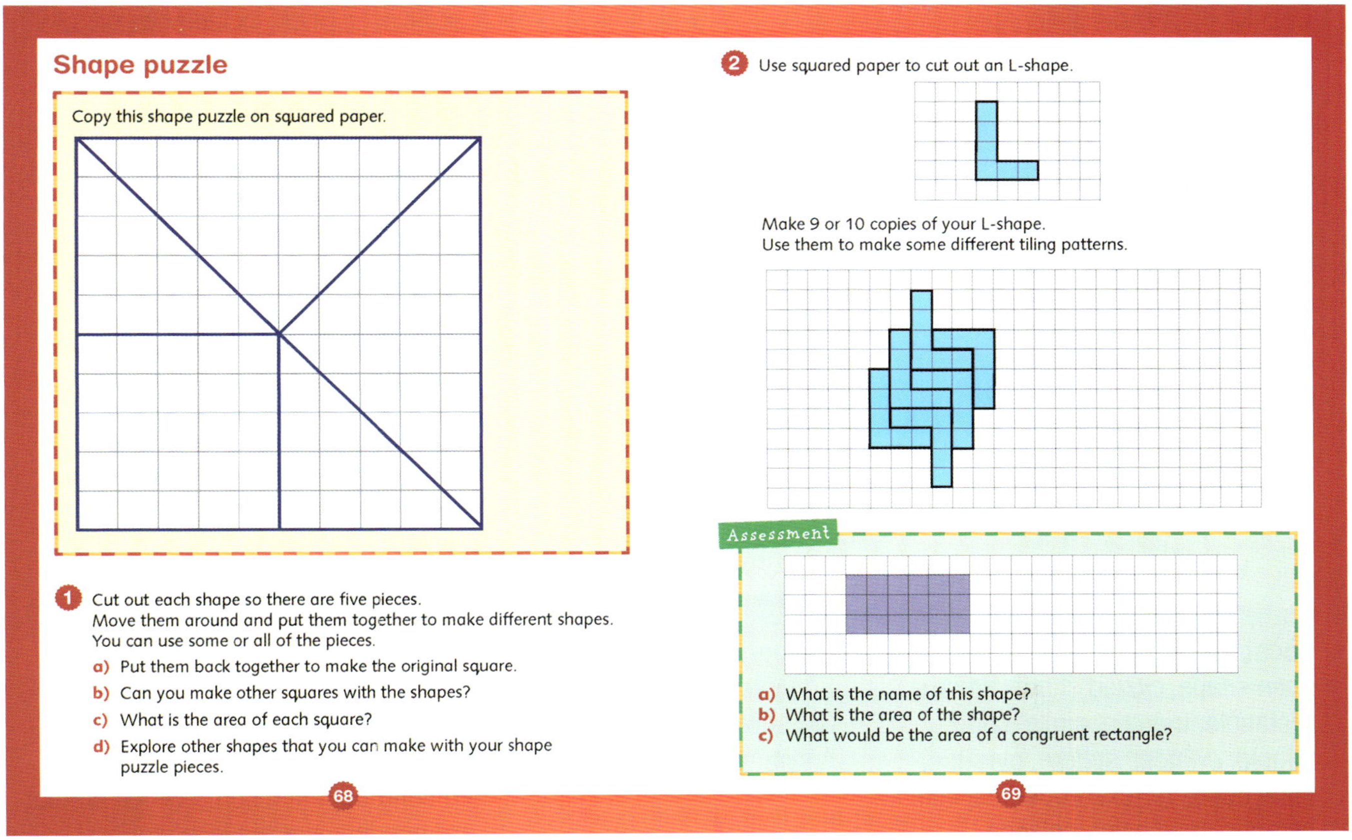

Shape puzzle

Copy this shape puzzle on squared paper.

1. Cut out each shape so there are five pieces.
Move them around and put them together to make different shapes.
You can use some or all of the pieces.
   a) Put them back together to make the original square.
   b) Can you make other squares with the shapes?
   c) What is the area of each square?
   d) Explore other shapes that you can make with your shape puzzle pieces.

68

2. Use squared paper to cut out an L-shape.

Make 9 or 10 copies of your L-shape.
Use them to make some different tiling patterns.

Assessment

a) What is the name of this shape?
b) What is the area of the shape?
c) What would be the area of a congruent rectangle?

69

Activities

- Look at page 68. Discuss the shape and the way in which the lines are drawn. 'Which shapes can you see on the large square? Are any of them congruent?' Establish that there are two sets of two congruent triangles and one square. 'Where on the large square do all the shapes meet?' Establish that they meet in the middle.
- Go through the instructions in question 1. Stress that pupils must draw the lines exactly as they are in the diagram and cut out the shapes very carefully.
- Towards the end of the lesson discuss the different shapes that pupils made in question 1. 'What was the area of the smallest square you made?' Discuss the areas of the five cut-out shapes, e.g. 'Which shapes have the same area? Which shapes have double the area of the small triangles?'

Answers

Assessment

a) rectangle b) 18 squares c) 18 squares

Unit 20 **Assess and review**

Term 2 Block E
Geometry
Unit 17 Flat and solid shapes
Unit 18 Lines and shapes
Unit 19 Area of shapes
Unit 20 Assess and review

Final evaluation
Check that pupils are able to:
1 Distinguish between open and closed lines, including curves.
2 Identify and name squares, rectangles, circles, triangles, cubes, cuboids, spheres, cylinders and pyramids.
3 Name some properties of shapes, e.g. number of sides, number of vertices, curved or straight sides, number and shape of faces, number of edges.
4 Visualise and name shapes from their description.
5 Identify lines, segments and rays.
6 Identify and draw polygons.
7 Identify symmetrical and non-symmetrical shapes and lines of symmetry.
8 Understand the concept of area and find areas of shapes on squared paper by counting whole squares.
9 Understand the concept of congruence and identify congruent shapes.
10 Arrange shapes to cover the least possible space.
11 Cut shapes into parts and rearrange them to make a new shape.

Vocabulary
open shape, closed shape, square, rectangle, triangle, circle, cube, cuboid, cylinder, sphere, pyramid, face, edge, vertex, properties, line, segment, ray, point, polygon, pentagon, hexagon, quadrilateral, symmetrical, fold line, line of symmetry, mirror line, reflection, distance, area, space, congruent, tiling pattern

Resources
Squared paper
Set of solid shapes (cube, cuboid, cylinder, sphere, pyramid)
A symmetrical picture
Set of shapes, some of which are congruent and some which are not
Set of flat shapes for pupils to arrange to cover the least space
Shapes for pupils to cut up and rearrange
Pupil's Book pages 70–75

Pupil's Book pages 70–75
1 Before looking at the Pupil's Book, ask pupils to describe a square, a rectangle, a triangle and a circle. (page 70)
2 Hold up a cuboid. Ask a volunteer to indicate a face, another to indicate an edge and another a vertex. Ask 'How many faces does a cuboid have? How many edges? How many vertices?' (pages 70–71)
3 Before looking at the Pupil's Book draw a line, a segment and a ray on the board and ask pupils to name them. (page 72)
4 Explain how to use and extract information from the Venn diagram. (page 73)
5 Ask a volunteer to explain what is meant by a symmetrical shape. (page 73)
6 Draw a shape on the board and ask a volunteer to come out and shade the area of the shape. Revise that the area is the amount of space inside the edges of the shape. (page 74)
7 Revise that in symmetrical patterns one side must match the other side exactly. (page 75)

Assessment activities
Use these to assess pupils' knowledge and understanding:
Draw a closed shape on this piece of paper. Now draw an open shape.

What is the name of each of these shapes? (cube, cuboid, cylinder, sphere, pyramid)
What shape are the faces on these shapes? (cube, cuboid, cylinder, pyramid)
In which ways is a cube the same as a cuboid? How is it different?
Show me a face on this cuboid, show me an edge, show me a vertex. Can you think of a shape which has no vertices and no edges? Which shape has two edges but no vertices?
Which of these is a line? Which is a segment? Which is a ray?
Draw me a polygon with five sides. Do you know its name? What do we call a polygon with three sides? Tell me all you know about triangles.
Why is a square a special rectangle?
Is this picture symmetrical? How do you know? Where could we draw a line of symmetry on it?
On this squared paper, draw me a square which has an area of 9 squares.
Show a set of flat shapes, some of which are congruent and some which are not. Which of these shapes are congruent?
Arrange these shapes so that they cover the smallest possible space.
Cut this shape into smaller shapes and make a new shape with them. Can you describe the shape you have made?

Assess and review activities

Use these activities taken from the previous three weeks to monitor, evaluate and consolidate pupils' knowledge and understanding.

- Ask 'Which closed shapes can you see in the classroom? Can you see any open shapes? Can you think of any open or closed shapes at home?'
- Hold up different examples of cubes, cuboids, cylinders, spheres and pyramids from the classroom collection. Ask the class to identify each one and to name it together on your signal. Ask for the names of particular faces on the shapes.
- Give out a selection cubes, cuboids, cylinders, spheres and pyramids to small groups of pupils so that each pupil has one shape but can see the others. Ask pupils to hold up their shape if it has: six faces, a curved face, one square face, two square faces, six square faces, triangular faces, rectangular faces, circular faces; twelve edges, eight edges, two edges, no edges; eight vertices, five vertices, no vertices.
- Draw two different examples each of lines, segments and rays on the board. Letter the segments and rays at each end and mark two lettered points on each line. Give the letters of each one in turn and ask the class to say line, segment or ray together. Each time ask 'How do you know?'
- Ask 'What do we call a polygon with 3 sides? … 4 sides? … 5 sides? … 6 sides?'
- Give paper squares, rectangles, equilateral triangles and circles out to small groups of pupils, sufficient for one shape per pupil. Ask them to choose a shape and fold it to make a line of symmetry, then to look at all the shapes in the group and check that they have been folded correctly.
- Give a set of squares and rectangles cut from squared paper to each group. Ask each pupil to take one of the shapes. Ask pupils to count the squares, write the number on the shape, then work with their groups to put the shapes in order of size, starting with the smallest area. Discuss the results, e.g. 'What is the area of your largest shape? How many squares larger is it than the next largest?' etc.
- Ask pupils to identify any congruent shapes they can see in the classroom, e.g. window panes, desk tops, front of Pupil's Books etc.

Unit 20 Assess and review

Flat and solid shapes

1 a) Complete this chart. Write the shape letters in the correct sections.

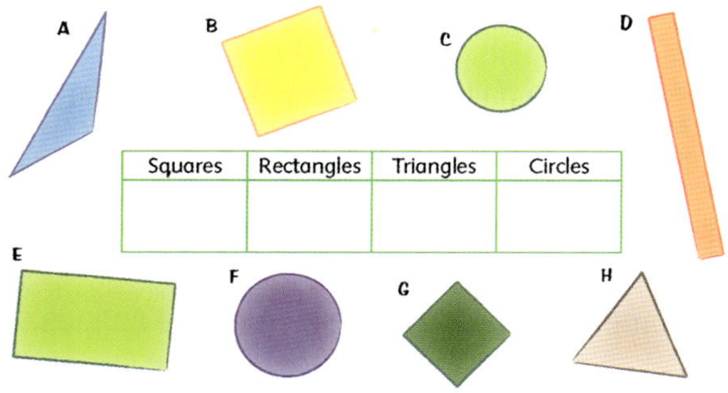

Squares	Rectangles	Triangles	Circles

b) Draw a shape in each box to match the names.
Make each shape different from the ones above.

2 Complete these sentences for each shape.

a)

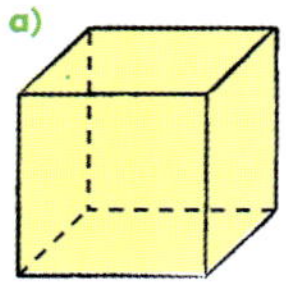

This shape has ☐ square faces.
This shape has ☐ rectangle faces.
This shape has ☐ vertices.
This shape has ☐ edges.
This shape is a ☐

b)

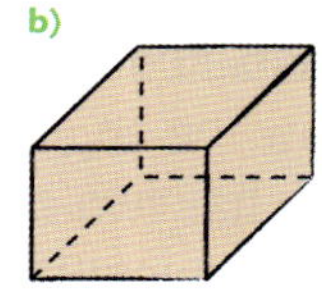

This shape has ☐ square faces.
This shape has ☐ rectangle faces.
This shape has ☐ vertices.
This shape has ☐ edges.
This shape is a ☐

c)

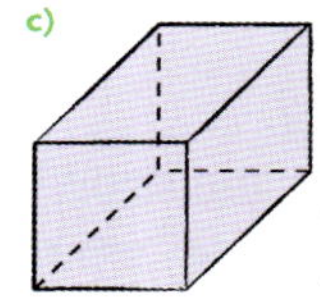

This shape has ☐ square faces.
This shape has ☐ rectangle faces.
This shape has ☐ vertices.
This shape has ☐ edges.
This shape is a ☐

3 Draw to complete each shape.

a) cone 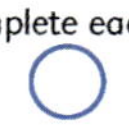

b) cylinder 

c) cube 

d) cuboid 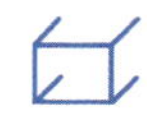

e) pyramid 

Try this

Draw a closed curve and an open curve.
How do they differ?

Lines and shapes

1

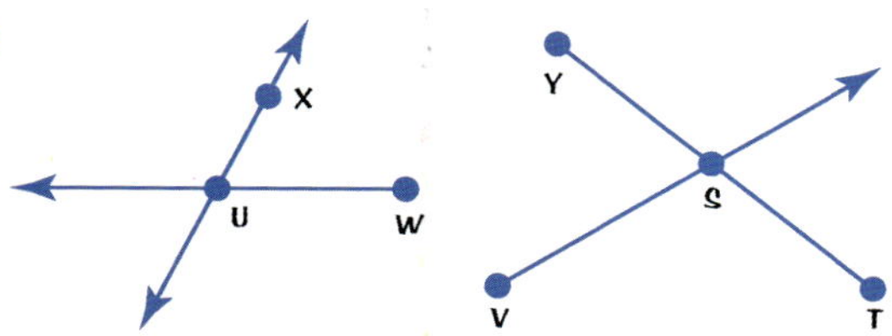

a) Name a line.
b) Name a line segment.
c) Name a ray.

2 Write the name for each shape.
Draw a line of symmetry on each shape.

a) 

b) 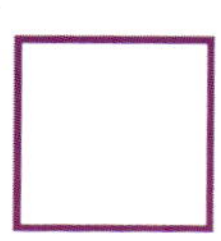

c) 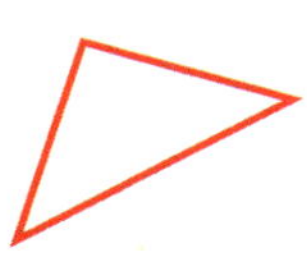

d) 

e) 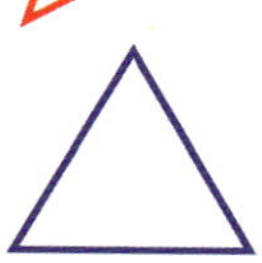

3 Some flat shapes have been sorted on to a diagram.

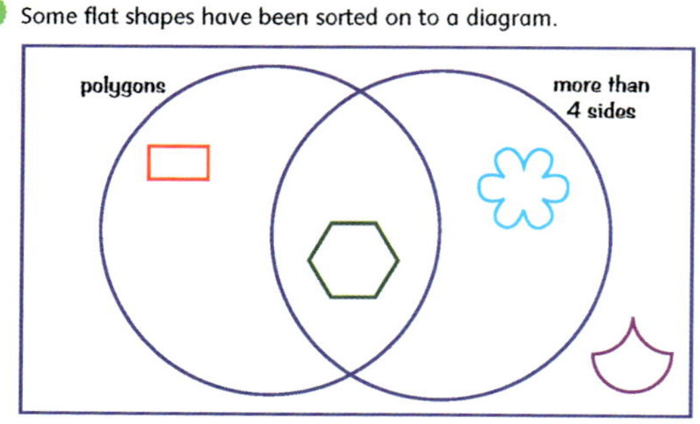

a) Copy the diagram on a large piece of paper.
b) Draw or cut out some shapes and stick them in the correct place on the diagram.

4 Look at the shapes you have put on the sorting diagram.

a) Which shapes are symmetrical?
b) Sort the shapes again so that you have a set of symmetrical shapes and a set that are not symmetrical.

Try this

Complete this pattern so it is symmetrical.

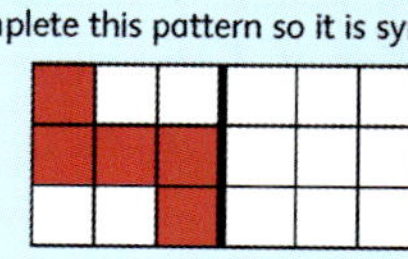

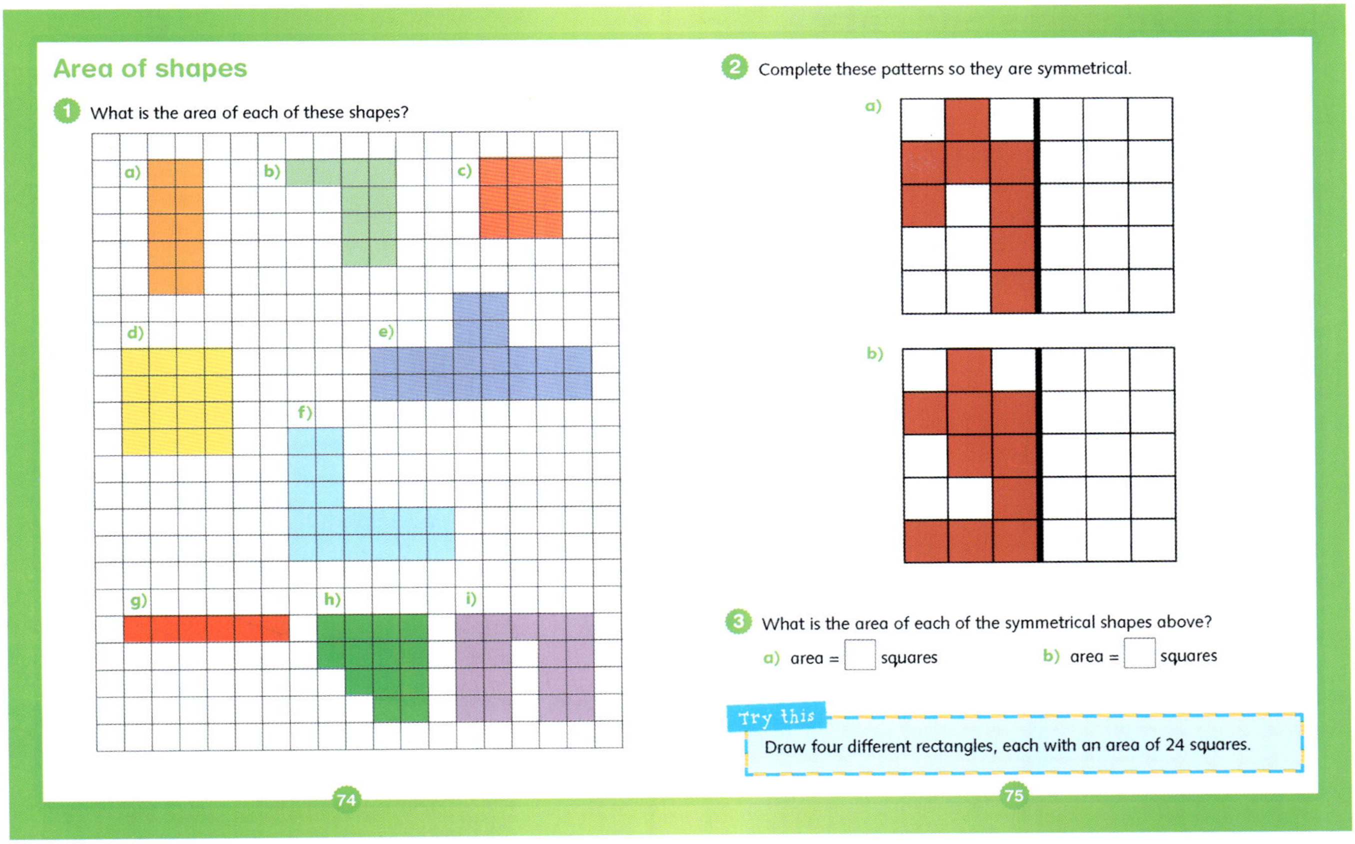

Area of shapes

1 What is the area of each of these shapes?

2 Complete these patterns so they are symmetrical.

3 What is the area of each of the symmetrical shapes above?

a) area = ☐ squares b) area = ☐ squares

Try this

Draw four different rectangles, each with an area of 24 squares.

74 75

Answers pages 70 and 71

1 a) Squares: B, G; rectangles: D, E; triangles: A, H; circles: C, F

2 a) 6 square faces, 0 rectangle faces, 8 vertices, 12 edges, cube
b) 0 square faces, 6 rectangle faces, 8 vertices, 12 edges, cuboid
c) 2 square faces, 4 rectangle faces, 8 vertices, 12 edges, cuboid

Answers pages 72 and 73

1 a) line UX b) segment YT c) ray WU or ray VS

2 a) rectangle b) square c) triangle
d) circle e) triangle

Try this

Answers pages 74 and 75

1 a) 10 squares b) 10 squares c) 9 squares
d) 16 squares e) 20 squares f) 18 squares
g) 6 squares h) 13 squares i) 17 squares

2 a)

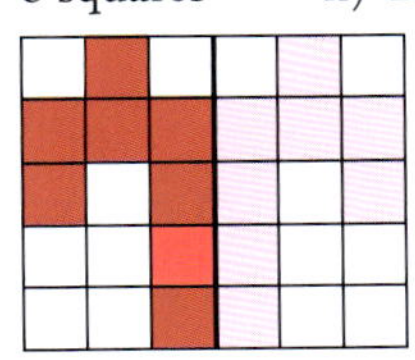

b)

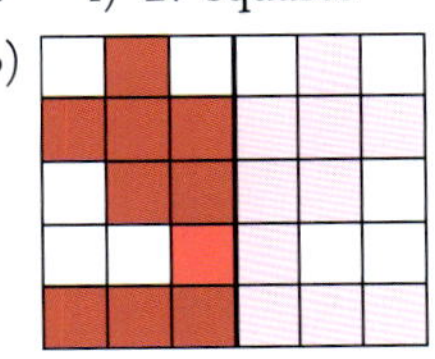

3 a) 16 squares b) 20 squares

Block F Measures and data

Maths Topic	National Standards from Government Guidelines	
Unit	*Curriculum area*	*End of year objectives / success criteria*
21 Measuring length	Understand the properties (features) of measurable items and the units, regulations and operations of measurements Application of appropriate methods, tools and rules of measurement	Solve simple everyday problems (word problems) that include units of measurement (length and height). Find the perimeter of some geometric shapes knowing the length of their sides. Identify the units of measuring length (m,cm). Convert from one unit of measuring length to another.
22 Measures problems	Application of appropriate methods, tools and rules of measurement Solving mathematical and everyday problems (word problems) using measurement Understanding Numerical Operations and relations between them	Identify the units of capacity (litre). Identify the units of measuring weight (kg, $\frac{1}{2}$ kg, $\frac{1}{4}$ kg). Convert from one unit of measuring weight to another. Solve simple everyday problems (word problems) that include units of measurement (capacity and weight). Choose the basic operation (addition – subtraction – multiplication) needed to solve mathematical or everyday problems (word problems). Check the results of any addition, subtraction or multiplication problem.
23 Handling data	Make enquiries (pose questions) and answer them by collecting the appropriate data, organising and displaying it	Record data using tallies. Collect and organise data. Display data in more than one way and explain them. Make enquiries (pose questions) and answer them. Categorise similar data and dissimilar data. Obtain data from different sources. Display the collected or given data using illustrations or simple geometric shapes and bars or columns.
24 Assess and review	Revision and assessment of previous 3 units – problems, formative and summative assessment. Monitor, assess, evaluate and consolidate pupils' knowledge and understanding.	

During this block of work, pupils will experience:

1 Estimating and measuring length in metres and in centimetres.
2 Comparing lengths given in centimetres with lengths in metres and fractions of metres.
3 Choosing appropriate units for measuring length.
4 Calculating perimeters of shapes.
5 Solving problems involving length, weight and capacity (both non-standard and standard units).
6 Estimating weight in kilograms, $\frac{1}{2}$ kilograms and $\frac{1}{4}$ kilograms.
7 Measuring and estimating capacity as equal to, less than or greater than 1 litre.
8 Using tally marks, interpreting and constructing tally charts.
9 Interpreting and displaying data in column graphs, pictograms and bar charts using given data and data that pupils have collected.

Unit 21 **Measuring length**

Term 2 Block F
Measuring and data
Unit 21 Measuring length
Unit 22 Measures problems
Unit 23 Handling data
Unit 24 Assess and review

Objectives
At the end of the unit, students should be able to…
Solve simple everyday problems (word problems) that include units of measurement (length and height).
Comprehend the concept of perimeter.
Find the perimeter of some geometric shapes knowing the length of their sides.
Identify the units of measuring length (metre, centimetre).
Convert from one unit of measuring length to another.

Vocabulary
estimate, measure, length, height, width, metre, metre stick, centimetre, ruler, division, unit of measurement, perimeter, rectangle, square

Lessons
1 Metres
2 Centimetres
3 Metres and centimetres
4 Measuring perimeter
5 Estimating and measuring lengths

Oral and mental starters
Hands up
Name it
Hidden fingers
Flash facts
In time

Resources
Metre sticks, rulers, marbles, bean bags
Sheets of paper and scissors (lesson 5)
A measuring box containing objects such as the following for pupils to measure when opportunities arise: pencils, sticks, strings, socks, ribbons, strips of card etc.
Pupil's Book pages 76–85

Prior learning
Comparing, ordering, estimating and measuring length using non-standard units

Background notes
Measurement is an important area across the curriculum and in everyday life in which number skills are used and applied. This unit develops previous learning to the use of standard units (metres and centimetres). Heavy emphasis is placed on estimating lengths prior to measuring them. Known benchmarks such as the height of a door (about 2 m), the length of a ruler (about 30 cm), known personal height, known length of thumb etc., are very useful comparisons when estimating length.

End of unit evaluation
Check that pupils are able to:
1 Estimate and measure lengths in metres and in centimetres.
2 Choose appropriate tools and units of measurement.
3 Convert from centimetres to metres and vice versa.
4 Find the perimeter of geometric shapes.

Supporting the topic
Discuss situations in real life involving length with which pupils are likely to be familiar, e.g. buying the correct amount of fabric to make curtains or clothes, measuring wood to make a shelf etc. Use opportunities in everyday classroom activities to reinforce the concept and vocabulary of length, e.g. distances to school, length/height of jumps in PE.
Provide opportunities for small groups to compare and measure the lengths of items in the measuring box.

Lesson 1 **Metres**

Pupil's Book pages 76 and 77 **Oral and mental starter: Hands up**

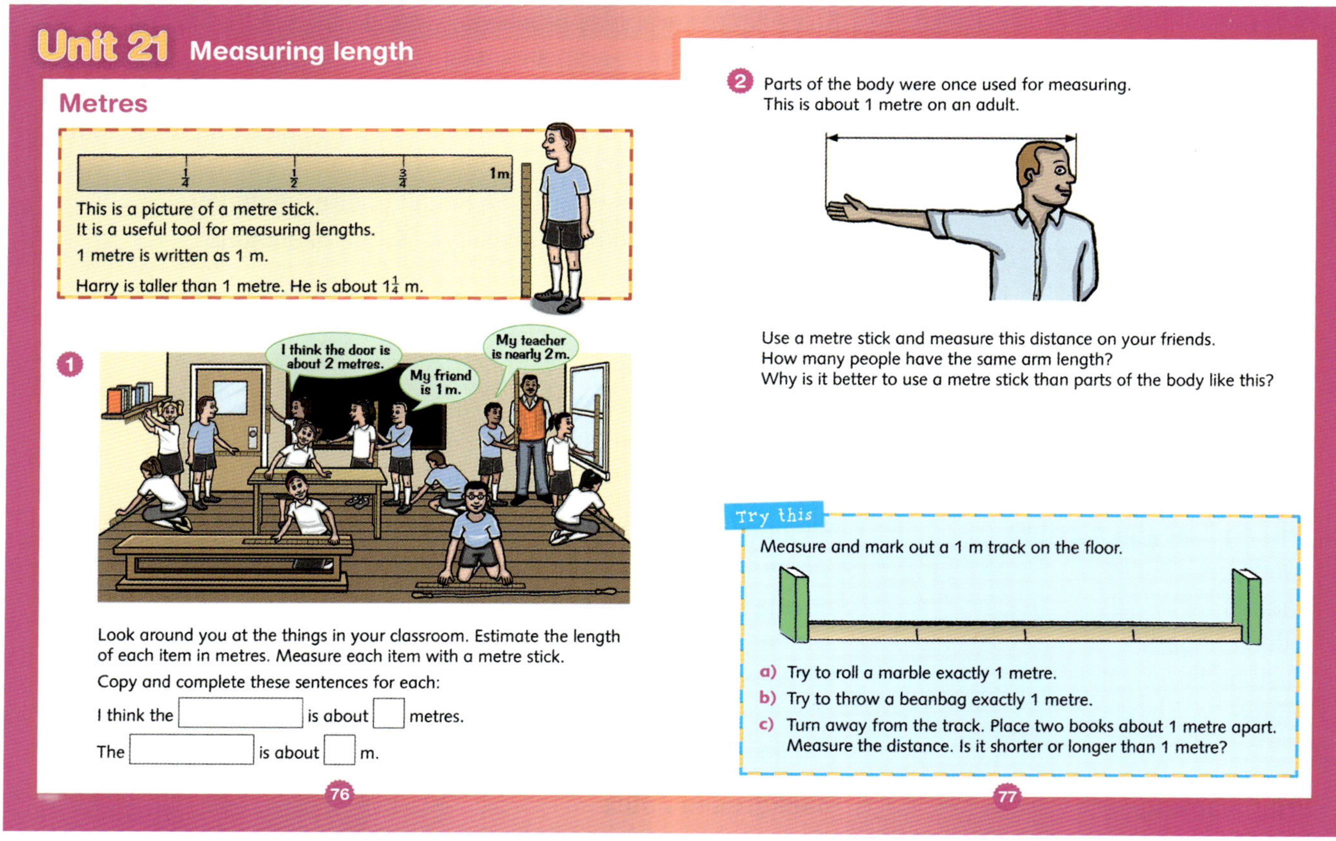

Unit 21 Measuring length

Metres

This is a picture of a metre stick.
It is a useful tool for measuring lengths.
1 metre is written as 1 m.
Harry is taller than 1 metre. He is about $1\frac{1}{4}$ m.

1

Look around you at the things in your classroom. Estimate the length of each item in metres. Measure each item with a metre stick.

Copy and complete these sentences for each:

I think the ☐ is about ☐ metres.

The ☐ is about ☐ m.

2 Parts of the body were once used for measuring.
This is about 1 metre on an adult.

Use a metre stick and measure this distance on your friends.
How many people have the same arm length?
Why is it better to use a metre stick than parts of the body like this?

Try this

Measure and mark out a 1 m track on the floor.

a) Try to roll a marble exactly 1 metre.
b) Try to throw a beanbag exactly 1 metre.
c) Turn away from the track. Place two books about 1 metre apart. Measure the distance. Is it shorter or longer than 1 metre?

76 77

Activities

- Ask three pupils to each hold a metre stick and to put them together to show they are all the same length. Explain that each stick measures 1 metre and write '1 metre' on the board. Explain that a metre is a standard unit for measuring, e.g. when shopping for fabric/wood etc. the shopkeeper will measure the length using metres. Where have pupils seen items being measured using metres?
- With the help of a pupil place one metre stick on top of another against a wall. 'How high from the floor is the top of the stick? How high would it be if I could put another metre stick on top?' Indicate the middle of the top stick. 'How high from the floor is this?' Establish that it is one and a half metres. Repeat for one and a quarter metres.
- Ask a pupil who is about 1.25 metres tall to come out and stand alongside the sticks. 'Approximately how tall is (name)? Approximately how high do you think the door is?'
- Go through the introduction on page 76. Emphasise that 'm' is a short way of writing metre.
- Emphasise that in question 1 pupils must record their estimate first, then measure the item and record that, then go on to the next item. Check that pupils are using the metre sticks accurately as they work, e.g. not leaving gaps for lengths over 1 m.
- Discuss the results from question 2 and the answers to the last question.

Answers

2 It is better to use a metre stick than body parts as people are not all exactly the same size.

Lesson 2 **Centimetres**

Pupil's Book pages 78 and 79 **Oral and mental starter: Name it**

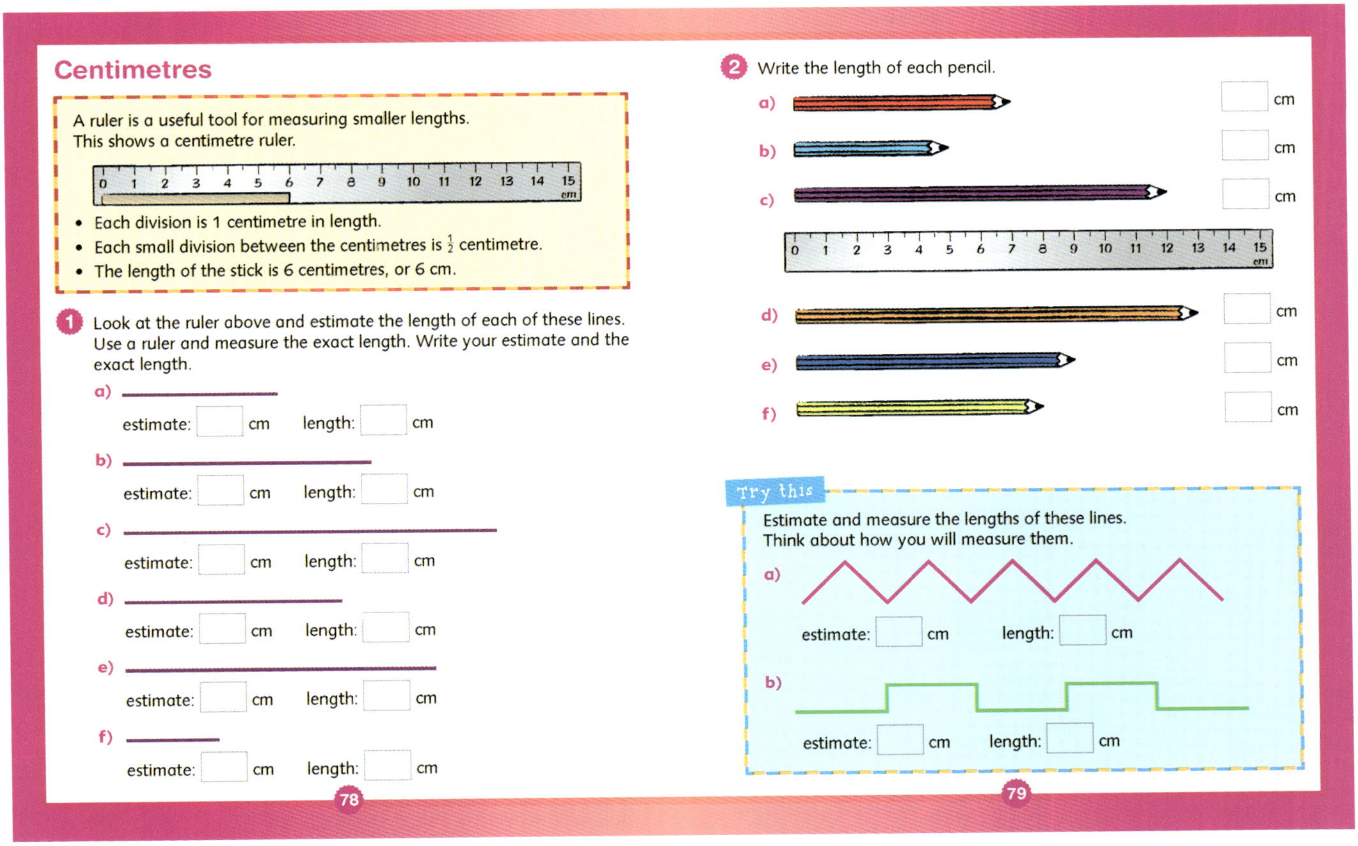

Centimetres

A ruler is a useful tool for measuring smaller lengths.
This shows a centimetre ruler.

- Each division is 1 centimetre in length.
- Each small division between the centimetres is $\frac{1}{2}$ centimetre.
- The length of the stick is 6 centimetres, or 6 cm.

1 Look at the ruler above and estimate the length of each of these lines. Use a ruler and measure the exact length. Write your estimate and the exact length.

a) estimate: cm length: cm
b) estimate: cm length: cm
c) estimate: cm length: cm
d) estimate: cm length: cm
e) estimate: cm length: cm
f) estimate: cm length: cm

78

2 Write the length of each pencil.

a) cm
b) cm
c) cm
d) cm
e) cm
f) cm

Try this

Estimate and measure the lengths of these lines.
Think about how you will measure them.

a) estimate: cm length: cm
b) estimate: cm length: cm

79

Activities

- Give a ruler marked in cm to each pupil and ask them to compare it with the illustration on page 78. Explain that a centimetre is another standard unit for measuring length. Go through the teaching points in the introduction, emphasising that one end of the stick being measured is at the beginning of the ruler, the 0 cm position, the other end is on 6 cm exactly.
- Ask pupils to estimate how wide their closed Pupil's Book is, then ask them to measure it to the nearest cm with their rulers. Ask them to estimate, then measure the length of their books. Check that they are using the rulers correctly as they do these activities.
- Towards the end of the lesson discuss the methods used in 'Try this', e.g. in part a) measuring one zigzag line and multiply by 10, in part b) counting each of the two different lengths.

Answers

1 a) 5 cm b) 8 cm c) 12 cm
d) 7 cm e) 10 cm f) 3 cm

2 a) 7 cm b) 5 cm c) 12 cm
d) 13 cm e) 9 cm f) 8 cm

Try this

a) 20 cm b) 19 cm

Lesson 3 **Metres and centimetres**

Pupil's Book pages 80 and 81 **Oral and mental starter: Hidden fingers**

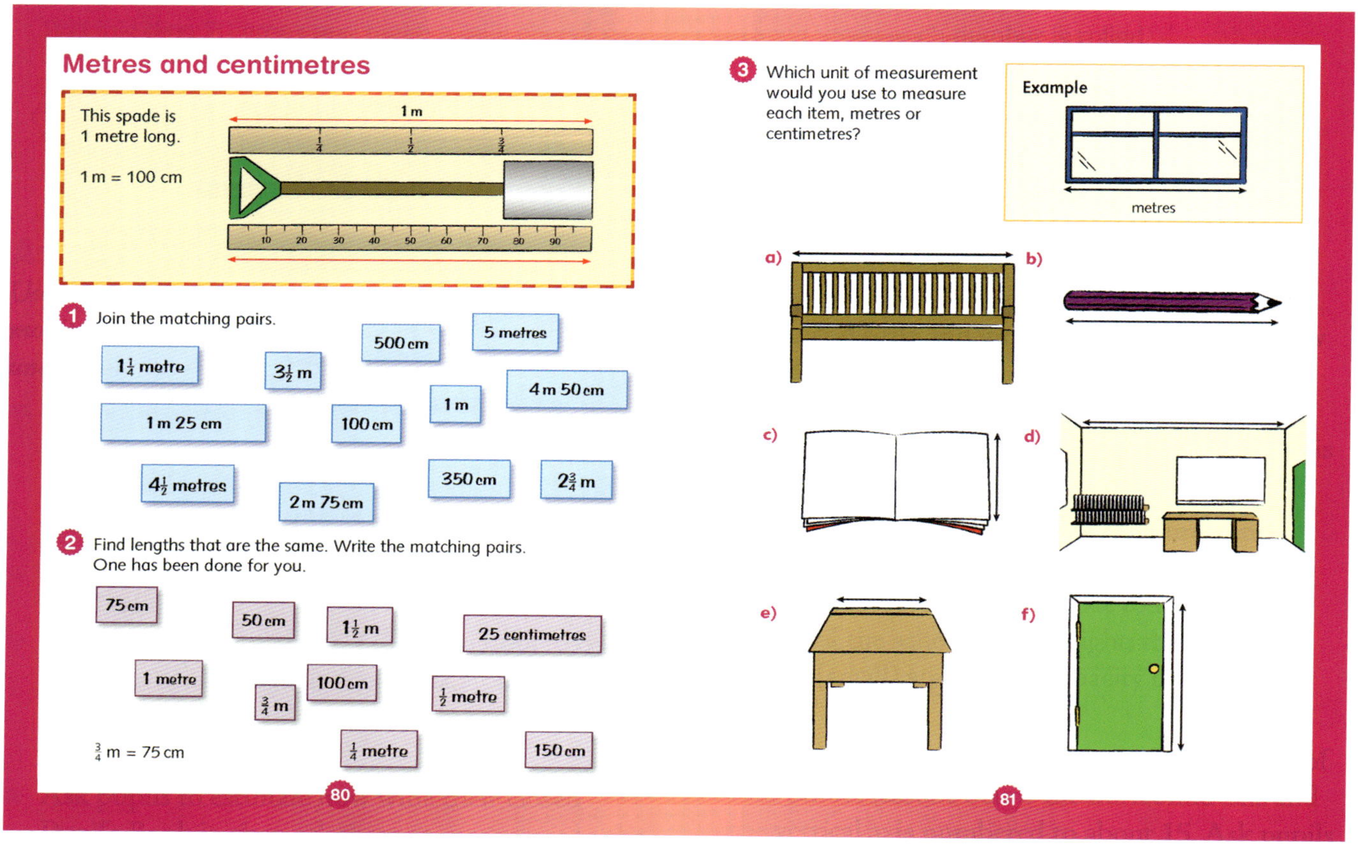

Activities

- Discuss different lengths that pupils can see in the classroom. Ask 'Would you use centimetres or metres to measure, e.g. the width of the clock; the height of the window; the length of your thumb; the height of the ceiling?' etc. Reinforce that metres and centimetres are both units of measurement.
- Look at page 80. Talk about the illustrations. Compare the metre sticks on the page with the sticks available in your classroom. Count the 10 cm marks on the second stick together to confirm that there are 100 cm in 1 m. Ask pupils to compare the two illustrated metre sticks to answer questions such as 'How many cm are there in $\frac{1}{2}$ m? … in $\frac{1}{4}$ m? … in $\frac{3}{4}$ m?'
- Hold up a metre stick. Indicate different points on the stick (multiples of 5 or 10 cm) and ask the class to say how many cm the point is from the beginning of the stick. Ask a child to come and hold up another metre stick alongside yours. Repeat the previous activity for lengths greater than 1 m, e.g. 150 cm, $1\frac{3}{4}$ m, 200 cm etc.
- Look at page 80 again. Ask pupils to put their fingers on given lengths on the stick marked in 10 cm intervals, e.g. 25 cm, 60 cm, 45 cm, $\frac{3}{4}$ m, 100 cm etc.

Answers

1 $1\frac{1}{4}$ metre → 1m 25 cm, $3\frac{1}{2}$ m → 350 cm,
500 cm → 5 metres, 100 cm → 1m,
4m 50 cm → $4\frac{1}{2}$ metres, 2m 75 cm → $2\frac{3}{4}$ m

2 1 metre = 100 cm, $1\frac{1}{2}$ m = 150 cm,
50 cm = $\frac{1}{2}$ metre, $\frac{1}{4}$ metre = 25 centimetres

3 a) metres b) centimetres c) centimetres
d) metres e) centimetres f) metres

Lesson 4 **Measuring perimeter**

Pupil's Book pages 82 and 83 **Oral and mental starter: Flash facts**

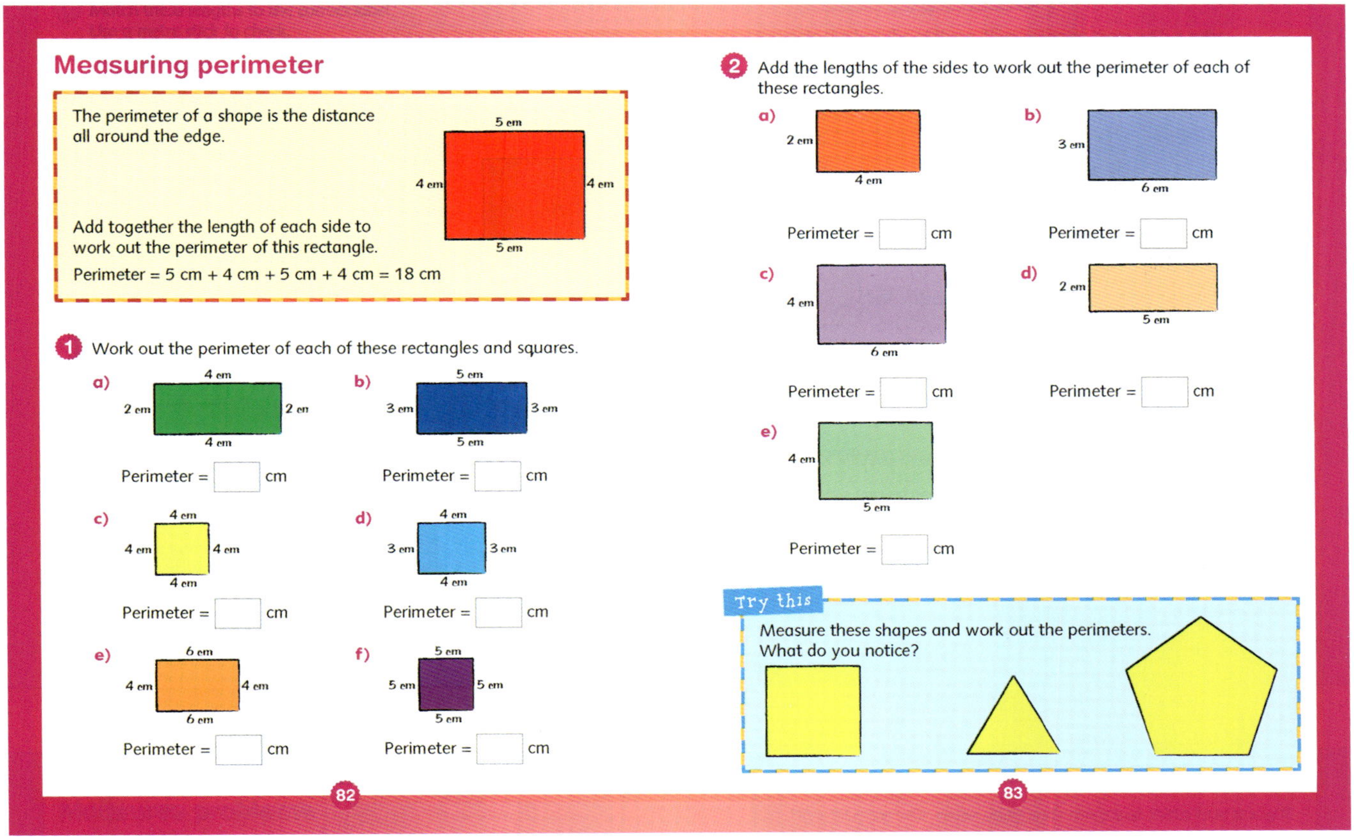

Measuring perimeter

The perimeter of a shape is the distance all around the edge.

5 cm, 4 cm, 4 cm, 5 cm

Add together the length of each side to work out the perimeter of this rectangle.

Perimeter = 5 cm + 4 cm + 5 cm + 4 cm = 18 cm

1 Work out the perimeter of each of these rectangles and squares.

a) 4 cm, 2 cm, 2 cm, 4 cm — Perimeter = ☐ cm

b) 5 cm, 3 cm, 3 cm, 5 cm — Perimeter = ☐ cm

c) 4 cm, 4 cm, 4 cm, 4 cm — Perimeter = ☐ cm

d) 4 cm, 3 cm, 3 cm, 4 cm — Perimeter = ☐ cm

e) 6 cm, 4 cm, 4 cm, 6 cm — Perimeter = ☐ cm

f) 5 cm, 5 cm, 5 cm, 5 cm — Perimeter = ☐ cm

82

2 Add the lengths of the sides to work out the perimeter of each of these rectangles.

a) 2 cm, 4 cm — Perimeter = ☐ cm

b) 3 cm, 6 cm — Perimeter = ☐ cm

c) 4 cm, 6 cm — Perimeter = ☐ cm

d) 2 cm, 5 cm — Perimeter = ☐ cm

e) 4 cm, 5 cm — Perimeter = ☐ cm

Try this

Measure these shapes and work out the perimeters. What do you notice?

83

Activities

- Ask 'What do we mean by the perimeter of a shape?' Allow time for pupils to make suggestions, then draw a rectangle on the board and indicate its perimeter. 'How could we find the length of the perimeter of this rectangle?' Discuss suggestions then measure the length and width of the rectangle to the nearest cm, write these lengths on the board and ask pupils to work out the perimeter.
- Ask pupils to measure the length and width of the front cover of their Pupil's Book and work out the total perimeter. Ask for the results. 'How did you work it out?'
- Look at page 82 and go through the introduction with the class.
- Towards the end of the lesson ask for the results pupils found in 'Try this'. 'Did anyone notice any connection between the number of sides and the perimeter of each shape?' (p = 3 cm × number of sides) 'Can anyone explain why?'

Answers

1 a) 12 cm b) 16 cm c) 16 cm
d) 14 cm e) 20 cm f) 20 cm

2 a) 12 cm b) 18 cm c) 20 cm
d) 14 cm e) 18 cm

Try this

Perimeter of square is 12 cm. Perimeter of triangle is 9 cm. Perimeter of pentagon is 15 cm. All sides are the same lengths.

Lesson 5 Estimating and measuring lengths

Pupil's Book pages 84 and 85 **Oral and mental starter: In time**

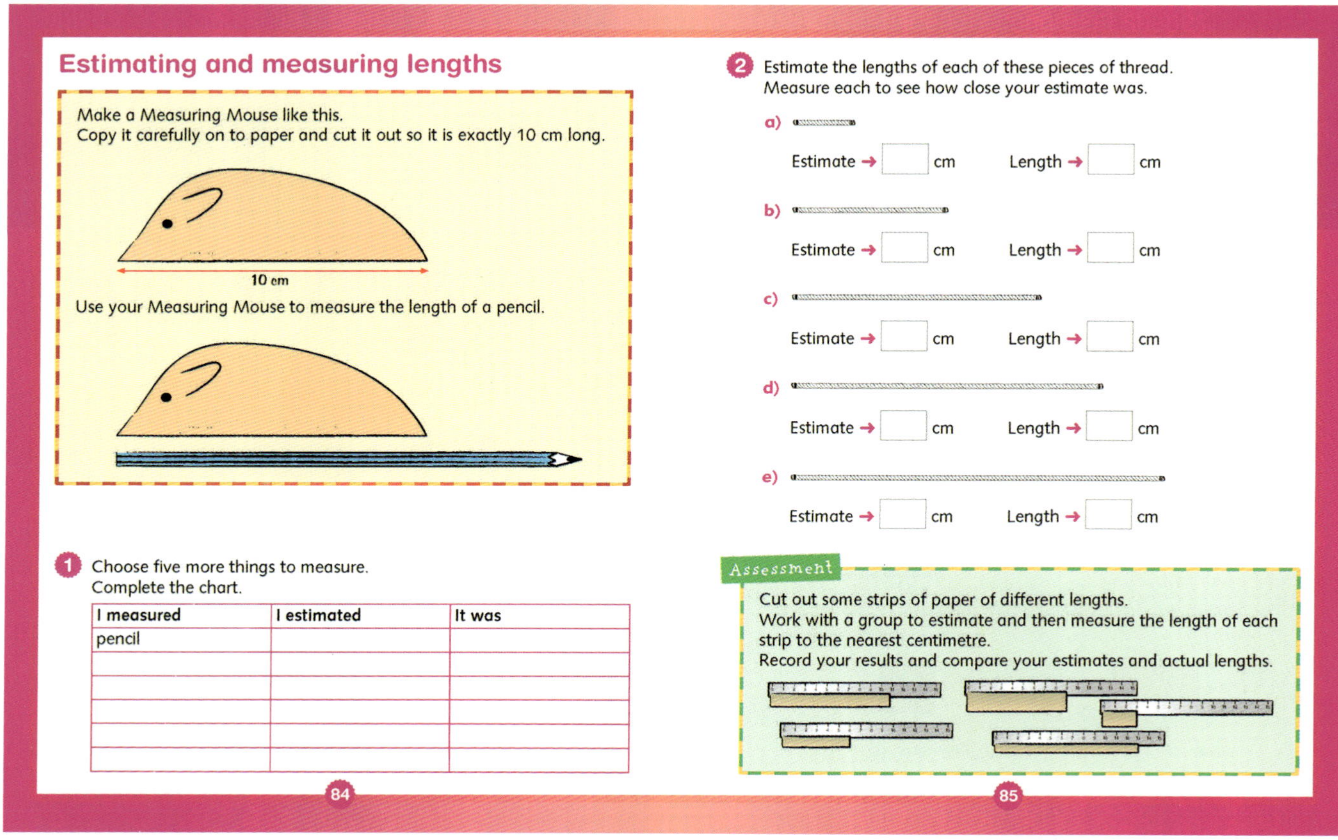

Estimating and measuring lengths

Make a Measuring Mouse like this.
Copy it carefully on to paper and cut it out so it is exactly 10 cm long.

10 cm

Use your Measuring Mouse to measure the length of a pencil.

1 Choose five more things to measure.
Complete the chart.

I measured	I estimated	It was
pencil		

84

2 Estimate the lengths of each of these pieces of thread.
Measure each to see how close your estimate was.

a) Estimate → ☐ cm Length → ☐ cm

b) Estimate → ☐ cm Length → ☐ cm

c) Estimate → ☐ cm Length → ☐ cm

d) Estimate → ☐ cm Length → ☐ cm

e) Estimate → ☐ cm Length → ☐ cm

Assessment

Cut out some strips of paper of different lengths.
Work with a group to estimate and then measure the length of each strip to the nearest centimetre.
Record your results and compare your estimates and actual lengths.

85

Activities

- Look at page 84. Go through the introduction with the class. Emphasise that the mouse is exactly 10 cm long and that pupils must copy it very carefully and make sure that theirs is exactly 10 cm long.
- Ask pupils to estimate the length of their pencils to the nearest cm. Ask them to record this estimate in their charts. Now ask them to use the mouse as a guide and give a more precise estimate based on 'measuring' with the mouse and estimating how much longer (or shorter) any extra part of the pencil is. Remind pupils not to leave gaps or overlap between mouse lengths as they are measuring. 'Was anyone's pencil more than 3 mouse lengths long? Was anyone's less than 1 mouse length long?' They then choose five more items to estimate and measure.
- Go through the instructions for the assessment activity with the class.

Answers

2 a) 2 cm b) 5 cm c) 8 cm d) 10 cm e) 12 cm

Unit 22 Measures problems

Term 2 Block F
Measures and data

Unit 21 Measuring length
Unit 22 Measures problems
Unit 23 Handling data
Unit 24 Assess and review

Objectives

At the end of the unit, students should be able to..

Identify the units of capacity (litre).
Identify the units of measuring weight (kilogram, $\frac{1}{2}$ kilogram, $\frac{1}{4}$ kilogram).
Convert from one unit of measuring weight to another.
Solve simple everyday problems (word problems) that include units of measurement (capacity and weight).
Choose the basic operation (addition – subtraction – multiplication) needed to solve mathematical or everyday problems (word problems).
Check the results of any addition, subtraction or multiplication problem.

Vocabulary

weight, balance, heavy, heavier, light, lighter, measure, kilogram, $\frac{1}{2}$ kilogram, $\frac{1}{4}$ kilogram, estimate, capacity, litre, standard unit, height

Lessons

1 Measuring weight
2 Kilograms
3 Comparing amounts
4 Litres
5 Measures problems

Oral and mental starters

Product pairs
Halve it
Language
Arrows away
Start here

Resources

Set up a measuring area with containers, e.g. bottles, bowls, cups, cans, spoons; water or sand; balance scales; sets of cubes, marbles or similar items; 1 kg, $\frac{1}{2}$ kg and $\frac{1}{4}$ kg weights; heavy and light objects, e.g. large stone, brick, pebble, bean, sock, cork, feather.
Pupil's Book pages 86–95

Prior learning

Comparing, ordering and measuring weight and capacity (non-standard units)

Background notes

This unit develops previous learning on capacity and weight to the use of standard units, including related word problems. These topics are important aspects of everyday life in which number skills are used and applied. Capacity should not be confused with volume. Capacity is the amount of material a container can hold; volume is the amount of space it occupies. A solid 10 × 10 × 10 cm cube has a volume of 1000 cubic cm, but it has zero capacity.

End of unit evaluation

Check that pupils are able to:

1 Estimate and measure and compare weights in $\frac{1}{4}$ kg, $\frac{1}{2}$ kg and 1 kg.
2 Estimate, measure and compare capacities using litres.
3 Solve word problems in the context of measures involving addition and subtraction.

Supporting the topic

Provide opportunities for pupils to use the resources in the measuring area. Talk about situations with which pupils are likely to be familiar in everyday life where capacity and weight are used, e.g. measuring liquids for cooking; capacity of drinks bottles; weighing ingredients for cooking; weighing babies to check growth.

Lesson 1 Measuring weight

Pupil's Book pages 86 and 87 **Oral and mental starter: Product pairs**

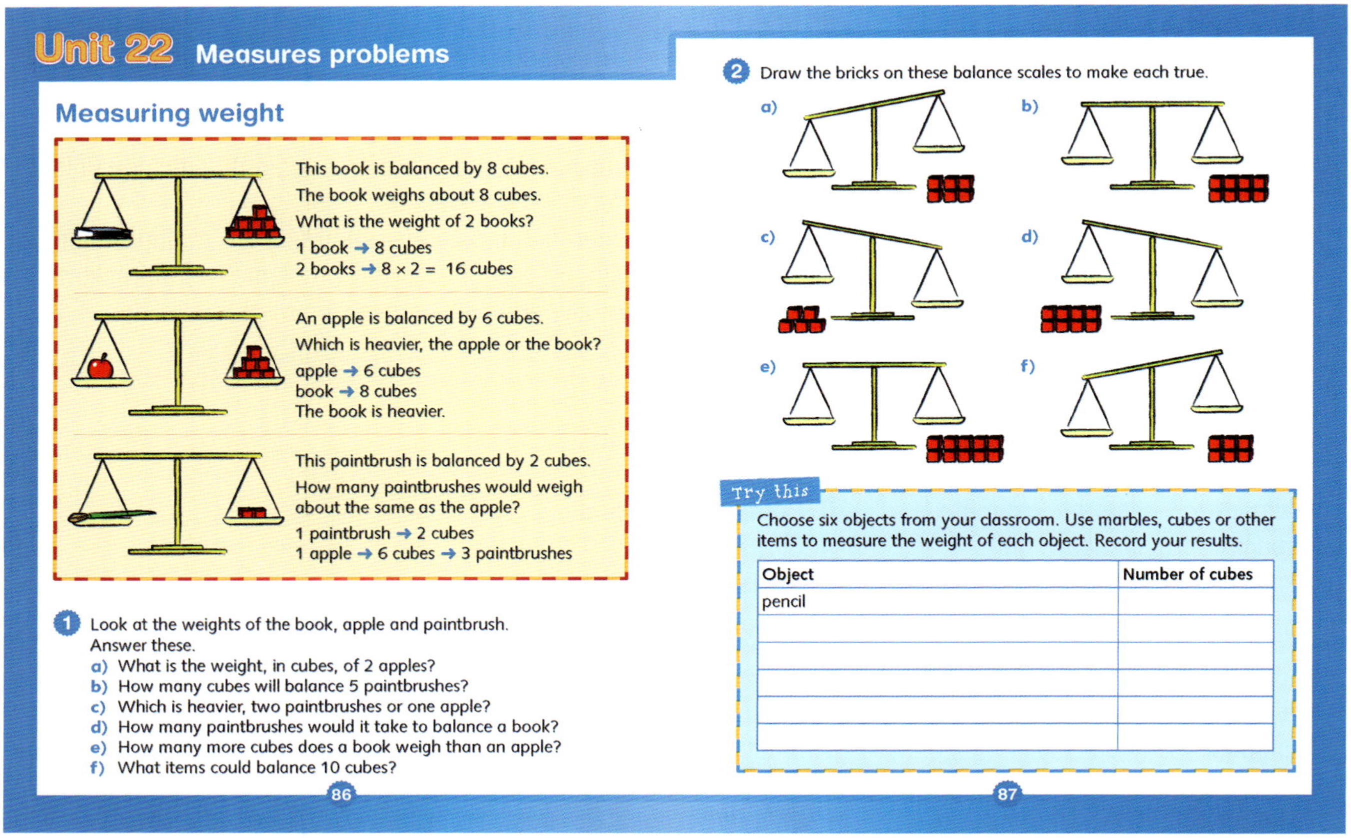

Unit 22 Measures problems

Measuring weight

This book is balanced by 8 cubes.
The book weighs about 8 cubes.
What is the weight of 2 books?
1 book → 8 cubes
2 books → 8 × 2 = 16 cubes

An apple is balanced by 6 cubes.
Which is heavier, the apple or the book?
apple → 6 cubes
book → 8 cubes
The book is heavier.

This paintbrush is balanced by 2 cubes.
How many paintbrushes would weigh about the same as the apple?
1 paintbrush → 2 cubes
1 apple → 6 cubes → 3 paintbrushes

1 Look at the weights of the book, apple and paintbrush. Answer these.
a) What is the weight, in cubes, of 2 apples?
b) How many cubes will balance 5 paintbrushes?
c) Which is heavier, two paintbrushes or one apple?
d) How many paintbrushes would it take to balance a book?
e) How many more cubes does a book weigh than an apple?
f) What items could balance 10 cubes?

86

2 Draw the bricks on these balance scales to make each true.
a) b) c) d) e) f)

Try this

Choose six objects from your classroom. Use marbles, cubes or other items to measure the weight of each object. Record your results.

Object	Number of cubes
pencil	

87

Activities

- Look at page 86. Go through the introduction, stressing that the weight of an object can be measured by balancing it against a number of identical objects, such as cubes (or marbles or whatever materials you have available). Revise that if an object on one side of the balance is lower than the cubes, it is heavier than the number of cubes and vice versa. 'What happens when an object weighs the same as the number of cubes?'
- Ask a pupil to weigh an item on your balance scales by balancing it against cubes (or marbles, bottle tops, etc.). 'How many (cubes) balance the (item)? So what is the weight of (item) in (cubes)? How many (cubes) would be needed to balance 2 (items)? Repeat with two or three other items and pupils.

Answers

1 a) 12 cubes b) 10 cubes c) 1 apple
d) 4 paintbrushes e) 2 cubes
f) 1 book and 1 paintbrush **or** 5 paintbrushes **or** 1 apple and 2 paint brushes

Lesson 2 **Kilograms**

Pupil's Book pages 88 and 89 **Oral and mental starter: Halve it**

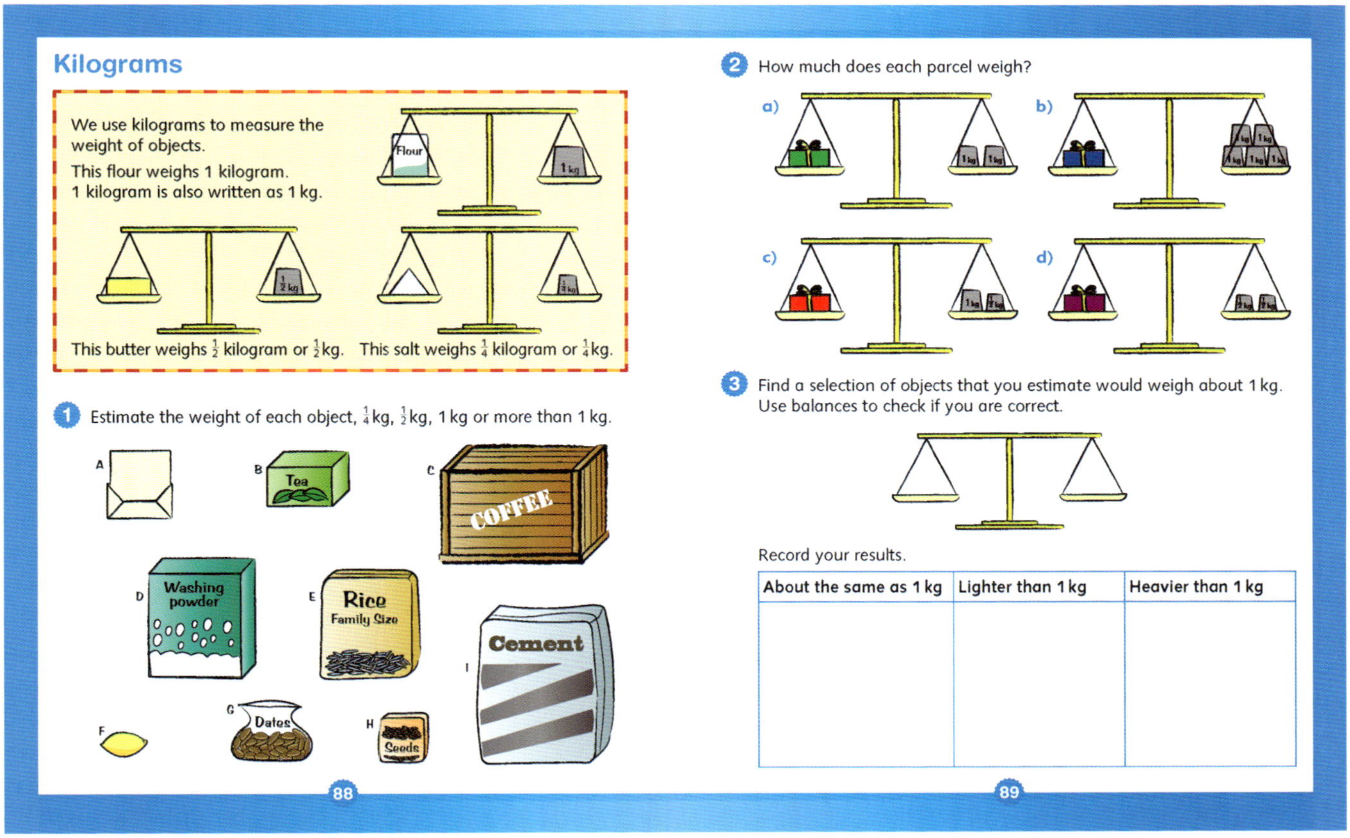

Kilograms

We use kilograms to measure the weight of objects.
This flour weighs 1 kilogram.
1 kilogram is also written as 1 kg.

This butter weighs $\frac{1}{2}$ kilogram or $\frac{1}{2}$ kg. This salt weighs $\frac{1}{4}$ kilogram or $\frac{1}{4}$ kg.

1 Estimate the weight of each object, $\frac{1}{4}$ kg, $\frac{1}{2}$ kg, 1 kg or more than 1 kg.

2 How much does each parcel weigh?

a) b) c) d)

3 Find a selection of objects that you estimate would weigh about 1 kg. Use balances to check if you are correct.

Record your results.

About the same as 1 kg	Lighter than 1 kg	Heavier than 1 kg

Activities

- Look at page 88. Go through the introduction with the class and explain that kilograms are standard units of weight. 'Why do we need standard units when weighing things?' Discuss the ideas suggested. 'Does anyone know their own weight in kilograms?'
- Pass round 1 kg, $\frac{1}{2}$ kg and $\frac{1}{4}$ kg weights for pupils to hold and have an idea how heavy they feel. Ask three or four pupils to come out and each select an object that they think will weigh about 1 kg, then test it against the 1 kg weight on the balance. Repeat with other pupils selecting and testing objects which they think are about $\frac{1}{2}$ kg and $\frac{1}{4}$ kg.
- Hold up a selection of obviously light and obviously heavy objects at random and ask pupils to say whether they would weigh the same as, more than or less than 1 kg. Each time ask different pupils to check using the balance and weights.
- For ease of classroom organisation it would be useful for half the class to begin on question 3 whilst the other half complete questions 1 and 2. As pupils work through question 3, check that they are using the apparatus correctly and that they understand the concept of measuring weight by balancing.
- Towards the end of the lesson ask for results in question 3. 'Did anyone have a different result for the same item?' Ask one of the pupils concerned to check by weighing the item again on the balance scales.

Answers

1 A $\frac{1}{4}$ kg, B $\frac{1}{4}$ kg (or $\frac{1}{2}$ kg), C more than 1 kg, D 1 kg, E $\frac{1}{2}$ kg (or 1 kg), F $\frac{1}{4}$ kg, G $\frac{1}{4}$ kg (or $\frac{1}{2}$ kg), H $\frac{1}{4}$ kg, I more than 1 kg

2 a) 2 kg b) 5 kg c) $1\frac{1}{2}$ kg d) 1 kg

Lesson 3 **Comparing amounts**

Pupil's Book pages 90 and 91 **Oral and mental starter: Language**

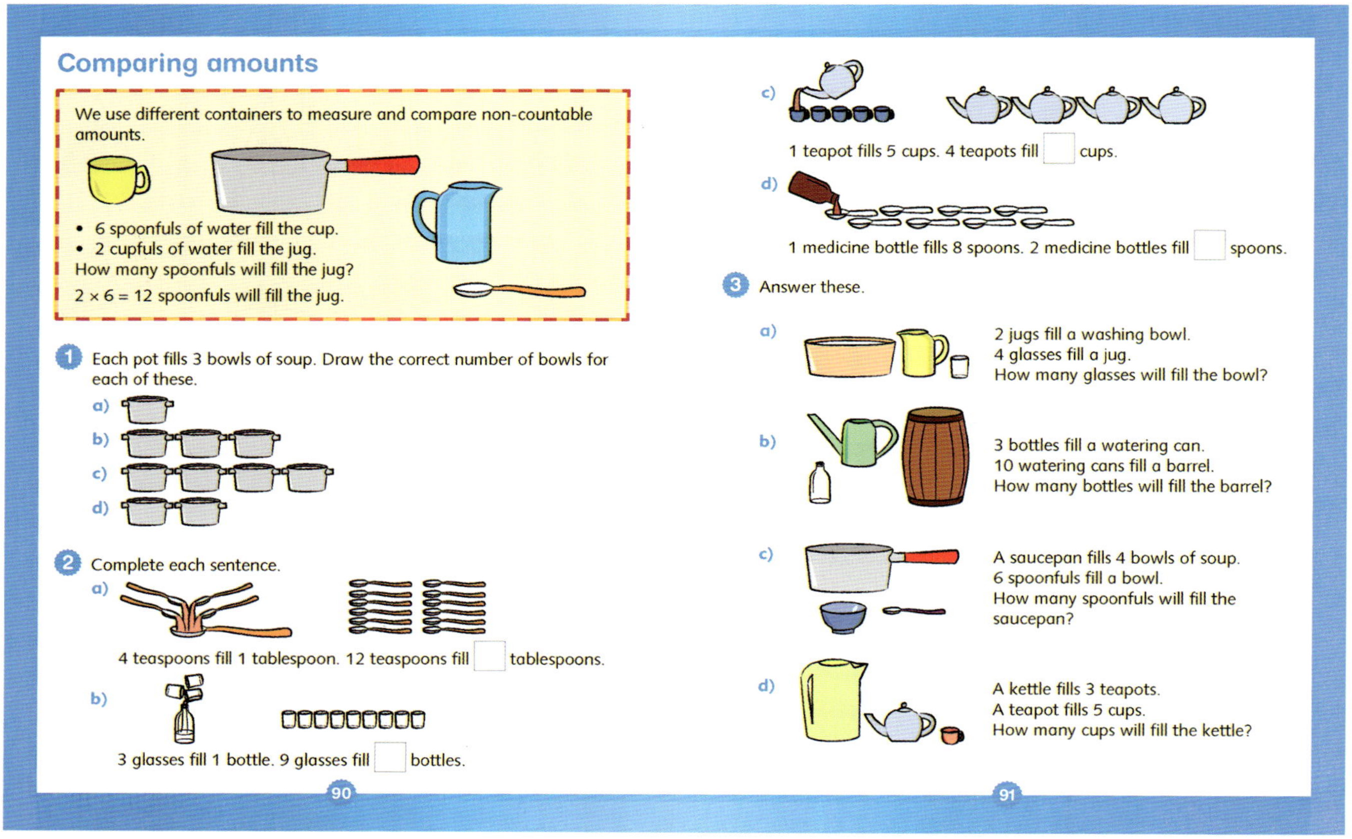

Comparing amounts

We use different containers to measure and compare non-countable amounts.

- 6 spoonfuls of water fill the cup.
- 2 cupfuls of water fill the jug.

How many spoonfuls will fill the jug?

2 × 6 = 12 spoonfuls will fill the jug.

1 Each pot fills 3 bowls of soup. Draw the correct number of bowls for each of these.

a)

b)

c)

d)

2 Complete each sentence.

a) 4 teaspoons fill 1 tablespoon. 12 teaspoons fill ☐ tablespoons.

b) 3 glasses fill 1 bottle. 9 glasses fill ☐ bottles.

90

c) 1 teapot fills 5 cups. 4 teapots fill ☐ cups.

d) 1 medicine bottle fills 8 spoons. 2 medicine bottles fill ☐ spoons.

3 Answer these.

a) 2 jugs fill a washing bowl.
4 glasses fill a jug.
How many glasses will fill the bowl?

b) 3 bottles fill a watering can.
10 watering cans fill a barrel.
How many bottles will fill the barrel?

c) A saucepan fills 4 bowls of soup.
6 spoonfuls fill a bowl.
How many spoonfuls will fill the saucepan?

d) A kettle fills 3 teapots.
A teapot fills 5 cups.
How many cups will fill the kettle?

91

Activities

- Have ready a large spoon, a small container and water or sand in a bowl. Explain that the lesson is about the capacity of containers. 'What do we mean by the capacity of a bottle?' Establish that capacity means the amount which a container can hold. Ask two pupils to come to the front and take turns to fill the spoon from the bowl then put the contents of the spoon into the container until it is full. Ask the class to count how many spoonfuls fill the container as the pupil does the activity. Record the number on the board, e.g. 3 spoonfuls fill the pot.
- Ask two more pupils to take turns to empty the small container into a larger container, refill the small container and repeat until the large one is full, with the class counting the number of times it takes to fill the larger container. Record on the board, e.g. 4 potfuls fill the bowl. 'How many spoonfuls would it take to fill the bowl? How did you work it out? Did anyone do it a different way?' Go over the suggested methods carefully for the benefit of those pupils who found it more difficult than others.
- Look at page 90. Go through the introduction and relate to the previous activity. Ask for the answer to the question and the methods used to work it out. Relate to previous work on multiplication.

Answers

1 a) 3 bowls b) 9 bowls c) 12 bowls d) 6 bowls

2 a) 3 tablespoons b) 3 bottles
c) 20 cups d) 16 spoons

3 a) 8 glasses b) 30 bottles
c) 24 spoonfuls d) 15 cups

Lesson 4 Litres

Pupil's Book pages 92 and 93 **Oral and mental starter: Arrows away**

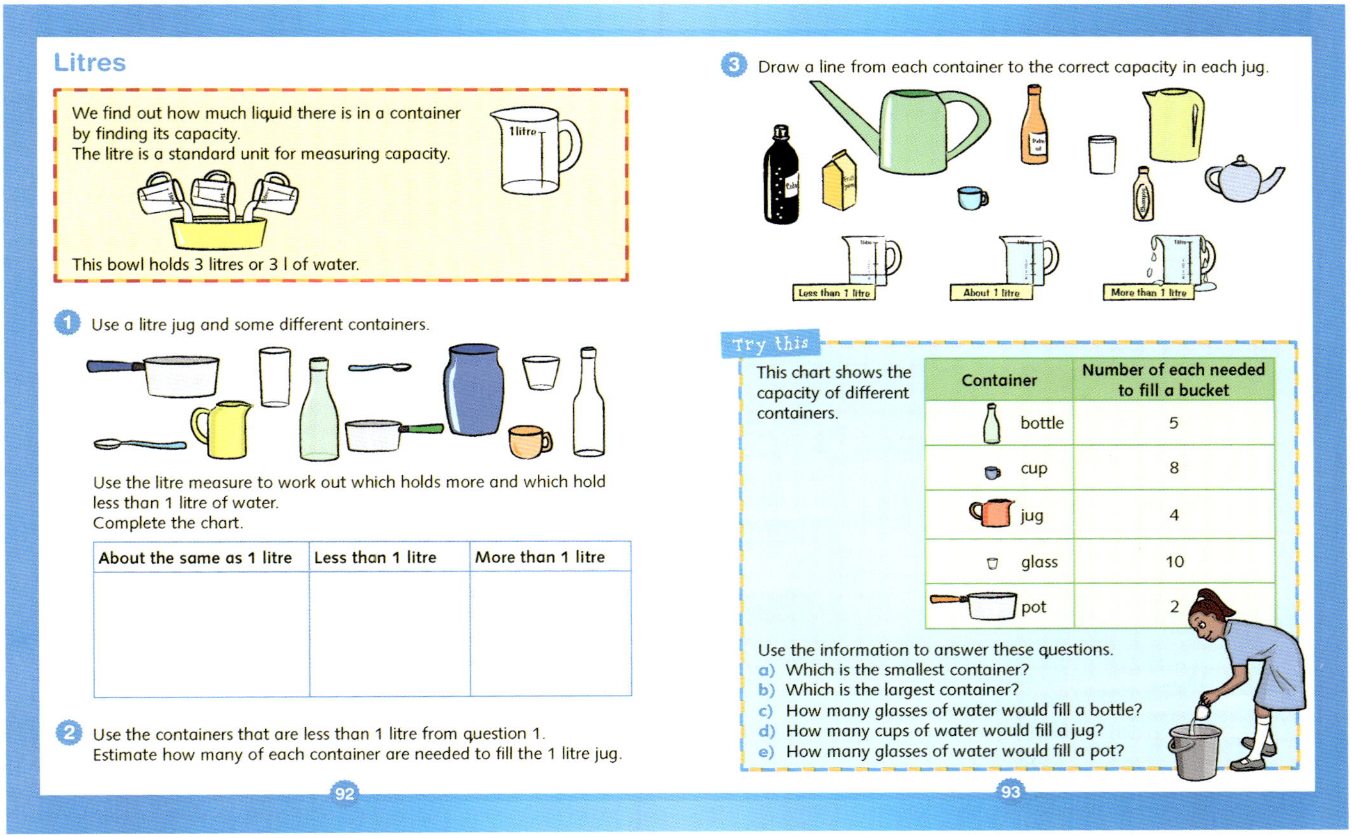

Litres

We find out how much liquid there is in a container by finding its capacity.
The litre is a standard unit for measuring capacity.

This bowl holds 3 litres or 3 l of water.

1 Use a litre jug and some different containers.

Use the litre measure to work out which holds more and which hold less than 1 litre of water.
Complete the chart.

About the same as 1 litre	Less than 1 litre	More than 1 litre

2 Use the containers that are less than 1 litre from question 1.
Estimate how many of each container are needed to fill the 1 litre jug.

92

3 Draw a line from each container to the correct capacity in each jug.

Less than 1 litre | About 1 litre | More than 1 litre

Try this

This chart shows the capacity of different containers.

Container	Number of each needed to fill a bucket
bottle	5
cup	8
jug	4
glass	10
pot	2

Use the information to answer these questions.
a) Which is the smallest container?
b) Which is the largest container?
c) How many glasses of water would fill a bottle?
d) How many cups of water would fill a jug?
e) How many glasses of water would fill a pot?

93

Activities

- Look at page 92. Go through the introduction with the class. Remind them that they have learned about metres and centimetres as standard units for measuring length and kilograms as standard units for measuring weight. 'What do we mean by standard units?' Establish that they are units which always mean the same amount and are commonly understood. Non-standard units, such as bottles, could be any size.
- Show a litre measure to the class. Point out the graduated scale and indicate the 1 litre line. 'How could we find out how many litres our bucket holds?' Ask different pupils in turn to measure 1 litre of water and pour it in the bucket until it is full, the rest of the class counting the litres.
- Ideally question 1 should be completed with pupils working in small groups. If there are insufficient capacity materials for this, then it could be done as a whole class with individual pupils coming out to test each container.
- Towards the end of the lesson ask for some of the results in 'Try this'. Ask pupils to explain how they worked them out.

Answers

3 less than 1 litre → cup, glass, shampoo;
about 1 litre → carton of juice, oil bottle, teapot;
more than 1 litre → watering can, kettle, bottle of cola

Try this

a) glass b) pot c) 2 d) 2 e) 5

Lesson 5 **Measures problems**

Pupil's Book pages 94 and 95 **Oral and mental starter: Start here**

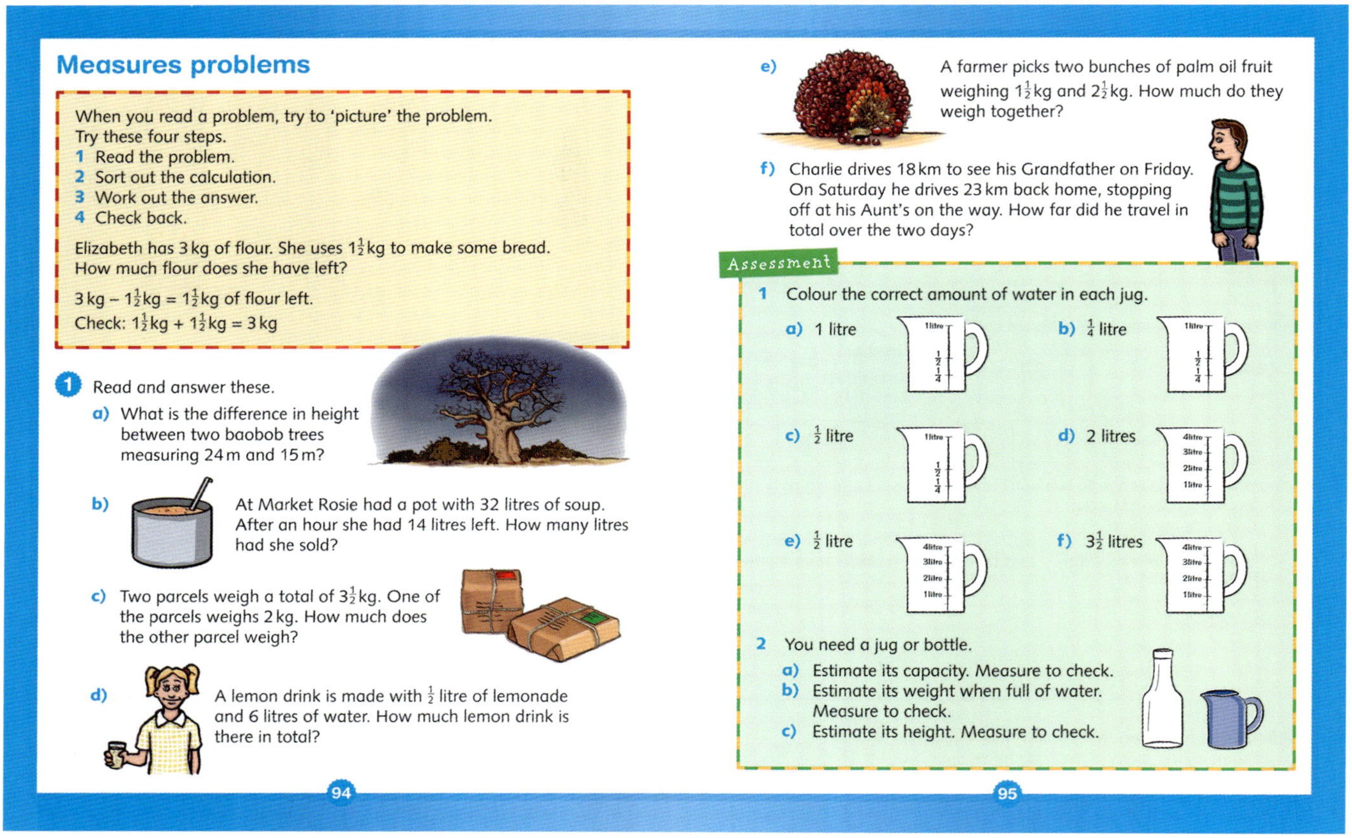

Measures problems

When you read a problem, try to 'picture' the problem.
Try these four steps.

1. Read the problem.
2. Sort out the calculation.
3. Work out the answer.
4. Check back.

Elizabeth has 3 kg of flour. She uses $1\frac{1}{2}$ kg to make some bread. How much flour does she have left?

$3\text{ kg} - 1\frac{1}{2}\text{ kg} = 1\frac{1}{2}\text{ kg}$ of flour left.
Check: $1\frac{1}{2}\text{ kg} + 1\frac{1}{2}\text{ kg} = 3\text{ kg}$

1 Read and answer these.

a) What is the difference in height between two baobob trees measuring 24 m and 15 m?

b) At Market Rosie had a pot with 32 litres of soup. After an hour she had 14 litres left. How many litres had she sold?

c) Two parcels weigh a total of $3\frac{1}{2}$ kg. One of the parcels weighs 2 kg. How much does the other parcel weigh?

d) A lemon drink is made with $\frac{1}{2}$ litre of lemonade and 6 litres of water. How much lemon drink is there in total?

e) A farmer picks two bunches of palm oil fruit weighing $1\frac{1}{2}$ kg and $2\frac{1}{2}$ kg. How much do they weigh together?

f) Charlie drives 18 km to see his Grandfather on Friday. On Saturday he drives 23 km back home, stopping off at his Aunt's on the way. How far did he travel in total over the two days?

Assessment

1 Colour the correct amount of water in each jug.

a) 1 litre
b) $\frac{1}{4}$ litre
c) $\frac{1}{2}$ litre
d) 2 litres
e) $\frac{1}{2}$ litre
f) $3\frac{1}{2}$ litres

2 You need a jug or bottle.

a) Estimate its capacity. Measure to check.
b) Estimate its weight when full of water. Measure to check.
c) Estimate its height. Measure to check.

94 95

Activities

- Discuss the standard units for measurement introduced over this and the previous unit, e.g. 'Which units would you choose to measure the height of the school; your weight; the perimeter of this (small) square ; the capacity of this (large) bottle?'
- Ask 'Does anyone know the units we would use to measure the distance between the school and (a town more than 5 kilometres from the school)?' Establish that kilometres are used to measure long distances. Hold up a metre stick and explain that 1 km = 1000 m. Write 'kilometre' and 'km' on the board and explain the abbreviation.
- Look at page 94 and go through the introduction with the class. Write a word problem on the board, e.g. 'My chair seat is 45 cm from the floor. My desk top is 70 cm from the floor. How much higher is my desk than my chair?' Discuss the four problem-solving steps set out in the introduction in relation to the problem, asking pupils where appropriate to explain their methods/reasoning, e.g. 'What sort of calculation is needed? How do you know? How did you work out the answer? Did anyone do it a different way? How should we write the answer to the problem?'

Answers

1 a) 9 m b) 18 litres c) $1\frac{1}{2}$ kg
d) $6\frac{1}{2}$ litres e) 4 kg f) 41 km

Assessment

a) 1 litre b) $\frac{1}{4}$ litre c) $\frac{1}{2}$ litre
d) 2 litres e) $\frac{1}{2}$ litre f) $3\frac{1}{2}$ litres

Unit 23 **Handling data**

Term 2 Block F **Measures and data** Unit 21 Measuring length Unit 22 Measures problems **Unit 23 Handling data** Unit 24 Assess and review	**Objectives** *At the end of the unit, students should be able to…* Record data using tallies. Collect data, independently or as part of a team, and organise them. Display the collected or given data in more than one way and explain them. Make enquiries (pose questions) and answer them. Categorise similar data and dissimilar data according to two standards. Obtain data from different sources (social – scientific – school activities). Display the collected or given data using illustrations or simple geometric shapes and bars or columns.
Vocabulary tally marks, tallying, chart, survey, pictogram, favourite, bar chart, graph	**Lessons** 1 Using tallies 2 Counting columns 3 Pictograms 4 Bar charts 5 Measuring and data
Oral and mental starters What's the question? Flash facts Pairs for sums My way Product pairs	**Resources** Paper for pupils to use when carrying out surveys and experiments Materials such as coloured counters, small cubes or beads per pair of pupils; coloured pencils; bags or boxes (lesson 3, question 3); paper strips, selection of different bottles, water and measuring jugs, balls (lesson 5) *Pupil's Book pages 96–105*
Prior learning Using tallying and reading data on tally charts Constructing and interpreting block graphs	**Background notes** This unit develops previous learning on data handling. It is important that pupils can interpret data displayed in charts and graphs which they have not constructed as well as being able to conduct a simple survey and display their results appropriately.
End of unit evaluation Check that pupils are able to: 1 Use and interpret tallying to show a count. 2 Interpret column graphs, pictograms and bar charts. 3 Ask questions, collect information and organise data. 4 Construct column graphs, pictograms and bar charts.	**Supporting the topic** Use opportunities in other curriculum areas to pose questions, collect data from different sources, represent and interpret it. Display pupils' charts, pictograms and graphs in the classroom and ask questions about them for other pupils to interpret the data.

Lesson 1 **Using tallies**

Pupil's Book pages 96 and 97 **Oral and mental starter: What's the question?**

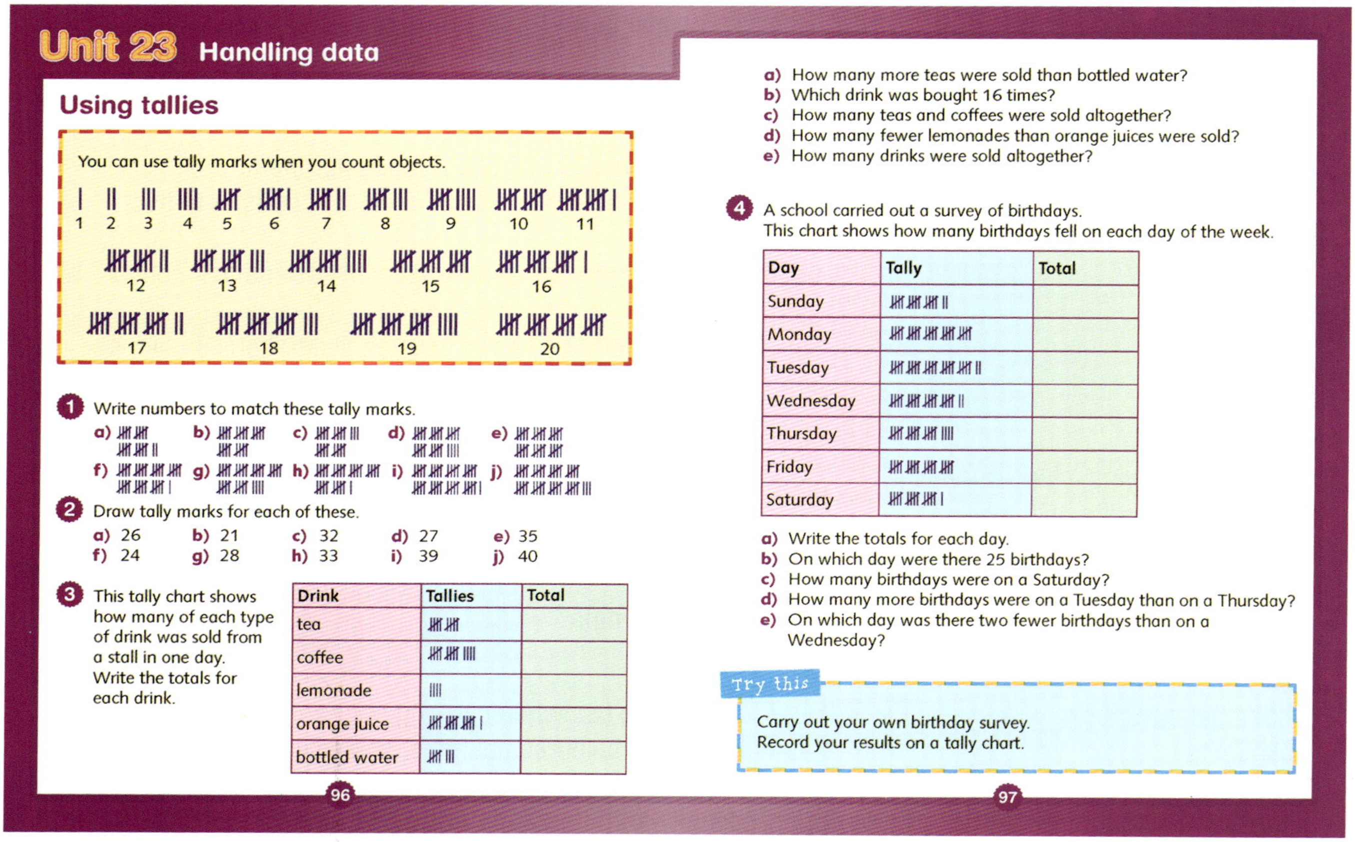

Unit 23 Handling data

Using tallies

You can use tally marks when you count objects.

|	||	|||	||||	卌	卌|	卌||	卌|||	卌||||	卌卌	卌卌|
1	2	3	4	5	6	7	8	9	10	11

卌卌||	卌卌|||	卌卌||||	卌卌卌	卌卌卌|
12	13	14	15	16

卌卌卌||	卌卌卌|||	卌卌卌||||	卌卌卌卌
17	18	19	20

1 Write numbers to match these tally marks.

a) 卌卌 卌卌\|\| b) 卌卌卌 卌卌 c) 卌卌\|\|\| 卌卌 d) 卌卌卌 卌卌\|\|\|\| e) 卌卌卌 卌卌卌
f) 卌卌卌卌 卌卌卌\| g) 卌卌卌卌 卌卌\|\|\|\| h) 卌卌卌卌 卌卌\| i) 卌卌卌卌 卌卌卌卌\| j) 卌卌卌卌 卌卌卌卌\|\|\|

2 Draw tally marks for each of these.

a) 26 b) 21 c) 32 d) 27 e) 35
f) 24 g) 28 h) 33 i) 39 j) 40

3 This tally chart shows how many of each type of drink was sold from a stall in one day. Write the totals for each drink.

Drink	Tallies	Total
tea	卌卌	
coffee	卌卌||||	
lemonade	||||	
orange juice	卌卌卌|	
bottled water	卌|||	

96

a) How many more teas were sold than bottled water?
b) Which drink was bought 16 times?
c) How many teas and coffees were sold altogether?
d) How many fewer lemonades than orange juices were sold?
e) How many drinks were sold altogether?

4 A school carried out a survey of birthdays. This chart shows how many birthdays fell on each day of the week.

Day	Tally	Total
Sunday	卌卌卌||	
Monday	卌卌卌卌卌	
Tuesday	卌卌卌卌卌||	
Wednesday	卌卌卌卌||	
Thursday	卌卌卌||||	
Friday	卌卌卌卌	
Saturday	卌卌卌|	

a) Write the totals for each day.
b) On which day were there 25 birthdays?
c) How many birthdays were on a Saturday?
d) How many more birthdays were on a Tuesday than on a Thursday?
e) On which day was there two fewer birthdays than on a Wednesday?

Try this

Carry out your own birthday survey.
Record your results on a tally chart.

97

Activities

- Ask the class to count in 5s to 50. Repeat if some pupils seem unsure. If necessary record the count on the board.
- Look at page 96. Remind the class that they used tallying to show counts in Grade 1. Discuss the way in which the tally marks are grouped to represent the numbers.
- Write 'boys' and 'girls' on the board. Ask pupils to come out in small groups and make a tally mark for themselves under the appropriate heading. Make sure the fifth marks are made across the previous four as they do so. When everyone has made their mark ask the class to 'read' the tallies and say how many boys and how many girls are present today.
- Check that pupils are tallying correctly as they complete question 2 and 'Try this'.

Answers

1 a) 22 b) 25 c) 23 d) 29 e) 30
f) 36 g) 34 h) 31 i) 41 j) 43

2 a) //// //// //// //// //// /
b) //// //// //// //// /
c) //// //// //// //// //// //// //
d) //// //// //// //// //// //
e) //// //// //// //// //// //// ////
f) //// //// //// //// ////
g) //// //// //// //// //// ///
h) //// //// //// //// //// //// ///
i) //// //// //// //// //// //// //// ////
j) //// //// //// //// //// //// //// ////

3 tea = 10, coffee = 14, lemonade = 4, orange juice = 16, bottled water = 8

3 a) 2 b) orange juice c) 24 d) 12 e) 52

4 a) Sunday = 17, Monday = 25, Tuesday = 27, Wednesday = 22, Thursday = 19, Friday = 20, Saturday = 16
b) Monday c) 16 d) 8 e) Friday

Lesson 2 **Counting columns**

Pupil's Book pages 98 and 99 **Oral and mental starter: Flash facts**

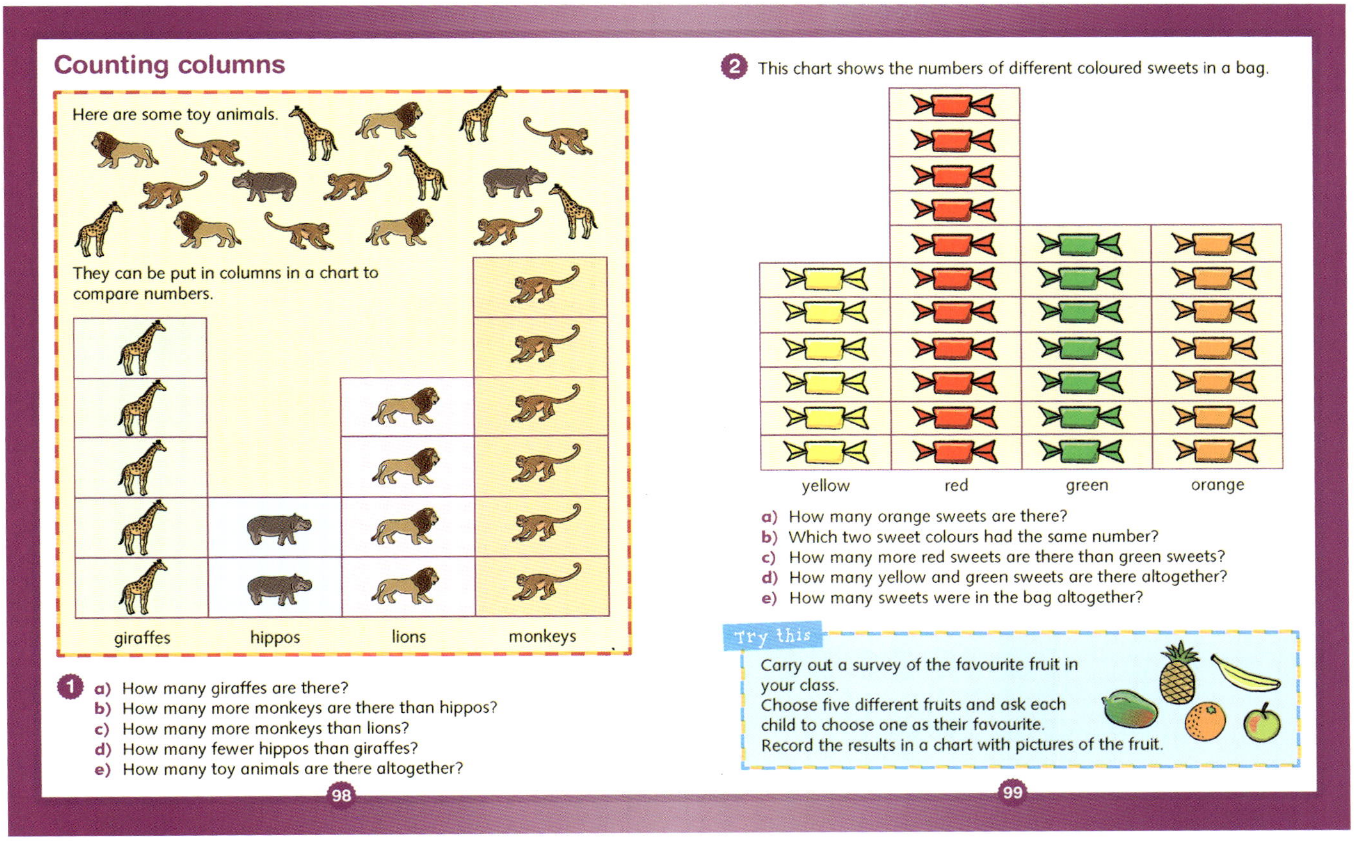

Counting columns

Here are some toy animals.

They can be put in columns in a chart to compare numbers.

giraffes hippos lions monkeys

1 a) How many giraffes are there?
b) How many more monkeys are there than hippos?
c) How many more monkeys than lions?
d) How many fewer hippos than giraffes?
e) How many toy animals are there altogether?

2 This chart shows the numbers of different coloured sweets in a bag.

yellow red green orange

a) How many orange sweets are there?
b) Which two sweet colours had the same number?
c) How many more red sweets are there than green sweets?
d) How many yellow and green sweets are there altogether?
e) How many sweets were in the bag altogether?

Try this

Carry out a survey of the favourite fruit in your class.
Choose five different fruits and ask each child to choose one as their favourite.
Record the results in a chart with pictures of the fruit.

98 99

Activities

- Ask pupils in pairs to each take a handful of coloured counters (or small cubes or anything similar which are in different colours). Ask them to sort their materials into columns for each colour so that the lowest in each column are in a horizontal row along a ruler and those above touching each other (to simulate a column graph).
- Ask questions such as 'How many red (counters) do you have? Do you have the same number of any other colour? What is the colour of your longest column? Which is the shortest? How many more are there in your longest column than in your shortest? How many (counters) do you have altogether?'
- Look at pages 98 and 99. Discuss the column graphs with the class, asking pupils to explain what they are about and to comment on what they show.

Answers

1 a) 5 b) 4 c) 2 d) 3 e) 17

2 a) 7 b) green and orange c) 4 d) 13 e) 31

Lesson 3 **Pictograms**

Pupil's Book pages 100 and 101 **Oral and mental starter: Pairs for sums**

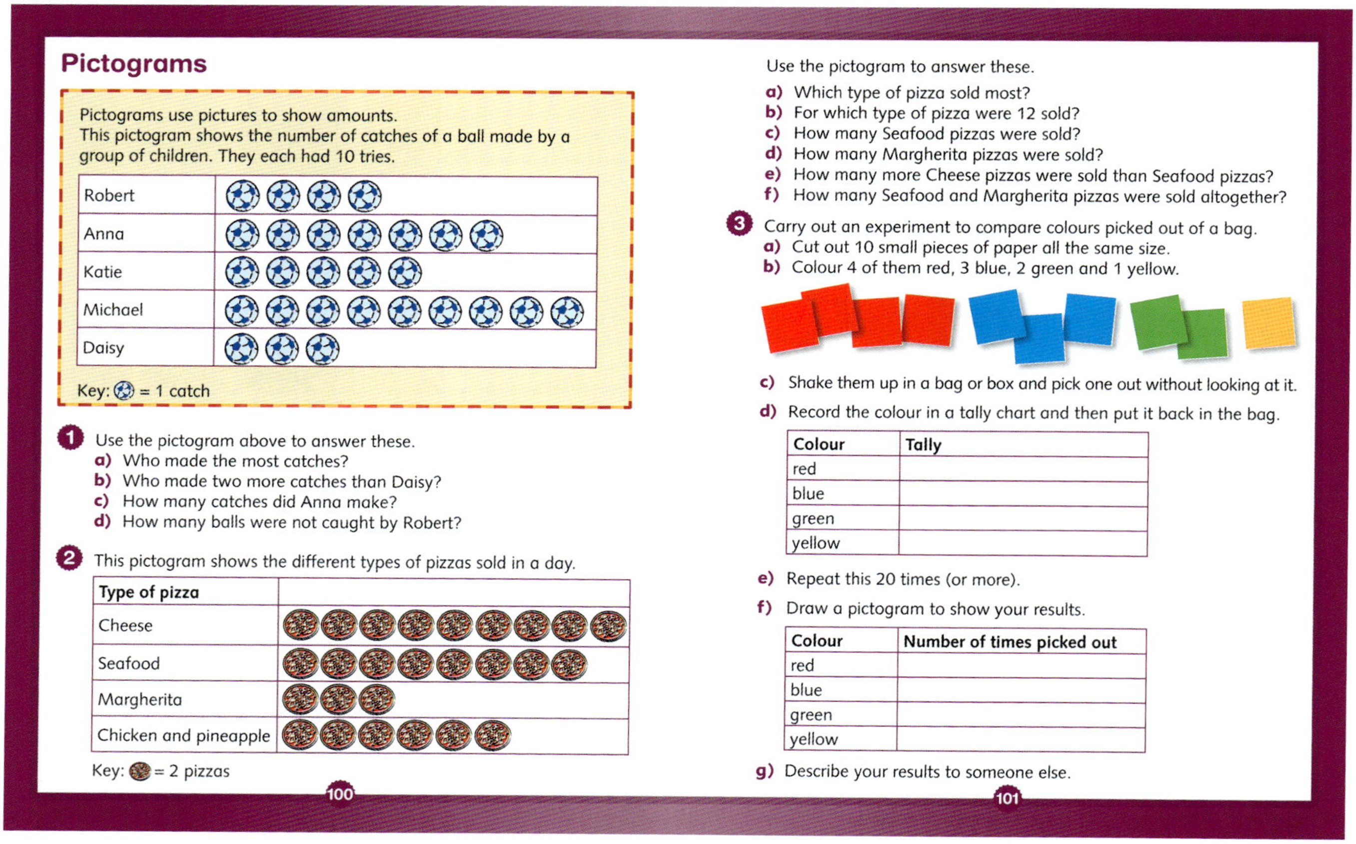

Pictograms

Pictograms use pictures to show amounts.
This pictogram shows the number of catches of a ball made by a group of children. They each had 10 tries.

Robert	
Anna	
Katie	
Michael	
Daisy	

Key: (ball) = 1 catch

1 Use the pictogram above to answer these.

a) Who made the most catches?
b) Who made two more catches than Daisy?
c) How many catches did Anna make?
d) How many balls were not caught by Robert?

2 This pictogram shows the different types of pizzas sold in a day.

Type of pizza	
Cheese	
Seafood	
Margherita	
Chicken and pineapple	

Key: (pizza) = 2 pizzas

100

Use the pictogram to answer these.

a) Which type of pizza sold most?
b) For which type of pizza were 12 sold?
c) How many Seafood pizzas were sold?
d) How many Margherita pizzas were sold?
e) How many more Cheese pizzas were sold than Seafood pizzas?
f) How many Seafood and Margherita pizzas were sold altogether?

3 Carry out an experiment to compare colours picked out of a bag.

a) Cut out 10 small pieces of paper all the same size.
b) Colour 4 of them red, 3 blue, 2 green and 1 yellow.
c) Shake them up in a bag or box and pick one out without looking at it.
d) Record the colour in a tally chart and then put it back in the bag.

Colour	Tally
red	
blue	
green	
yellow	

e) Repeat this 20 times (or more).
f) Draw a pictogram to show your results.

Colour	Number of times picked out
red	
blue	
green	
yellow	

g) Describe your results to someone else.

101

Activities

- Look at page 100 and go through the introduction with the class.
- Look at question 2 together. Point out that each pizza symbol represents 2 pizzas, as shown by the key.
- Go through the instructions for the activity in question 3. Demonstrate the process by drawing a tally chart on the board and recording the tally as different pupils pick from a bag of coloured counters (or coloured paper pieces), say the colour, then replace it in the bag. Stress that pupils must colour their papers as detailed in part b).
- At the end of the lesson discuss the results in question 3, e.g. 'Which colour did you pick out most often? Did anyone have a different colour? How many people had red? Which colour did you pick out least often? How many people had yellow least often? Can anyone explain why?'

Answers

1 a) Michael b) Katie c) 7 d) 6

2 a) Cheese b) Chicken and pineapple
c) 16 d) 6
e) 2 f) 22

Lesson 4 **Bar charts**

Pupil's Book pages 102 and 103 **Oral and mental starter: My way**

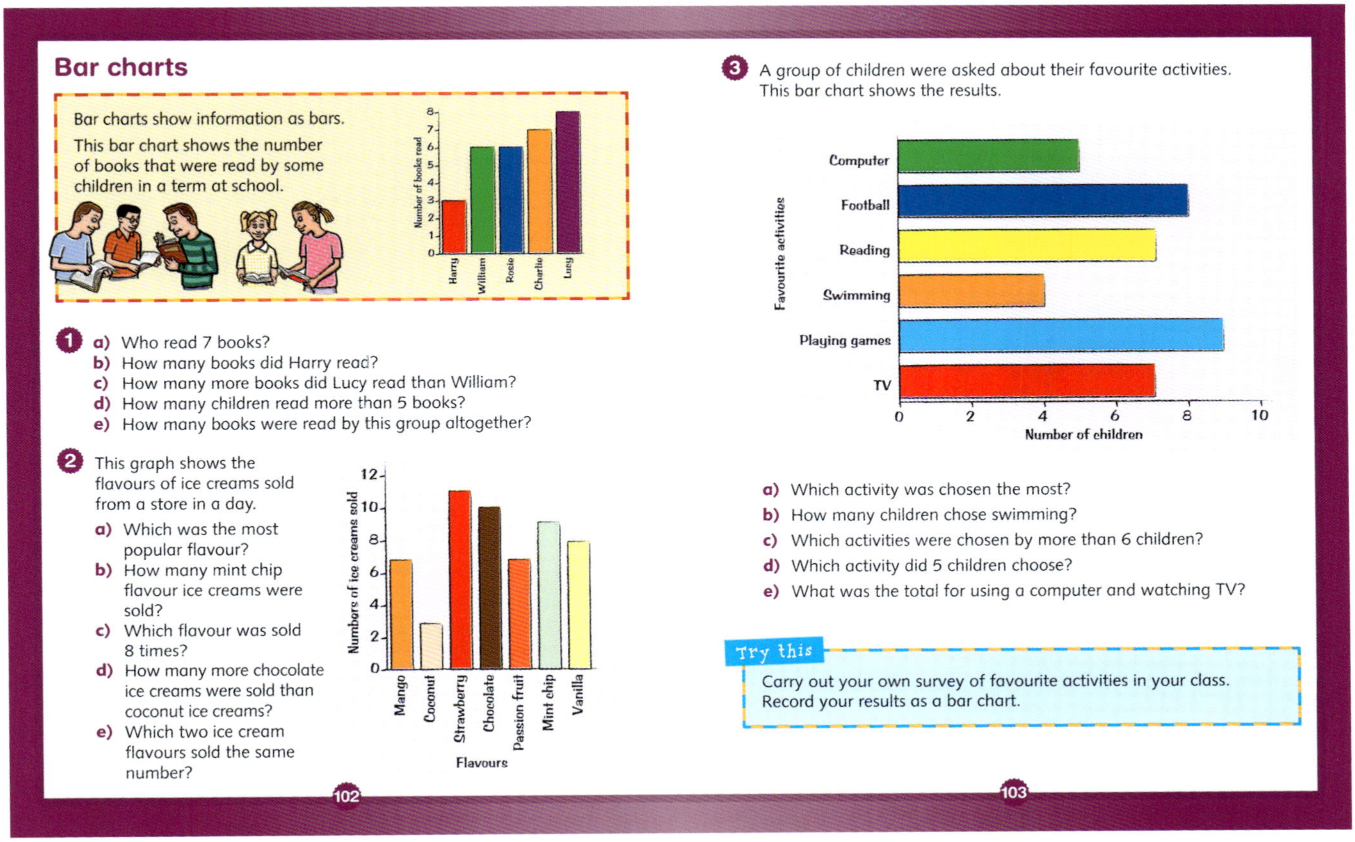

Bar charts

Bar charts show information as bars.

This bar chart shows the number of books that were read by some children in a term at school.

1 a) Who read 7 books?
b) How many books did Harry read?
c) How many more books did Lucy read than William?
d) How many children read more than 5 books?
e) How many books were read by this group altogether?

2 This graph shows the flavours of ice creams sold from a store in a day.
a) Which was the most popular flavour?
b) How many mint chip flavour ice creams were sold?
c) Which flavour was sold 8 times?
d) How many more chocolate ice creams were sold than coconut ice creams?
e) Which two ice cream flavours sold the same number?

3 A group of children were asked about their favourite activities. This bar chart shows the results.

a) Which activity was chosen the most?
b) How many children chose swimming?
c) Which activities were chosen by more than 6 children?
d) Which activity did 5 children choose?
e) What was the total for using a computer and watching TV?

Try this

Carry out your own survey of favourite activities in your class. Record your results as a bar chart.

102 103

Activities

- Before the lesson prepare the axes for a bar chart with the names of four school lessons below the horizontal axis and the vertical axis numbered to about 15.
- Ask pupils to each choose the lesson from the board which they like the most. Ask them to raise their hands if they chose the first lesson. Count the total and construct a bar on the chart to show that number. Repeat with the other three lessons. Discuss the results displayed with the class, e.g. 'Which is the most popular lesson? Which is the least popular? How many more people chose (lesson) than (lesson)?' etc.
- Look at page 102 and go through the introduction with the class.
- Towards the end of the lesson ask pupils who did 'Try this' to share their results with the class.

Answers

1 a) Charlie b) 3 c) 2 d) 4 e) 30

2 a) Strawberry b) 9 c) Vanilla
d) 7 e) Mango and Passion fruit

3 a) playing games b) 4
c) football, reading, playing games and TV
d) computer e) 12

Lesson 5 **Measuring and data**

Pupil's Book pages 104 and 105 **Oral and mental starter: Product pairs**

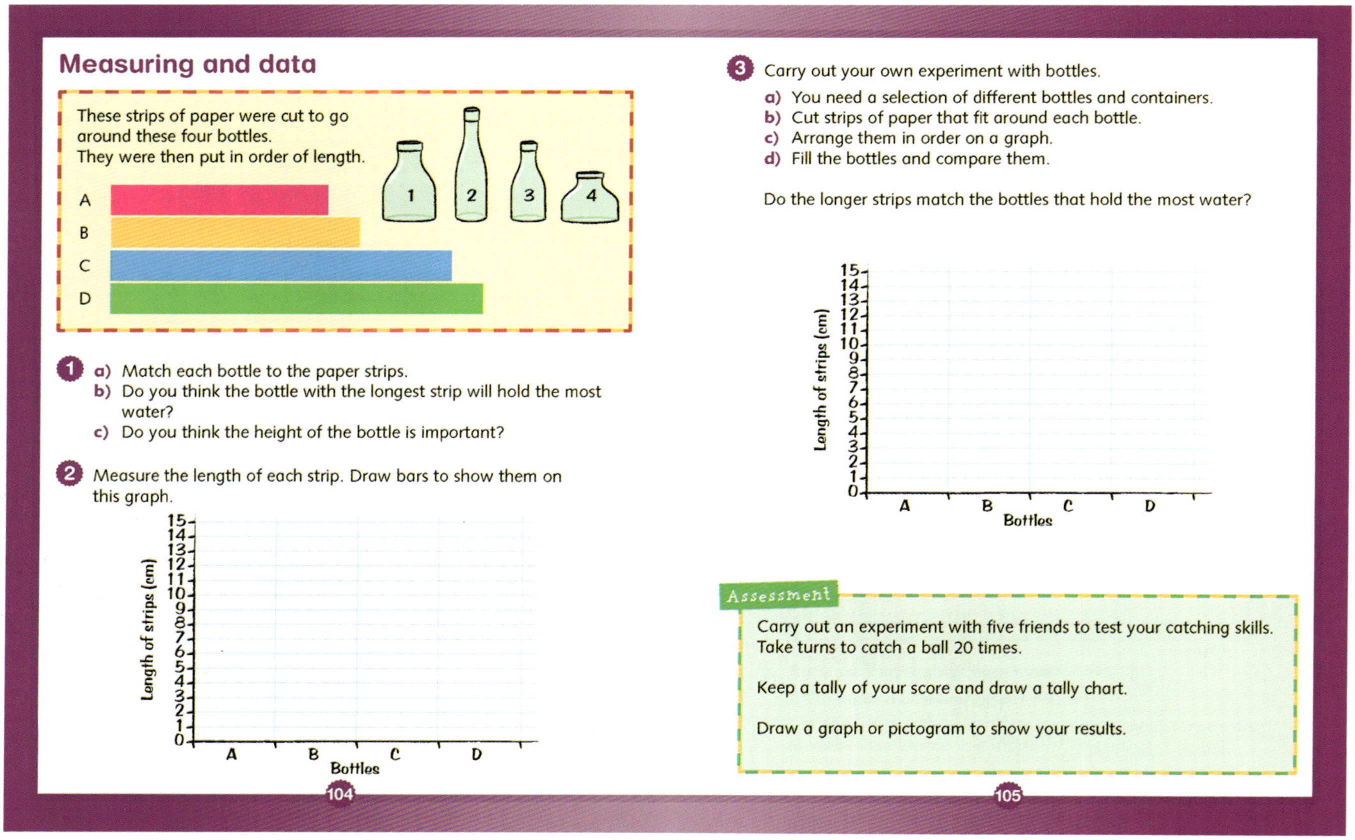

Measuring and data

These strips of paper were cut to go around these four bottles.
They were then put in order of length.

1. a) Match each bottle to the paper strips.
   b) Do you think the bottle with the longest strip will hold the most water?
   c) Do you think the height of the bottle is important?

2. Measure the length of each strip. Draw bars to show them on this graph.

3. Carry out your own experiment with bottles.
   a) You need a selection of different bottles and containers.
   b) Cut strips of paper that fit around each bottle.
   c) Arrange them in order on a graph.
   d) Fill the bottles and compare them.

   Do the longer strips match the bottles that hold the most water?

Assessment

Carry out an experiment with five friends to test your catching skills. Take turns to catch a ball 20 times.

Keep a tally of your score and draw a tally chart.

Draw a graph or pictogram to show your results.

104 105

Activities

- Look at pages 104 and 105 and go through each question with the class. Demonstrate a method for cutting a paper strip to fit around a bottle. Emphasise that the strip should fit round the widest part of each bottle for the experiment in question 3. (Make sure that some tall bottles with greater capacities than some wide ones are available.)
- When pupils have finished the experiment discuss the results. Encourage them to explain their findings, e.g. 'Did anyone find a bottle which held more water than the bottle with the longest strip? Can you explain why?'

Answers

1 a) Bottle 1 = C, Bottle 2 = A, Bottle 3 = B, Bottle 4 = D

2

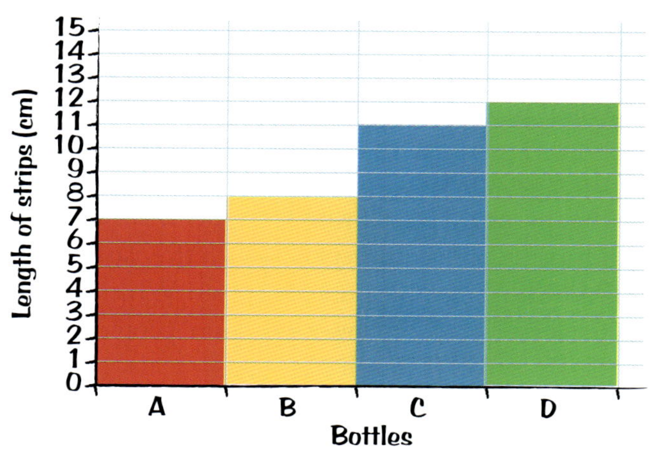

Assess and review

Term 2 Block F

Measures and data

Unit 21 Measuring length

Unit 22 Measures problems

Unit 23 Handling data

Unit 24 Assess and review

Final evaluation

Check that pupils are able to:

1 Understand the concepts of length, capacity and weight.
2 Measure lengths in metres and in centimetres and convert between the two.
3 Measure weight in kg, $\frac{1}{2}$ kg and $\frac{1}{4}$ kg.
4 Measure capacity in litres.
5 Solve simple problems in the context of measures.
6 Use, interpret and construct tally charts, column graphs, pictograms and bar charts.
7 Collect information to answer a question and display it appropriately.

Vocabulary

estimate, measure, length, height, width, metre, metre stick, centimetre, ruler, division, unit of measurement perimeter, rectangle, weight, balance, heavy, heavier, light, lighter, kilogram, $\frac{1}{2}$ kilogram, $\frac{1}{4}$ kilogram, capacity, litre, standard unit, tally marks, tallying, chart, survey, pictogram, favourite, bar chart, graph

Resources

Metre sticks, rulers

Measuring jugs (1 litre), cups, spoons, small bottles, water or sand or grains

Balance scales, 1 kg, $\frac{1}{2}$ kg and $\frac{1}{4}$ kg weights

Footballs, empty bottles, full bottles of water, pencils, books, pencil cases, chalk, shoes (see Pupil's Book p.108)

Balls

Pupil's Book pages 106–111

Pupil's Book pages 106–111

1 Revise the vocabulary relating to length, e.g. hold up a metre stick and ask how long it is; hold up a ruler and ask which unit of length it uses; ask pupils to explain what is meant by 'height', 'width', 'length' and 'perimeter'. (pages 106–107)
2 Check that pupils are using metre sticks and rulers accurately as they work. (pages 106–107)
3 Hold up a 1 kg weight and ask how much it weighs. Ask pupils to suggest things which are lighter than 1 kg and others which are heavier than 1 kg. (page 108)
4 Hold up a litre jug and a cup. Ask 'Which will hold the most? Which has the smaller capacity? How much do you think the jug holds?' (pages 108–109)
5 Check that pupils understand the hourly periods on the pictogram. (page 110)
6 Revise the meaning of 'to the nearest centimetre'. (page 111)
7 Air flow balls would be ideal for the 'Try this' activity. (page 111)

Assessment activities

Use these to assess pupils' knowledge and understanding:

What would you use to measure this line? (cm) How long is it? How would you measure the height of the window? Approximately how high do you think it is?

How many cm are there in 1 metre; $\frac{1}{2}$ m; $\frac{1}{4}$ m?

What is the perimeter of this rectangle?

(name) is $1\frac{1}{4}$ m tall, (name) is $1\frac{1}{2}$ m tall. Which is the tallest? How many cm taller?

Choose two things that are heavier than 1 kg and two that are lighter. Check with the balance.

Choose a container which has a capacity of less than 1 litre. Check to see if you are correct.

Roll this dice 20 times and make a tally chart to show how many times each number is rolled.

Find out which is the most popular of your favourite five books with other people in the class. Show your findings in a bar chart or other type of graph.

Assess and review activities

Use these activities taken from the previous three weeks to monitor, evaluate and consolidate pupils' knowledge and understanding.

- With the help of a pupil place one metre stick on top of another against a wall. 'How high from the floor is the top of the stick? How high would it be if I could put another metre stick on top?' Indicate the middle of the top stick. 'How high from the floor is this?' Repeat for $1\frac{1}{4}$ metres.
- Ask a pupil who is about 1.25 metres tall to come out and stand alongside the sticks. 'Approximately how tall is (name)? Approximately how high do you think the door is?'
- Ask pupils to estimate how wide their closed Pupil's Book is, then ask them to measure it to the nearest cm. Ask them to estimate, then measure the length of their books. Check that they are using the rulers correctly as they do these activities.
- Hold up a metre stick. Indicate different points on the stick (multiples of 5 or 10 cm) and ask the class to say how many cm the point is from the beginning of the stick.
- 'How could we find the length of the perimeter of this rectangle?' Discuss suggestions then measure the length and width of the rectangle to the nearest cm, write these lengths on the board and ask pupils to work out the perimeter.
- Pass round 1 kg, $\frac{1}{2}$ kg and $\frac{1}{4}$ kg weights for pupils to hold. Ask three or four pupils to come out and each select an object that they think will weigh about 1 kg, then test it against the 1 kg weight on the balance. Repeat with other pupils selecting and testing objects which they think are about $\frac{1}{2}$ kg and $\frac{1}{4}$ kg.
- Show a litre measure to the class. Point out the graduated scale and indicate the 1 litre line. 'How could we find out how many litres our bucket holds?' Ask different pupils in turn to measure 1 litre of water and pour it in the bucket until it is full, the rest of the class counting the litres.
- Discuss the standard units for measurement introduced over this and the previous unit, e.g. 'Which units would you choose to measure the height of the school; your weight; the perimeter of this (small) square; the capacity of this (large) bottle?'
- Prepare the axes for a bar chart with the names of four school lessons below the horizontal axis and the vertical axis numbered to about 15. Ask pupils to each choose the lesson from the board which they like the most. Ask them to raise their hands if they chose the first lesson. Count the total and construct a bar on the chart to show that number. Repeat with the other three lessons. Discuss the results displayed with the class, e.g. 'Which is the most popular lesson? Which is the least popular? How many more people chose (lesson) than (lesson)?' etc.

Unit 24 Assess and review

Measuring length

1 Match these lengths to the correct label.
Use a metre stick to check.

about 1 metre | about 2 metres | less than 1 metre | more than 2 metres | between 1 metre and 2 metres

2

Estimate the lengths of these, then measure them with a ruler.

3 Draw a line from each spot to exactly the length given.

a) 10 cm •
b) 6 cm •
c) 13 cm •
d) 2 cm •

4 What is the perimeter of this piece of paper?

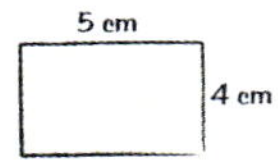

Perimeter = ☐ cm

5 Which of these shapes has the largest perimeter?

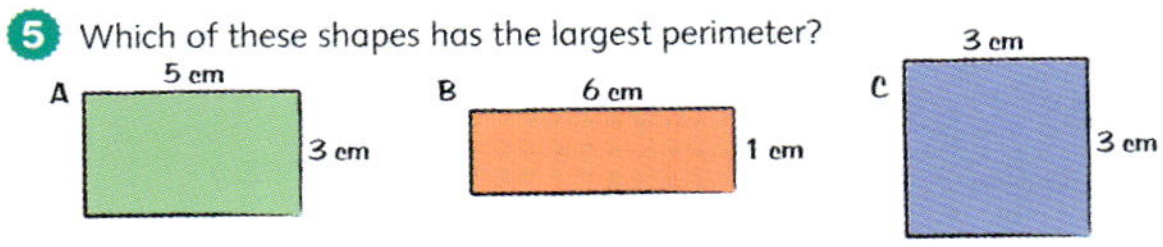

☐ has the largest perimeter of ☐ cm.

Try this
Draw four different rectangles.
Each of them must have a perimeter of 20 cm.

Measures problems

1 Look at these objects and complete the chart.

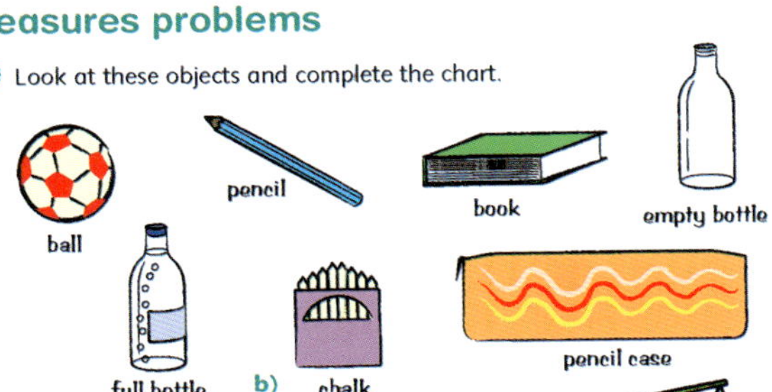

b) Use some balance scales and test each object.
Record your results.

Heavier than a shoe	Lighter than a shoe	About the same as a shoe

2 Balance the objects above with a 1 kg weight.
a) Which objects weigh more than 1 kg?
b) Which items can you put together to weigh exactly 1 kg?

3 **a)** Write how many you think it will take to fill the jug with these containers.

b) Now fill a jug with water using each container. Write how many it took to fill the jug.

Container	Estimate	Check
	☐ cups	☐ cups
	☐ spoons	☐ spoons
	☐ bottles	☐ bottle
	☐ jars	☐ jars

Choose two of your own containers to complete the table.

4 Estimate how many cups can be filled from a litre jug.
Check by pouring. Use tallies to record.
Try this with other containers.

I used	My estimate	My measure
cup		
spoon		
bottle		

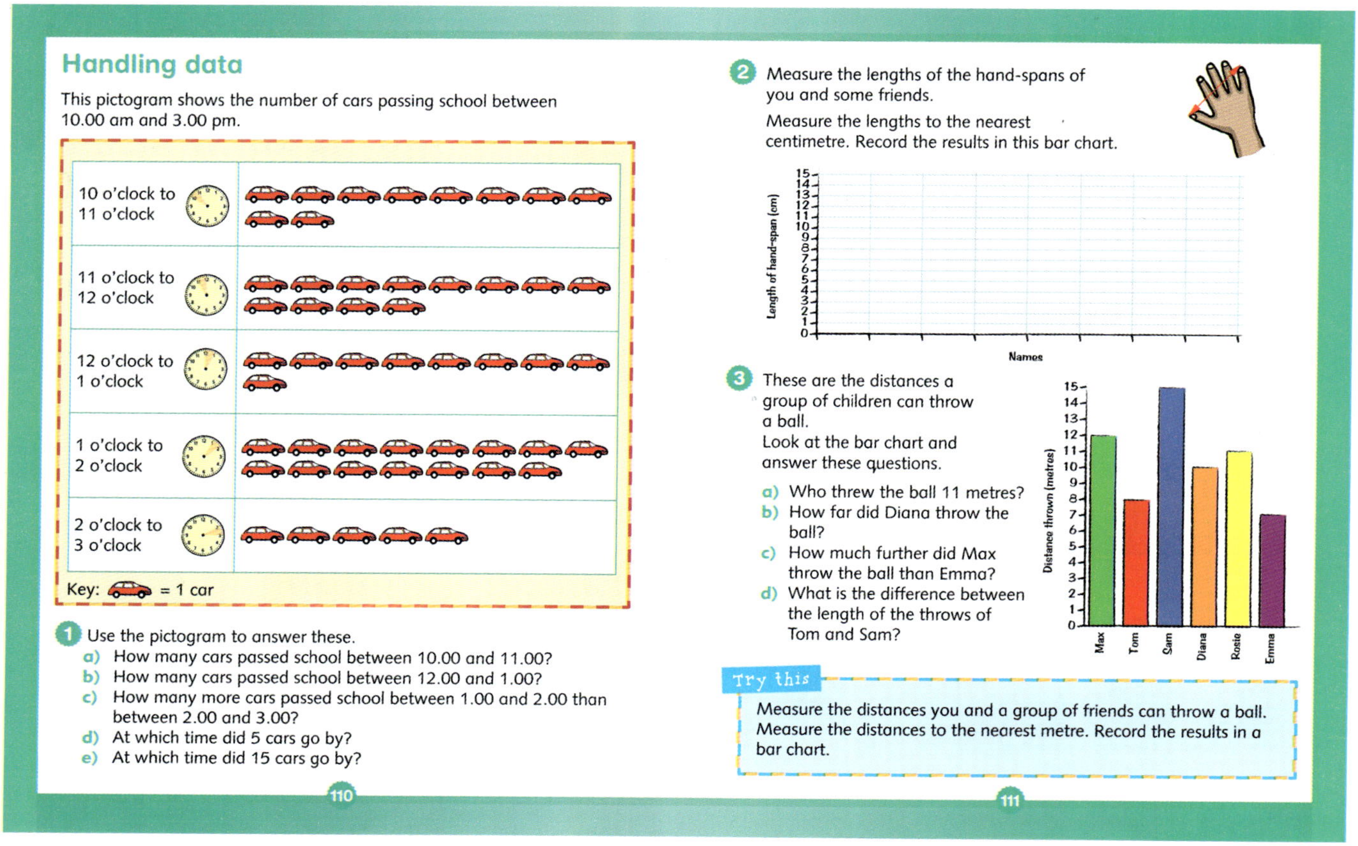

Handling data

This pictogram shows the number of cars passing school between 10.00 am and 3.00 pm.

10 o'clock to 11 o'clock	10 cars
11 o'clock to 12 o'clock	12 cars
12 o'clock to 1 o'clock	9 cars
1 o'clock to 2 o'clock	15 cars
2 o'clock to 3 o'clock	5 cars

Key: (car) = 1 car

1. Use the pictogram to answer these.
   a) How many cars passed school between 10.00 and 11.00?
   b) How many cars passed school between 12.00 and 1.00?
   c) How many more cars passed school between 1.00 and 2.00 than between 2.00 and 3.00?
   d) At which time did 5 cars go by?
   e) At which time did 15 cars go by?

2. Measure the lengths of the hand-spans of you and some friends.
   Measure the lengths to the nearest centimetre. Record the results in this bar chart.

3. These are the distances a group of children can throw a ball.
   Look at the bar chart and answer these questions.
   a) Who threw the ball 11 metres?
   b) How far did Diana throw the ball?
   c) How much further did Max throw the ball than Emma?
   d) What is the difference between the length of the throws of Tom and Sam?

Try this

Measure the distances you and a group of friends can throw a ball. Measure the distances to the nearest metre. Record the results in a bar chart.

110 111

Answers pages 106 and 107

1 Height of chair – about 1 metre,
Width of table – between 1 and 2 metres,
Length of window – about 2 metres,
Your height – between 1 and 2 metres,
Height of door – about 2 metres,
Width of room – more than 2 metres,
Length of stride – less than 1 metre

2 a) 3 cm b) 5 cm c) 6 cm d) 8 cm

4 18 cm

5 A has the largest perimeter of 16 cm

Answers pages 108 and 109

1

Heavier than a shoe	Lighter than a shoe	About the same as a shoe
ball, full bottle	pencil, chalk, empty bottle, pencil case	book

Answers pages 110 and 111

1 a) 10 b) 9 c) 10 d) 2 o'clock to 3 o'clock
e) 1 o'clock to 2 o'clock

3 a) Rosie b) 10 m c) 5 m d) 7 m